Spirit Walk

Daily Devotions
on the Holy Spirit

—— COMPILED BY ——
ROBERT WHITE

Pathway Press
Cleveland, Tennessee 37311

Library of Congress Catalog Number: 95-070531

ISBN: 0871489678

Copyright © 1995 by Robert White

Printed by Pathway Press

Cleveland, Tennessee 37311

All Rights Reserved

Printed in the United States of America

SpiritWalk
Daily Devotions on the Holy Spirit

Floyd D. Carey
and
Tom George,
Editors

EDITORIAL COMMITTEE
Robert White
Floyd D. Carey
Tom George
Homer G. Rhea
Marcus V. Hand
Daniel L. Black
Hoyt E. Stone
Lewis J. Willis
Benjamin B. McGlamery

DEDICATION

Each Wednesday morning, Prayerborne senior-adult prayer group meets in the chapel at Church of God International Offices in Cleveland, Tennessee. This faithful band of men and women—retired ministers, their spouses, and retired laypersons—averages more than 1,000 hours a year praying together for prayer requests that come to the International Offices from individuals and churches all over the world.

During this century, the Pentecostal Movement has come from a handful of sincere people who sought God for revival to a mighty worldwide army numbering more than 400 million Spirit-filled Christians. Prayerborne's veteran soldiers of the Cross have participated in and contributed to the Pentecostal revival. They have served God and the church as evangelists, pastors, missionaries, teachers, and administrators. Today, these pioneers of the Pentecostal Movement continue to serve God in their retirement years as faithful prayer warriors.

This book is dedicated to the faithful men and women of Prayerborne and to the memory of the Prayerborne members who have already gone home to be with their Lord.

ACKNOWLEDGMENTS

SpiritWalk—Daily Devotions on the Holy Spirit is the work of many people. To compile such a monumental book required the efforts of a team of dedicated individuals who carried the book from concept to completion in less than a year.

More than 350 men and women submitted a daily devotional for inclusion in this book. Without the Bible expositions and testimonies they shared, this daily devotional book would not have been possible.

Floyd D. Carey and Tom George, who served as editors of *SpiritWalk*, diligently shepherded the book through the long process of compiling the devotionals and editing the manuscripts. They were assisted by an editorial committee composed of Homer G. Rhea, Marcus V. Hand, Daniel L. Black, Hoyt E. Stone, Lewis J. Willis, and Benjamin B. McGlamery.

Paul F. Henson provided valuable assistance in contacting family members of deceased ministers and securing permission to include material by these ministers.

Marcus V. Hand, editorial assistant at Pathway Press, went beyond the call of duty to guide the manuscript through the copyediting phase.

Lonzo T. Kirkland masterfully designed both the four-color cover and the inside page layout and graphics.

Pat Bradbury, sales coordinator for Pathway Press, offered many helpful suggestions about the design and promotion of *SpiritWalk* and prepared the advertising campaign.

To these and all others who made a contribution to the completion of this project, I extend my heartfelt thanks.

INTRODUCTION

The Prophecy

During the Old Testament era, when a priest or a king took office the customary procedure was to anoint him by pouring oil on his head. This consecrated him to God and set him apart for holy service.

Aaron received this anointing by the hand of Moses: "And he poured some of the anointing oil on Aaron's head and anointed him, to sanctify him" (Leviticus 8:12). King Saul also received this anointing: "Then Samuel took a flask of oil and poured it on his head" (1 Samuel 10:1). David too received this anointing: "Then Samuel took the horn of oil and anointed him in the midst of his brothers; and the Spirit of the Lord came upon David from that day forward" (1 Samuel 16:13).

The anointing by the hand of the prophet of God denoted God's blessing and favor upon the one anointed and the presence of God's Spirit in his life. However, this anointing was only for a chosen few.

The prophet Joel, writing under the inspiration of God approximately 800 years before Christ, foretold a time when God would pour out His Spirit, not upon just a chosen few but upon all people.

Joel probably had witnessed anointing ceremonies and was familiar with the symbolism of the poured out oil when he prophesied, "And it shall come to pass afterward that I will pour out My Spirit on all flesh; your sons and your daughters shall prophesy, your old men shall dream dreams, your young men shall see visions; and also on My menservants and on My maidservants I will pour out My Spirit in those days" (2:28, 29).

The Fulfillment

While Joel looked down through the ages to prophesy of the outpouring of the Holy Spirit, John the Baptist, preaching only a few years before the outpouring at Jerusalem, saw the time in the near future when Joel's prophecy would be fulfilled.

John declared, "I indeed baptize you with water unto repentance, but He who is coming after me is mightier than I, whose sandals I am not worthy to carry. He will baptize you with the Holy Spirit and fire" (Matthew 3:11).

Only a few days before the outpouring of the Holy Spirit, Jesus assembled His disciples and commanded them not to leave Jerusalem, but to wait for the promise of the Father.

He told them, "John truly baptized with water, but you shall be baptized with the Holy Spirit not many days from now" (Acts 1:5).

After receiving these instructions from Jesus, the disciples waited in prayer in an upper room at Jerusalem. The Scriptures record:

When the Day of Pentecost had fully come, they were all with one accord in one place. And suddenly there came a sound from heaven, as of a rushing mighty wind, and it filled the whole house where they were sitting. Then there appeared to them divided tongues, as of fire, and one sat upon each of them. And they were all filled with the Holy Spirit and began to speak with other tongues, as the Spirit gave them utterance (Acts 2:1-4).

God, who has within His power to determine the times and seasons, chose the Day of Pentecost as the specific time when the fulfillment of Joel's prophecy would take place and His Spirit would be poured out on all flesh.

The disciples were all with one accord in one place. Little bands didn't meet at different places, but they were all moved upon by the Holy Spirit to go to an upper room to prepare their hearts for this church-empowering, world-shaking event.

For 10 days they no doubt testified, prayed, and sang praises to God. Thus, their hearts were prepared to receive from the Lord the promise of the Father.

Suddenly—abruptly, without warning—the event ordained from the council room of God as surely as the manger event happened in the Upper Room. Throughout history God has at times moved dramatically. When the earth was dark and without form, suddenly God said, "Let there be light," and there was light. When Noah had preached repentance for many years and the people wearied of Noah's warnings, the ark was completed and suddenly the sky darkened and it rained 40 days until the earth was destroyed.

When the sins of Sodom came up before God, suddenly two angels appeared and led Lot from the city before fire consumed Sodom. When the Israelites cried because of their afflictions, suddenly Moses came from the back side of the desert and told Pharaoh, "God said, 'Let My people go.'" When the voices of the prophets had been silent for 400 years, suddenly an angel appeared to Mary and said, "You will . . . bring forth a Son, and shall call His name Jesus" (Luke 1:31).

The 120 people in the Upper Room had been praying, singing, and worshiping for 10 days, and suddenly there came a sound from heaven. It wasn't a voice, a trumpet, a song, or a sermon. It was a sound like the sound before a storm hits. This sound was not from hell, as some claim. It was not born out of the trance of the mystical or the imaginations of the fanatical. It was not founded in heresy. Neither did it come from the polity of a denomination or the doctrine of a seminary.

The sound was from heaven. It came like a rushing mighty wind—not a gentle, swaying breeze but a rushing, mighty, forceful, powerful wind from heaven. The disciples were all filled with the Holy Spirit. They all began to speak in tongues as the Spirit of God gave them utterance.

The Affirmation

At that time there were in Jerusalem devout Jewish men from every nation. They had come there for the Feast of Pentecost. When news of the happenings at the Upper Room spread abroad, a multitude of people soon gathered. They were amazed at the strange actions of the disciples.

Even more confounding was the fact that the disciples were speaking in the tongues of the nations of the assembled Jews. Many in the crowd began to question this unusual event. Others simply mocked and said the disciples were drunk.

But Peter, standing up with the eleven, raised his voice and said to them, "Men of Judea and all who dwell in Jerusalem, let this be known to you, and heed my words. For these are not drunk, as you suppose, since it is only the third hour of the day. But this is what was spoken by the prophet Joel: 'And it shall come to pass in the last days, says God, that I will pour out of My Spirit on all flesh; your sons and your daughters shall prophesy, your young men shall see visions, your old men shall dream dreams. And on My menservants and on My maidservants I will pour out My Spirit in those days; and they shall prophesy' " (Acts 2:14-18).

The outpouring Joel had foreseen hundreds of years before had come to pass! The power for which Jesus had commanded His disciples to tarry had been given! The anointing for all people had come!

The Anointing

Jesus told His disciples, "But you shall receive power when the Holy Spirit has come upon you; and you shall be witnesses to Me in Jerusalem, and in all Judea and Samaria, and to the end of the earth" (Acts 1:8).

The records of the early church show the dramatic fulfillment of that promise. The growth and expansion of the Christian church was nothing less than phenomenal! There could be no doubt that the Holy Spirit was working through the church, anointing them to do great exploits for God!

The power given to the church always exalts Christ. When the

Jewish priests and the Sadducees questioned Peter and John about the healing of the lame man, they asked, "By what power or by what name have you done this?" Peter, full of the Holy Spirit, answered, "By the name of Jesus Christ of Nazareth, whom you crucified, whom God raised from the dead, by Him this man stands here before you whole" (Acts 4:7, 10).

This power is effective; it accomplishes things for God. In Acts 6, Stephen was chosen to serve the church. He was "a man full of faith and the Holy Spirit. . . . And the word of God spread, and the number of the disciples multiplied greatly in Jerusalem, and a great many of the priests were obedient to the faith. And Stephen, full of faith and power, did great wonders and signs among the people" (vv. 5, 7, 8).

The Pentecostal Revival

The Pentecostal revival began inauspiciously in the closing years of the 19th century and the opening years of this century. From humble beginnings the Pentecostal Movement has grown into a globe-circling religious force.

Unlike other great movements, the Pentecostal Movement was not led by any one man or group of men. Instead, this latter day outpouring of the Holy Spirit can be ascribed to nothing less than a sovereign move of God.

Jesus said, "The wind blows where it wishes, and you hear the sound of it, but cannot tell where it comes from and where it goes" (John 3:8). On the Day of Pentecost, the Spirit came like a rushing mighty wind. The same wind of the Spirit is blowing across the world with a force that cannot be stopped. This mighty move of God transcends language and culture, race and religion. Political boundaries cannot keep the Spirit out. Hostile governments cannot forbid His work. Wherever the gospel is preached, the Spirit is falling upon hungry hearts.

And wherever the wind of the Spirit blows, people are being filled with the Holy Spirit as on the Day of Pentecost. At least 400 million people are Spirit-filled Christians today. Some estimates place the total number closer to a billion.

This mighty move of God is bringing unprecedented revival. While religionists lament about a falling away, hungry hearts are abandoning the cold confines of religiosity and embracing the warmth of the Spirit-filled life.

Even in environments hostile to Christianity, the Holy Spirit is at work preparing a people for the coming of the Lord. "And the Spirit and the bride say, 'Come!' And let him who hears say, 'Come!' And let him who thirsts come. Whoever desires, let him take the water of life freely" (Revelation 22:17).

Jesus said He would send the promise of the Father (Luke 24:49; Acts 1:4). The promise came on the Day of Pentecost and is yours today! "For the promise is to you and to your children, and to all who are afar off, as many as the Lord our God will call" (Acts 2:39).

As you read these daily devotions prepared by many different people from different eras, different places, and different backgrounds, you will see a common thread woven through the fabric of this book: the Holy Spirit working with extraordinary power through the lives of ordinary people, equipping them to do extraordinary exploits for God.

And that is what He is doing for us even now! At this very moment He is filling us with joy and peace and hope through the power of the Holy Spirit! He is working through us to bring a mighty last-days revival to this earth!

God has indeed given us "the exceeding greatness of His power" (Ephesians 1:19). "If we live in the Spirit, let us also walk in the Spirit" (Galatians 5:25).

—Robert White

THE HOLY SPIRIT GIVES US ASSURANCE

And we are His witnesses to these things, and so also is the
Holy Spirit whom God has given to those who obey Him
(Acts 5:32).

When my wife, Kathy, was stricken with a heart attack, the local doctor told us we needed to get her to a hospital equipped to do open-heart surgery. He recommended University Hospital in Birmingham. I admitted Kathy to the hospital and checked into a nearby motel. The heart attack happened so suddenly I didn't have time to contact anyone to pray with me. I knew only the Lord could help me in this emergency.

I stretched out on the floor and began to pray. I started by asking forgiveness for the coldness of my heart and the prayerlessness of my life. I repented of every failure and shortcoming I could think of. Then I sought the Lord for Kathy solely upon the merit of Jesus' blood. In my anguish and desperation I cried out to God from my innermost being.

The Holy Spirit spoke to my heart and gave me 2 Kings 4:25, 26: " 'Look, there is the Shunammite woman. Please run now to meet her, and say to her, "Is it well with you? Is it well with your husband? Is it well with the child?" ' And she answered, "It is well." ' "

The Lord had witnessed to my heart that everything was going to be all right. I rushed to Kathy's bedside and told her the Lord has spoken to me and said, "It is well."

After an arteriogram the surgeon came to Kathy's room and told her, "Mrs. White, your heart will be the envy of all Cleveland, Tennessee. The muscles and arteries around your heart are perfect."

I went to the motel and spent time praising and worshiping God. I didn't have the vocabulary to express my gratitude, so I opened my Bible to the Psalms and read them aloud. I started with Psalm 100: "Make a joyful shout to the Lord, all you lands! . . . Come before His presence with singing. . . . Enter . . . into his courts with praise." I read the psalm very loudly as I continued to use the words of David as my own words in a prayer of praise and thanksgiving.

· · · PRAYER · · ·

Lord, I am thankful that in the difficult times of life the Holy Spirit
speaks to us and gives us the assurance everything is going to be all right.

· · · TODAY'S THOUGHT · · ·

God did indeed perform a miracle—and He gave me the assurance before the miracle.

—Robert White

A VICTORIOUS HOMEGOING

*Yea, though I walk through the valley of the shadow of
death, I will fear no evil; for You are with me; Your rod and
Your staff, they comfort me* (Psalm 23:4).

My father, the Reverend W.L. Shires, was a pastor for 35 years. After his retirement, he continued to be very loyal in his church attendance, support, and worship. On Sunday, June 11, 1972, in the Hurst Church of God in Hurst, Texas, my dad left a message of victory in his homegoing that was as powerful as the sermons he preached. He was given the opportunity to testify and he stated: "The world can't feel what we feel here tonight. I am so thankful for the sweet, wonderful spirit that we have felt in our midst. It's just wonderful. I am thankful for a church like this where we can come and receive these great blessings. Thank God for knowing our needs and for supplying them. I feel so good. I love the Lord better tonight than I've ever loved Him. I hope I feel just like this when it comes time for me to meet my Maker. Thank God for the power of this church tonight!"

He shouted, "Hallelujah," and began to speak in tongues. His face was shining with happiness as he continued to speak in a heavenly language. Suddenly he collapsed to the floor. The last words he spoke were praises to the Lord in tongues.

My brother, the Reverend M.A. Shires, also a minister, said he wanted to leave this world with the same victory and joy as our dad. On February 22, 1993, the Lord granted his request. Arriving home after a day of pastoral duties, he began to praise the Lord in tongues, slipped to the floor, and the Holy Spirit escorted him into the presence of the Father.

· · · PRAYER · · ·

Lord, as I reflect on the homegoings of my dad and my brother, I am reminded that You defeated death's sting and robbed the grave of its victory. Help me to live a victorious life and be ready to move to the heavenly home You are preparing for Your people.

· · · TODAY'S THOUGHT · · ·

Living for Jesus in this world is victory; but when we cross Jordan to our new home, we can experience even greater victory.

—Kathy Shires White

APPOINTED BY THE HOLY SPIRIT

"Therefore take heed to yourselves and to all the flock, among which the Holy Spirit has made you overseers, to shepherd the church of God which He purchased with His own blood" (Acts 20:28).

The church was purchased with the blood of God himself. This immediately speaks both to the divinity and humanity of Jesus. Therefore, we cannot look upon His death as that of an ordinary man but as the death of the God-man, who is totally God and totally man. He is totally God in that He can touch God for us and totally man in that He can feel our infirmities and represent them to the Father.

As the apostle Paul was leaving Ephesus, he committed the oversight and government of the church to the Ephesians. However, he made certain they understood it was the Holy Spirit who had made them overseers. He impressed upon them that the Spirit was the chief administrator in all church affairs. They did not take this honor to themselves, neither was it conferred upon them by man. The Spirit had selected, appointed, and ordained them. The Spirit is the leader controlling all offices occupied by Spirit-filled men.

The Holy Spirit played a major role in the leadership of early Christians, and they depended upon Him for strength and guidance. When decisions were made, it was said, "It seemed good to the Holy Spirit, and to us" (Acts 15:28). When we have the consolation that the Spirit is directing the church's affairs, He unites with us in our conclusions and seals them with His approval. Often have I seen the Spirit resolve difficulties and give direction when congregations realized He is the chief administrator and committed themselves and their problems to Him.

・・・ PRAYER ・・・

Heavenly Father, I approach Your throne with boldness, knowing that You entered into the Holy Place by Your own blood to make a way for me and that I am now a part of Your church. Thank You for making me a part of Your body, filling me with the Holy Spirit, and directing my life.

・・・ TODAY'S THOUGHT ・・・

The more we rely upon the Spirit, the less we will rely upon the flesh. The Spirit must not only become resident in our lives, but He must also become president of our lives.

—Ray H. Hughes

January 4

THE SPIRIT IS NOT RESTRICTED

You who are named the house of Jacob: "Is the Spirit of the Lord restricted? Are these His doings? Do not My words do good to him who walks uprightly?" (Micah 2:7).

The Holy Spirit is not restricted in power, presence, or potential. He is God the Holy Spirit, and all the attributes of God apply to Him.

He is not restricted in power. Through Him all things are possible. His power is unlimited. If we are to know His power toward us, we must be open to His guidance. When His anointing comes upon us, He provides power to accomplish our Christian tasks. His power which dwells in us is not ours to use as we please, but it is His to work through us for His own good pleasure.

He is not restricted in His presence. He can be everywhere at once. My finite mind cannot comprehend the idea that anyone can be everywhere at the same time, but I believe it. I have experienced His presence under many different circumstances. One of His titles, the Comforter, means one who goes alongside to help. Everyone who is baptized in the Holy Spirit has this constant companion. We are never left alone. He abides.

He is not restricted in knowledge. Since He knows all things, He knows our needs and will supply them according to the riches of Christ in glory. He knows all about us and cares for us in every respect. When I was 9 years old, I received the Holy Spirit baptism. That same year I saw my mother brought back from the dead. As she sat up in the bed, she gave a number of prophecies—one being that I would be engaged in the work of the Lord. This prophecy has kept me in good stead when things were difficult. I know the Holy Spirit has directed my life and He will take me through every difficulty. His power gives assurance.

· · · PRAYER · · ·

O God, I give thanks to You for the unrestricted Spirit who works through me. Help me to lean more fully upon Him for direction, and give me a deep insight into the Word.

· · · TODAY'S THOUGHT · · ·

After more than 50 years, the Holy Spirit still abides with me. His presence in the past gives me hope for tomorrow.

—Euverla Hughes

THE HOLY SPIRIT AND FIRE

*"I indeed baptize you with water unto repentance, but He
who is coming after me is mightier than I, whose sandals I
am not worthy to carry. He will baptize you with the Holy
Spirit and fire"* (Matthew 3:11).

The 400-year interlude that followed the close of the Old
Testament abruptly ended by a voice crying in the wilderness:
"Repent, for the kingdom of heaven is at hand!" As the river-
bank evangelist awakened the hope of a messianic kingdom,
he told a demoralized and discouraged nation there was more coming
than the baptism of repentance he was preaching—in the person of the
Lamb of God.

John the Baptist's ministry prepared the people to receive the Holy
Spirit and fire that would come only after repentance and cleansing.
John identified Jesus as the Holy Spirit baptizer. Before His ascension,
Jesus breathed on His disciples and commanded that they receive the
Holy Spirit. This was fulfilled on the Day of Pentecost. Just as John
had plunged people into Jordan's water, Jesus sent the Holy Spirit on
the Day of Pentecost in a rushing mighty wind riding on tongues of fire
and plunged the disciples into a Spirit baptism.

The precedent was set. The first priority is to receive Christ as
Savior by the drawing and wooing of the Spirit. After repentance and
sanctification, a spiritual vessel is ready for the infilling of the Holy
Spirit and fire.

Fire indicates the intensity of the Spirit. The effects of the Spirit can
be described as a fire. A.B. Simpson gave these characteristics of fire:

Fire is a penetrating, purifying, consuming, refining, quickening,
and protective element. Fire is necessary in preparing almost every
article of food. Fire is a great energizer. Fire warms; the Holy Spirit is
the source of one's zeal and holy earnestness. Holy Spirit fire melts the
rigid heart and molds it after God's holy will.

Salvation is an unforgettable event. Old things pass away and all things
are new. Yet there is more for us in the Holy Spirit and fire baptism.

· · · PRAYER · · ·

*O God, grant that we would hunger for more. Fill us and refill us
with Your Holy Spirit and fire baptism.*

· · · TODAY'S THOUGHT · · ·

I want all God has promised me as I walk this earthly path.

—G. Dennis McGuire

FULL OF POWER

But truly I am full of power by the Spirit of the Lord
(Micah 3:8).

Shortly before the Day of Pentecost, Jesus told His followers, "You shall receive power when the Holy Spirit has come upon you" (Acts 1:8). The records of the early church show the dramatic fulfillment of that promise. The growth and expansion of the Christian church was nothing less than phenomenal! There could be no doubt that the Holy Spirit was working through the church, anointing them to do great exploits for God!

Yet the church was not made up of supernatural, spiritual giants but ordinary men and women much like you and me. They were . . .

Common people with uncommon resources

Finite believers with infinite support

Ordinary persons with extraordinary reserves

Usual Christians with unusual means

Natural disciples with supernatural power.

The key word is *power*. It is used repeatedly to refer to the Holy Spirit's work in us and through us. Power implies resources, capability, and strength. The early church had supernatural resources through the Holy Spirit. They possessed powerful capabilities to do mighty deeds for God. Through the Spirit they were strong enough for any task.

We are full of power by the Spirit of the Lord! The power working through us comes from God.

"Power belongs to God" (Psalm 62:11), but He "gives strength and power to His people" (Psalm 68:35). In fact, He gives us "the exceeding greatness of His power" (Ephesians 1:19).

· · · PRAYER · · ·

Lord, I thank You for the power You give to Your people. Help me to be full of power by the Spirit of the Lord.

· · · TODAY'S THOUGHT · · ·

In a world obsessed with power, no power can match the exceeding greatness of God's power.

—DeRosa McGuire

LET THE SPIRIT SPEAK

"But when they arrest you and deliver you up, do not worry beforehand, or premeditate what you will speak. But whatever is given you in that hour, speak that; for it is not you who speak, but the Holy Spirit" (Mark 13:11).

 As a teenager new to the Pentecostal faith, my instruction concerning how to receive the Holy Spirit came mostly from observation. Extremely shy, I found it difficult to raise my hands and pray aloud.

One summer at camp meeting, I had an embarrassing experience. During an altar service, a very zealous lady began to pray for me. She asked the Lord to fill me with the Spirit and urged me to lift my hands and cry out to God. After several minutes of praying and prodding, she finally pleaded in desperation, "God, save this young man!" I left the altar that night wondering where I stood spiritually.

Back home, I became more and more discouraged in my efforts to be filled. Then one Sunday night after a fruitless session at the altar, the Lord impressed me to go to the prayer room alone—just the Lord and me. In that darkened room, I heard this message: "You seek God and let the Spirit speak." Tears flowed as I told the Lord how much I loved Him and how I wanted to live for Him. I didn't worry about manifestations. I was lost in communion with God. When I came to myself, I sensed the powerful outflow of the Spirit and heard myself speaking in tongues.

That experience taught me a great lesson: When human methods fail, let the Spirit speak. I have relied on that word. When my efforts end in frustration, when trouble looms and there seems to be no answer, the Lord reminds me to let the Spirit speak. Sometimes that word has been to me; sometimes it has been through me.

Whatever you need today, put away your preconceived ideas, open your heart, and let the Spirit speak.

· · · PRAYER · · ·

Lord, in the midst of life's pressures, help me not to worry beforehand or premeditate how I will answer; but let me hear Your voice and speak as the Spirit empowers me.

· · · TODAY'S THOUGHT · · ·

The Scriptures admonish: "Be swift to hear, slow to speak" (James 1:19). Usually we reverse that formula. We would save ourselves much heartache by consistently obeying this command.

—Robert E. Fisher

DO NOT FEAR

"I will pray the Father, and He will give you another
Helper, that He may abide with you forever" (John 14:16).

For 32 years our ministry was exciting and fruitful. Ministering alongside my husband, I was privileged to work in the area where I feel best qualified. I worked at West Coast Bible College and in state offices. I had been executive secretary to Executive Committee members for eight years when we were assigned to state overseer work again. We would have to sell our home; the children were in college and we would be breaking up the family by leaving them behind. Our first child would be marrying, I would have to give up the job I enjoyed, and I was turning 50.

Six major events were happening to me. "Job's comforters" said they would give me six months before I would have a nervous breakdown.

As state Ladies Ministries president I would be following Kohatha Culpepper, a talented and godly woman who was also a minister. Fear gripped me. How could I follow someone like her? I desperately wanted to be a good spiritual leader and to be loved by those I would work with.

On Tuesday morning at the camp meeting right after our appointment, a scripture from the devotional spoke directly to me: "Arise, for this matter is your responsibility. We also will be with you. Be of good courage, and do it" (Ezra 10:4). That said to me that in this new responsibility, this new direction, our family would be fine and God would lead me as He had in the past. I was encouraged. The Holy Spirit had once again given me the assurance needed for the road ahead.

A nervous breakdown never came! My fears faded away. The Holy Spirit was the comforter He promised to be.

· · · PRAYER · · ·

Thank you, Lord, for being a keeper of Your promises, and an ever-present help in time of need. I love you.

· · · TODAY'S THOUGHT · · ·

"God does not hold me responsible for success, but for faithfulness."

—Mary Fisher

THE GREAT COMMUNICATOR

"But the Helper, the Holy Spirit, whom the Father will send in My name, He will teach you all things, and bring to your remembrance all things that I said to you" (John 14:26).

 President Ronald Reagan was acclaimed as the "great communicator" during his tenure in office. His communication skills could transcend culture and age. He had a unique ability to get a message across to people, but he was limited.

Jesus presented the Holy Spirit as the great communicator from heaven. He is an omniscient communicator. The triune God is the basis of all truth. The scope of His knowledge is unlimited.

The Spirit is able to teach all things. He can teach the best-educated, the most brilliant, and the wisest. There is nothing He cannot communicate to a willing heart. A sincere and open mind is His invitation to impart knowledge and understanding. He brings new and unlearned truths to those who submit themselves to God. He leads followers into vast new dimensions of spiritual understanding and makes deep truths that are beyond human comprehension easily understood.

The Spirit not only introduces the believer to new truths, but He also restores to memory truth learned in the past. "He will . . . bring to your remembrance all things that I said to you." Straying children who have been taught the Word will be reminded of the truth as the Spirit convicts them. He will restore the memory of truth to witnesses for Christ in a marvelous manner.

Look at Christ's disciples. They were bound by human ideas, plagued by pressures from people, and bewildered by the events of the Crucifixion. After their baptism in the Holy Spirit, they entered a new dimension of understanding as the Spirit gave them illumination. They spoke the wonderful works of God to the amazement of the hearers.

· · · PRAYER · · ·

Dear God, I want to know You and to know Your perfect will for my life. I open my mind to Your Spirit for His fullness and direction. Speak and I will hear, lead and I will follow, direct and I will obey.

· · · TODAY'S THOUGHT · · ·

More important than having great knowledge of many things is knowing the Holy Spirit, who knows all things and can enlighten the mind as the need arises. He is near and desires to be a divine Helper to those who will listen.

—Walter P. Atkinson

THE SPIRIT THAT MOVES MOUNTAINS

*So he answered and said to me: "This is the word of the
Lord to Zerubbabel: 'Not by might nor by power, but by My
Spirit," says the Lord of hosts. 'Who are you, O great
mountain? Before Zerubbabel you shall become a plain!
And he shall bring forth the capstone with shouts of
"Grace, grace to it!"'"* (Zechariah 4:6, 7).

Zechariah was a prophet during the reign of Zerubbabel the
governor and Joshua the high priest. For over 12 years the
project of rebuilding the temple had been left uncompleted.
Zechariah was commissioned to motivate the people to finish
the project. The task loomed like an insurmountable mountain.

An angel showed Zechariah "a lampstand of solid gold, with a bowl
on top of it, and on the stand seven lamps with seven pipes to the seven
lamps. Two olive trees are by it . . . [with] branches that drip into the
receptacles of the two gold pipes" (4:2, 3, 12).

The receptacles for the oil were routinely to be filled by the priests.
However, the angel showed Zechariah that God would divinely furnish
the supply of oil. This was symbolic of the Holy Spirit.

Before the mountain is moved, repentance is necessary (1:3). The
Holy Spirit never demonstrates His power through lives which are not
submitted to Him. He must be received in His baptismal power for the
miraculous to be demonstrated.

Cleansing must come from God (3:4). Unclean and unfit garments
are gone and "rich robes" of His righteousness are given. God does not
perform mountain-moving miracles where sin exists. He makes
Himself strong on behalf of the righteous (Psalm 5:12).

Satan must be rebuked (Zechariah 3:2). Satan cannot overcome a
believer who walks in the Word and submits to the Holy Spirit.

Even after repentance, cleansing, and rebuking of Satan, the mountain
of obstacles or impossible tasks cannot be moved by human effort. Only
the power of the Holy Spirit moves mountains in the spiritual realm.

· · · PRAYER · · ·

*O God, I open my life to Your holy presence. Flow into me in Your
power, and flow out of me as a river of blessing to others.*

· · · TODAY'S THOUGHT · · ·

He cares! He is able! Allow Him to move the mountain now!

—Oleda Atkinson

GRACE FOR GRIEF

Likewise the Spirit also helps in our weaknesses. For we do not know what we should pray for as we ought, but the Spirit Himself makes intercession for us with groanings which cannot be uttered (Romans 8:26).

The silence that surrounded me prior to daybreak was comforting. Not fully awake but unable to return to a sound sleep, I reflected on the Thanksgiving holiday that the family had spent at Grandmother's house. It had been a day of laughter, songs, and play. It was a perfect day of family fellowship and reunion.

Suddenly the shrill ring of the telephone pierced the stillness.

"Your son and his wife have had an accident. Your daughter-in-law is seriously injured. Your son was killed instantly."

In one terrible moment the joyful closeness of Thanksgiving changed to the empty loss of death. Joy of a firstborn son who fulfilled every expectation and. brought nothing but pleasure and pride was changed to numbness. *This can't be true*, I kept thinking. *Somebody please tell me that this is all a big mistake.*

How could we cope? In our time of tragedy and grief, our family turned to the Word and received this grace for grief:

In all things God works for the good of those who love Him (Romans 8:28). When we put together everything that happens in our lives, it all combines for an ultimate, eternal good.

God will finish that which He has begun in our lives. It doesn't matter how small or how large our faith may be, God will nourish it until it grows to the size which He desires.

The Spirit makes intercession for us when we are struggling. God acts on our behalf and promises to give victory in the midst of crises.

God will keep us in His love. Nothing "shall be able to separate us from the love of God which is in Christ Jesus our Lord" (Romans 8:39).

· · · PRAYER · · ·

Father, thank You for the power that gives us grace for grief. In our times of grief You speak and heal.

· · · TODAY'S THOUGHT · · ·

Our son, Paul, said it best that Thanksgiving Day when he wrote: "It is time for me to be quiet; / It is time for me to be still; / For Jesus Christ, the light of my life, / Is about to speak and heal."

—Paul L. Walker

GOD'S HOLY SPIRIT SUSTAINS US

Now may the God of hope fill you with all joy and peace in believing, that you may abound in hope by the power of the Holy Spirit (Romans 15:13).

For several weeks I had been experiencing a horrible accumulation of pressure, both mental and emotional. My work had piled up, and schedule demands were burning me out. Through a combination of circumstances, I was riding the ragged edge of a nervous breakdown.

Some nights I would dream of being chased—and then crushed—by a massive object relentlessly pursuing and slowly gaining on me as I ran to escape it. Other nights I feared closing my eyes to go to sleep, feeling that if I did I would not awaken again—that my heart would stop or my breath cease. I was rational enough to know this wasn't true but too weak in my emotionally drained condition to break the tormenting thoughts.

Then I discovered the words of the songwriter: "I will both lie down in peace, and sleep; for You alone, O Lord, make me dwell in safety" (Psalm 4:8). And another lyric read, "I lay down and slept; I awoke, for the Lord sustained me" (3:5).

I can hardly describe the power of those words as they flowed across my weary soul. I grasped them for the reliable, eternal words of truth that they are. They were all the more meaningful to me when I remembered they were written by a very busy man—a man of accomplishment and crushing responsibilities. David was a successful king and a conquering hero, yet a man who needed release from pressures that threatened his sleep.

Let God's words buoy your soul. He's there for you right now. You don't need to fear anymore. "Whoever calls on the name of the Lord shall be saved" (Acts 2:21).

· · · PRAYER · · ·

Thank You, Lord, for Your protection and Your sustaining power. Abiding in You, I have nothing to fear.

· · · TODAY'S THOUGHT · · ·

Long ago God promised, "As your days, so shall your strength be" (Deuteronomy 33:25). That promise still holds today.

—Jack W. Hayford

KNOWING THE WILL OF GOD

Teach me to do Your will, for You are my God; your Spirit is good. Lead me in the land of uprightness (Psalm 143:10).

The will of God for the believer should not be one of uncertainty or mystery. It is in the providence of God that we know His will for our life. How do we determine that? I have used "The Witness of the Three W's" to help an individual make a determination.

First, there is the witness of the Spirit. God has made us a spirit being, and He gives direction as to the way His Spirit will guide us. He speaks to our spirit man. Sometimes there is a red light that says *stop*, or a yellow light that means *caution*; and then there are times when we get a green light indicating that we should *move ahead*. If we learn to obey these signals, it will bring a sense of direction to our life.

There is also the witness of the Word. God's will is always contained within the framework of His Word. The psalmist said, "Your word is a lamp to my feet and a light to my path" (Psalm 119:105). We should be very careful when instruction, counsel, or advice concerning the will of God cannot meet the test of the Word. God's will is revealed through His Word.

Then there is the witness of circumstances. When we look to God for His will, I believe He allows us to use the witness of circumstances. It is like putting together a jigsaw puzzle. When the right piece is found, it drops in; but if it is the wrong piece, even though one tries to force it, it won't fit. In determining God's will, the circumstances will be such that we will not have to force it to happen, but the right piece will fall into place naturally. We will feel the witness of the Spirit, and we will sense an easiness when it happens.

· · · PRAYER · · ·

Father, help me to feel the reassuring witness of Your Spirit as I seek to know Your will for my life. I am depending on the leadership of the Spirit in all of life's decisions.

· · · TODAY'S THOUGHT · · ·

Once we have found the will of God and live in that will, assurance will come, as well as faith, confidence, and trust; and the blessing of God will rest upon us.

—Thomas E. Trask

THE FREEDOM OF THE SPIRIT

*Now the Lord is the Spirit; and where the Spirit of the Lord
is, there is liberty* (2 Corinthians 3:17).

The Holy Spirit brings liberty. This is comforting and exciting
truth. The Holy Spirit brings freedom from sin, guilt, and fear.
He brings freedom in worship. The uninhibited worship of
Pentecostals is the result of the ministry of the Spirit.

He also gives believers freedom to love with the unconditional love
of God. He enables the church to give unfettered witness for Christ.
The life of the Spirit-led, Spirit-filled believer is a life of wonderful
freedom.

Paul urged the Thessalonians, "Do not quench the Spirit" (1
Thessalonians 5:19). The fire of the Spirit may be extinguished by
those who are uncomfortable with the "fire." The full-orbed ministry
of the Spirit fulfills the prophetic vision of John the Baptist, who said,
"He will baptize you with the Holy Spirit and fire" (Matthew 3:11).
Quenching the Spirit puts out the fire.

Stephen accused the Jewish leaders of his day of resisting the Holy
Spirit. He said, "You stiff-necked and uncircumcised in heart and ears!
You always resist the Holy Spirit" (Acts 7:51). They resisted the ministry of the Spirit in their midst. The freedom of the Spirit was abridged
by these religious leaders.

Paul instructed the Ephesians, "And do not grieve the Holy Spirit of
God, by whom you were sealed for the day of redemption" (Ephesians
4:30). He indicated the sources of this grief—lying, anger, stealing,
corrupt communications, bitterness, wrath, and malice. The miscon-
duct of believers grieves the Spirit.

Let us join the Spirit in a mutual gift of freedom. The church gives
Him freedom to operate in the life and ministry of the church. He gives
the church freedom in worship and witness. The mutual freedom is
essential to the health of the church. We participate in this mutual gift
by refusing to quench, resist, or grieve this divine Helper.

· · · PRAYER · · ·

*Father, we thank You for the promise of the Spirit. Help us always to
be receptive to the Spirit and to give Him freedom to work among us.*

· · · TODAY'S THOUGHT · · ·

When the Spirit has freedom to work, the work will be done!

—B.E. Underwood

YOUR GIFTEDNESS

Having then gifts differing according to the grace that is given to us, let us use them: if prophecy, let us prophesy in proportion to our faith (Romans 12:6).

"According to the effective working by which every part does its share" (Ephesians 4:16) is how Paul spoke of the means for increase of the body. Elsewhere he wrote about "having . . . gifts differing according to the grace that is given to us" (Romans 12:6). Such gifting is not of one's own volition. It rather is of God's sovereign choice and is imparted by the Holy Spirit.

For the work of the ministry in a local church, too often there has been too great a dependency upon one man, the pastor. This must change. Even as many members comprise the human body, so it is with the body of Christ. God places these members in the body for specific functions, and they are gifted accordingly.

The eye does not resemble the ear in either appearance or function; neither the ear the hand. Remember, what you are and the function you perform is by God's choice. It is important also to remember that each of us is part of the whole. We work in harmony for the good of the entire body of Christ to accomplish His purposes on earth.

Only the Spirit can orchestrate this harmony, reminding us pointedly of the need for a Spirit-filled and Spirit-led body. This can be so only as individual believers are Spirit-filled and Spirit-led.

Appreciate your giftedness, though it differs from that of a fellow believer. What you are, you are by the grace of God!

· · · PRAYER · · ·

Father, I thank You for the gifts You have placed in Your church. Help us to discover the special gifts we have received according to the grace You have given us.

· · · TODAY'S THOUGHT · · ·

God has given us different gifts, and He desires us to use them for His glory.

—Billy Murray

HIS GLORIOUS PROVISION

But you, beloved, building yourselves up on your most holy
faith, praying in the Holy Spirit . . . (Jude 20).

Everyone has an "Aunt Ida." Mine moved back to Texas from California shortly after World War II. Accompanying her was a grown son who had been the victim of two very serious mistakes by physicians at the time of his birth. His eyesight was 80 percent destroyed, and he was unable to drive. Now, in Hamlin, Texas, my mother asked me to drive my aunt to church.

Driving my aunt to her church was humiliating. The church met in a most tortured building, was filled with those of lower income, and was pastored by a woman. The music was loud, and shouts of "Amen" and "Hallelujah" could be heard above the singing. People spoke in tongues and testified. It was not the place of choice for a proud 15-year-old junior in high school.

One Sunday morning, my Sunday school teacher said, "I've been praying for you. The Lord has told me He has called you into the ministry. Is that true?" I turned red, as she put her arms around me and began to pray and weep. One week later, during a Sunday night service, she invited, "Johnny, if you want to go up for prayer, I will go with you." I was converted and submitted my life to God's call. The change that took place in my life was astounding.

The congregation began to pray that I would be baptized in the Holy Spirit. A new hunger began to grow for prayer and Bible reading. During a tarrying service, the Holy Spirit came upon me, bringing sweet peace and release for ministry. I became a confident witness for the Lord.

The baptism in the Holy Spirit has been a great equipping experience. When words are insufficient to express life's agonies or to satisfy my need to praise the Lord, I have the privilege of returning to God's wonderful flow and enabling strength. He empowers me to fulfill my calling and to confront the kingdom of darkness.

· · · PRAYER · · ·

Father, I thank You for the baptism in the Holy Spirit and for the
blessing of speaking to You in the language of Your Spirit.

· · · TODAY'S THOUGHT · · ·

When we do not know what we should pray for, the Spirit will intercede for us.

—John Holland

CAN WORK BE SPIRITUAL?

"And I have filled him with the Spirit of God, in wisdom, in understanding, in knowledge, and in all manner of workmanship" (Exodus 31:3).

It is not just preachers who are to seek God's anointing for their daily work. The biblical truth evident in Exodus 31:3 is that the whole realm of human activity called work is under the authority of God's Spirit. The Spirit anointed Bezaleel in all his craftsmanship labors. It was the Spirit of God who enabled Bezaleel and all the other workers to build the wilderness tabernacle. Every day's labor, in any job imaginable, can be submitted to God and carried out under the Spirit's anointing.

Work is a part of God's plan for every person. God assigned Adam and Eve to the work of cultivating and maintaining the Garden of Eden before sin entered the world (Genesis 2:15). It is through work that men and women find fulfillment for the creative nature God has given them.

Without a doubt, sin changed the realm of work for humankind. After the fact of sin, work became burdensome (Genesis 3:17-19). It also became idolatrous as people sought to find meaning in life in their work instead of finding it in God. The Book of Ecclesiastes describes this problem candidly: "Then I looked on all the works that my hands had done and on the labor in which I had toiled; and indeed all was vanity and grasping for the wind. There was no profit under the sun" (2:11). The meaning of life lies outside the workplace. Human achievement cannot ultimately satisfy. Work is intended to be a meaningful part of human existence but not the meaning of it.

The gospel calls us to dedicate our work to God. In doing that we open ourselves to receive the anointing of the Spirit to be laborers for the Lord in all things.

· · · PRAYER · · ·

Our Father, let our labors each day be dedicated to You. Our work is so much of what we do and who we are. Help us to render all our labor to You as we strive to serve humankind and build up the kingdom of God.

· · · TODAY'S THOUGHT · · ·

Whatever your hand finds to do, do it with your might" (Ecclesiastes 9:10).

— R. Jerome Boone

IN THE SPIRIT AND INTO THE WILDERNESS

So he carried me away in the Spirit into the wilderness
(Revelation 17:3).

If asked to chart their spiritual course, most people would tell you that their desire is to dwell on the mountain, or perhaps even to take a trip to Canaan. Few, if any, would choose to travel the uncharted roads into the wilderness. I too would choose Canaan. The wilderness is for next time, sometime, or maybe even for someone else. There is a fear of the unknown. We have all experienced it.

There was a time when the thought of being in the wilderness frightened me greatly. Testimonies given by others made my imagination run wild—pain, hours of loneliness, tears, heartbreak, temptation, brushes with death, and emotions no one even dared to utter. I was truly convinced that the valley of the shadow of death was just beyond the wilderness. Surely God loved me too much to take me down this road. I was wrong.

Romans 8:14 tells us the sons of God are led by the Spirit. God charts our path. God told Israel it was He who led them into the wilderness to teach them, to prove them, and to humble them.

Jesus himself was also led into the wilderness by the Holy Spirit. Though weakened in the flesh and tempted by Satan, through the power of the Word He overcame the wilderness trial and embarked on a ministry of miracles.

I too was led into the wilderness. For me, the wilderness experience was a severe illness. Pain screamed out of the darkness; fear gripped my soul. I was tired, hungry, and thirsty, but God provided manna and water from the Rock. The Spirit led and I trusted His guidance. My faith increased as I was nurtured daily by the Spirit. Finally, He led me to the milk and honey of Canaan.

If you are in the wilderness, the Holy Spirit will lead you out.

· · · PRAYER · · ·

Dear Father, I thank You today for Your love and for the divine guidance of Your Holy Spirit. Grant me and all Your children the strength to face whatever wildernesses we may have to go through.

· · · TODAY'S THOUGHT · · ·

The road that leads to the wilderness also leads to Canaan. Today's suffering and trials are tomorrow's victories.

—Roy Stewart

LIVE A LIFE WITHOUT REPROACH

If we live in the Spirit, let us also walk in the Spirit
(Galatians 5:25).

When Johnny was 6 years old, his father was caught speeding. Dad handed the officer a $20 bill along with his driver's license. "It's OK, son," his father said. "Everybody does it."

When Johnny was 8, he heard his uncle George explaining how to shave points off the income tax form. "It's OK, kid," Uncle George explained. "Everybody does it."

At 9, Johnny's mother took him to his first live theater production. The box-office man couldn't find any seats until his mother discovered an extra five dollars in her purse. "It's OK," she said. "Everybody does it."

At 12, Johnny broke his glasses, and Aunt Francine told the insurance company that his glasses had been stolen so they could collect $75. "It's OK. Everybody does it."

At 15, Johnny made right guard on the high school football team, and his coach showed him how to block and at the same time to grab the opposing end's shirt in a manner the officials couldn't see. "It's OK, Johnny," the coach explained. "Everybody does it."

At age 19, Johnny was offered college test scores for $50. "It's OK, kid," the upperclassman explained. "Everybody does it."

Johnny was caught cheating and was kicked out of school in disgrace.

"How could you do this to your mother and me?" his father lamented. "You never learned such at home." His aunt and uncle were also highly shocked. If there's one thing the adult world can't stand, it's a kid who cheats.

Paul tells us to live in the Spirit. If we Christians, as we profess, have the Spirit of Christ in our lives, if we have been renewed by His Spirit, our minds and actions are changed. We will show forth proper fruit of the Spirit rather than the actions of the world. The true believer no longer wants to walk after the flesh but after the Spirit.

· · · PRAYER · · ·

Lord, You have sent the Holy Spirit to help us live pleasing to You. May we live and walk according to Your calling. May others see and sense Your presence in and through our lives.

· · · TODAY'S THOUGHT · · ·

Action speaks louder than words .

—Larry Miller

PUTTING YOURSELF TOGETHER

*But you, beloved, building yourselves up on your most
holy faith, praying in the Holy Spirit* (Jude 20).

We live in a world not unlike Jude's as it relates to the attacks on our faith. If we accept all the Bible as absolutely true and as a foundation on which to build a lifestyle, we are out of step with this modern society. Many professing Christians are constantly trying to reinterpret or put a new face on the faith. We must guard against such error and continue to build our lives on the most holy faith.

The faith we received was not something we manufactured. That faith came from Jesus to the apostles, from the apostles to the church, from the church to blood-washed, Spirit-filled teachers and ministers and to us. Our faith is not merely someone's personal opinion but a revelation preserved and transmitted within His church, under the care and guidance of the Holy Spirit, from generation to generation.

This faith is a most holy faith. Holy faith is different from other faith because it is God-given—not opinion but revelation, not guessing but certainty. It is different because it has power to make those who believe different. It is mind-changing and life-changing.

Jude said we are to build ourselves up on this most holy faith. We are to take the building materials of life and put ourselves together daily in accordance with the revelation of God's Word. The building materials that do not fit must be discarded and replaced with those that do. We can only discern which materials are the right ones by praying in the Holy Spirit. When the Holy Spirit takes full possession, our desires are so purified that our prayer becomes right. This is why it is so essential that we pray in the Spirit, which cannot be done until we have been filled with the Spirit.

· · · PRAYER · · ·

Gracious Father, put me together today like You want. Help me to follow the blueprint. I do not know in myself what I need to do; but as the Spirit prays through me, give me those needed building blocks and make me the person You want me to be.

· · · TODAY'S THOUGHT · · ·

Praying in the Spirit will assure you of proper life building, and the human spirit cannot fail if it is based on that foundation.

—Daniel Boling

GOD STILL FILLS BELIEVERS' SPIRIT

They were all filled with the Holy Spirit and began to speak
with other tongues, as the Spirit gave them utterance
(Acts 2:4).

———————

The experience of receiving the baptism in the Holy Spirit some 42 years ago is still fresh in my mind. An evangelist from the United States came to our church at Pointe-a-Pierre, Trinidad, and I went there to hear him on a Saturday evening. The overseer's son said to me, "Brother Arnold, the Holy Spirit is falling, you better go in and get yours."

I slipped into a pew and began seeking the Lord. I prayed, saying, "Pass me not, O gentle Savior, hear my humble cry; while on others Thou art calling, do not pass me by." At that point a surge of spiritual power moved through me and I fell to the floor shouting praises to God. I got up feeling happy, thinking I had received the baptism in the Spirit. But my pastor, the Reverend Sam Mathura, questioned me, "Brother, did you get filled?" I answered in the affirmative. Then he asked, "Did you speak in tongues?" I said, "No." To my dismay, he said, "You ain't got it yet, brother; you got to speak in tongues."

The next day, on Sunday evening, I was in church again. This time, as I prayed, I again felt the spiritual power I had felt before. I heard a brother saying, "Fill him, Lord! Fill him, Lord!" Suddenly, I heard myself speaking in a language I did not know. This went on so long I began to wonder if I would ever be able to speak in English again. But now I knew that I had been filled with the Holy Spirit.

Today, after so many years have passed, and after 29 years of missionary service, I still believe in and preach the baptism in the Holy Spirit with the initial evidence of speaking with other tongues, as the Spirit gives the utterance.

· · · PRAYER · · ·

Thank You, God, for the wonderful experience of the baptism in the
Holy Spirit. Thank You for the initial evidence of the baptism in the Spirit,
which gives us unshakable assurance of our experience of Your Spirit.

· · · TODAY'S THOUGHT · · ·

God still fills believers with the Holy Spirit and enables them to speak with other tongues as the Spirit gives the utterance.

—Selwyn E. Arnold

THE SPIRIT, A FOUNTAIN PEN, AND ME

"However, when He, the Spirit of truth, has come, He will guide you into all truth" (John 16:13).

Born November 20, 1914, the son of a minister in Dandridge, Tennessee, going to church became old hat to me. In my early teen years I began to skip church services every time I could, but God was working on His plan for my life.

Unknown to me, my older sister was praying for my salvation. One evening she coaxed me into accompanying her to church by promising to give me a new fountain pen. That night the Holy Spirit drew me to an altar of confession and forgiveness. I was saved and given a hunger for God.

When I was 18 God filled me with the Holy Spirit. From then on, I tried to follow the quiet inner leading of the Holy Spirit. Over the next nine years, as I worked for the Lord in my local church (Eighth Avenue Church of God in Knoxville, Tennessee), I felt called to the ministry, but I wanted to be sure. Being a minister's son, and married to the daughter of a minister, I knew the difficulties to be faced in the ministry.

Finally, I went to the General Assembly, praying, "Lord, if You are calling me to the ministry, let one of the state overseers ask me to come work in his state." Sitting alone in the balcony after one of the services was dismissed, I was approached by State Overseer Houston R. Morehead. He said, "I feel led of the Lord to offer you the pastorate in Potosi, Missouri." Thus did the Holy Spirit confirm my calling, and I became an ordained minister in the Church of God on August 6, 1942.

Over the years I was privileged to serve as pastor of seven churches, overseer of six states, a member of the Church of God Executive Council, and I served on the Church of God World Missions Board for 18 years.

· · · PRAYER · · ·

Lord Jesus, thank You for the Holy Spirit who leads us to saving faith in You. Thank You for the Holy Spirit, who guides us all through life.

· · · TODAY'S THOUGHT · · ·

All the good things about which we preach and for which we live will, by the guidance and help of the Holy Spirit, become ours.

—Donald A. Biggs

THE CURRENCY OF THE KINGDOM

Likewise the Spirit also helps in our weaknesses. For we do not know what we should pray for as we ought, but the Spirit Himself makes intercession for us with groanings which cannot be uttered (Romans 8:26).

The Bible has a different view of weakness than the one held by our generation. The apostle Paul said that when he was weak, then he was strong (2 Corinthians 12:10). The chorus says, "Let the poor say, 'I am rich'; let the weak say 'I am strong.'" Jesus said, "Come to Me, all you who labor and are heavy laden, and I will give you rest" (Matthew 11:28).

The Bible indicates that supernatural strength is available through the prayer of faith. Prayer is the currency of the kingdom of God. Money operates the kingdoms of this world, but prayer operates the kingdom of God. Faith in God and His Word gives authenticity to the currency of prayer. Money is used to meet needs in worldly kingdoms. Prayer is used to meet the needs presented to God.

Prayer is so important the Bible exhorts us to "pray without ceasing" (1 Thessalonians 5:17). Prayer is so important that Jesus Christ is ever interceding to the Father for His children (Hebrews 7:25). Prayer is so vital that the Holy Spirit helps us in our weaknesses and in our ignorance by praying through us and for us.

Jesus is praying for you. The Holy Spirit is praying for you. Christian brothers and sisters are praying for you. Are you praying? Can the Holy Spirit pray through you? There is nothing more important you can do about any problem than to join in this supernatural prayer meeting each day. Let your needs open you to more of Christ and His Word. Pray!

· · · PRAYER · · ·

Blessed Father, I thank You for sending Christ to respond to my greatest need—forgiveness for sin. Thank You for sending the Holy Spirit to help with my weaknesses. Thank You for understanding my needs and using them as an opportunity to love me and help me. I rejoice in Christ my Savior and in the Holy Spirit, my Comforter.

· · · TODAY'S THOUGHT · · ·

Because of Christ's presence in our life, we can say with Paul, "When I am weak, then I am strong."

—Al Taylor

WAITING IN THE SPIRIT

For we through the Spirit eagerly wait for the
hope of righteousness by faith (Galatians 5:5).

 The person and work of the Holy Spirit is usually understood in terms of a dynamic, forceful, and empowering ministry. We are transformed by, baptized with, guided through, and will be caught away in the *power* of the Holy Spirit.

Paul, however, set forth another dimension of the Spirit's dynamic work in a believer. It is an eager, yet patient and peaceful, waiting "for the hope of righteousness." The believer lives in an environment of flash, fury, and futility. We are surrounded by a fast-food, instant-on, 24-hour-shopping, fax-connected, cellular-networked, running, walking, jogging, stressed-out society.

To be *eager* and to *wait* seems like a contradiction—and it would be were it not for the residential ministry of the Holy Spirit. It is contrary to the natural impulses of the human person to eagerly hope and patiently wait. It is the Holy Spirit who enables us to do both.

What Paul describes is a beautiful spirit-controlled temperament—one in which we are able to live the full Christian life in a straining, stressed-out, and sinful society. It is exciting to live in the miraculous tension of *hoping* and *waiting*. In the midst of a sea of restless people, impatient to "go nowhere," hearing the rumble and feeling the musical vibrations of the spiritually dead, surrounded by people so emotionally low they need a fix to get high, is a group of Spirit-filled believers living in eager hope and yet patiently waiting! This is what Jesus promises to His faithful followers.

· · · PRAYER · · ·

Holy Spirit, I am prone to such eagerness for the hope which right-
eousness promises that I get impatient in this life. Slow me down, so
that in the waiting I can share my hope with someone lost in the rush
and rumble of life. Help me to learn how to appreciate living in fellow-
ship with eternity while walking in rhythm with time.

· · · TODAY'S THOUGHT · · ·

Christianity, by its very nature, creates a yearning for a better time and place, while on the other hand, the Holy Spirit whispers, "Wait in restrained eagerness."

—J. Anthony Lombard

THE HOLY SPIRIT, OUR TEACHER

*But into the second part the high priest went alone once a
year, not without blood, which he offered for himself and for
the people's sins committed in ignorance; the Holy Spirit
indicating this, that the way into the Holiest of All was not
yet manifest while the first tabernacle was still standing*
(Hebrews 9:7, 8).

All the works of the Holy Spirit in the believer are sublime! It
is impossible to explain in our limited human words His role in
bringing us to Christ to receive forgiveness. Neither can we
describe the way He works in our consciences to produce
repentance. Nor can we scientifically outline step-by-step what happened when we were born again. But the Holy Spirit works continually
in our lives to accomplish these things, even though we don't understand
them.

The Holy Spirit, through His indwelling and through the Scriptures,
teaches us about the mysteries and riches of Christ. The Lord knew it
was impossible for us as imperfect humans to plumb the depths of the
kingdom of God. Therefore, He advised His disciples—and us His
people—not to be discouraged, for He would send the Spirit to dwell
in us (John 14:16, 17), to guide us into all the truth (John 16:13, 14), to
teach us all things, and to bring to our remembrances all that He had
taught (John 14:26).

When the apostle Paul wrote his first letter to the Corinthians, he let
the church know what a privilege Christians possess in having the eternal wisdom that comes from God and the knowledge of heavenly
things that we enjoy. All this has been revealed to us by the Holy
Spirit (1 Corinthians 2:10).

Because the Holy Spirit has told us, we know that we can approach
the throne of grace with confidence and receive God's mercy and find
His grace is sufficient to help us in our times of need (Hebrews 4:16).
It is the Spirit who reveals to us our position in Christ.

· · · PRAYER · · ·

*Father, help us to surrender our lives totally to the influence of Your
Holy Spirit, that we may comprehend the things You want us to know.*

· · · TODAY'S THOUGHT · · ·

God has chosen to reveal to us the treasures of the Kingdom through
the Scriptures, the church, and his servants. These, however, are mere
channels—it is the Holy Spirit who teaches us.

—Hiram Almirudis

BAPTIZED IN THE HOLY SPIRIT

"Then I remembered the word of the Lord, how He said,
'John indeed baptized with water, but you shall be baptized
with the Holy Spirit'" (Acts 11:16).

I remember well the year 1921. That was when the Pentecostal message, the message about the baptism in the Holy Spirit, first came to our area. I was 16 years old, living in Mississippi, out from Brookhaven. My father was a farmer and the Sunday school superintendent of the local Baptist church, but the preaching about the Holy Spirit was new to us. I was saved, but the Lord began to deal with me about the baptism in the Spirit.

My brother-in-law Lum Adams had been called of God to preach, and God had baptized him in the Holy Spirit. With much desire to learn, he and I searched the Scriptures for a better understanding of the baptism in the Spirit. One day, as we were plowing the watermelon field, we stopped for a time of prayer. All of a sudden, a light shone down from above, the Lord appeared to me, and I was filled with the Holy Spirit and began to speak in other tongues. At the same time, God called me to preach the gospel.

My first sermon was preached not in a church but on a Mr. Sullivan's front porch. Many people gathered around to hear the Word of God.

Sometime later I began to feel the need to attend Bible school and prepare myself for the ministry. My father wanted me to be a farmer, but after much prayer and persuasion on my part, he consented to my going to Bible school and even agreed to help me, since I was so determined.

Another young preacher, named A.V. Beaube, and I loaded up our families and went to Bible Training School in Cleveland, Tennessee. Over the course of my ministry, I pastored a total of 12 churches in Louisiana, Texas, Arkansas, and California; conducted 127 revivals; organized five churches; and gave a helping hand to many young preachers.

· · · PRAYER · · ·

God, help us to never forget the words of our Lord Jesus, who said, "You shall be baptized with the Holy Spirit." Thank You for transforming and molding my life to Your will by the baptism in the Holy Spirit.

· · · TODAY'S THOUGHT · · ·

The gospel is good news, and part of that good news is that we can be filled with the Holy Spirit.

—W.F. Ainsworth

SPEECH THAT SPEAKS TO THE HEART

*And my speech and my preaching were not with persuasive
words of human wisdom, but in demonstration of the Spirit
and of power* (1 Corinthians 2:4).

Paul was a brilliant scholar. His background skilled him in
debate. However, the apostle's goal was to present the message of Jesus Christ and Him crucified. His confidence was
the gospel. The result was awesome. Anything Paul lacked,
God made up for in power.

I still remember going with my wife to hear Paul Harvey speak one
evening in the early '60s. Parking was inadequate. It was a long walk
to the auditorium. The seating was uncomfortable in the old building
on the vacated Navy base in Norman, Oklahoma. But for an hour I
was spellbound with Mr. Harvey's articulate speech and colorful
vocabulary. He interested me in his subject. He spoke of the greatness
of America and what it meant to be a citizen. He made me proud. But
for all the talent and ability displayed that evening, I wasn't changed.

In His providence, God has sent men of lesser talent into my life but
who preached the gospel by the power of the Holy Spirit and brought
me from darkness into the marvelous light of salvation.

Enticing words are enjoyable. Words of man's wisdom are wonderful. But the demonstration of the Spirit of God and the power of God
bring entrance into the kingdom of God. Thank God for those who
follow Paul's pattern. They keep Christ central and the message basic.

The same Spirit who enriches and confirms the believer also gives
gifts and sustains as we wait for the coming of the Lord Jesus Christ.
Paul spoke and preached about Christ crucified. Our witness must
always be the same. Thank God for the story of His love (John 3:16).

· · · PRAYER · · ·

*Heavenly Father, we thank You for the men and women You use to
communicate Your truth to our hearts. Reveal Your glory to us and
through us. Use us to reach others with Your love and grace. Let Your
Spirit and power flow through us to further Your kingdom.*

· · · TODAY'S THOUGHT · · ·

Our world needs most desperately to "see" Christ in our lives and to
"hear" Christ in our words. It is He who inspires and transforms men
and women into children of God.

—Kenneth Adams

THE HOLY SPIRIT, MY INSTIGATOR

And we know that all things work together for good to those who love God, to those who are the called according to His purpose (Romans 8:28).

I was born in the Republic of Panama and reared in the Roman Catholic faith. When I was 17 years old, the Holy Spirit unquestionably instigated my conversion. Like Saul of Tarsus, I was not seeking the Lord but going in the other direction. Then the Holy Spirit literally arrested me and led me to a humble Church of God where I was convicted of my sins and wonderfully saved.

I could not remain quiet about this new truth I'd found. I began to preach to family and friends about my conversion.

God wondrously opened a way for me to attend Zion Bible Institute in Rhode Island. After three years of study and one year of general evangelistic activities, I returned to Panama. As pastor of a local congregation I had the privilege of seeing my parents and my brothers and sisters converted. I baptized them in water with my own hands.

In Bible college I developed a disease that almost took my sight in one eye. After a while the other eye began to deteriorate also. I prayed with faith and confidence—but to no avail. Then the Holy Spirit spoke and said, "If you really believe the promise of Mark 16:18, that they shall lay hands on the sick and they shall recover, what better way to begin than with yourself?" I knew then that God was going to heal me.

Instead of getting better, my sight got worse. My doctor said my disease was incurable. Then five days after the doctor made his diagnosis, at 10 o'clock at night, I was led by the Holy Spirit to pray. At midnight I opened my eyes, the black turned to gray, the gray turned to light! The very first thing my eyes fell on was a plaque on the wall which read, "God answers prayer."

· · · PRAYER · · ·

Lord, I am so thankful that You have instigated the great things in my life! Through Your Holy Spirit, make me an instigator of truth and love.

· · · TODAY'S THOUGHT · · ·

My blindness gave me a new perspective on ministry, life, destiny, and even eternity.

—Horace Spragg

THE HOPEFUL EXPECTATION

*Not only they, but we also who have the firstfruits of the
Spirit, even we ourselves groan within ourselves, eagerly
waiting for the adoption, the redemption of our body*
(Romans 8:23).

In the three years my brother, Bob, fought a losing battle with cancer, the family rode an emotional roller coaster. There were some very encouraging days, but there were also some days when pain and death pressed so heavily upon his frail body that Bob would say to us, "Pray that I'll die."

He had reached that point when the flesh realized it would be best to enter a finer life—a diviner life—waiting beyond death's veil. Nearing the end, Bob roused to say, "I'm looking for Him, I'm looking for Him." His wife, Barbara, asked, "Who are you looking for, Bob?" He replied, "I'm looking for Jesus." A short time later, he triumphantly declared, "I've found Him, I've found Him!"

As Bob closed his eyes in death, the Spirit of God flooded the room. My mother raised her hands and began to speak in a heavenly language. It was as if God said, "Don't worry about a thing. I've just put My big fingers on his eyelids and kissed away his soul at his lips, and I've taken him to be with Me."

How does a man and his family hold on faithfully when it seems prayers are unanswered and death claims a saint in the prime of his ministry? It can only be attributed to the blessed Holy Spirit, the seal of our present and future life in Christ, whose firstfruits tell us there is a higher life to share.

· · · PRAYER · · ·

Dear Father, I thank You for redemption that will be complete when Your Son returns. May Your Spirit continue to endorse my longing for total redemption. Let me help others to find the full salvation You alone can give.

· · · TODAY'S THOUGHT · · ·

Christ suffered on the cross, but the writer of Hebrews said He endured its agony for the "joy that was set before Him" (12:2). Suffering may come, but it comes to sanctify. Faith looks up, knowing that redemption draws near. How can we lose if we are living in the Spirit?

—T. David Sustar

MEASURABLE OR IMMEASURABLE

*For He whom God has sent speaks the words of God, for
God does not give the Spirit by measure* (John 3:34).

 By measure or without measure, limited or unlimited, this is
the heart and core of a wonderful verse which explains so
much about the outpouring of the Holy Spirit in the life of
every believer.

In the Old Testament, the Spirit was given by measure. Remember
the portion of Moses which was divided and given to 70 others
(Numbers 11:16, 17, 25-29). Elijah's portion was powerful enough but
he asked for a double portion (2 Kings 2:9, 10) and received it. John
the Baptist also had a measure of Elijah's portion (Luke 1:15-17).

But things change in Acts 2, for "when the Day of Pentecost had fully
come," there was an outpouring of the Holy Spirit and power in immea-
surable proportions. John the Baptist spoke of this baptism with these
words: "I indeed baptize you with water unto repentance, but He who is
coming after me is mightier than I, whose sandals I am not worthy to
carry. He will baptize you with the Holy Spirit and fire" (Matthew 3:11).

Finis Dake, in his *Annotated Bible,* illustrates the principle this way:
"Take a pitcher of water and a small glass. The glass is filled by pouring
from the pitcher. It could be divided into 70 portions. If half-full it
could be doubled. Even if filled, it could be dropped into the pitcher and
baptized, no longer by measure, but now without measure. Submerged,
inundated, saturated inside and outside, filled to overflowing."

Rest assured, it is not possible to be baptized without being filled.
God's Word calls for all believers to be both filled and baptized with
the Holy Spirit. He doesn't want you to be limited but totally unlimited for Him.

· · · PRAYER · · ·

*Thank You, our Father, that You do all things well. Thank You for the
Niagara of Your love and grace showered daily upon us. Here's my cup,
Lord; fill it up, Lord. Baptize me that I may bless others by the overflow.*

· · · TODAY'S THOUGHT · · ·

The psalmist David exclaimed, "My cup runs over. Surely goodness
and mercy shall follow me all the days of my life; and I will dwell in
the house of the Lord forever" (Psalm 23:5, 6).

—Bennie S. Triplett

HOLY SPIRIT DIRECTION

*As they ministered to the Lord and fasted, the Holy Spirit
said, "Now separate to Me Barnabas and Saul for the work
to which I have called them." Then, having fasted and
prayed, and laid hands on them, they sent them away*
(Acts 13:2, 3).

While in prayer one night in November 1950, I had a unique experience relative to my call to preach. Under a heavy burden to get started actively conducting revival services, the Holy Spirit began speaking through me in other tongues. My wife's father, who was in an adjoining room, received and gave an interpretation to the message. It was about 1 a.m. The message was a distinct affirmation of my call and a promise that the Lord would use my life in His work.

In January 1951, I was invited to conduct a revival in Canton, Georgia. I have never been without a preaching appointment since that time. As the men cited in the scripture above, God spoke to me through the Holy Spirit.

I believe the Holy Spirit still moves today so we can be aware of ministry for a specific purpose. We must not read into every feeling or experience a change in our work—it is imperative that we stay within the context of an event—but the Holy Spirit is certainly involved in God's work here on earth. The Holy Spirit will minister to us as we glean truth and direction from the inspired Word, which is in essence an interpretation of God's will for all mankind: "For prophecy never came by the will of man, but holy men of God spoke as they were moved by the Holy Spirit" (2 Peter 1:21).

· · · PRAYER · · ·

Dear Lord, grant that we will be filled with the Spirit. May we walk in the way of revealed truth, one body indwelt and sustained by the Holy Spirit, to complete our purpose as effective witnesses for Jesus.

· · · TODAY'S THOUGHT · · ·

The Spirit-filled believer can always depend on the leading of the Holy Spirit. We must remain sensitive and keenly aware of what He is saying. He will never lead us astray.

—E.J. Reynolds

Febr

LED TO PLANT NEW CHURCHES

*"However, when He, the Spirit of truth, has come, He will
guide you into all truth; for He will not speak on His own
authority, but whatever He hears He will speak; and He will
tell you things to come"* (John 16:13).

The year was 1960, the place England. I had graduated from Birmingham Bible Institute in July of the previous year and had been invited to the city of Manchester 86 miles away. That was not unusual, but it was unusual the way God had prepared the hearts of the people to receive the gospel. We soon moved from a tent to a school auditorium and finally into our own building. The Spirit of the Lord descended mightily upon me, giving me a vision and a burden for those challenging times.

Six churches were planted in the space of seven and a half years—five in adjacent towns and one as far as 215 miles away, in the city of Southampton.

The Holy Spirit raised up workers from the Manchester church who accompanied me in towns and cities across the northern part of that country.

On one occasion the Lord healed a woman who had suffered a stroke and had not been able to close her mouth or eat anything for a whole day. Immediately, she was able to sit up in bed and have something warm to drink.

On going into a new field of harvest, the Holy Spirit always impressed upon me a heavy burden for that town or city. This was the sign which gave me boldness and assured me that there were many people in that city to be won for the Lord. In my later ministry, this sign appeared also in Montreal; in Ottawa; in Trenton, New Jersey; and all the 13 places that the Holy Spirit has guided me to establish local congregations.

· · · PRAYER · · ·

Lord, bless Your children today in all that we do. Teach us to listen closely to what Your Spirit would tell us, and give us grace to follow the Spirit's guidance at all times and under all circumstances.

· · · TODAY'S THOUGHT · · ·

Just as the Holy Spirit led the early disciples, and the apostle Paul, so will He lead us today into those places where the harvest is ripe for the reaping.

—Jeremiah McIntyre

FILLED WITH JOY AND THE HOLY SPIRIT

And the disciples were filled with joy and
with the Holy Spirit (Acts 13:52).

 The prominence of the Holy Spirit in divine redemption is evident throughout the Bible. When God created the world, it was the Spirit of God that moved upon the face of the earth, fashioning it to conform to God's spoken word.

Time and again throughout the Bible the Spirit of God moved upon and especially anointed individuals chosen to bring His message to His people and to deliver them from their enemies. Many of these instances involved ordinary people who experienced extraordinary power and ability as the Spirit touched their hearts, their minds, their lips.

The anointing of the Holy Spirit is real! I remember one of the first times I experienced His anointing. There were a couple of men in my home church who would travel to the small towns of the surrounding area on Saturdays, set up a public-address system, and preach on the street. As a teenage Christian, I would sometimes accompany them. I still remember when they gave me opportunity to testify and, as I spoke, the Spirit of God anointed me to speak in a way I had never known before. When I had finished testifying, I was visibly shaken and humbled by the experience.

What I experienced that day as I testified on the street in a small south Georgia town was the joy and the fullness of the Holy Spirit which the disciples of Jesus experienced in Acts. The Holy Spirit is a real person, a real presence, a real power—the source of our joy and our strength.

The fullness of the Holy Spirit is necessary. Jesus knew His disciples could not possibly survive the opposition they would face without the Spirit working in their lives. This was not an optional "equipping for service." They were commanded to tarry until they were endued with power from on high. The fullness of the Holy Spirit enables us today. Through His working in our lives we become pliable, powerful, usable, and real. Those early disciples were filled with joy and with the Holy Spirit. There is no greater source of strength for us today.

· · · PRAYER · · ·

Father, help us to truly be full of the Holy Spirit, and help us to live
and serve in the joy and ability which the Spirit gives.

· · · TODAY'S THOUGHT · · ·

Of all Christian resources, joy in and of the Holy Spirit is paramount.

—Aubrey D. Maye

SHARING GOOD NEWS

"You shall receive power when the Holy Spirit has come upon you: and you shall be witnesses to Me in Jerusalem, and in all Judea and Samaria, and to the end of the earth" (Acts 1:8).

 The fact that the witnessing was to be "to the end of the earth" shows that the commission did not apply to the apostles alone. They did not go to the end of the earth. Therefore, the commission reaches to Christians of all ages.

When Saul of Tarsus fell under glaring light from heaven, the Lord said He had come to make him a minister and a witness. Paul wasn't at that moment able to witness for Jesus. He was prostrate on the ground, a penitent, inquiring what the Lord would have him do. The Lord said, "I will make you a witness" (see Acts 26:16).

Paul was to witness about the happening of that day, also to what would yet appear to him. His experience was great on that special day, but he received a greater experience after he, in his blinded condition, had prayed for three days and received the Holy Spirit. He was then able to successfully witness about the great light, the voice of the Lord, and his healing from blindness.

The more we have to share with people, the more they shall receive. Paul did not have enough power to complete his testimony in his first experience, but after he received the other two experiences (sanctification and the Holy Ghost baptism), he was able to share with others.

You will notice in the verse it says, "You shall receive power when the Holy Spirit has come upon you." The question might arise, "Power for what?" The remaining part of the verse says, "And you shall be witnesses to Me." Their witnessing was to be a consequence of having received the Holy Ghost.

Today, timid women are testifying. Also, little children are giving testimonies the same as grown people. Why can they do this? The answer is "The power of the Holy Spirit has come upon them."

· · · PRAYER · · ·

O gracious God, breathe upon us with Your Holy Spirit until we are filled with Your grace and glory and enabled to share with others the testimony of Your wondrous salvation.

· · · TODAY'S THOUGHT · · ·

When the Holy Ghost comes upon us, He gives us power to share the good news of salvation.

—F.J. Lee

February 4

THE HOLY SPIRIT AS HELPER

"And I will pray the Father, and He will give you another Helper, that He may abide with you forever" (John 14:16).

I was a 12-year-old boy. I was sitting on a slatted pew in the old Clegg Street Church of God in Shelby, North Carolina, when something wonderful happened to me. I remember well that there was a large potbellied coal stove sitting square in the middle of the church. There were no rugs or carpets, just dusty wood floors with splinters. The altar was an old wooden pew turned backward.

But there in that rustic place, the Holy Spirit of God spoke to me one night and said, "I love you!"

I responded, "Not me, Lord. I don't love You, so how can You love me?"

But again the Spirit said, "I love you . . . and if you will give Me your heart, I will come in and make a new creature of you."

I could not resist His pleading call; and rushing to the old slatted altar, I gave my heart and all that I was and had to Jesus. The next weekend I received the baptism in the Holy Spirit, with the evidence of speaking in tongues.

Since that night, the Holy Spirit has been with me as my helper, friend, guide, teacher, and constant companion. Today, I have been in the ministry for 47 years, been married for 51 years, and have raised two marvelous sons, who were also called into the ministry.

How glad I am that God loved a small boy enough to send His Spirit to convict him of sin—and then loved this man sufficiently to give that same Spirit as Helper through all these years. I cannot thank Him enough!

The Church of God was born in the fire of the Spirit. If we allow that fire to go out, even this church will die.

· · · PRAYER · · ·

Father, I have leaned on Your Spirit for more than 56 years. I have learned that I can trust Him. I don't know what I would have done without Him. Thank You for giving me this wonderful gift.

· · · TODAY'S THOUGHT · · ·

Luke 4:1 tells us that even Jesus was "filled with the Holy Spirit." If our Lord needed to be filled with the Spirit, do we need such a filling any less?

—S. A. Lankford

SEASONED WITH SALT

Let your speech always be with grace, seasoned with salt,
that you may know how you ought to answer each one
(Colossians 4:6).

 My wife and I were converted in a small mining town in northeast Oklahoma. Shortly after our conversion we began attending the Church of God in Chetopa, Kansas. We knew nothing about the Holy Spirit and speaking in tongues as the initial evidence of the baptism of the Spirit.

My pastor, J.J. Weatherby, preached under the anointing of the Holy Spirit, creating in us a thirst for more of God. The Word says, "As the deer pants for the water brooks, so pants my soul for You, O God. My soul thirsts for God, for the living God. When shall I come and appear before God?" (Psalm 42:1, 2). "I spread out my hands to You; my soul longs for You like a thirsty land" (Psalm 143:6).

The saints in that church testified of being saved, sanctified, and filled with the Holy Ghost, with the evidence of speaking in tongues. My, how the power of God would fall during testimony services. When the altar call was given, we would immediately go and tarry at the altar for the Holy Ghost to come. About six months after my conversion, I received the Holy Spirit in my life and spoke with other tongues.

In church revivals and camp meetings where the minister preaches about the Holy Spirit and the gifts of the Spirit, a continual thirst is created for more of God's power. The psalmist wrote, "O God, You are my God; early will I seek You: my soul thirsts for You, my flesh longs for You in a dry and thirsty land where there is no water. So I have looked for You in the sanctuary to see Your power and Your glory" (Psalm 63:1, 2). David remembered the "good old days" when he had seen the manifestations of God's power in the house of the Lord.

· · · PRAYER · · ·

Lord, let the gospel we preach, the testimony we give, and the life we live make those around us thirsty for an experience with You. Let our speech be with grace, seasoned with salt.

· · · TODAY'S THOUGHT · · ·

These are still the good old days; the Holy Spirit is still relevant for these times—and He is still available for those who "hunger and thirst for righteousness, for they shall be filled" (Matthew 5:6).

—Billy L. Olds

February 6

AND HE REMAINED

*And John bore witness, saying, "I saw the Spirit descending
from heaven like a dove, and He remained upon Him"*
(John 1:32).

Each morning before our children leave for school, we have a
family prayer. We pray not only for God to protect them
throughout the day or to give them a good day or to help in
remembering what they have studied, but we also pray for the
Holy Spirit to help our children to be aware that He is always
with them. No matter what pressures they may encounter, whatever
exams are to be taken or reports to be given, we want them to always
sense the presence of the Holy Spirit. We want them to know they are
never alone.

Our lives are filled with uncertainties. Our society is more transi-
tional than ever. More of us are likely to relocate our residence or
change our careers than at any time in the past. This breeds uncertainty for us and our families.

How do we cope? It is important for us to understand what happened to Jesus in our text. The Holy Spirit moved upon Jesus as He
had moved upon others in years gone by. However, this time it was
different—the Holy Spirit *remained* on Him.

For us, the Holy Spirit came on the Day of Pentecost, and He has
remained even until now. The Holy Spirit also dwells in us to be a
source of stabilization, security, and power. When we receive the Spirit,
we are no longer alone. No matter where our paths may lead us, He
remains. No matter what we encounter, He remains. He is a constant
presence, a continuing guide, providing a secure relationship at all times
and under all circumstances. We can live with certain knowledge that
Jesus will be with us and go with us always, even to the end of the world.

· · · PRAYER · · ·

*Heavenly Father, keep us ever aware that this day the Holy Spirit is
with us as our constant source of inspiration and encouragement.
Help us to effectively yield to and obey that presence that we may minister to and encourage others. Grant that whatever we encounter or
wherever our feet take us, we will know Christ always remains.*

· · · TODAY'S THOUGHT · · ·

Life may be unstable and uncertain; but when we receive the Holy
Spirit, He is a sure and stabilizing factor in our lives.

—Martin Taylor

THE PENTECOSTAL REVIVAL

*"And it shall come to pass afterward that I will pour out My
Spirit on all flesh; your sons and your daughters shall
prophesy, your old men shall dream dreams, your young
men shall see visions; and also on My menservants and on
My maidservants I will pour out of My Spirit in those days"*
(Joel 2:28, 29).

Although my grandparents, the Reverend and Mrs. W.M.
Collins, were members of the Baptist church and he an
ordained minister and pastor, my grandmother Roxie experienced the baptism of the Holy Spirit with the evidence of
speaking in tongues.

My grandmother not only had received the baptism in the Holy
Spirit but also the gift of faith, the working of miracles, and the gifts of
healings. People came from near and far to be prayed for in her home.
We hardly knew what it was to go to a doctor. Grandmother would
pray for us, and God would heal us. Her experience of the Holy Spirit
and anointing of His power was not widely accepted by the people of
my grandfather's church. However, when there was a need from God,
they would come for her prayers.

The Spirit is being poured out upon all flesh. Millions of people of
traditionally non-Pentecostal persuasion are being filled with the Spirit,
speaking in tongues, and manifesting gifts of the Spirit in their lives.

How did this change come about? What caused this wide acceptance of the Holy Spirit's power? I believe it came because the message of Pentecost has been preached throughout the land. The scriptural message is irrefutable and undeniable: "I will pour out My Spirit on
all flesh."

· · · PRAYER · · ·

*Thank You, Father, for the latter rain that is making Your message of
love to be heard around the world through the power of Pentecostal
revival. Let there be a mighty outpouring upon all nations, preparing the
harvest for the reaping.*

· · · TODAY'S THOUGHT · · ·

These are exciting days. Greater and more glorious things are
ahead.

—F. Douglas Morgan

WHEN THE HOLY SPIRIT MOVES

Now the birth of Jesus Christ was as follows: After His mother Mary was betrothed to Joseph, before they came together, she was found with child of the Holy Spirit (Matthew 1:18).

A virtuous Mary was moved upon by the Holy Spirit. This was no ordinary event. Every time the Holy Spirit is involved, supernatural things happen. At this moving, the Lord Jesus came forth into the world, a thought which leaves three very distinct impressions.

First, Mary was prepared. She knew her God personally, in service and in purity. When we observe Mary, we are aware of the preparation that must be made in our own life. We must know God personally. The angels should be able to say to us, "The Lord is with you" (Luke 1:28). Every action and thought must be in preparation to receive and accomplish the will of God.

Second, Mary was submissive. In order for the Holy Spirit to move in us, with powerful anointing, we must be submissive. Mary said, "Let it be to me according to your word" (Luke 1:38). When the Spirit finds an openly submissive vessel, He will move in. Mary was totally open to her heavenly Father. There were no preconditions or selfish contracts to be signed and notarized. She recognized the awesome authority and holiness of God. Our society relishes the concept of being your own person, but true submission declares your willingness to allow God room in which to work. Preconceived ideas and theories must go. God requires all of the heart. We must remember He is the Creator and we are His creation.

Third, Mary was obedient. The Holy Spirit always requires an obedient individual. Obedience takes great effort—resisting temptation, maintaining integrity, shutting out the whispers of Satan.

· · · PRAYER · · ·

Heavenly Father, prepare our hearts to be submissive and open to Your divine will. May we obey Your Word, and let the Holy Spirit move upon us so that we may be vessels of honor unto You. Bring forth in us the Spirit of Christ so that others may see and know of Your love and concern for them.

· · · TODAY'S THOUGHT · · ·

"Let it be to me according to your word" (Luke 1:38).

—Joseph Mirkovich

PURIFYING OUR SOULS

Since you have purified your souls in obeying the truth
through the Spirit in sincere love of the brethren, love one
another fervently with a pure heart (1 Peter 1:22).

 A farmer in west Texas planted cotton. It came up but died from lack of moisture. He planted again. A dust storm blasted the tender plants level with the ground. A hailstorm ruined the next crop. Discouraged, he left the farm, never to return.

So it can happen for the young Christian without the work of the Holy Spirit. We plant love and mercy, but carnality and anger devour the seed before it can mature.

The Holy Spirit brings power to protect and nourish the fruit of love and to purify our souls in obeying the truth. "We know that we have passed from death to life, because we love the brethren. He who does not love his brother abides in death" (1 John 3:14).

My father, A.O. Robertson, went into the oil fields around Burkburnett and Wichita Falls, Texas, during the rough and tumble Depression days. Not a Christian at that time, he soon learned to survive with his wits, his fists, and alcohol. As a young boy, I saw him come home many times drunk, bloody, and mean.

One day during revival Dad was under deep conviction. As he started up a ladder to gauge the oil in a tank, he said, "God, if there is anything to that Holy Ghost power, let me feel it." Such a move of God came over him that he had to hold tightly to the rail to keep from falling. That night, he rushed to the altar and was filled with the Holy Spirit.

We witnessed a transformed personality. Instead of going to the bar or pool hall after work, Dad went into the pasture to pray. The Spirit taught him to love and forgive instead of hating.

· · · PRAYER · · ·

Holy God, we yield ourselves to You today. Flood our souls and personalities with the Holy Spirit. Let the love of God be shed abroad in our hearts that we may deal with others in love.

· · · TODAY'S THOUGHT · · ·

As believers today, we can watch with great joy as the Spirit manifests power over alien forces of life and causes the good crop to grow.

—O.D. Robertson

WHEN THE SPIRIT COMES

Now his father Zacharias was filled with the Holy Spirit,
and prophesied, saying . . . (Luke 1:67).

A beautiful, inspired hymn followed the filling of Zacharias by the Spirit (vv. 68-79). Before we are filled with the Spirit, there must also be a Christ-exalting preparation for His coming. An old song says, "Come, Holy Spirit, I need You; come, sweet Spirit, I pray; come in Your strength and Your power; come in Your own gentle way."

We need the Spirit to come as our *connector.* Sin separated us from the Father and marred His image in us. Now we are being transformed into Jesus' image "by the Spirit of the Lord" (2 Corinthians 3:18). The Holy Spirit connects us with all that is righteous and pure.

We need the Spirit to come as our *protector.* There are so many wicked and evil influences from which we need to be protected. Jesus said He would be with us always (Matthew 28:20) and that He would give us another Comforter who would abide with us forever (John 14:16). The Holy Spirit protects us from Satan, sin, and the storms of life. He is there in every circumstance and problem.

We need the Spirit to come as our *director.* "The steps of a good man are ordered by the Lord, and He delights in his way" (Psalm 37:23). The way is dark and uncertain unless the Holy Spirit leads the way.

We need the Holy Spirit to come as our *revelator.* We do not know how to pray or for what to pray unless the Spirit reveals it to us (Romans 8:26, 27). He shows us Christ, the truth and things to come (John 16:13).

Remember the words of that blessed old hymn: "Have Thine own way, Lord! Have Thine own way! Hold o'er my being absolute sway! Fill with Thy Spirit till all shall see Christ only, always, living in me."

"Nevertheless I tell you the truth. It is to your advantage that I go away; for if I do not go away, the Helper will not come to you; but if I depart, I will send Him to you" (John 16:7).

· · · PRAYER · · ·

Holy Spirit, fill my life each day so I may show others the way.

· · · TODAY'S THOUGHT · · ·

The Holy Spirit gives us two wonderful things—a love for Jesus and a commitment to the gospel truth.

—W.C. Ratchford, Sr.

THE HOLY SPIRIT, A PRICELESS GIFT

Therefore he who rejects this does not reject man, but God,
who has also given us His Holy Spirit (1 Thessalonians 4:8).

 The apostle Paul's advice to the Thessalonians is timely advice for Christians today. Through the indwellng of the Holy Spirit, God has made it possible for us to live clean, exemplary, and godly lives.

As a boy of about 10 years of age, I attended a Pentecostal church and then later a Pentecostal mission in downtown Findlay, Ohio. I went to the altar often, prayed, and did my best to live right. However, I had never really been converted until a few years later when, in a service one night at the mission, I was convicted by the Holy Spirit in a most definite way. I was born again and have lived for God these last 63 years.

Through the years I have been guided by the preaching of Spirit-anointed ministers and teachers who instructed me in God's ways. I am so thankful I accepted God's truth and the guidance which came to me through them.

The Holy Spirit desires purity and holiness in the lives of God's children. To live sinfully is to disregard the Holy Spirit and His guidance. It is to disregard the Word of God. We are to flee from the slightest hint of impurity—the thought, the look, the word. Nothing is more honorable than to be pure of heart and holy in living.

When a true servant of God proclaims God's Word to us and we reject it, we may try to excuse our nonacceptance for one reason or another. However, when we reject God's Word, we are rejecting God—the One who makes it possible for the Holy Spirit to dwell in us.

The Lord abides in His people by the indwelling of the Holy Spirit. All holy desires, all good counsels, and all just works come from Him—from His inspiring, elevating presence. This is the will of God.

· · · PRAYER · · ·

Heavenly Father, thank You for giving us Your Holy Spirit. Help us to never disregard Him and His guidance. We sincerely want to live daily a life of holiness in the purity of Your love so our influence will lead sinners to accept Your Son, Jesus, as their Savior.

· · · TODAY'S THOUGHT · · ·

When the Holy Spirit dwells in the life of an individual—and definitely when he or she is filled with the Holy Spirit—the person for whom this individual prays will be touched by the presence of God's power

—O.W. Polen

WE MUST BEAR FRUIT

For the fruit of the Spirit is in all goodness, righteousness, and truth (Ephesians 5:9).

I have known many Holy Spirit-filled people who have made a lasting impression on my life. One was Sister Dessie Beeler. She was never the most obvious person in the church—never sang in the choir, never gave a message in tongues—but she was a tower of strength until she died at age 97.

What made her life so meaningful? She bore the fruit of the Spirit. The Holy Spirit led her to do good things, to live righteously, and to stand on the truth. Her determination to uplift and encourage was a constant testimony of deep commitment to a life of righteousness, and her support of ministry always exemplified her belief in the truth.

In an age when people search for real meaning and purpose for their lives, the greatest testimony is a life manifesting the fruit of the Spirit: "love, joy, peace, longsuffering, kindness, goodness, faithfulness, gentleness, self-control" (Galatians 5:22, 23).

How do we do this? By dying to self and allowing the Holy Spirit to have complete control. Only the Holy Spirit can produce goodness in our lives. He is continually causing us to grow into vessels of honor to the glory of God the Father. As He molds us, our character and demeanor exemplify the love of God. The Holy Spirit also produces in us the righteousness of the Lord. Righteousness permits us to walk with integrity before men. We can do this only when free of guilt and shame in terms of the flesh, and only when justified by the blood and through the Spirit. This justification allows us to have the righteousness of God; therefore, we conduct ourselves in a manner that brings glory to God because of His own righteousness.

· · · PRAYER · · ·

Holy Father, let Your Holy Spirit so control our lives that we are made into perfect examples of Your Son.

· · · TODAY'S THOUGHT · · ·

There is more in what we do than in what we say. Let us strive every day to do the will of our heavenly Father, with goodness, righteousness, and truth manifested in our actions.

—Tommy D. Patterson

THE CHURCH PRAYED

He shall call upon Me, and I will answer him; I will be
with him in trouble; I will deliver him and honor him
(Psalm 91:15).

In October 1936, the General Assembly, in session at Chattanooga, Tennessee, commissioned my father and mother, Herman and Lydia Lauster, as missionaries to Nazi-occupied Germany. They had emigrated to America from Germany just 10 years before, and the return to their homeland at such an uncertain time was a great sacrifice.

Herman, Lydia, Walter (10), Mary (5), and I, still in my mother's womb, sailed for Germany. The ministry was hazardous, and the new missionaries met with opposition from an uninterested populace and the German government. Dad was forbidden to preach; but with tenacious faith and unbelievable strength, he clung to the words of Peter that "we ought to obey God rather than men" (Acts 5:29).

After several warnings by the Gestapo, he was arrested on August 22, 1938, and taken to a concentration camp in Welzheim. In this awful place, Dad continued to preach and win souls.

While Dad was in prison, Mother and a few faithful lay ministers kept the church at home alive. In despair, and risking her own incarceration, Mother sent a letter to the church in America through a sister from Grasonville, Maryland, who was visiting in Germany.

General Overseer J.H. Walker set aside March 5, 1939, as a day of prayer and fasting for Dad's release. On March 16, just 11 days later, a guard told him, "Lauster, you are going to be released today."

When he was called to the prison office to sign his release papers, he found that among them was a promise that he would never preach again. While he was praying, the guard was called out of the office. When the guard returned, he "forgot" to have Dad sign the paper. What a time of rejoicing my father had all the way home.

· · · PRAYER · · ·

Precious Lord, Father of our Lord Jesus, give me the courage of my
father. Let me go where You call without regard to consequence or cost.

· · · TODAY'S THOUGHT · · ·

In the records of Welzheim prison, the file of Herman Lauster contains no document of his release.

—Paul H. Lauster

THE HOLY SPIRIT, OUR GUIDE

My help comes from the Lord, who made heaven and earth.
He will not allow your foot to be moved; He who keeps you
will not slumber (Psalm 121:2, 3).

 In September 1989, while the Pentecostal churches in the Soviet Union were still underground, Robert White, Kenneth Dismukes, Paul Lombard, and myself combined a visit to the churches in Romania with a side trip into Russia.

We had only a name and phone number in Moscow—which we called. Somehow, we were able to communicate our hotel room number to the lady who answered. A half hour later another lady called, spoke briefly, and asked us to call her from a phone booth on the street, since the phones in the hotels were known to be bugged.

The second lady was named Marina. The man whose name and number we had been given was her pastor. Marina asked us to meet her at a train station called Shelkoskaya the following day. Since none of us spoke Russian, getting to the station would have been almost impossible if it hadn't been for a Russian soldier who spoke English.

Without realizing he was aiding the cause of Christ, the soldier explained the layout of the Moscow metro system to us. I memorized the information and knew where to go the next day.

We were able to meet Marina's family and her pastor, Sergeii Riachowsky, a courageous leader in the underground church movement.

Pastor Riachowsky introduced us to other leaders in the Russian underground church. During a Spirit-directed meeting, groundwork was laid for future relationships with the Pentecostals of Russia—one that would flower during the next several years as the Berlin Wall and the Iron Curtain fell and Eastern Europe was opened to the gospel.

· · · PRAYER · · ·

Lord, help us to be open to the guidance of the Holy Spirit. Even when we cannot see where He is leading, let us go in faith, believing that He knows what is ahead.

· · · TODAY'S THOUGHT · · ·

Throughout my ministry I have experienced few times when I was more aware of the leadership, protection, and guidance of the Holy Spirit than during those five days spent in Moscow.

—Paul H. Lauster

F e b r u a r y   1 5

A MIRACLE IN A DEATH PENALTY

"This is the word of the Lord to Zerubbabel: 'Not by might,
nor by power, but by My Spirit,' says the Lord of hosts"
(Zechariah 4:6).

While serving as a missionary in Central America, the country experienced a dreadful war. Missionaries were threatened by guerrilla forces. The government asked all missionaries to leave, but I failed to get the message. I was the only foreign missionary left in the country.

One of our churches was bombed and the parsonage burned. I traveled five hours to get there. On arrival, I was captured by the guerrillas. They took away my shoes and my shirt, tied my hands behind my back, and blindfolded me.

I overheard some of the guerrillas talking about killing me, but others argued that since they had brought me back to their base camp they should wait for their commander to arrive. As I waited, still blindfolded and tied, and knowing I was about to die, I was so confused and frightened that I could remember only one verse of Scripture: "The Lord is my shepherd; I shall not want" (Psalm 23:1).

For 13 days I remained in darkness. I could not tell what time of day it was, except by the kind of food brought to me. But during it all the Lord gave me a great peace. I was ready for whatever was going to happen to me.

On the 14th day, they took off my blindfold. It took 15 to 20 minutes to get used to the sunlight. Quite suddenly, a superior came out of his tent and screamed at his subordinates: "Don't do anything to this man! Don't touch him! Let him go!"

One of the guerrillas whispered to me, "Go that way . . . and don't look back!"

When I got back home, I found several pastors had been in prayer for me. It was through their prayers and the leading of the Holy Spirit that I was spared and found my way back to civilization.

· · · PRAYER · · ·

Thank You Lord for Your sustaining Spirit!

· · · TODAY'S THOUGHT · · ·

The Holy Spirit is most real in our lives when we are totally at His mercy and standing on His grace alone.

—Osvaldo A. Orellana

EMPOWERED BY THE SPIRIT

*Then the Spirit lifted me up, and I heard behind me a great
thunderous voice: "Blessed is the glory of the Lord from
His place!"* (Ezekiel 3:12).

 The challenge, the charge, and especially the call to ministry
are all of God. Within himself, a man is not able to fulfill the
requirements of that call. He needs a power greater than his
own—a power found only in the Holy Spirit.

The spiritually conscientious servant will surrender to the call of
God, though it is sometimes with great reluctance and fear that he does
so. Like Moses, some who are called try to shift the responsibility
onto another by explaining to God that the other person is better qualified or more gifted.

But He who calls will also equip those He calls. The Holy Spirit can
calm our fears, erase our doubts, and strengthen our commitment to do
God's will and work. How futile it would be to try to carry out the call
to ministry without the divine enabling and grace of the Holy Spirit.

We live in a rootless society. If we don't like our job or neighborhood, we move to another one. Marital commitments and the stability
of the home are undermined. Churches change pastors with the wind.
There is little of substance to hold together home, church, or family.

Ministers, too, seem to be caught up in this trend, and many start out
well only to abandon their calling after a short while. Ezekiel must
have seen his task as one of awesome proportions, but he recognized
that the reservoir of God's power was bigger than his need. When God
calls, God provides.

Then, too, there is the fact that Ezekiel was sent by God. He did not
choose the task nor the way to accomplish it. If we are sensitive to the
leading and presence of the Holy Spirit, we can be sure we will be successful in whatever ministry God calls us to.

· · · PRAYER · · ·

*Our Lord, help us to make the best choices by yielding our lives to the
Holy Spirit and allowing Him to lead, empower, and bless
whatever we do for You.*

· · · TODAY'S THOUGHT · · ·

Don't worry about when or to where God calls you. His purpose
and timing are always right. The man who honors God by surrender-
ing everything into the hands of the Holy Spirit will always be God's
man for God's task . . . in God's time.

—Keith D. Williams

BAPTIZED WITH FIRE

"For John truly baptized with water, but you shall be baptized with the Holy Spirit not many days from now" (Acts 1:5).

Nearing the hour of His ascension, Jesus exhorted His disciples to wait in Jerusalem for the "promise of the Father." Delicately nestled within this exhortation is a contrast aimed at holding the disciples in captive anticipation. Jesus announced the arrival of the kingdom of heaven and the sealing of its presence in power and glory. It is a contrast between the symbol of the transformed and repentant soul and the dynamic alteration of the man from the soul outward to the very tip of his tongue, between that which has been sufficient in its season and that which is about to be—a sufficiency for every season and every day to come until the Kingdom is complete.

John baptized with water, but we are to be infused with the power that moved upon the face of the deep, the power that moved Samson against the Philistines, the power that moved David against Goliath. So will we be moved in power. Without fear of the Serpent, we will tread upon him. Without fear of kings and rulers, we will stand boldly and pronounce the rule of the kingdom of heaven. Without fear of tomorrow or guilt of the past, we will march forward until we encompass the earth with the gospel proclaimed in this power of the Holy Spirit.

We will be baptized with fire. This power will burn upon our head and upon our tongue. It will consume us with a zeal and anointing that cannot be shut up in our bones. This baptism of fire will ignite us in servitude to the Lord. As one afire, we will shout God's message from the rooftops. As one afire, we will give constant praise and glory to the God of hosts. As one afire we will lay hands on the sick and they will recover. As one afire, we will pray upon the altar until this same fire burns within the soul of another, and thus the fire will spread.

· · · PRAYER · · ·

Father, I thank You for baptizing me with the Holy Spirit and filling me with fire. Let this fire burn in my soul every day of my life, that I may accomplish the mission You have for me on earth.

· · · TODAY'S THOUGHT · · ·

The success of ministry has always been in direct proportion to the amount of power in one's life.

—W.F. Williams

AND THE SPIRIT OF THE LORD CAME

Then Samuel took the horn of oil and anointed him in the midst of his brothers; and the Spirit of the Lord came upon David from that day forward. So Samuel arose and went to Ramah (1 Samuel 16:13).

When Samuel was sent to the house of Jesse to anoint one of his sons to be king, the old prophet apparently assumed that since Saul was a man of striking physical appearance, God would choose another like him. As Eliab, Jesse's oldest son, stood before him, Samuel said in his heart, "Surely the Lord's anointed is before Him." It was then that God showed Samuel the divine standard was not according to physical appearance but according to the inner attitude toward God. "But the Lord said to Samuel, 'Do not look at his appearance or at the height of his stature, because I have refused him. For the Lord does not see as man sees; for man looks at the outward appearance, but the Lord looks at the heart'" (1 Samuel 16:7).

Paul referred to this when he said, "And when He had removed him, He raised up for them David as king, to whom also He gave testimony and said, 'I have found David the son of Jesse, a man after My own heart, who will do all My will.' From this man's seed, according to the promise, God raised up for Israel a Savior—Jesus" (Acts 13:22, 23).

God's choice was a heart choice. In spite of David's imperfections, two excellent qualities stand out: he cast himself upon God's mercy, and he trusted God implicitly. He put God's will ahead of his own desires. David's life was a life of obedience to the will of God (Psalm 57:7). Because of this "the Spirit of the Lord came" and God made a covenant with David in which his kingdom was established forever. God said, "I have made a covenant with My chosen, I have sworn to My servant David: 'Your seed I will establish forever, and build up your throne to all generations.'" (Psalm 89:3, 4).

· · · PRAYER · · ·

My precious heavenly Father, let your Spirit come upon me as never before. Help me to daily walk in full obedience to your will, that I may be that vessel you can daily fill as I pour it out to others in need.

· · · TODAY'S THOUGHT · · ·

We will always have all we need . . . to do all that God wants us to do . . . as long as He wants us to do it.

—Robert W. Clagg

SUSTAINED BY THE HOLY SPIRIT

*And do not be drunk with wine, in which is dissipation; but
be filled with the Spirit* (Ephesians 5:18).

The Pentecostal message was first preached in our community
in Webster County, Mississippi, in early fall of 1916. Two
revivals later, in February 1917, my father, an ordained Baptist
deacon, embraced Pentecost and was baptized in the Holy Spirit
and became a charter member of the first Church of God organized in
Webster County. I was 14 years old. From that time on, my father, J.C.
Byrd, by precept and example, influenced my life for good, as I observed
his dedicated life and perseverance in holy living, daily reading of God's
Word, and prayer. His testimony was always positive and encouraging.

As was common in those days, strong persecution was his lot. He
was ostracized by his church, his siblings, and many of his friends. I am
fully convinced he could not have endured the persecution and trials
without the power and comfort of the Holy Ghost.

He loved and respected the Reverend Hal Presgrove, the only pastor
he had in the Church of God. In the fall of 1917 we moved to Sunflower
County, Mississippi. From that time on, my father never lived within
commuting distance of a Church of God. However, he would find a few
church folk and they would meet in cottage prayer meetings or community buildings for worship and to encourage one another in the Lord.

Farm work was hard and the days long. Yet he was never too tired
for Bible reading and family prayer. I can still hear him call my name
as he would earnestly and fervently plead with God to save his family.

My dad was only 47 years old when God called him home in August
1922. His faith sustained him during his illness. He fought a good
fight. He kept the faith.

My father did not have worldly goods to leave his children. Yet he
left us something far more precious than silver and gold. By his example of righteous living, he showed us the way home.

· · · PRAYER · · ·

Lord, let me die the death of the righteous and let my last end be like his.

· · · TODAY'S THOUGHT · · ·

The greatest gift one can leave to his family is not measured in dollars but in character, ethics, integrity, and righteousness.

—John L. Byrd

THE COMFORTER

"And I will pray the Father, and He will give you another
Helper, that He may abide with you forever" (John 14:16).

The deep sorrow, terrible disappointment, and heavy gloom
provoked by Christ's arrest, mock trial, crucifixion, and burial
mercilessly obliterated all His disciples' optimism for the
future. To them Christ was dead and His cause, upon which
and for which they had staked their all, was buried with Him in the
borrowed tomb.

However, shortly after the Resurrection He suddenly appeared
before the disciples who were secured behind doors because of their
fear of the Jews. He reminded the disciples of His promise to give
them another Comforter: "'Peace to you! As the Father has sent Me, I
also send you.' And when He had said this, He breathed on them, and
said to them, 'Receive the Holy Spirit'" (John 20:21, 22).

During the post-Resurrection period that Christ spent with the disciples, He prepared His followers for His ascension. He inspired the
hearts and minds of the disciples to such a happy attitude that instead
of gloom and sorrow filling their hearts when the cloud of glory
enveloped Him and swept Him out of their sight they "returned to
Jerusalem with great joy, and were continually in the temple praising
and blessing God" (Luke 24:52, 53).

"When the Day of Pentecost had fully come, they were all with one
accord in one place. And suddenly there came a sound from heaven, as
of a rushing mighty wind, and it filled the whole house where they
were sitting. Then there appeared to them divided tongues, as of fire,
and one sat upon each of them. And they were all filled with the Holy
Spirit and began to speak with other tongues, as the Spirit gave them
utterance" (Acts 2:1-4).

The Comforter had come!

· · · PRAYER · · ·

Father, help us to assuredly know that the presence of the Holy
Spirit within us will not only comfort us but also secure us against evil.

· · · TODAY'S THOUGHT · · ·

Because the Holy Spirit represents the Godhead with all the divine
power to provide for and protect us, we have every reason to be comforted.

—J.D. Bright

EQUIPPED FOR SERVICE

For to one is given the word of wisdom through the Spirit,
to another the word of knowledge through the same Spirit
(1 Corinthians 12:8).

Many years ago in Omaha, Nebraska, after viewing my mother in the casket, I walked into the garden behind the funeral chapel, with seemingly unbearable grief and pain in my heart. Although it was dark and I was alone, I knew I really was not alone, for the Holy Spirit was there. Having ministered to many in similar circumstances as a pastor, I now had to personally deal with this earthly loss. The Holy Spirit walked in the garden that night with me, and I experienced true comfort and joy in the midst of sorrow.

I still have fond memories of how excited my mother was about her homegoing. The Holy Spirit helped me to understand that the Savior has full ability to restore the sleeping, scattered dust of all those who have died in the faith.

A helper of the great chemist Faraday knocked a small silver cup into a jar of acid. The acid immediately dissolved the little cup. Mr. Faraday was called and he quickly poured a chemical into the jar. In a moment every particle of silver was precipitated into the bottom of the jar. He simply sifted out the shapeless mass of silver and sent it to a silversmith who restored the cup to shining luster, brighter than ever before.

In order for all phases of the ministry of the church to be carried out, God gives varying gifts through the Holy Spirit to different persons. The gifts are to be used for service in Kingdom work. The wisdom and knowledge of spiritual gifts come from God in heaven. Our responsibility is to seek God for the gifts and allow the Holy Spirit to use them freely as He wills.

· · · PRAYER · · ·

Heavenly Father, help me to recognize that You have equipped me for service. Move me to minister to others and to always reflect praise and honor upon Christ's name by what I say and by what I do.

· · · TODAY'S THOUGHT · · ·

The Holy Spirit is the Person with the responsibility for guiding God's people through heartaches, trials, and struggles.

—Paul F. Barker

THE GIFT THAT KEEPS ON GIVING

"If you then, being evil, know how to give good gifts to your children, how much more will your heavenly Father give the Holy Spirit to those who ask Him!" (Luke 11:13).

One Christmas, my son, then a 3-year-old, became the proud owner of what he thought were some pretty neat toys. There was a fire truck with flashing red lights and a siren, a police car with flashing lights and a siren, and a set of electric drums, complete with cymbal tempo masters.

However, as attractive as all these toys seemed to be, my son, within minutes, was dissatisfied with all of them. The problem with the toys was that we had forgotten to install batteries in them. Without the batteries, the toys were quite ordinary and could not do the things they were supposed to do. The lights flashed, the sirens whined, and the drums and cymbals sounded, only after being empowered by the batteries.

The Holy Spirit in us is just as necessary for our spiritual life as batteries are for the proper operation of a toy. Although batteries eventually run down, while they last they give energy to operate the toy. The Holy Spirit keeps on giving the spiritual energy needed for Christian living; the Holy Spirit never runs down.

Many Christians seem to be uncertain about what they should ask of God. According to Scripture, we can ask anything of God that is consistent with His will. According to Jesus' own words, we know it is God's will to give us the Holy Spirit. Jesus, emphasizing that God can be trusted to act in our best interest, said, "How much more will your heavenly Father give the Holy Spirit to those who ask Him!"

· · · PRAYER · · ·

Heavenly Father, help me to desire and ask You daily for the fullness of Your Spirit. By the gift of Your Spirit, make me receptive to Your will for my life.

· · · TODAY'S THOUGHT · · ·

There is a constant spiritual battle in us between whether we shall depend on our own abilities, energies, and experiences for Christian living or depend on the Holy Spirit. Dependence on the Holy Spirit is the only way to really live as Christians.

—Randy L. Ballard

THE SPIRIT OF CHRIST

But you are not in the flesh but in the Spirit, if indeed the Spirit of God dwells in you. Now if anyone does not have the Spirit of Christ, he is not His (Romans 8:9).

Believers come from an entirely different perspective than unbelievers. Believers are not "in the flesh"; that is, they are not controlled by, nor do they obey, the baser nature. Rather, they are "in the Spirit"; that is, they live under the control of the Spirit. The Holy Spirit takes possession of them and makes His home with them. Where the Spirit resides, Christ resides.

The apostle Paul referred to the Holy Spirit as "the Spirit of Christ" because Christ sent Him into the world to carry out His mission. The Spirit continues Jesus' work—calling, convicting, and transforming persons into the likeness of Christ and communicating to them the benefits of redemption.

The Holy Spirit is involved in all the elements of redemption. Not only does He convict the sinner of his sins, but He also leads him to godly sorrow for those sins. He prompts the sinner to change his behavior, to make restitution where he has wronged others, to understand how repulsive sin is, and to confess the error of his ways. The Spirit provides the faith which enables the sinner to personally trust in the Savior. Then He quickens the individual to newness of life. By the Spirit, one is born again and adopted into the family of God. Further, He empowers the Christian life with a daily refreshing as He indwells the believer.

Queen Victoria once visited the home of a widow. Later, the widow said Queen Victoria was the most honored guest ever to be in her cottage. Knowing the widow was a Christian, neighbors chided her with "How about this Jesus you are always talking about? Seems He would be more honored than the queen." The lady replied, "But He's not a visitor. He lives here all the time."

· · · PRAYER · · ·

Lord Jesus, help us to walk in the Spirit and not in the flesh. Enable us to live in such fashion that we can say with Paul, "It is no longer I who live, but Christ lives in me."

· · · TODAY'S THOUGHT · · ·

One cannot feel alive without being alive. It is the work of the Holy Spirit to bring life to believers. By faith, Christ's life and the believer's life become one.

—Homer G. Rhea

AS UPON US AT THE BEGINNING

"And as I began to speak, the Holy Spirit fell upon them, as upon us at the beginning. Then I remembered the word of the Lord, how He said, 'John indeed baptized with water, but you shall be baptized with the Holy Spirit'"
(Acts 11:15, 16).

Because God's work is grounded upon His own sovereignty, it transcends the structured thinking of the human mind. God breaks the structured pattern of our thinking and manifests Himself as eternal God.

When Peter spoke to the apostles and brethren in Judea about what happened at the house of Cornelius, a Gentile, they were all stunned. To their structured way of thinking, the Gentiles were spiritually corrupt. The metaphors Peter used in his vision before his visit suggest the same. What they were hearing from Peter could not be true according to all the logic they could employ. Nevertheless, the Spirit of God fell upon the house of Cornelius just like at the beginning on the Day of Pentecost.

My faith journey began in a Presbyterian church when I was a teenager. From that initial contact with the gospel, I have tried to remain faithful in my Christian life. Later, I felt God's call to ministry and started my theological training in a nearby Presbyterian Bible seminary. Upon graduation, I was assigned to pastor a local Presbyterian church.

The most crucial turning point of my faith journey came during a week when I went to a mountain prayer house to wrestle with God about church matters. At the end of the week of prayer and fasting, a rushing mighty wind of the Spirit fell upon me and I began to speak in tongues.

That experience shattered my established ways of thinking. I became broken and the Spirit gave me a burning passion for God and His work.

· · · PRAYER · · ·

Gracious God, let me not insist on my own ways, but instead let me be led by Your divine Spirit. Help me to learn more of Christ and to be a faithful steward of Your kingdom.

· · · TODAY'S THOUGHT · · ·

When the Spirit comes, He changes the way we think about spiritual matters and gives us a burning passion to win people to the Lord.

—Yung-Chul Han

SHARE CHRIST WITH THE WHOLE WORLD

*There is one body and one Spirit, just as you were called in
one hope of your calling* (Ephesians 4:4).

Born into a Pentecostal home and church, in my teen years I
taught a Sunday school class of children, was involved in church
youth activities, fasted and prayed, and sought to know and do
God's will for my life. Already I wanted to be a missionary.

In my senior year of high school, the Lord directed me to go preach
a revival at a schoolhouse in Slaughter's Creek, West Virginia, where
Baptists often conducted services. I made many excuses to God as to
why I should not do this, but He worked out the arrangements and we
had an outstanding revival at Slaughter's Creek.

With God's help and an initial gift of money from Rancel, my older
brother, I attended Bible Training School (now Lee College) and completed four years of credits in three years while working at various jobs
to help earn my way. While at Lee I became certain about my desire to
be a missionary. There I met John Herbert Walker, who also felt called
of God to be a missionary. After we earned degrees from Scarritt
College and Vanderbilt University, we were married and spent the first
five years of our marriage as missionaries in Haiti.

Our children, Dianne and Crystal, were born in Haiti. Today, both are
in the service of the Lord. Dianne is a clinical psychologist in California,
and Crystal is a medical technologist and missionary to the Chinese.

My calling has always been that of special love for all people everywhere. Some are called to specific places, but wherever I have been, I
have always enjoyed being among the people. I regard myself as a
"world Christian." This means I care about all people and want to
share Christ with the whole world.

Since the church is one body, we all worship the same Lord, we all
have the same Holy Spirit, and we all have the same hope of eternal
life, it is only right that we should share the love of Christ with everyone everywhere.

· · · PRAYER · · ·

*Thank You, God, for bringing together in Your church people of all
nationalities. Thank You for letting me be a world Christian.*

· · · TODAY'S THOUGHT · · ·

Let's all be active world Christians and complete the task of preaching the gospel in all the world.

—Lucille Walker

EFFECTIVE LEADERSHIP

Then he remembered the days of old, Moses and his people, saying: "Where is He who brought them up out of the sea with the shepherd of His flock? Where is He who put His Holy Spirit within them?" (Isaiah 63:11).

 Some people are looking for a Moses to be their leader when they should look to the Spirit of God for power to meet the need of the hour. Man is not the source of power. The Holy Spirit is our answer.

When Saul, the son of Kish, was chosen to be the first king of Israel, the Holy Spirit came upon him to equip him for his position and work. David received the kingly anointing when Saul's disobedience disqualified him. Then, as now, the assurance the angel gave to Zerubbabel concerning the enabling of the Holy Spirit (Zechariah 4:6) is what qualifies leaders.

One of the most amazing people I have ever met helped to win me to the Lord. Evangelist Minnie Danley, who was so very thin she worried me, was one of the most powerful leaders I have ever known. From the time she would walk to the platform, I could sense the power of God at work in her ministry. Her words, so soft yet so powerful under the divine unction of God, would pierce the heart and soul of those who listened. As the gifts of the Spirit operated through her in each service, I became aware of the mighty power of God. God's power was magnified even more as His glory shone from this wisp of a woman.

Seeing God's power work through Minnie Danley made me hungry for His mighty anointing to fall on me as well. The same God that made a shepherd boy's sling greater than a giant's sword still enables the weakness of man to overpower the might of Satan's modern-day attacks.

· · · PRAYER · · ·

Blessed Father, fill us with Your enabling power so that we might reach our highest potential. Please fill us to overflowing so that others may partake of Your blessings through us.

· · · TODAY'S THOUGHT · · ·

To quote Ray H. Hughes, one of our prolific authors, "The anointing makes the difference."

—John L. Walker

GO WHEREVER THE LORD SENDS YOU

Then the Spirit said to Philip, "Go near and overtake this chariot" (Acts 8:29).

Born in 1914, I was converted in January 1932, at the depth of the Great Depression. While working on a farm in 1933, God called me to be a missionary to India. Then a year later, while at home with my widowed mother and my brothers, I received from the Lord a definite call to preach the gospel. A week later I began to evangelize and traveled from church to church by hitchhiking. My income in those days was less than $10 a month, and my expenses had to be deducted from that.

In 1934 I saw Ellen Merritt Brown in a convention worship service, and the Lord told me she would be my companion for my life and ministry. We both attended Bible Training School in Cleveland, Tennessee; and on our graduation day in 1936, we were married by Pastor W.T. Milligan in the home of General Overseer J.H. Walker. We both were licensed as ministers in the Church of God in 1936.

That was the beginning of more than 60 years of continuous ministry for the Lord at home and abroad. We served as missionaries in Puerto Rico, Santo Domingo, India, Peru, and Haiti. I traveled extensively as a Church of God World Missions representative. Other ministry opportunities included evangelizing, pastoring churches, serving in state youth leadership, and teaching in 33 states, Canada, and Germany.

Ellen, who is professor emerita, taught at Lee College for 15 years, becoming chairperson of the Language Arts Department the last two years of her tenure. I was honored to be designated pastor emeritus of North Cleveland Church of God in 1989.

God has given us a wonderful life. We are the parents of five sons—Chancel, David, Joseph, Samuel, and Gordon. Ellen and I will celebrate our 60th wedding anniversary in 1996.

· · · PRAYER · · ·

Thank You, God, for directing our lives. For every divine promise, for every divine call, for every divine commission, and for Your great faithfulness, we praise You.

· · · TODAY'S THOUGHT · · ·

Are you an ambitious Christian? Do you aspire to do great things for Christ? Go wherever the Holy Spirit sends you. Say and do and be whatever He bids you.

—Chancel E. French

A JOURNEY WITHOUT DOUBT

Then the Spirit told me to go with them, doubting nothing.
Moreover these six brethren accompanied me, and we
entered the man's house (Acts 11:12).

Life is more than a single journey that begins at birth and ends in death. Life is the great gift of God that is made up of many journeys and numerous adventures.

In our scripture we find Simon Peter, that most colorful of apostles, sharing with the Jewish Christians of Jerusalem his most recent crusade that had taken place at the home of a Gentile believer named Cornelius. To the shock of his listening audience, this most recent convert to the Pentecostal persuasion was a centurion of the hated Roman Empire; and yet, not only had Peter shared the gospel with Cornelius' household, but the Holy Spirit had fallen upon each of them just as had happened in Jerusalem. In one grand leap of faith Peter had seen cultural and religious boundaries cast aside, and all this had developed as the result of a vision received on a housetop in Joppa (Acts 10:9-16). Peter shared with his skeptical listeners that he was commanded of the Spirit to go to Cornelius, "doubting nothing."

The story of God's grace being extended to the Gentiles involves most of the remainder of the Book of Acts and the Epistles and Revelation. But the first part of this glorious mission of worldwide mercy began with a command to doubt nothing.

Doubt is a robber and a thief. It depresses and hinders the believer's progress. Hesitancy often comes with nagging doubt. The father with the possessed child was himself so hampered and distressed by his doubt that he cried to Jesus, "Lord, I believe; help my unbelief!" (Mark 9:24).

This is the heart of the matter. We need God's help to combat doubt. It was the assurance of the Holy Spirit that told Peter to make the journey, "doubting nothing." So it is with us.

· · · PRAYER · · ·

Father, may faith be our daily companion. May it grow until we need no longer worry about what is in sight, for faith becomes our eyes and our feet walk in Your Word where doubts are faded memories.

· · · TODAY'S THOUGHT · · ·

The wind may take a kite into the sky until it is out of sight, but the one holding the string knows it is there. He feels the tug. The Spirit of God may not be seen, but we can always feel the tug.

—David M. Griffis

DEVISED PLANS, BUT NOT OF GOD

"Woe to the rebellious children," says the Lord, "who take counsel, but not of Me, and who devise plans, but not of My Spirit, that they may add sin to sin" (Isaiah 30:1).

Judah's failure to obtain direction from the Lord led to an unholy alliance with Egypt. The prophet saw this as an affront to God and a grieving of the Holy Spirit.

The Spirit of the Lord was saying that Judah had committed an act of idolatry, adding sin to sin by sending an ambassador to Egypt. This alliance, formed without seeking guidance from God, placed their trust in man rather than the strength and wisdom of God.

People have often been guilty of devising plans and entering relationships without seeking God and then expecting Him to bless their efforts. Such was the case with Bill and Ted.

Bill was a born-again believer who desired to start a business with his childhood friend Ted, who professed no relationship to God and was not interested in receiving Christ as his Savior. Bill came to my office to seek advice concerning this business venture. I advised him that he needed to seek the mind of God and to make no decision until he had heard from Him. I further instructed him that from a biblical standpoint it was inadvisable to become unequally yoked with an unbeliever.

Bill told me he had to make the decision immediately. From all the facts he and Ted had gathered, it should be a prosperous endeavor. Bill and Ted's restaurant opened for business, and everything seemed to go well until Ted wanted a license to sell alcohol. Bill was frustrated. In the beginning they had agreed no alcoholic beverages would be sold. Now Ted wanted to make all the money he could in any way he could.

Bill returned to my office. This time he was defeated. Ted would buy Bill's half for only the initial investment. His friendship was broken, his dream shattered.

· · · PRAYER · · ·

Father, lead us today and help us to accept that the steps of a righteous man are ordered of the Lord. Fill us with wisdom and keep us ever sensitive to Your voice that we may obey and be found in the center of Your will.

· · · TODAY'S THOUGHT · · ·

God speaks to us in many voices. We should listen with a heart that says with Samuel, "Speak, Lord, for Your servant hears."

—Walter H. Hall

STRENGTHENED BY THE HOLY SPIRIT

*That He would grant you, according to the riches of His
glory, to be strengthened with might through His Spirit in
the inner man* (Ephesians 3:16).

My grandmother was the first Pentecostal in my family, and
she influenced me to love the Lord. In my childhood, the
Lord spoke concerning me that my heavenly Father would
save me, as it is written in the Bible: "He sent from above, He
took me; He drew my out of many waters" (Psalm 18:16). And so, He
saved me at the age of 17.

After my conversion I was baptized in water at night in August
1941. At that time in Romania, all Evangelical churches were closed
by authority of the government. The brother who baptized me was
condemned to prison for one year and seven months. Because I was a
minor, I was not sent to prison, but I was persecuted by my parents
until, after a few years, my mother was converted and baptized in
water and in the Holy Spirit.

On the morning of January 6, 1942, I received the baptism in the
Holy Spirit. While praying, I felt the presence of the Lord. Like electric power, His presence penetrated my whole body. At the same time
I received a new language. In spite of the severe winter weather, I felt
that all nature was smiling on me. I was full of happiness.

The Spirit strengthened me, and I received power to preach the
gospel and became one of the leaders of the Pentecostal Movement in
Romania. I was a helper to George Bradin, the man who pioneered the
Church of God in Romania.

The Holy Spirit helped me to overcome when on two occasions (in
1958 and 1965) the government revoked my authorization to be a pastor. The Spirit spoke prophetically, saying God would help me to build
a church in Bucharest. In time, a church was built at 43 Sebastian
Street. It became famous as a place where miracles occurred and
preachers such as Billy Graham, Robert White, Ray Hughes, Richard
Wurmbrand, and others came to preach.

· · · PRAYER · · ·

*Thank You, gracious God, for the spiritual strength given to us by Your
Holy Spirit. I pray that I may be strengthened by Your Spirit this day.*

· · · TODAY'S THOUGHT · · ·

For more than 50 years the Holy Spirit has given me strength, light,
and guidance.

—Trandafir Sandru

THE PRIMARY PURPOSE OF THE SPIRIT

"But when the Helper comes, whom I shall send to you from the Father, the Spirit of truth who proceeds from the Father, He will testify of Me" (John 15:26).

It is not unusual for us to get so caught up in manifestations of the Spirit that we miss the purpose of His presence. I use the word *purpose* (singular) because I refer to His primary purpose. He has, of course, more than one purpose, but each purpose relates to the primary purpose.

Just what is the primary purpose of the Holy Spirit in the world today? His *primary* purpose is to bring to Jesus a spotless bride! Everything the Holy Spirit does relates to that eternal purpose. Every manifestation of His presence, power, and glory has behind it the purpose of preparing us for Christ.

In Genesis 24 we find a type of the Holy Spirit's *primary* purpose. Abraham sent Eliezer to find a bride for Isaac. In this story, Abraham represents God the Father, Isaac represents God the Son, and Eliezer represents God the Holy Spirit. Eliezer's name means "divine helper"—certainly a type of the Holy Spirit. Rebekah represents the bride of Christ. Eliezer had one mission—to bring back a bride for Isaac. That was his primary mission. He gave gifts, he blessed, he communicated, he created excitement and joy. But his goal was to get the bride.

So it is with the Holy Spirit. He will speak. He does so with tongues, interpretation of tongues, and prophecy. He also gives gifts, wonderful gifts. He creates excitement and joy. But the purpose for all this is to get a bride for Christ. He will make us happy, but He is more concerned with our holiness than our happiness. The Holy Spirit is calling and preparing a spotless bride for Jesus Christ, the Son of God.

· · · PRAYER · · ·

Heavenly Father, we desire to be the bride of Your Son, Jesus Christ. Help us to be sensitive to the work of the Holy Spirit in our lives. Help us not to miss His purpose by just enjoying His presence. Help us to understand His calling and respond without hesitation.

· · · TODAY'S THOUGHT · · ·

Our response to the Spirit's invitation must be that of Rebekah. We must be quick to say, "I will go." The Holy Spirit will always lead us to Jesus, for He testifies of Him.

—Rich Bowen

GUIDING OUR STEPS

*And finding disciples, we stayed there seven days. They told
Paul through the Spirit not to go up to Jerusalem*
(Acts 21:4).

I placed the receiver on the hook. Memories began to flood
my mind. Eva, who had been hospitalized with phlebitis in
her third trimester of pregnancy, told me she had fainted earlier that day. To reassure her, I suggested that her medication
had possibly made her imagine it.

A month earlier I had an unusual dream—the kind that stays with
you long after you get up in the morning. In the dream I read her obit-
uary in the newspaper in detail. Of course, that bothered me and I
called to check on her. She explained that she was having difficulty
getting over the flu. I assured her of my prayers.

She began to feel better, and the dream was stored away until this
day in May. Somehow I realized that my dream had indicated an
unexpected death, so my husband and I drove several miles to visit her.
Her doctor thought she would be fine, so I felt much better. The next
day the telephone rang—Eva had suffered a cardiac arrest. She and the
baby were gone.

As I pondered the reason for the forewarning, my first thought was
only that God loved her so much He sent me to her on her last night
here. Years later, however, I began to think of this experience as also
"my piece of the Rock." I can boldly proclaim that He does know and
care where we are!

Circumstances are easier to handle when we are certain God is
directing our steps. The disciples urged Paul not to go to Jerusalem, but
he felt he must. He had told them, "And now, compelled by the Spirit,
I am going to Jerusalem, not knowing what will happen to me there. I
only know that in every city the Holy Spirit warns me that prison and
hardships are facing me" (Acts 20:22, 23, *NIV*).

· · · PRAYER · · ·

*Heavenly Father, accept my gratitude for the work of the Holy Spirit
and for the assurance that our steps are directed according to
Proverbs 3:5, 6.*

· · · TODAY'S THOUGHT · · ·

We can have a personal relationship with God that gives us an
assurance of His divine presence as real as Paul's.

—Rebecca J. Jenkins

THE MIGHTY SPIRIT OF THE LORD

*And the Spirit of the Lord came mightily upon him, and he
tore the lion apart as one would have torn apart a young
goat, though he had nothing in his hand. But he did not tell
his father or his mother what he had done* (Judges 14:6).

Samson's birth was announced to his father and mother by the
angel of the Lord. They were told that he would be a Nazarite
from birth. No razor was to pass on his head, and he was to
drink no strong drink. Samson was a man like other men until
"the Spirit of the Lord" would come mightily upon him. Then, he
could slay a lion with his bare hands, lift up city gates and walk away
with them, kill a thousand Philistines with the jawbone of a donkey,
and pull down a pagan temple with his hands.

The Holy Spirit still works in the lives of men and women today,
helping them to pull down the strongholds of Satan. When the Spirit of
the Lord comes on us, there will be revival, believers will return to
holy living, and the church will be empowered to go into all the world
and preach the gospel.

Samson forgot his mission, lost his power, and wound up in prison.
His hair, the symbol of his Nazarite vows and his strength, was shorn.
Samson prayed, "O Lord God, remember me" (Judges 16:28); and the
God of the second chance gave him another opportunity to accomplish
what he was born for. His hair grew back and his strength returned.

At times the church seems to have lost its way, its zeal, and its commitment to carry the gospel message to all men. But as we pray, fast,
repent, and seek the face of God, the Spirit will come again. He will
give us a second chance . . . or third . . . or fourth! "If My people who
are called by My name will humble themselves, and pray and seek My
face, and turn from their wicked ways, then I will hear from heaven,
and will forgive their sin and heal their land" (2 Chronicles 7:14).

· · · PRAYER · · ·

*Heavenly Father, pour out Your Spirit on us. Use us to reach the
lost. Make us an instrument of Your peace throughout the world.*

· · · TODAY'S THOUGHT · · ·

God wants to bring revival much more than we want to be revived.
If we take a step toward Him, He will bound a thousand miles toward
us.

—Wayne P. Chelette

GOD INSTRUCTS THROUGH THE SPIRIT

Then the Lord came down in the cloud, and spoke to him,
and took of the Spirit that was upon him, and placed the
same upon the seventy elders; and it happened, when the
Spirit rested upon them, that they prophesied, although they
never did so again (Numbers 11:25).

In the summer of 1977, while attending Bible college in Pensacola, Florida, I was seeking the will of the Lord for my life and facing a major decision about my ministry. During the Northwest Florida Camp Meeting at Fort Walton Beach, the Holy Spirit moved mightily in each meeting. During one of the services, the Holy Spirit spoke to me and instructed me to move to Jackson, Mississippi. I took Him at His word, shared the revelation with my wife, and immediately made plans to move.

This began a ministry of obeying the leading of the Lord as given to me through the Holy Spirit. On many occasions since then, the Holy Spirit has directed me about a particular thing and shown me the will of the Lord or what He desired of me in His work. Every pastoral change has been at the express direction of the Spirit. The Holy Spirit goes before me—guiding, leading, and often showing what the future holds, enabling me to prepare for it. Since the day I said yes to His first instructions for me and my family, God the Father, through the Son and the Holy Spirit, has guided my steps.

To be Spirit-directed in our own ministry only is not enough. We must also share the Spirit the Lord has given us, so that others beginning their service with the Lord can also be led by Him. The Lord took the Spirit that was on Moses and placed it on 70 elders of Israel. That is, the Lord shared the Spirit which was on Moses with those who would minister to His people.

· · · PRAYER · · ·

Heavenly Father, let me be overshadowed and moved on by the Holy Spirit in an even greater measure. Instruct me in all my ways and keep my feet that I may serve You better.

· · · TODAY'S THOUGHT · · ·

Like love that is given away, the Holy Spirit when shared becomes richer in our own life.

—Pettis E. Brewer

I WILL POUR OUT MY SPIRIT

"Turn at my reproof; surely I will pour out my spirit on you;
I will make my words known to you" (Proverbs 1:23).

 James Alexander Stewart wrote a history of the outpouring of the Holy Spirit in Wales in 1904-1905. The stories of the wonderful move of the Spirit during that Welsh revival have been written indelibly on my mind since I read this work many years ago.

Among the outstanding features of that great move of the Spirit was the fact that there were no committees or organizers. Many of the meetings had no song leaders, no hymnbooks, no musicians or choir. Nor was there great scholarly preaching. The Holy Spirit was in control completely.

Evan Roberts was mightily used of God during the revival. In preparation for one of the greatest outpourings of the Spirit during the revival, God led Roberts to preach a sermon on "The Four Great Tenets." He told the congregation that four conditions for an outpouring of the Spirit were essential:

1. Is there sin in your past that you have not confessed? "On your knees at once," he exhorted, "for your past sins must be put away and yourself cleansed."

2. Is there anything in your life that is doubtful? Anything you cannot decide whether it is good or evil? "There must not be a cloud between you and God," he declared. Then he asked, "Have you forgiven everybody. . . everybody. . . everybody? If not, don't expect forgiveness of your own sins. You won't get it."

3. Do what the Spirit prompts you to do. Obedience—prompt, implicit, unquestioning obedience to the Spirit—is imperative.

4. Publicly confess Christ as your Savior. Roberts explained the vast difference between profession and confession.

· · · PRAYER · · ·

My blessed Lord, I thank You because it is still Your desire to pour out Your Spirit upon Your people today. Help me to meet the conditions prescribed by Your Holy Word, that I may be a blessing to others and bring glory to Your name.

· · · TODAY'S THOUGHT · · ·

"When we are filled with the Spirit, we do not have more of the Spirit, but the Spirit has all of us" (W.B. Knight).

—Curtis Grey

THE TRANSFORMING POWER OF GOD

*"Then the spirit of the Lord will come upon you, and you
will prophesy with them and be turned into another man"*
(1 Samuel 10:6).

A purpose of the Holy Spirit is to "teach . . . all things" (John
14:26). The Spirit has a threefold ministry in teaching the
truth. First, the Spirit is the *repository of the truth* (John
14:25, 26)—all truth rests in Him. Second, He is the *communicator of the truth* from God to man (John 16:13-15; 1 Corinthians
2:11-14). Third, He is the *convincer of the truth*, who alone can draw
sinners to Christ (Matthew 16:17; John 16:8).

While there are earthly things man can know, the wisdom of God
comes only through the Spirit of God. Knowledge of spiritual things is
by analogy or comparison, therefore imperfect and incomplete without
the Spirit's help (1 Corinthians 2:11-14). Perverseness of heart shuts
out the light so that the mind cannot receive the truth unless the Spirit
enlightens (John 3:19-21). Prejudice also obstructs the reception of
truth (Mark 8:31-33).

The Spirit uses at least three methods to teach the truth. He anoints
men to declare truth so He can reveal truth to the hearer (Luke 4:18-21).
He manifests truth through Christlike disciples (John 15:8). He demonstrates and confirms truth by empowering men and women to do supernatural works (1 Corinthians 2:4, 5). Knowledge without the Spirit
hardens hearts; it does not change them (2 Corinthians 3:5, 6). It may
convince one of duty, but it can never transform life. No degree of
learning or power of persuasion makes one a successful preacher or
teacher without the illuminating power of the Holy Spirit. It is the
Spirit who empowers for witness (John 15:26, 27).

Paul told us how to maintain our Christian life: "Put on the Lord
Jesus Christ, and make no provision for the flesh, to fulfill its lusts"
(Romans 13:14).

· · · PRAYER · · ·

*Lord, You have given me a mind to know the truth, a conscience to
approve the truth, a body to desire the truth, and a will to choose the
truth. Help me to put on Jesus and make no provision for the flesh.*

· · · TODAY'S THOUGHT · · ·

"Oh, that a MAN would arise in me; that the man I am would cease
to be."

—Jerry F. Chitwood

SPIRITUAL MANIFESTATIONS

What is the result then? I will pray with the spirit, and I will
also pray with the understanding. I will sing with the spirit,
and I will also sing with the understanding
(1 Corinthians 14:15).

To be able to communicate with God in the Spirit is one of the unique blessings given to the church. That God has chosen to indwell believers with the Holy Spirit and that this same Spirit enables us to speak with God in heavenly languages is marvelous indeed. God has also given in the gifts of the Spirit the interpretation of tongues to allow the continuing revelation of His message to His church. Paul admonished the church to desire spiritual gifts but also to understand the need for the gifts to be used orderly and for the edification of the whole church.

Spiritual gifts were misused in the Corinthian church, so Paul's instructions to them have been interpreted by some to prohibit the operation of the gifts completely in corporate worship. This is not God's intent. He wants the gifts to operate for both edification and encouragement. The Spirit-filled believer should be ready to be used of God for praying, singing, and other manifestations of the Spirit.

I remember the first time I experienced the powerful presence of God's Holy Spirit in tongues and interpretation. A holy awe swept over me. Sinners came to the altar to find God. The Spirit in the service exalted Christ and brought us nearer to God. I am still moved when I realize that God speaks directly to the church through tongues and interpretations.

I have two sons, both of whom have been filled with the Holy Spirit with the evidence of speaking in tongues. I have accepted the responsibility to teach them the fear of God and respect for the Spirit of God.

· · · PRAYER · · ·

Father, draw us nearer to You today. Make us vessels of honor fit
for Your service. Help us to teach our children about the Pentecostal
blessing and strive to see them filled with the Holy Spirit and become
instruments for Your daily use.

· · · TODAY'S THOUGHT · · ·

"For the promise is to you and to your children, and to all who are afar off, as many as the Lord our God will call" (Acts 2:39).

—Bill Isaacs

BEING CHRISTLIKE

But the fruit of the Spirit is love, joy, peace, longsuffering,
kindness, goodness, faithfulness, gentleness, self-control
(Galatians 5:22, 23).

When a plant, tree, or plan comes to a full realization of its purpose, potential, or capacity, we say it has come to fruition. It bears fruit. Likewise, when the Holy Spirit has achieved His full purpose in the life of a believer, it is evidenced by the influence and effect Christ has on character, personality, and behavior.

The purpose for which the Holy Spirit was sent to the church, and to the believer, was made clear by the Lord himself: "He will testify of Me" (John 15:26); "He will guide you into all truth" (16:13); "He will glorify Me" (16:14). These things must be visible in the life of the believer. If we have received the Spirit, we will bear witness of Jesus.

To witness is not simply to talk about Jesus but to be like Him as well. The fruit of the Spirit demonstrates the indwelling of the Spirit of Christ, showing His character and nature revealed in us.

In an age which seeks manifestations and demonstrations, we are called to remember that the Word shows us "a more excellent way" (1 Corinthians 12:31—13). Singing, shouting, and praising God is good! Showing the love of God in our lives all week long is better. When others see Jesus in us, we indeed become the "praise of His glory" (Ephesians 1:12).

I will never forget an elder colleague, Pastor Maldwin Oliver. A district pastor, he encouraged me to "preach the Word." In him I found a man who, by the power of the Holy Spirit, followed close behind Christ (Psalm 63:8) and revealed Christ's likeness in word and deed. *Preaching* and *living* should not be strangers but partners in the life of the man of God.

· · · PRAYER · · ·

Father, cause Thy Spirit to reach full fruition in my life that I might come "to a perfect man, to the measure of the stature of the fullness of Christ," according to Ephesians 4:13.

· · · TODAY'S THOUGHT · · ·

An old saying reminds us: "What you are speaks so loud I can't hear what you are saying." The crowd, looking on the disciples, "realized that they had been with Jesus" (Acts 4:13).

—C. J. van Kerken

PROPHECY AND THE HOLY SPIRIT

Then one of them, named Agabus, stood up and showed by
the Spirit that there was going to be a great famine through-
out all the world, which also happened in the days of
Claudius Caesar (Acts 11:28).

 The Bible clearly allows for personal prophecy. Nathan brought David a word from God (2 Samuel 12), Isaiah predicted Hezekiah's death (38:1), and Agabus told Paul he faced trouble in Jerusalem (Acts 21:11).

The Scripture reveals safeguards against abusive uses of personal prophecy.

First, the word of prophecy will usually not be new to the person addressed, but will confirm something God is already dealing with him or her about. Paul was already sensitive to the issue Agabus raised (Acts 20:22-24).

Second, the character of the person bringing the word should be weighed. Agabus' credibility is related to his record as a trustworthy man used in the exercise of this gift (Acts 11:28; 21:10).

Third, prophecy is not to be controlling. Such messages should never violate anyone's free will. Christian living is not cultism—governed by omens or the counsel of gurus. Personal prophecy should be evaluated by those present (1 Corinthians 14:29).

Paul did not change his plans because of Agabus' prophecy or the urging of others (Acts 21:12-14). He received the word graciously but continued his plans nonetheless.

Fourth, all prophecy is "in part" (1 Corinthians 13:9); it does not give the whole picture. Personal prophecy is not risky if kept on biblical footings, but neither is it to become the way we plan or direct our lives.

The incident with Agabus resulted in the church's rising to meet a challenging situation. This is a valid test of the prophetic office. It is for edification—to enlarge and refresh the body—and not for entertainment.

· · · PRAYER · · ·

Lord, we desire to be used of You. Help us to be filled with the Holy Spirit and yield ourselves to Your service, so that we can stand and show by the Spirit Your divine direction for the Church of God.

· · · TODAY'S THOUGHT · · ·

God uses men and women who are guided by the Word and who are willing to yield to the work of the Holy Spirit.

—Orville Hagan

CHRISTLIKE MINISTRY

By purity, by knowledge, by longsuffering, by kindness, by
the Holy Spirit, by sincere love (2 Corinthians 6:6).

We've encountered a brand of stinging criticism and general-ized judgmentalism that hurts and startles us. It goes "I would be a Christian if it weren't for Christians!" "Don't even think about joining the church—they're just a bunch of hypocrites!" "You won't catch me trusting a minister—all those preachers are fakes!"

Paul shared our consternation. In 2 Corinthians 6, he embarked on a bold attempt to establish the authenticity of his ministry. He made it clear that he wanted to "put no stumbling block in anyone's path, so that our ministry will not be discredited" (v. 3, *NIV*). Paul was pre-pared for the accusations of the world; they had come and would con-tinue to come. But as a faithful servant of the Lord, he was committed to commending, defending, and celebrating the legitimacy of God's work through his ministry.

Christ's work through the apostle was to be received as fully authentic by the Corinthians because it bears a striking resemblance to the work of Jesus himself. It is real ministry, characterized by purity, knowledge, patience, and kindness and accomplished through the Holy Spirit with sincere love. The message is powerful and clear. The work of the Holy Spirit in Paul's life and ministry had served to bring forth a bumper crop of spiritual fruit. The character traits of Jesus had been reproduced in the apostle—in who he was and in what he did in obedi-ence to his Lord. The ultimate commendation of Paul was that his ministry was truly the ministry of Jesus Christ. It was initiated, moti-vated, sustained, purified, and made victorious through the Holy Spirit.

· · · PRAYER · · ·

Holy Spirit, I need You to overflow me with Your presence and release Your power afresh in me. Legitimize and energize my ministry for Your glory and for the good of Your world today.

· · · TODAY'S THOUGHT · · ·

"All the graces and characteristics of God are to be modeled in the daily life and relationships of God's children" (Lloyd John Ogilvie, Chaplain of the U.S. Senate).

—Joe E. Edwards

THE SPIRIT OF LOVE

"The Spirit of the Lord is upon Me, because He has anointed Me to preach the gospel to the poor . . . to heal the brokenhearted, to preach deliverance to the captives and recovery of sight to the blind, to set at liberty those who are oppressed" (Luke 4:18).

 He walked down ghetto street, past sleazy bars and dark-eyed men, kicking away trash and trying to ignore the stench of uncollected garbage. Fear tugged at his mind. "Lord, if You want me to pastor here, help me to love these people."

A voice said, "Preach on love!"

He began his first sermon with the words "Though I speak with the tongues of men and of angels, but have not love, I have become as sounding brass or a clanging cymbal." His eyes filled with tears and he felt as if his heart would burst with compassion.

"Pastor, my neighbor had a stroke; would you come?" a small voice asked. He went, and touching the trembling forehead of the stroke victim, there arose a spirit of compassion. "Lord, we thank You for Your healing touch," he prayed.

Rising, the pastor saw four young men staring at him through the doorway. He knew them—the ringleaders of the neighborhood's notorious gang. Speechless, he stared back as fear rose inside him.

The most unkempt of the bunch lunged toward the pastor, who stood his ground. Then gruffly, but sincerely, he reached out to grip the minister's hand. "Thank you for coming to pray for Dad," he muttered.

"They don't mean to be impolite," the mother said softly. "They just didn't think anyone cared."

A few weeks later, two of the young men came and said, "Preacher, pray for us. We want to learn to love like these people love." A revival broke out that lasted for almost a year. One of the city's most violent gangs became a new-convert class . . . because of a *spirit of love.*

· · · PRAYER · · ·

Lord, fill us with compassion, that we may hear the silent screams and feel the hurting hearts.

· · · TODAY'S THOUGHT · · ·

To merely talk about love is like jingling coins in your pocket while `a child starves. Love is a coin spent in a bakery so that child can have bread.

—H. Lynn Stone

A GODLY LIFE ENSURED

And if Christ is in you, the body is dead because of sin, but
the Spirit is life because of righteousness (Romans 8:10).

 Two themes run through this verse: one is *domination* and the other is *absorption*. Paul declared that a person's life is determined by the force, or forces, dominating it, and by the things in which it is absorbed.

There is the life dominated by sinful human nature. The focus and center of this life is self. It is satisfying the ego. It can be described as passion- and lust-dominated, or pride- and ambition-dominated. This life is fully absorbed in things which gratify the desires of the flesh.

Then, there is the life dominated by the Holy Spirit of God. When one accepts Jesus Christ as Lord, he or she finds that the law of the Spirit is the dominant force in life. This operative force of the Holy Spirit awakens spiritual life and sustains it. It is, in fact, the very source of life. Life, then, becomes absorbed in things of the Spirit, so that matters of the flesh no longer occupy the paramount place in life. The spiritual law is set against the carnal and overcomes it.

Most people live with people; only a few are able to live the life of a hermit. Positive forces in society have tended to curb the darker nature of man, allowing people to live together in community. Modern society seems determined to destroy these positive forces, however, and replace them with lawlessness. These days call for greater personal discipline than ever.

This discipline cannot come from within ourselves without the direct power of the Holy Spirit. The Spirit must operate to generate the kind of righteousness advocated by Paul. The answer for an ordered society is Christlike people living their lives in the power of the Holy Spirit.

· · · PRAYER · · ·

Our Father in heaven, let the Holy Spirit so dominate my life that I will always be absorbed only in those things which edify my life, glorify You among men, and bring honor to Your holy name.

· · · TODAY'S THOUGHT · · ·

In September 1953, God sent the Holy Spirit and filled me. The Pentecostal experience of Acts 1:8 then became a reality for me and since then has empowered and invigorated me.

—Gene D. Rice

THE GLORIOUS HOLY SPIRIT

"Stand up and bless the Lord your God forever and ever!
Blessed be Your glorious name, which is exalted above all
blessing and praise!" (Nehemiah 9:5).

My father passed away when I was quite young, and my family did not have many material possessions. We were not totally devoid of spiritual influence, however, for we had a godly grandmother.

I was a rebellious child. I got into any mischief I could find; I even bootlegged whiskey for a while in Atlanta and spent one night in jail. The Holy Spirit often convicted me of the life I lived. When I thought of my grandmother's prayers, it seemed that with each step I took away from God, I felt her tears slosh in my shoes.

One Sunday afternoon at the corner of Humphrey and Hightower streets in Atlanta, I was led of the Spirit to enter an old-fashioned brush arbor building. The floor was sawdust strewn over the hard-packed ground. The preacher rolled his Bible in his hand, paced up and down the aisles, and preached a "hell fire and brimstone" message.

My sinner's heart trembled as God made me conscious of my need to give Him my heart and life. I "hit the sawdust trail" and fell into the altar. A dear sister named Anna Belle, whose husband was a prize fighter—a lady who loved to dance and rejoice before the Lord— prayed with me.

Oh, what a glorious experience it was to be saved! Heaven and earth came together with a smack and I was right in the middle of it all! Not only was I saved, but I also received the baptism in the Holy Spirit that same afternoon.

The glorious Holy Spirit has been so wonderful to me through the years.

· · · PRAYER · · ·

Sweet Holy Spirit, let us never become so big or so important that we fail to hear You when You speak. Guide and direct us in all things.

· · · TODAY'S THOUGHT · · ·

The Holy Spirit echoes softly in our minds the sounds of a mother or grandmother at prayer. Like the aromas from the kitchens of our childhood, they draw us back home and eventually into the arms of Jesus.

—John Thomas (Jake) Roberts

OLD-TIME HOLY GHOST BAPTISM

*"But the Helper, the Holy Spirit, whom the Father will send
in My name, He will teach you all things, and bring to your
remembrance all things that I said to you"* (John 14:26).

 I was born on a south Georgia farm. My parents were share-croppers, so my eight brothers and I had little opportunity or desire to attend church. The Lord showed His love for me, however, by giving me a wonderful Christian girl as my wife.

The turning point in my spiritual life came in January 1916, when an evangelist, Brother Anderson, and song director E.W. Williams came to the little town of Branford, Florida, where I worked as a sawmill super-intendent. The revival tent was pitched a block from my house, so my wife and I could sit on our porch and listen to the services.

My wife persuaded me to go to the meetings with her, and she received the baptism in the Holy Spirit. Seeing her enthusiasm for this then-new "tongues-speaking" movement, I accepted the Lord as Savior; but I wasn't ready yet to seek for the Holy Spirit. Brother Williams needed a job and I hired him at the mill. I gave him hard, dirty work to see how he would react. He sang and smiled.

So I began to seek the Holy Spirit also. Before I was filled with the Spirit, I was called to preach the gospel. When I talked to my wife about it, she responded, "Get the Holy Ghost and the preaching will work out." She promised she would go wherever the Lord sent us, and for 55 years of ministry she remained faithful to that promise.

Now, the Lord could fill me with the Holy Spirit. He did—glorious-ly! Thus I, a bashful and uneducated young man, teamed up with Brother E.W. Williams to take the gospel to nearby communities. I am overwhelmed to think how God has blessed this country boy through the years. I didn't have much formal schooling, but God said, "When He, the Spirit of truth, has come, He will guide you into all truth" (John 16:13). And He has!

· · · PRAYER · · ·

*Thank You, Father, for loving me enough to send Your Son and Your
sweet Holy Ghost into my life.*

· · · TODAY'S THOUGHT · · ·

The Holy Spirit takes the most common cloth and makes a scarlet robe. Adopting the son of a sharecropper as a son of God is the great-est miracle of all.

—R.P. Johnson

THE HOLY SPIRIT ENABLES US

"This dream I, King Nebuchadnezzar, have seen. Now you, Belteshazzar, declare its interpretation, since all the wise men of my kingdom are not able to make known to me the interpretation; but you are able, for the Spirit of the Holy God is in you" (Daniel 4:18).

As a small child, I was impressed by my father's ability to handle difficult situations. Preachers' children are sometimes exposed to the negatives of church problems by their parents' open discussion, but this was not the case in our home. My father discreetly handled church difficulties with grace and finesse.

His wisdom was displayed in family situations as well. At times, I thought he was the most intelligent man alive. When I came across a terrifying problem, I knew I could seek Dad's wisdom and usually resolve the problem.

When I was 12, a teenager several years older attacked me as I delivered newspapers. I was humiliated, hurt, and enraged, so I ran to my father, who saw I was troubled. When he asked why, I responded with an eruption of negative words and emotions. Then, he touched my shoulder tenderly and spoke a few soft words that comforted me instantly.

Years later, I came to realize that this great ability Dad possessed was not a natural ability. He was a mere human who had been empowered by the Holy Spirit. His wisdom was spiritual, not just human intellect. The Holy Spirit provides this wisdom for each believer. Through Him, we can know the answer to adverse situations that we may encounter daily.

The Spirit not only allows us this supernatural wisdom, but He also offers the privilege of a prayer language, an emotional stirring, and exciting Pentecostal worship. More importantly, He endues us with power to be Christ's witnesses.

· · · PRAYER · · ·

Father, fill me with the Spirit so individuals may see You, the author of salvation, in me. Create in me an attitude that is ready to listen when the Spirit speaks, to talk when the Spirit commands, and to walk where the Spirit leads.

· · · TODAY'S THOUGHT · · ·

The Holy Spirit enables us to experience true and ultimate wisdom which cannot be obtained through man's intellect alone.

—V.R. LeBuhn

POWER FOR THE TASK

And when they had prayed, the place where they were assembled together was shaken; and they were all filled with the Holy Spirit, and they spoke the word of God with boldness (Acts 4:31).

The apostles had been beaten, put in prison, and ordered not to speak in the name of Jesus. They had not come together, however, to nurse wounded egos, to complain, or to draft a retraction of their declarations. They had assembled to ask God to empower them to do more of what got them into trouble in the first place.

Their victory was not because of their aptitude or resourcefulness but because of the power they received on the Day of Pentecost. They were given an opportunity, in a practical way, to trust in the promise of endowment which accompanied the Holy Spirit baptism.

We are called to be His witnesses. The message we share is in direct opposition to the world; therefore, adversity cannot be avoided. We must have divine assistance. God has made that help available to the humblest believer. The same Holy Spirit who enabled early believers is promised and available to us today.

Most everyone in the Christian world trusts in the Holy Spirit as a matter of creed. Only those who know the inwardness of His presence, however, understand what it is like to cling to Him in times of external oppression. The Spirit-filled person knows what it is like to live from the inside out, to be driven by an inward assurance, to be comforted by an inward security, and to be replenished from an inward reservoir.

In speaking of the Holy Spirit, Jesus said to His disciples, in John 14:17, "For He dwells with you and will be in you."

We need to understand that all we need for victory in this world is within us—the Holy Spirit!

· · · PRAYER · · ·

O Lord, You know the threats of the hostile world. Make us brave enough to speak Your message. Help us speak with boldness and clarity so those who hear will understand. Show Your mighty power. Save, heal, work miracles and wonders in the name of Your Son, Jesus Christ.

· · · TODAY'S THOUGHT · · ·

Our children and a new century wait expectantly for the transforming power and the miraculous impact of Pentecost. May the Lord help us to lead them to that reality.

—R. Lamar Vest

THE HOLY SPIRIT AS ADMINISTRATOR

Now may He who supplies seed to the sower, and bread for food, supply and multiply the seed you have sown. . . . For the administration of this service not only supplies the needs of the saints, but also is abounding through many thanksgivings to God (2 Corinthians 9:10, 12).

I am a child of the Church of God—born in what is now the girls dormitory of Lee College. I was saved at the age of 5 in the old auditorium where the Church of God Publishing House now stands. Alda B. Harrison, founder of *Lighted Pathway*, was my youth leader; Hoyle Case, veteran missionary, my Sunday school teacher. I was baptized in the Holy Spirit under the ministry of D.B. Yow.

I planned to be a civil engineer, but God thought differently and I entered the ministry. In chapel at Bible Training School (BTS), God called me to the mission field. At BTS, I met Lucille Settle. I graduated from Vanderbilt University at age 19; Lucille got her degree from Scarritt College, and we were married on August 29, 1947.

Two weeks later we arrived in Haiti, where I was acting overseer. A 65 percent increase in church membership and 70 percent increase in congregations marked our first five years there. Friends tell me that surely one of the Holy Spirit's gifts to me is the gift of administration. Most of my ministry has been with colleges or missions administration. While president of the Church of God School of Theology, studies and materials were prepared for the seminary's approval by two accrediting associations.

God has performed many miracles in our lives. Traveling behind the Iron Curtain, we worked with Christians in the underground church. Our daughter, Dianne, was healed at birth of an intestinal blockage and later of a tropical infection. Our daughter, Crystal, is a missionary who helped establish the China Church of God in Taiwan. The Holy Spirit has been my administrator.

· · · PRAYER · · ·

To God—Father, Son, and Holy Spirit—be the glory both now and forever.

· · · TODAY'S THOUGHT · · ·

God's message to me at BTS was, "Thou shalt not count this as a small thing. Unto you it is given to know the will of God. Then that which I have done among you, ye shall not despise."

—John Herbert Walker, Jr.

GOD'S CONTINUING SPIRIT

"As for Me," says the Lord, "this is My covenant with
them: My Spirit who is upon you, and My words which I
have put in your mouth, shall not depart from your mouth,
nor from the mouth of your descendants, nor from the
mouth of your descendants' descendants," says the Lord,
"from this time and forevermore" (Isaiah 59:21).

Israel had so many great promises from God. What could be greater than for God to say to a person or nation, "My Spirit will never depart from you or your children"? Verse 20 says, "The Redeemer will come to Zion . . . to those who turn from transgression."

Through the Redeemer, Isaiah's prophesy was a new covenant made with the church. As long as we follow the example of Christ, the same promise of His Spirit is for us today. Peter proclaimed, "The promise is to you and to your children, and to all who are afar off, as many as the Lord our God will call" (Acts 2:39).

God's Word will never be broken. The Holy Spirit will continue in His church throughout all generations. Christ, as Head of the church, was first filled with and led by the Spirit. The anointing was first on Him, and from His head that precious ointment flows to each of us if we so desire.

Many things are important to the church for progress and growth. Nothing, however, will take the place of the Spirit of God. As long as Christ prolongs His coming, we can rest assured that the Holy Spirit will continue in His church. We can be sure that the gates of hell shall not prevail against the church. He has brought us this far, and He is not going to turn us away now.

It is up to us to agree with Him and enter into this covenant. As long as we obey Him, He will not forsake us.

· · · PRAYER · · ·

Dear Father, I thank You for sending the precious Holy Spirit. I covenant with You today to seek Your will and follow Your way in all of life. I rejoice in Your promise that the Holy Spirit will abide forever.

· · · TODAY'S THOUGHT · · ·

I will honor the covenant with Jesus for the continuing presence of the Spirit.

—Terrell Taylor

THE HOLY SPIRIT AND FIRE

John answered, saying to them all, "I indeed baptize you with water; but One mightier than I is coming, whose sandal strap I am not worthy to loose. He will baptize you with the Holy Spirit and with fire" (Luke 3:16).

I grew up in a farm family in Jamaica. When I was 15, I was given responsibility for tending my father's prize Jamaican Red Poll bull. I underestimated the strength and tenacity of the bull, who got loose and destroyed a neighbor's newly planted sugarcane. My father paid for the damage and then gave me a thorough lashing, despite the pleas of the rest of the family. In anger I went out and beat the bull to death, and open war began between my father and me.

Fearing to leave me at home with my father that night, my mother took me with her to the Young People's Endeavor (YPE) service at the church. The message by the minister drew me to the altar, where I accepted Christ. God changed my life.

I began taking part in the activities of church—Sunday school, YPE, and testimony meetings. But something was missing from my spiritual life. My elders told me, "You need the baptism with the Holy Ghost."

I was asked to drop all church activities and concentrate on my infilling. I wanted God more as I studied His Word and waited before Him. Three years went by. Then the power came and God filled me with His Holy Spirit with the evidence of speaking in other tongues.

My ministry was immediately enhanced, and God began to work through my life. The Holy Spirit and fire empowered this sanctified believer like a mighty locomotive into divine service. How wonderful it is to have God's Spirit as my strength and guide.

· · · PRAYER · · ·

Holy Spirit, fill us anew with the fire of Pentecost. Make us power-houses of energy, consumed with a desire to win the lost. Let us blaze like divine flames in Your service.

· · · TODAY'S THOUGHT · · ·

Foxe's Book of Martyrs tells us that early Christians were sometimes tied to stakes, doused with oil, and set afire as the light for games in the amphitheaters of the Roman world. There they were offered as "lights" and "fire" for the Christ they loved.

—Fedlyn A. Beason

RESTORING THE JOY

Restore to me the joy of Your salvation, and uphold me with Your generous Spirit (Psalm 51:12).

Recently, as I was riding behind a large motor home, I observed a bumper sticker which read, "He who dies with the most toys wins." To this materialistic culture, joy depends on the accumulation of "stuff." The Lord said in Luke 12:15: "Take heed and beware of covetousness, for one's life does not consist in the abundance of the things he possesses." People still don't understand that kind of thinking.

In contrast, I reflected on my heritage in the Church of God. I remember the attitude of joy that was a constant companion of the saints in those earlier years of the church. Joy was based on a relationship with Jesus Christ rather than on "toys." Joy wasn't dependent on *novelty* but on *newness* in His Spirit. Many testified: "I am not feeling well in my body, but I feel good in my soul" or "The way has been hard at times, but God has been good to me."

How can this generation of Pentecostal believers recapture that joy in the midst of such agitating and perturbing times? The Psalmist declared, "We need a restoration of the joy of Your salvation." We also need to be renewed in the joy of His salvation to us. In Christ, we have everything we need to live an abundant life. In Christ we are full! The presence of the Spirit bears witness of our heirship and helps us in our weaknesses. He enables us to take to heart the words of the Lord in John 16:33: "In the world you will have tribulation; but be of good cheer, I have overcome the world." Because of His generous restoring presence, we know we too can overcome. We can be full of joy!

· · · PRAYER · · ·

Lord Jesus, generously restore and uphold me with Your Spirit of joy. Because of Your salvation I know I am delivered from the darkness of gloom and translated into the light of Your joyous Presence..

· · · TODAY'S THOUGHT · · ·

"Joy is not in things, it is in people." Embrace this principle and live above the world through the power of the Holy Spirit.

—A. Ray Garner

THE MIND OF THE SPIRIT

Now He who searches the hearts knows what the mind of the Spirit is, because He makes intercession for the saints according to the will of God (Romans 8:27).

The Holy Spirit is a person as much as the Father and the Son are persons. The Spirit is the third person of the Trinity. He has intelligence, feelings, and will. He teaches, guides, commissions, prays, and speaks to humankind. He is to be obeyed and reverenced.

The Holy Spirit deals with people on a personal basis. He works, communicates, and speaks through individuals to others. His ministry is not restricted to gifts, for He has all attributes of God.

The ministries of the Spirit are diverse and manifold. The Holy Spirit is important to us for spiritual growth, power in prayer life, and witnessing for Jesus. In Creation, the Holy Spirit moved on the waters. He is the author of the Word of God. He reveals to us the message of salvation. He guides, enlightens, and ministers to the church.

The Holy Spirit baptism on the Day of Pentecost was a new happening. This blessing is for all, great and small, who by adoption are sons and daughters of God. The experience is permanent, remaining with us until the day of Rapture.

My Italian immigrant parents found Christ as their Savior in a small Pentecostal mission in Brooklyn, New York. My grandparents asked them why they would change their faith. They were reared in a beautiful church with stained–glass windows, altar benches between pews, and statues of saints around the sanctuary. Why would they exchange that for a little storefront mission with no beauty at all? Mother responded by saying, "The church you brought me up in has a beauty that satisfies the eyes. But when I accepted Christ and received His Spirit I found a beauty that satisfies my soul!" Now He who searches the hearts "knows what the mind of the Spirit is."

· · · PRAYER · · ·

Father, teach us to exert a wholesome influence on those we contact. May the world be better tomorrow because we are living in it today.

· · · TODAY'S THOUGHT · · ·

I will live confidently, in the power of the Holy Spirit—today!

—Thomas Grassano

THE HOLY SPIRIT, MY HELPER

If you love Me, keep My commandments. And I will pray the Father, and He will give you another Helper, that He may abide with you forever (John 14:15, 16).

When I was a young girl, my mother taught men's Bible class in the Sunday school of a Methodist church. She told them that the things she read about in the Book of Acts were not happening in her life or theirs. She became so hungry for God that she began to go early every morning to an old washhouse behind our house to pray.

I remember well the morning my mother came out of that washhouse praising God and speaking in a language I had never heard. My father was a physician in the small town of Artesia, Mississippi. My older brother ran to get him to come see what was wrong with our mother. After examining her, our dad said Mama was fine physically, "and spiritually she appears to be filled full of the Holy Ghost."

I too wanted to be filled with the Spirit, and during a prayer meeting I received the baptism. I began helping my mother in meetings by standing at the door and greeting people and giving out songbooks and leaflets. In my teen years I learned to play the piano and became involved almost full–time in evangelistic work with my mother and aunt, who were ministering together throughout Mississippi.

I decided to attend Fort Wayne Bible College. Although this was not a Pentecostal college, a number of my close friends in the school received the baptism in the Holy Spirit while I was there. I graduated with a major in music—the youngest student on campus.

Through these years the Holy Spirit has been my Helper. I have been enabled by Him to establish and pastor churches, build schools, do youth and ladies ministries, help build an orphanage, speak in numerous camp meetings and conferences, be a wife to a wonderful husband, and raise three fine children. Yes, the Holy Spirit has been my Helper.

· · · PRAYER · · ·

Lord, thank You for the Holy Spirit You have sent to be our Helper. I want to reverence and obey Him and never grieve Him.

· · · TODAY'S THOUGHT · · ·

In life we have many helpers, but the Holy Spirit is *the* Helper.

—Mary Graves

GOD'S SEARCHLIGHT

But God has revealed them to us through His Spirit. For the
Spirit searches all things, yes, the deep things of God
(1 Corinthians 2:10).

As a young boy I was fascinated by lights. I remember walking under a magnolia tree, shining a miner's headlamp on the birds as they perched for the night. It still amazes me to watch a spotlight dispel darkness in its path, revealing what lies before it.

This verse tells of the wonderful work of the Holy Spirit through uncovering the untold mysteries of God regarding His actions, activities, and work. Much of God's grace, gifts, and goodness are before us unseen and often unrealized. They are, as it were, hidden in the blackened darkness of the unknown. The Holy Spirit, like a huge spotlight, simply uncovers, unfolds, and exposes to us the very mind and purpose of God's counsel.

Paul spoke to the Ephesians concerning our comprehending to the fullest all of the will of God for us. He, the Holy Spirit, takes something of God's mind or nature and presents it to man's mind directly—things such as the meaning of the acts of God, the secret of the person of the Lord Jesus, the character of God as Father, the will of God for the conduct of His children, the mind of God for His people.

· · · PRAYER · · ·

Father, would You commission the Holy Spirit to lift the veil, dispel the darkness, and allow us to see all You have in store for us and all You are to us? Show us Your provisions, Your strengths, and Your divine hand guiding every aspect of our lives. Let trials, problems, heartaches, and disappointments fade into nothingness as we learn now to trust You and Your counsel. In the wonderful name of Jesus.

· · · TODAY'S THOUGHT · · ·

It is the Holy Spirit's work to unveil, or uncover for us precious truths of God's Word and will. By simply removing the covers and revealing the treasures of God's blessings, promises, and comforts, He gives us strength, joy, and peace through Christ.

—D. Keith Gunter

THE SPIRIT RESTS ON HIM

The Spirit of the Lord shall rest upon Him, the Spirit of wisdom and understanding, the Spirit of counsel and might, the Spirit of knowledge and of the fear of the Lord (Isaiah 11:2).

Isaiah prophesied that the Savior, the Messiah, when He should come into the world, would be endowed by the Holy Spirit with wisdom, discernment, and might. In confirmation of this prophecy, John the Baptist, after he baptized Jesus, said of Him, "I saw the Spirit descending from heaven like a dove, and He remained upon Him" (John 1:32). Not long thereafter, in the synagogue at Nazareth, Jesus himself announced, "The Spirit of the Lord is upon Me" (Luke 4:18).

The Holy Spirit rested on Jesus and we have His promise that the Holy Spirit will also rest on us. Jesus said, "I will pray the Father, and He will give you another Helper, that He may abide with you forever" (John 14:16). And He added, "For He dwells with you and will be in you" (v. 17). Jesus promised, "You shall receive power when the Holy Spirit has come upon you" (Acts 1:8).

The promise of the Holy Spirit was not made only to the apostles and immediate disciples of Jesus. The promise is to all who will believe in Him as Savior and Lord (Acts 2:39). The Savior still bestows the Holy Spirit on those who believe in Him.

It is not by human might or power that we serve the Lord Jesus but by the power of the Holy Spirit. The Spirit resting on us equips us to meet life's challenges. We are not helpless, defenseless, or powerless to face the challenges of life. The Holy Spirit imparts to us the wisdom and understanding, counsel and might, knowledge and reverence needed for victorious Christian living.

The Spirit upon us is not a now–and–then occurrence but an enduring and constant experience. The Holy Spirit gives us moral values and the power to put them into action according to the will of God.

· · · PRAYER · · ·

Heavenly Father, fill me with Your Holy Spirit that I may have the wisdom, knowledge, and might to fulfill Your will for my life.

· · · TODAY'S THOUGHT · · ·

We ought not underestimate the power and influence of the Holy Spirit in our lives.

—G. Evett Guyton

KNOWING THE THINGS OF GOD

For what man knows the things of a man except the spirit of the man which is in him? Even so no one knows the things of God except the Spirit of God (1 Corinthians 2:11).

Christianity is on the rise—particularly in the Pentecostal Movement—and believers are multiplying around the world. Yet, hundreds of millions do know God through a personal relationship with His Son, Jesus Christ. Our Scripture verse talks about knowing God and the things of God, which would indicate those intimate aspects of God that only those closest to Him could possibly know. There are individuals who apparently rise above the crowd and come into an intimate relationship with God.

These persons who, because of their intense love for God and devotion to Him, know the things of God as revealed to them by the Holy Spirit. I do not believe these people are superspiritual or even favored by God above others. Rather, they reflect the love God demonstrates to them back to Him in a greater measure than do others.

I once heard Dr. Charles W. Conn explain that he loved each of his children with equal intensity. But because several of his children reflected that love back to him in such an openhearted and intense manner, these children, though certainly not loved more by their father, had a different relationship with him. I believe we have a similar opportunity with God. Even when duty says we have done enough, even when God's Word states we have fulfilled what is required of us, yet our heart cries out, "Lord, I want to know You more, I want to know You better." If we from a heart of love choose to pursue Him with such an intense love, I am confident there are things we will discover in the Lord that we could never learn any other way.

· · · PRAYER · · ·

Father, I want to know You in a more intimate way than I have ever known You before. By Your Spirit, reveal Yourself to me afresh and help me reflect the love You shower on me daily back to You.

· · · TODAY'S THOUGHT · · ·

The privilege of knowing God is the result of His grace, freely given.

—B. Randall Hamon

WHERE THE HOLY SPIRIT DWELLS

Do you not know that you are the temple of God and that the Spirit dwells in you? (1 Corinthians 3:16).

So often people look for God and His Spirit in their surroundings. We hear statements such as "I see God in the sun, moon, stars, trees, flowers, birds, and animals." The whole creation shows the handiwork of God and testifies of His creative genius, but the Spirit of God dwells in us—His people redeemed from sin by Christ.

Scripture refers to all of God's people collectively as "the temple of God." Scripture also refers to each of His people individually as "the temple of the Holy Spirit" (1 Corinthians 6:19).

When you think of a temple, you probably think of a magnificent building, overwhelming in size or architectural design, like Solomon's temple, described in the Bible. The Bible says of us that we are marvelously made in the image and likeness of God. We are God's building. To Him we are the magnificent temple. In us He is to find the praise, glory, and honor.

What a privilege it is to be a temple of God, a temple of the Holy Spirit! We are living temples, not temples made of lifeless materials. As living temples of the Lord, we must present ourselves to the Lord to be used for His glory and in His service.

In regeneration the Holy Spirit comes to dwell in us. Then, as we are yielded to the Spirit, we can be filled with the Holy Spirit. We can be a temple of the Lord filled with His power and used of Him to bring others to Jesus Christ.

The Spirit–filled temple displays the character of the One who dwells within. In the Spirit–filled temple are the treasures of love, joy, peace, long–suffering, kindness, goodness, faithfulness, gentleness, and self–control (Galatians 5:22, 23). Such a temple will cause others to inquire about the hope we have in Christ.

· · · PRAYER · · ·

Father, in the name of Jesus Christ, we desire to have the presence of Your Spirit fill us to overflowing now. Spirit of God, You are welcome in this temple. You are invited to abide here always.

· · · TODAY'S THOUGHT · · ·

Temples are places of worship. As living temples, let us live so that all who pass by our temple will see that we represent the true God, and want to worship Him—the God and Father of our Lord Jesus Christ.

—Daniel W. Hampton

THE SPIRIT OF THE LORD

Then the Spirit of the Lord fell upon me, and said to me,
"Speak, thus says the Lord: thus you have said, O house of
Israel; for I know the things that come into your mind'"
(Ezekiel 11:5).

 When the Spirit of the Lord comes upon us, we are prepared and commissioned for spiritual service.

The Spirit of the Lord came on Ezekiel and commanded him to speak to a defiant nation.

The Spirit of the Lord came on the elders of Israel (Numbers 11:25) and gave them new authority and leadership. They prophesied and were anointed with wisdom, discernment and great spiritual insight.

The Lord said to Ezekiel, "I will put My Spirit within you and cause you [enable you] to walk in My statutes, and you will keep My judgments and do them" (Ezekiel 36:27).

When the Spirit of the Lord comes on us today, we are changed in a miraculous way. My father was a pastor. Shortly after I was filled with the Holy Spirit, I was testifying in his church. Suddenly, the Holy Spirit fell on me. My body warmed all over and I shook and trembled under the anointing of the Spirit. I was lifted into a new sphere, another dimension of His mighty presence. Words began to pour out of my mouth in a way I had never experienced before. It seemed someone was standing behind me, speaking through the back of my head the most gracious thoughts I had ever heard.

When I came to myself. I was saying things I had never heard or read, and the place was literally shaken by the mighty power of God. God had sovereignly spoken through me. I did not understand it, nor could I comprehend the depth of what had happened. But now I have come to realize that my experience was comparable to Ezekiel's when the Spirit of the Lord fell upon him and commanded him to speak.

· · · PRAYER · · ·

Lord, let your Spirit fall fresh on me today. Put your words in my mouth that I may speak for you.

· · · TODAY'S THOUGHT · · ·

Each of us is to be a vessel, a conduit, and a channel through which the Holy Spirit may flow out into the lives of others.

—T. L. Lowery

THE SENSITIVE EAR

*He who has an ear, let him hear what the Spirit says to the
churches. To him who overcomes I will give some of the
hidden manna to eat. And I will give him a white stone, and
on the stone a new name written which no one knows except
him who receives it* (Revelation 2:17).

 Walking in a large shopping mall during the Christmas season
I heard my name called. Immediately I stopped and looked
around. A sea of faces clamored in every direction. Having
recognized my wife's familiar voice, I remained still and, sure
enough, from among the crowd she appeared.

A sensitive ear to the voice of the Holy Spirit is primal for the
Christian. Hearing Him above the noise all around is crucial. Just as
the art of listening in our human relationships must be purposely culti-
vated, so it is with the Holy Spirit. To hear what the Spirit speaks goes
beyond merely recognizing His presence. Many are attracted by the
warmth and feeling of a beautiful worship service where He is manifested. However, the real issue is what does the Holy Spirit want me to
hear, understand, and do?

Not everyone listens attentively to His voice. But to those who will
He directs them through the maze of daily confusion. Just as I listened
to the voice of my dearest friend in the mall, we too can hear Him.

The church is much more than a place we go on Sunday. It is more
than a building or a group of individuals. It is the fellowship of the
Holy Spirit, and we are family members in communion with Him.
This means that as we walk in fellowship with Him, we are the church.
Our privilege is not to be another face in the crowd but to reflect His
face in the crowd.

· · · PRAYER · · ·

*Dear Lord Jesus, I eagerly seek You. Commune with me as I abide
in Your presence. It is my deepest desire to constantly be sensitive to
Your Holy Spirit that I may be an overcomer in this world and reflect
Your face in the crowd.*

· · · TODAY'S THOUGHT · · ·

As Jesus told His disciples, "I have food to eat of which you do not
know" (John 4:32), so you too have the divine privilege of a spiritual
ear that is sensitive to hear Him.

—J. David Stephens

ANOINTED TO PREACH

*"The Spirit of the Lord is upon Me, because He has anoint-
ed Me to preach the gospel to the poor. He has sent Me to
heal the brokenhearted, to preach deliverance to the captives and recovery of sight to the blind, to set at liberty those
who are oppressed"* (Luke 4:18).

People try to justify themselves for the lack of success in ministry by blaming others for lack of prayer. We often hear such
expressions as "If we have a revival, you will have to pray it
down," "I did not bring a revival in my suitcase," "If you are
expecting me to bring a revival, you will be disappointed," Seemingly,
they want to impress the church that they are to blame because they
have not prayed.

Who do you suppose went around with Jonah, or Peter, or Paul, or
Philip to pray down a revival? When God got through dealing with
Jonah, he preached the word of the Lord to Nineveh, and more than
120,000 souls fasted and prayed to God to save them.

Was Peter preaching or praying on the Day of Pentecost when 3,000
souls were added to the number? It was when Paul was preaching and
reasoning of righteousness, temperance and judgment to come that
Felix trembled and Agrippa said, "You almost persuade me to become
a Christian" (Acts 26:28).

When the angel spoke to Philip and the Spirit said to him, "Go near
and overtake this chariot," Philip ran to the Ethiopian eunuch. He did
not get down and pray for him. He opened his mouth, and beginning at
this Scripture, preached Jesus to him" (Acts 8:29, 35).

The success of Jonah's preaching was accomplished while he prayed
from the belly of the whale. Paul's power for preaching the gospel
came when the light shone around him and he prayed, "Lord, what do
You want me to do?" (Acts 9:6). Peter's power came as he prayed,
"Now, Lord, look on their threats, and grant to Your servants that with
all boldness they may speak Your word, by stretching out Your hand to
heal, and that signs and wonders may be done through the name of
Your holy Servant Jesus" (Acts 4:29, 30).

· · · PRAYER · · ·

*Help us to truly know, O God, that holy anointing comes only when
we enter into Your presence through earnest prayer and supplication.*

· · · TODAY'S THOUGHT · · ·

Our help must come from God.

—Zeno C. Tharp, Sr.

SUFFICIENCY IN THE SPIRIT

Who also made us sufficient as ministers of the new covenant, not of the letter but of the Spirit; for the letter kills, but the Spirit gives life (2 Corinthians 3:6).

At age 16 I lost my mother to cancer. Up until that time in my life I could turn to her for the solution to almost any problems I faced. If she could not solve them herself, I knew that she could touch God for the answer. She would pray until the Spirit would take over and pray through her, then the answer would come. When Mom was taken from me, I knew I would have to get help myself. Then and only then did I learn that my sufficiency was in God's Holy Spirit, for I learned to pray in the Spirit.

I had been a Christian all my life and never knew what open sin was, yet I hungered for a deeper experience with God. One night, as a 17–year–old high school student, I prayed in the altar for approximately one hour to receive the Holy Spirit. A friend of mine asked me, "How bad do you want the Holy Ghost?" I stated, "Pretty bad." He asked me if I was willing to spend the night at the altar if necessary. I stated that I was, and at midnight I was filled with the Spirit.

When I entered the Navy, young and naive, I was told that I would not last as a Christian. At that moment a scripture came to me and stayed with me the entire time I was in the service: "My grace is sufficient for every need" (see 2 Corinthians 12:9). Each time I needed help, the Spirit was there to lead.

Finding the source of our sufficiency is one of the greatest lessons one can learn in life. It is easy for a person to think that he or she is sufficient because of intelligence or religious background—and these things are helpful—but as Christians we are never equipped for service until we realize our sufficiency is only in God. The Bible says, "We do not wrestle against flesh and blood, but against principalities [and] powers" (Ephesians 6:12).

· · · PRAYER · · ·

Holy Spirit, guide me that I may walk the walk and talk the talk that will be acceptable in Your sight and perform service that will exalt You and expand Your kingdom.

· · · TODAY'S THOUGHT · · ·

The Holy Spirit is what I need and He is all I need.

—Douglas J. Johns

RETURN IN THE POWER

*Then Jesus returned in the power of the Spirit to Galilee,
and news of Him went out through all the surrounding
region* (Luke 4:14).

In the story of Christ's temptation, it should be observed that He was prepared for battle beforehand, because He was full of the Holy Spirit. The same Spirit who had descended on Him like a dove at His water baptism led Him into the wilderness also. He was led as a champion onto the field, to fight an Enemy He was sure to conquer.

Christ had shown His indifference to the world by His willingness to endure the wilderness experience. By His fasting, He showed His power over the flesh. Satan cannot touch a life that is loosed from, and dead to, the world and flesh. The more we discipline the body and bring it into subjection, the less advantage Satan has over us (see 1 Corinthians 9:27).

We too are tempted through appetite, ambition, and presumption. But by the power of the Holy Spirit, we can resist the Enemy. The Enemy used all his force and yet was defeated. After failing in his temptation, the devil departed from the Lord. He saw it was futile to attack Christ, for Jesus had nothing Satan's fiery darts could fasten upon. There was no blind side, no weak or unguarded wall. Therefore, Satan gave up the cause.

In the same way, we must take up the weapons of the Spirit. As we follow Christ's example, we will minister as fully equipped saints who will have the victory over the Enemy every time.

· · · PRAYER · · ·

Heavenly Father, I ask for strength to endure whatever wilderness experience I must confront. I know that when I conquer and overcome, I will find a treasure from You. I need fresh courage and new strength to overcome temptation. I desire to return to my family, to my church, to my workplace, and to my community victorious in the power of the Spirit!

· · · TODAY'S THOUGHT · · ·

"Temptations that find us dwelling in God are to our faith like winds that more firmly root the tree".

—Jimmy D. Smith

LEAVING A LEGACY

In mighty signs and wonders, by the power of the Spirit of God ... I have fully preached the gospel of Christ (Romans 15:19).

 The Holy Spirit was truly the guiding light in the life of my father, J.H. Walker, Sr. A "heavenly glow" radiated around him as he preached. It penetrated congregations as he told how God led him into a deeper understanding of the Holy Spirit.

W.A. Capshaw, early Pentecostal minister, laid hands on little Jewel, Dad's sister, who was ill with epileptic convulsions. He prayed, and she was healed. The Walkers embraced the Holy Spirit in a new and different way. Dad was the second person in northern Louisiana to receive the baptism in the Holy Spirit and speak in tongues. It was a glorious experience that changed his life forever.

My father began preaching as a teenager, emphasizing divine healing through the Holy Spirit. Soon he contracted malaria. Chills and fever lasted for weeks and at times left him unconscious. He was close to death when State Overseer M.S. Haynes drove 200 miles to pray for him. Dad was healed immediately!

When Dr. Julian Sullivan came to our home to assist in my birth. Dad lay ill with a ruptured appendix. As he was superintendent of education for the Church of God, the doctor said, "I'm sorry, professor—it's too late. Nothing can be done."

But something could be done! As ministers prayed for him, Dad was healed!

Every time I heard him tell this, anxiety would fill me, thinking of Dad almost dying when I was born. But with face shining and tears in his eyes, he would tell of a large silvery sheet floating from the top of the room. A long glittering sword in it pierced his side. His body trembled and he felt a heavenly anointing of the Holy Spirit. Healing was complete.

· · · PRAYER · · ·

Thank You, dear God, for the power of the Holy Spirit, who develops ordinary people into saints whose lives are so marvelously filled with the glory of God that they radiate His grace long after their death.

· · · TODAY'S THOUGHT · · ·

I will follow the examples of Spirit–filled men and women and let God shine in my life.

—Grace Walker Delatour

LIGHT ON MY PATH

If by the Spirit you put to death the deeds of the body, you will live (Romans 8:13).

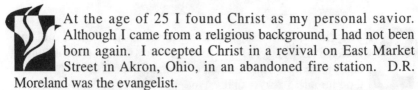 At the age of 25 I found Christ as my personal savior. Although I came from a religious background, I had not been born again. I accepted Christ in a revival on East Market Street in Akron, Ohio, in an abandoned fire station. D.R. Moreland was the evangelist.

As a heavy drinker, I brewed my own beer; but after receiving Christ, I poured my beer, whiskey, and wine down the sewer. While I poured, my wife shouted. We had camp meeting that night.

I was told that I must be sanctified and baptized with the Holy Ghost. One evening my family and I had dinner with a Carter family. As we prepared to leave, it was suggested that we pray. They prayed for more than an hour for me to receive the Baptism. Suddenly, I began to speak in tongues. Just before the Holy Spirit came, my son, Ray, heard me say, "Yes, Lord." On the way home, I explained why.

As a country boy, raised in the red clay hills of North Georgia, the country was still in me. I continued the practice of butchering hogs, using a room in my basement as a smokehouse for curing hams. I worked at Goodyear Tire and Rubber Company, and we used large knives three feet long to cut rubber. I thought one of these would be just the thing for butchering hogs. So, I put one down my trouser leg and took it home. While seeking the Baptism, that knife came before me, and I said, "Yes, Lord, I'll take it back."

The next day I took the knife to my foreman and told him what had happened, thinking I might lose my job. As tears welled in his eyes, he said, "Joe, any man that would receive an experience like that . . . let's just forget it." I had favor with Goodyear as long as I worked there––the day God called me to preach.

· · · PRAYER · · ·

The Pentecostal way is a blessed way. Thank You, God, for shedding Your light on my path.

· · · TODAY'S THOUGHT · · ·

After my Holy Ghost experience, I could understand messages in tongues. Not being learned in the Spirit, I thought that everyone who had the Holy Ghost understood the messages too. I was shocked to realize that God was giving me a special gift—interpretation.

—J.H. Hughes

GOD'S COMMON DENOMINATOR

*For by one Spirit we were all baptized into one body
whether Jews or Greeks, whether slaves or free and have all
been made to drink into one Spirit* (1 Corinthians 12:13).

 We gravitate toward people who are most like ourselves. We find friends who share common interests and values with us, and we feel comfortable and secure in "our own group." But God has His own special way of bringing people together. Our children sing a song that says:

God likes people, any shape, any color, any size;
You don't have to be an angel, to be special in His eyes;
He said it in John 3:16, and He proved it on Calvary too;
God likes people, ordinary people, people like you and me.

The composition of the church is diverse and all–inclusive because God welcomes any person who will trust in Christ as Savior and Lord.

As Christians the Holy Spirit has baptized us all into one body. In regeneration He immerses us into the death of Christ and raises us up with Christ to a new life in His body, the church. The Holy Spirit has worked to make us who we are by the grace of Jesus Christ.

As members of the body of Christ, we are accepted and approved by God for Christ's sake. No matter who we are, or what we may have been, when God looks at His church, He sees us in the body of Christ.

That we all have been "made to drink into one Spirit" indicates that the Spirit dwells in us by regeneration. We are not only baptized into the body of Christ, but we also become partakers of the Holy Spirit of Christ. The Holy Spirit is God's common denominator for His people.

· · · PRAYER · · ·

Father, thank You for the Holy Spirit by whom we all have equal access to You. I submit myself to the leadership of Your Spirit and invite His presence in my life and work.

· · · TODAY'S THOUGHT · · ·

God is the architect of the church. He is putting it together to please Himself. By His Spirit He has brought us together in Christ, diverse though we are in our ethnic origins, cultural backgrounds, and natural and acquired abilities.

—Jerry Irwin

THE SPIRIT GIVES

"But one and the same Spirit works all these things, distributing to each one individually as He wills"
(1 Corinthians 12:11).

One of the greatest frustrations for me as a pastor is the realization that many Christians are not aware this verse is in the Bible! While that may seem at first a shocking statement, many born–again men and women do not study their Bibles, and therefore many important truths remain hidden in God's Word.

This verse tells us the Holy Spirit gives gifts to each child of God, just as He determines. The Greek word *charismata* (translated "gifts") is very diverse and speaks of "divine gratuities, spiritual endowments, religious qualifications, and miraculous faculties," to name but a few of its usages.

I understand the above scripture to mean that the Holy Spirit of God has given to every one of us at least one "spiritual endowment," and possibly even more than one.

Satan does not want us to be aware of this. If he can keep us in the dark about spiritual gifts, he can hinder us from becoming productive saints in God's kingdom. It is spiritual warfare to keep the flesh under subjection, and it requires the continuing work of the Spirit.

We all have opportunities to use our gifts in ministry, as well as in personal spiritual warfare. If we will study God's Word daily and renew our minds and "earnestly desire the best gifts" (1 Corinthians 12:31), we will learn who we are in Christ and what His Holy Spirit has prepared for us to use for God's service.

· · · PRAYER · · ·

Father, I know You have given to each of us spiritual gifts to use as stewards in Your work here on earth. Forgive us for our failure to apprise ourselves of all that You have for us, and give us a proper perspective on the gifts of the Spirit. Let us use them for Your glory and not ours, to advance Your kingdom and not our programs. In Jesus' name.

· · · TODAY'S THOUGHT · · ·

Yes, we have been gifted and sent! Now, let us go and grow in the power of His Spirit, that we may be found faithful stewards of the manifold grace of God.

—Alan D. Humphries

RELY ON THE HOLY SPIRIT

You are manifestly an epistle of Christ, ministered by us,
written not with ink but by the Spirit of the living God, not
on tablets of stone but on tablets of flesh, that is, of the
heart (2 Corinthians 3:3).

A truth I have learned has been especially helpful is that my ministry cannot succeed without sincere devotion to God and reliance on His Spirit.

How many recollections I have of working in vain—in vain because it was done by me alone, not by relying on the Holy Spirit. My actions were well–intended, but I lacked the wisdom to sincerely ask for the Holy Spirit's help and intervention in the things I was trying to accomplish. I have learned by experience that it is necessary to ask the Holy Spirit to accomplish in my life, and in the lives of others, what I cannot possibly accomplish by my efforts alone.

As a young pastor, I discovered that my task was not to make people into epistles that would reflect me, but to help them become epistles that would reflect Christ. God has not called us to save souls by our own power, since we have no such power. Our only power is that of calling on the Spirit of the living God to make our witness of Christ effective by transforming lives from the inside, from the heart.

Once when there was much confusion in the church I served—some of the members had left and others were threatening to resign from their ministries—panic settled on me, followed by discouragement. I did not know what to do. Then the Lord gave me a dream. He showed me that all I needed to do was to trust in Him to take care of the church. That is what I did.

I knelt in prayer, asking God to send His Spirit to accomplish through me the work to be done. That is exactly what He did. Soon the church the Lord had given me to serve was restored to vitality and back on course.

· · · PRAYER · · ·

God, help us to always have the wisdom to trust in You and to rely on Your Spirit to accomplish Your work in us and in others, the people to whom we minister for Christ's sake.

· · · TODAY'S THOUGHT · · ·

Remember, anything that needs to be accomplished for Christ's sake should never be undertaken by our own effort alone but by depending on the Holy Spirit.

—Jacques Houle

POSSESSED BY THE SPIRIT

Come near to Me, hear this: I have not spoken in secret from
the beginning; from the time that it was, I was there. And now
the Lord God and His Spirit have sent Me (Isaiah 48:16).

As a child, I often became extremely fearful each night at bedtime. Each time I crawled into my bed, it seemed that mon-
sters were about to overwhelm me. There were times when I
became so afraid that I would cry out, "Daddy, Daddy." Dad
would cal back, "Son, don't be afraid. I am in the next room."

Though that would suffice for a short time, I would soon call out
again, "Daddy, I'm afraid!" The voice of my dad would ring out
through the darkness, "Come on in here, Son, Dad's here." With great
relief, I would crawl into the bed beside my father, and when I felt the
touch of his presence, I knew everything would be O.K.

I never once saw my father, J.G. Houck, afraid of anything. In his
ministry in the Church of God, in whatever situation, he was always a
tower of strength. Where did his strength come from? Why was he
never afraid of even the most frightening circumstances? He taught
me, "Son, you are never alone as long as you stay near the Father and
depend upon His Spirit."

Dad was an extraordinary person. I would hear him pray for hours
each day, and I knew he possessed the presence of the Holy Spirit and
the Holy Spirit possessed him. No wonder he felt secure. No wonder
he maintained a serenity. He understood the comfort and strength
brought about by knowing that He was there.

Dad always seemed prepared to tackle the giants of life. He faced
the problems as they came, and fought the battles when they became
necessary. He knew the Holy Spirit had sent him and was with him.

· · · PRAYER · · ·

Heavenly Father, help me every day to know You are present in
every situation. Help me to understand, "Just because You are silent
does not mean that you are not at work.

· · · TODAY'S THOUGHT · · ·

The greatest power available to us each day is the assurance from
God "I am with you." He is to provide whatever is necessary to live
abundantly and victoriously.

—Kenneth R. Houck

THE SPIRIT'S WITNESS

For you did not receive the spirit of bondage again to fear,
but you received the Spirit of adoption by whom we cry out,
"Abba, Father" (Romans 8:15).

Prior to conversion, we lived as prisoners to sin, the flesh, and the devil. Our bondage was absolute, total, and complete. We had no power to extricate ourselves, no strength to resist sin, and no will or desire to do otherwise. We lived in fear. It was such pervasive fear that Paul describes it as a spirit of bondage to fear.

Then we became conscious of God's Holy Spirit, who is the agent of salvation. It was the Holy Spirit who had constrained us and restrained us in our sins, lest we would have utterly destructed. The Holy Spirit convicted us of personal sin. He persistently wooed us to God the Father. He constantly honored and presented Christ to us as the eternal expression of the Father's love.

Finally, our stubborn wills crumbled. This happened rather quickly for some of us, after many years of wooing from the Spirit for others. We repented, accepted Christ, and found new birth.

It was the Holy Spirit who witnessed then. It was the Spirit who continues to witness even now. He assures us we have been transformed by God's grace into new people and adopted into the family of God. None of us can fully explain the miracle of this witness. We cannot describe it in a fashion the world can grasp.

But we do know.

And it is the miracle of knowing, through this witness of the Holy Spirit that constantly reassures us and always reminds us that we now belong to God. He is our Father and we can and do say with impassioned conviction, "Abba, Father."

· · · PRAYER · · ·

Thank You, Father, for the witness of Your Spirit and for the strength, courage, and confidence that abides with us every hour and through every difficulty of life. Teach us more of Christ's virtues. Lead us yet nearer to You in love, holiness, and Christlikeness.

· · · TODAY'S THOUGHT · · ·

I am not a slave to fear. I am a child of my heavenly Father. I affirm my position in Him today!

—Hoyt E. Stone

April 9

WHEN THE SPIRIT SAYS "NO"

"After they had come to Mysia, they tried to go into Bithynia, but the Spirit did not permit them" (Acts 16:7).

It is a wonderful thing to be led by the Holy Spirit. It is important to understand that the Holy Spirit sometimes restrains us in our efforts, even though our goals are worthy. This is what happened to the apostle Paul and his missionary party in Acts 16:7. They were establishing churches regularly. They were in Mysia and reasoned, "Since we are this close, why not cross over into Bithynia, preach the gospel to them, and establish a church?" But the Holy Spirit did not agree, and led them to Troas instead.

This account raises several questions: *Aren't people in one place just as important as the people in another?* Of course, but some people are not as ready to receive the gospel as others. The Spirit was not so much *restricting* as *redirecting*. The gospel did reach Bithynia, but there was only one of Paul and there were receptive hearts in Philippi. It was necessary for him to go there first. *If you are about to make a mistake, will the Spirit check you?* Notice the text again: "They tried to go into Bithynia, but the Spirit did not permit them." The Holy Spirit closed one door and opened another one. A few nights later in a vision, a man came to the apostle Paul and pleaded, "Come over to Macedonia and help us" (v. 9). The *restriction* was in fact a *redirection*.

I recall in the earliest days of my ministry I was invited by a single preacher to accompany him to Florida to evangelize. On the way I felt a strange urging of the Spirit to stop and visit a pastor friend. When my friend saw me, he threw his arms around me and rejoiced. He told me they were desperate for a revival, and he felt God had sent me. A few weeks later I learned that the minister I was traveling with had fallen into disgrace through homosexual activity. The Spirit redirected my steps, although my motives were to serve God wholeheartedly.

· · · PRAYER · · ·

Lord, we do not know where we go from this familiar scene. But You are here, and You are there, and everywhere between. Please guide us.

· · · TODAY'S THOUGHT · · ·

We should always remember that *restrictions* can be used as a source for *redirection*.

—Paul F. Henson

116

ONLY A LOOK

*Then Saul, who also is called Paul, filled with the Holy
Spirit, looked intently at him* (Acts 13:9).

How many times have you looked at a person and make an
instant judgment before the person spoke a word? Have you
reacted to how a person looks, dresses, or acts?

Nonverbal communication is an important topic at business
seminars, professional workshops, and leadership training sessions. It
is believed that people receive more through our tone of voice, our ges-
tures, our posture, and our appearance than through our words.

Paul, filled with the Holy Spirit, looked at an unbeliever and understood him. Before he ever said a word to him, Paul looked intently,
with strained or eager attention. Paul was "sent out by the Holy Spirit"
(v. 4). It was the Spirit of God that called him and sent him forth (see
Acts 13:1–4), and it was the Spirit that guided him in discernment.

The leadership of the Spirit is critical to the servant of God. Those
led by the Spirit are filled with the greatest encouragement, but those
not led by the Spirit are often filled with the greatest discouragement.
Paul and Barnabas were led by the Spirit; therefore, they were able to
march forth triumphantly with these assurances:

• They were sons of God (Romans 8:14).

• The Holy Spirit was abiding with them (John 14:16, 17).

• The Holy Spirit was guiding them (John 16:13).

• The Holy Spirit was giving them the words to say (John 14:26).

• The Holy Spirit was giving success, convincing the hearers (John
16:8–11).

We have these same assurances today. We are the children of God
and the Holy Spirit abides in us, guiding us, giving us words to say,
convincing hearers, and saving the lost.

· · · PRAYER · · ·

*Father, enlist me with Your Holy Spirit–filled army that must stand
against false teachers and erroneous doctrines. I want to be a
20th–century soldier whose eyes are set on You.*

· · · TODAY'S THOUGHT · · ·

Your eyes may convey a message stronger than the words you
speak. Focus your eyes on Christ and let His Spirit become the focus
of your life.

—Kenneth T. Harvell

I AM ONE OF THEM

But be doers of the word, and not hearers only, deceiving yourselves (James 1:22).

While serving as a missionary and superintendent in Latin America, one experience stands out above the rest. The president of Colombia believed the Church of God was a false religion and severely persecuted it. He assigned a group of special police to find Overseer Moreno. He had him arrested and brought to his office, where he was questioned about his "strange religion." Finally, he was told if he did not recant he would be executed.

Brother Moreno refused to obey and told the president he would rather die than give up the Lord Jesus Christ. The president was so amazed that he asked him who was over the church and demanded the overseer come to Colombia to talk to him.

Early Saturday morning I received a call. Brother Moreno advised me of the circumstances and asked if I could come. I told him I would catch the first flight to Colombia. He told me to come praying because he did not know what was going to happen.

When I arrived in Bogota, Colombia, I was met by Brother Moreno and two police officers. We were taken directly to the president's office. He was respectful and asked me about our religion. As I told him about our loving heavenly Father, he began to cry. He said there must be something to this religion that a man would die before recanting. I told him he could go directly to Jesus for forgiveness of his sins. He buried his face in his hands and wept his way to Calvary.

The president sent out orders to every part of the country to cease the persecution of Christians, saying, " I too have received Christ into my heart. Now I am one of them."

· · · PRAYER · · ·

I am thankful, Lord, for the timely ministry of the Holy Spirit. He is always there at the right time, to give the right instructions, and to issue the right equipment.

· · · TODAY'S THOUGHT · · ·

We must always be ready to practice what we preach. We must be doers of the Word in order to influence the unconverted.

—Vessie D. Hargrave

POWER TO SPEAK THE TRUTH

"Therefore I make known to you that no one speaking by the Spirit of God calls Jesus accursed, and no one can say that Jesus is Lord except by the Holy Spirit" (1 Corinthians 12:3).

In the farming area where I was raised, when men agreed to do something, they would shake hands as a bond of their word. You didn't need notarized papers to back it up. Things have changed since then. Now you need signed documents, lawyers, and witnesses. And you still might not have the assurance the person you are dealing with is speaking truth.

In the verses leading up to 1 Corinthians 12:3, Paul drew a contrast between his readers' experience as unconverted idolaters with their present experience as Christians.

Old Life	New Life
• They worshipped dead idols.	• They now belonged to the living God.
• Their idols never spoke to them.	• God spoke to them by His Spirit.
• They were under the control of demons and led astray.	• The Spirit lived in them and directs them.
• They didn't follow Christ.	• Now Jesus is Lord.

Paul knew the difference between the old and new life. He had come full circle from persecutor of Christ to preacher of Christ. Paul, who was Saul of Tarsus, called the Christ–message false, but at his miraculous conversion on the road to Damascus, he called Him Lord.

The Holy Spirit is the "Spirit of truth" and cannot be misled or deceived. The Spirit of truth authorizes us to say, "Jesus is Lord." Lordship is a mark of ownership; and when we say Jesus is Lord, we are saying He is in charge by the Holy Spirit. The baptism in the Holy Spirit makes truth available to us in every experience of life.

· · · PRAYER · · ·

Father in heaven, I proclaim that Jesus is Lord of my life by the Holy Spirit. Please help me. I pray to always be filled with the power to speak the truth about Jesus Christ in every area of life.

· · · TODAY'S THOUGHT · · ·

Truth is the foundation that will enable you to stand in times of trouble and temptation. The Holy Spirit is the source of truth and I will look to Him.

—W.A. Davis

THE HOLY SPIRIT AND THE WORD

While Peter was still speaking these words, the Holy Spirit
fell upon all those who heard the word (Acts 10:44).

Cornelius was excited. This Gentile had been visited by a shining angel who had told him his prayers had been heard and God had seen his good works of almsgiving. The divine messenger also told him that the great preacher, Simon Peter, would be coming from Joppa. So Cornelius gathered in all his friends and relatives to hear what the man of God was going to say.

As Peter entered the home, Cornelius fell down as if to worship him. Peter patiently lifted Cornelius and told him that he was just a man. However, God had instructed him to teach the Gentiles as well as the Jews.

Then Peter began telling the wondrous story of Jesus to this eager crowd. Their hearts must have been arrested and captivated. As they listened to the words of Peter, the Holy Spirit fell on all who received the message of Christ.

Peter's Jewish traveling companions were astonished when they heard these Gentiles speak in tongues in the same manner Jewish believers had done on the Day of Pentecost. Peter organized a water baptismal service for the new converts to Christ.

It was the power of the Word of God that brought about the miracle of the conversion of these Gentiles and the demonstration of the Holy Spirit in their lives. Although the people were eager to receive Peter, the man, it was not his skill as a speaker that changed them. It was the message and not the man that was effective for this occasion.

Fertile hearts are eager to receive the seed of God's Word. They are waiting for us to explain and proclaim to them the gospel message. Miracles happen when we talk of Jesus, His life, and His love.

・・・ PRAYER ・・・

Dear Father, please give me an opportunity to be a speaker for You today, to tell the message of Jesus to someone who needs Your love. Please send the Holy Spirit to fulfill the work of grace in someone's life today.

・・・ TODAY'S THOUGHT ・・・

"A word is dead when it is said, some say. I say it just begins to live that day" (Emily Dickinson).

—Dan R. Dempsey

A GRACIOUS AND MERCIFUL GOD

"Yet for many years You had patience with them, and testified against them by Your Spirit in Your prophets. Yet they would not listen; Therefore You gave them into the hand of the peoples of the lands. Nevertheless in Your great mercy You did not utterly consume them nor forsake them; for You are God, gracious and merciful" (Nehemiah 9:30, 31).

God's Spirit is moving in our land today. The Spirit of God is speaking through people to call our nation to repentance. God wants revival. It is not the reluctance of God that hinders revival but rather the condition of hearts. Our prayer focus should be agreeing with God in behalf of revival and believing that hearts will be changed.

Why am I so convinced of God's commitment to a spiritual awakening? It is because of the great investment He has already made. He gave His Son so the world could be saved. You do not give your most precious possession for something that is secondary to your purposes. His sacrifice tells us about the passion of His heart. God is at work every day on behalf of the spiritual condition of our nation.

What is true about our nation is also true about individuals. God chastens those He loves (Hebrews 12:6). You may be engaged in a battle because you have stepped out for God and the Enemy is opposing your advancement. Or you might be at rest and out of the will of God. If it is the first situation, God will fight the battle with you. If it is the second circumstance, you will find yourself fighting the battle alone until you have reconciled yourself to God's purposes. Be assured, God wants the best for you and is with you in both situations. He is always working for your good!

· · · PRAYER · · ·

Dear heavenly Father, I agree with You in prayer on behalf of my nation. Turn the hearts of the people back to You. I trust You to use whatever means is necessary to accomplish this end. I also want You to work in my life and help me to walk in the center of Your will.

· · · TODAY'S THOUGHT · · ·

Former American president John F. Kennedy made this challenge: "Ask not what your country can do for you—ask what you can do for your country." We can do nothing greater for our country than to pray for repentance and to be renewed by the Spirit in revival.

—Richard Dial

DESCENDING FROM HEAVEN

*"And it shall come to pass afterward that I will pour out My
Spirit on all flesh; your sons and your daughters shall
prophesy, your old men shall dream dreams, your young
men shall see visions"* (Joel 2:28).

I had completed my devotions and prayers and, hoping for a
good night's sleep, I turned off the lamp and closed my eyes.
But this night turned out to be different than most.

In a dream I was brought to a place I had never been before
—in the middle of freshly plowed field, and my wife was there with
me. Looking to the north, I could see a storm approaching. It was
moving rapidly toward us with large dark clouds spinning as if with
anger. It seemed we would surely be killed by the storm, but then I
noticed a small house in the distance, at the end of the field.

Grabbing my wife's hand, I told her we would be safe if we could
reach that little house. Racing the storm, we ran to the house and
slammed the door behind us. However, our relief quickly vanished
upon seeing that the roof of the house was missing. As the storm
closed in and swirled about us, we felt doomed. But then we noticed
doves descending from the heavens one by one. They kept coming, and
huddling together, they formed a roof for the house. Peace settled over
us, the storm subsided and sunlight began to break through the clouds.

The meaning of that dream unfolded a few months later, when my
physician reported that he was 90 percent sure that I had cancer. Now I
clung to the outcome of that dream. The cancer was the storm I had
seen coming; the field and the house my life. The doves represented
divine protection. I had the assurance that God's Holy Spirit was covering and protecting me. This gave me peace, and my peace turned to
joy when, after the third visit to my physician, what had at first been
diagnosed as cancer had disappeared. The storm had passed!

· · · PRAYER · · ·

*Heavenly Father, thank You for pouring out the Holy Spirit on us.
Thank You for the Dove of heaven who comes to give us peace in the
storm.*

· · · TODAY'S THOUGHT · · ·

God, by the outpouring of His Spirit, has brought to pass His
promise: "Your old men shall dream dreams, your young men shall see
visions."

—James Dill

THE ADORNING SPIRIT

"By His Spirit He adorned the heavens; His hand pierced the fleeing serpent" (Job 26:13).

 Job had lost his children, his possessions, and his health. Now his faith was being further tested by the accusations of his friends, whose theology could not accommodate the suffering of the righteous.

Though his friends could find no fault in Job, Bildad reasoned that there must be some imperfections in him. Why, even the heavens were not perfect. How could God make Job perfect if He had failed to make the heavens perfect? To support his contention, Bildad protested that the moon shows its face differently every night— neither are the stars the same each night. As Bildad summed up his argument against Job, he concluded that if God could not make the heavens perfect, it must follow that He could not make Job perfect either (see ch. 25).

Job responded by declaring perfect faith in the work of the Holy Spirit. He stated that the heavens do not *appear* to be perfect because the clouds obscure our view. By faith in God, Job proclaimed the heavens to be perfect because the Holy Spirit adorned them. He further stated that God has power over the clouds to bind them up until He is ready to release them.

Thus the Holy Spirit had adorned his spirit, but clouds now distorted the view of the perfect work the Holy Spirit had done in him.

Job gave us words to live by through this beautiful analogy. Even though clouds come into our lives to distort the view, we must know by faith that the Holy Spirit has adorned us with salvation. We must not allow tragedy, losses, or just common place experiences of life to cause us to doubt the perfect work He has done in us.

· · · PRAYER · · ·

God, make me sensitive to the working of the Holy Spirit in my life even when Your will is that the foundations of my life be shaken. Help me to trust You and to know that You are always leading me to greater faith, greater commitment, and greater understanding.

· · · TODAY'S THOUGHT · · ·

Helen Keller said about her blindness and deafness: "I thank God for my handicaps, for through them I have found myself, my work, and my God."

—Kenneth Dismukes

THE HOLY SPIRIT REVEALS JESUS

He, being full of the Holy Spirit . . . said, "Look! I see the heavens opened and the Son of Man standing at the right hand of God!" (Acts 7:55, 56).

I received the Holy Spirit baptism at the East Chattanooga Church of God in 1928, when I was 13 years old. My father, the Reverend E.M. Ellis, was pastor, and revival services were being conducted by the Reverend Earl P. Paulk, Sr. Several of my friends and I received the baptism of the Holy Spirit at the same time, and many of them would later become leaders, ministers, and outstanding workers in the Church of God.

The Holy Spirit has been a great help to me as I have served the Church of God for 54 years as a member, pastor, state overseer, state evangelism director, and chairman of the World Missions Board.

Throughout my life, God has always been there for me. He has never failed me. I have never regretted a single day that I have walked with God.

One of the most memorable experiences of my life occurred when I was pastoring a church in Anderson, South Carolina. It was a difficult time. I was suffering and my "flock" was suffering too. I had been praying in my study at the church, asking for God's intervention in the service.

During the service I was praying, when at the back of the church I saw Christ! He was dressed in a beautiful purple robe and had His hands outstretched. He said to me, "Fear not, My son, everything is in My hands. I rose to my feet and saw the whole congregation in the altar crying out to God. The Holy Spirit had intervened and things were going to be OK in the church.

I thank God for the Holy Spirit and His work in my life, and I thank Him for all my brethren in the Church of God. The day God called me to work for Him was the greatest day of my life.

· · · PRAYER · · ·

Dear Father, help me to see Jesus in the severest trials and the most difficult times in my life. Lift my vision so that I can see beyond my present circumstances. Give me an eternal perspective and I will ever praise You. In Jesus' lovely name.

· · · TODAY'S THOUGHT · · ·

I will live this day open to the Holy Spirit for His encouragement, inspiration, and guidance.

—B.E. Ellis

THE ANOINTED ONE

" . . . how God anointed Jesus of Nazareth with the Holy Spirit and with power, who went about doing good, and healing all that were oppressed by the devil, for God was with Him" (Acts 10:38).

A well–known emblem of the Spirit of God is the anointing oil (Exodus 29:7, 21; 30:23– 25, 30; Psalm 133:2). This oil was a perfumed mixture of olive oil and various spices. It was used to anoint Israelite priests when they were installed in office. Kings were anointed with oil by having it poured on the heads. The prophet Elisha was anointed in this manner.

God anointed Jesus with the Holy Spirit and with power. The words *Christ* and *Messiah* mean, literally, "the anointed One. The Spirit's anointing denotes divine power. Isaiah prophesied of One who would announce, "The Spirit of the Lord God is upon Me" (61:1).

What did the Anointed One do? He went about doing good. Powerful, wonderful, marvelous works were accomplished by Jesus. He was anointed to heal those oppressed by the devil. Jesus never turned away a sick person who came to Him. He healed the demon–possessed, epileptic, and paralytic.

In my early ministry I preached in Chicago and gave an altar appeal. A middle–aged lady who had been raised in a Pentecostal home and attended a Pentecostal Bible school responded by coming for prayer. She had been backslidden for years. As she prayed for forgiveness, she said that evil spirits were choking her. Saints laid hands on her and commanded the spirits to come out. She was gloriously delivered—saved, sanctified, and filled with the Holy Spirit.

The anointing binds Satan and his evil forces. Jesus commands us to be "endued with power from on high" (Luke 24:49). We too can have the anointing of the Spirit.

· · · P R A Y E R · · ·

Holy Father, fill me with Your Spirit and power that I might go about doing good, seeing the oppressed healed in the name of Jesus. Lord, please give me the testimony that will cause others to say, "God was with him."

· · · T O D A Y ' S T H O U G H T · · ·

Since I know His anointing rests on me, I will live today with this thought in my mind.

—Junus C. Fulbright

INDISPENSABLE POWER

"But you shall receive power when the Holy Spirit has come upon you"(Acts 1:8).

On October 3, 1954, desperate and hopelessly sick, I sought refuge in the Full Gospel Church of God on 23rd Avenue in Guatemala City. Eighteen specialists had recommended surgery to replace my deteriorated intestine with tubes and a waste receptacle. They told me that without surgery I would live only 15 days.

As I prayed, a yellow and red fireball flew toward me and struck me powerfully. I fell to the floor. Instantly, God forgave me, healed me, and gave me a new intestine. He also filled me with the Holy Spirit and called me to ministry. I saw angels singing praises to God. One angel gave me a stick that turned into a book. He told me, "You will be a witness. Do not fear, because I am with you."

Pastor Felix Cifuentes taught me in doctrine and how to witness, and the Holy Spirit gave me the power. As I ministered, I experienced miracles. On one occasion, God paralyzed a woman's hand when she tried to attack me. Later, the Lord restored her and forgave her. Another time, an angel miraculously guided me on roads I had never traveled. The Lord used that particular occasion to help us gain church property where a church was established.

Later, I left Guatemala, without any fiancial support, taking my family by faith to Costa Rica. Once at a meal, we had only water. We thanked the Lord for the water, and as we prayed a full meal was brought to us. We never missed a meal nor went hungry. When we had no rent money, God spoke to Orendes Visquez, a rich man in the province of Alajuela in Costa Rica, to provide enough money to build a church *and* a house for the pastor.

· · · PRAYER · · ·

Lord, thank You for the abiding presence of the Holy Spirit, without which we can do nothing.

· · · TODAY'S THOUGHT · · ·

During the ministry of this writer, God accomplished much. While serving as overseer of El Salvador, 220 churches were organized in 10 years. In Costa Rica, 450 churches were organized in 12 years. Truly, we can do so much more in the power of the Spirit.

—Jose Enrique Guerra

SUPPLYING THE SPIRIT

Therefore, He who supplies the Spirit to you and works mir-
acles among you, does He do it by the works of the law, or
by the hearing of faith? (Galatians 3:5).

There is a crisis moment of receiving the baptism in the Holy
Spirit, yet there is a sense in which the Spirit is being supplied
richly and abundantly to us every day. We are never without
His presence and availability.

The Greek word for *supplies* used in this passage (*epichoregon*)
comes from a root word from which we get the English word *chorus* or
choir. It refers to the one responsible to supply a chorus or to defray
the expenses of a choir to sing at a public festival. The phrase could be
translated: "He who furnishes you with the fullness of the Holy Spirit"
or "He who supplies you abundantly with the Spirit" or "He who lav-
ishes His Spirit on you, enabling you to perform miracles."

God gives us an abundant supply of His Spirit in order for us to live
fruitful lives. He pours out His Spirit to fill to overflowing our empty
vessels. This outpouring in our lives is in response to our faith and is
for our ministry on His behalf.

A pastor friend's wife died unexpectedly. He was left to care for
five children. He told me that he did not know how he could handle
the task. He could not understand why this had happened. As we
prayed, the Holy Spirit witnessed through him. In the days ahead God
continued to pour out the richness of the Spirit upon his life enabling
him to cope with every situation.

It is reassuring to know that the same Spirit who works miracles,
raised Jesus from the dead, and operates the gifts in the church is being
furnished to me. What a resource!

· · · PRAYER · · ·

Father, I thank You for giving the Holy Spirit to me. I praise You
that Your Spirit abides within and provides abundant resources so that
my life can glorify You.

· · · TODAY'S THOUGHT · · ·

Why not pause today for a time of self–examination. Has God supplied His Spirit abundantly in your life? If so, reflect on those occasions for a few moments. Then, give praise to God.

—Douglas LeRoy

THE AFFIRMING PRESENCE

*And the Holy Spirit descended in bodily form like a dove
upon Him, and a voice came from heaven which said, "You
are My beloved Son; in You I am well pleased"* (Luke 3:22).

 A memorable moment occurred for me in second grade in
Shreveport, Louisiana. On field day every student was
required to participate, and the teacher assigned me the
100–yard dash. This sounds easy, but in my case it wasn't.

I was born with bilateral clubfoot. Physicians at Birmingham's
Crippled Children's Clinic had done an excellent job correcting the
physical impairment, but my coordination was lacking. Never before
had I been so aware of awkwardness.

Awaiting the starter's whistle, my heart seemed to beat in my head.
I had spent exasperating years tripping over my feet doing easy things,
yet a desire to win overwhelmed the fear of my inability to safely run.
I believed this moment would be different. I would run like the wind,
gliding gracefully across the dirt track, handily taking the blue ribbon.

Suddenly, the race began. All my positive thoughts quickly came to
a screeching halt as wobbly legs tangled together, plummeting me face
first into the dirt. I was crushed, publicly embarrassed, humiliated
before the crowd.

Dad put an arm around me and began to encourage me. He told me
how great it was that I tried. He recounted obstacles I faced that others
didn't. He told me how proud he was of me. His affirming presence
turned a broken moment into one of wholeness. I recognized I was uncon-
ditionally accepted, regardless of my awkward stumbling. Knowing I was
loved was suddenly more important than winning the race.

The Holy Spirit communicates our Father's thoughts toward us. The
Spirit reminds us our heavenly Father has planned for us a future and a
hope. The Spirit is alongside when we stumble. He assures us we are
loved.

· · · PRAYER · · ·

*Father, I thank You for recognizing my needs. As Your Spirit affirms
Your presence, help me to be an affirming presence to those I see daily.*

· · · TODAY'S THOUGHT · · ·

You impact those you meet in a delightful or deadly way. Negative
people make a negative impact. Reflect the affirming presence of the
Holy Spirit.

—Donnie W. Smith

WALKING IN THE SPIRIT

"I will put My Spirit within you and cause you to walk in My statutes, and you will keep My judgments and do them" (Ezekiel 36:27).

I do not know about your devotional life—whether certain scriptures or words seem to leap out at you. When I first looked at this scripture, several key words caught my attention. The first was *Spirit*, as God said, "I will put My Spirit within you." The word *Spirit* is translated from the Hebrew word *ruwach* (wind, breath of life, or life itself). The second word, *statutes*, comes from the Hebrew word *choq* (appointments, a future event). The third word that caught my attention was *judgments*, which is translated from the Hebrew word *mishpat* (verdicts already decided, a past event). The last word, *do*, comes from the word *asah* (to accomplish, in the present). Once I understood the root meaning of these key words, this scripture took on a much more personal and reassuring quality.

God is saying that His personal presence will be in us to fulfill the appointments He has planned for us. His presence is also with us to support and carry out all His verdicts (judgments) that He has already decided upon.

What reassurance this is when we feel as if life is crashing in around us and that no one seems to care! Walking in the Spirit does not mean that every appointment or step along life's road will be pleasurable. Some may even be bitter or painful experiences. Nevertheless, as we both keep His judgments and take part in their fulfillment, we have God's promise that He will never leave us.

· · · PRAYER · · ·

Dear Lord, help me to realize that You are directing my life; that every day I can rest, knowing I am in You and You are in me.

· · · TODAY'S THOUGHT · · ·

The glowing face of Moses was not received by a quick bedtime prayer. It was obtained by dwelling in the Lord's presence for 40 days. David's skill in slinging stones was not acquired when he met Goliath. It was polished by practice in the wilderness. The power of Pentecost came after tarrying in prayer. If we are to walk in the Spirit, we must tarry in His presence.

—Mark S. Abbott

HARD HEARTS, REBELLIOUS SPIRITS

Therefore, as the Holy Spirit says: "Today, if you will hear
His voice, do not harden your hearts as in the rebellion, In
the day of trial in the wilderness" (Hebrews 3:7, 8).

 The examples we learn from the Israel in the wilderness are endless. The events that take place during their 40-year wanderings are portrayed to us by Scripture as one filled with glorious privileges and fearful judgments.

The Israelite people reacted to testing time by rebelling. Their attention was consistently diverted to others things. In most circumstances these were selfish ideals. They regularly complained of their circumstances and often made reference to their past days of Egyptian slavery. They said: "For it would have been better for us to serve the Egyptians, than that we should die in the wilderness" (Exodus 14:12). Although they had prayed for deliverance during times of crisis in Egypt, slavery was now enticing.

God knew the hearts of the Israelite people. "God did not lead them by way of the land of the Philistines, although that was near; for God said, 'Lest perhaps the people change their minds when they see war, and return to Egypt.'" (Exodus 13:17). God wanted them to press toward their glorious future, not to return to the past. Relentless hunger, privation, weakness, and temptation hardened their hearts toward God and caused their spirit to be rebellious against His will.

While this example is from history past, we often find that similar circumstances produce the same results today. The world is a wilderness to the Christian. Simple cares of life cast shadows over our spirits. Our personal relationship with God is constantly challenged by things which seem secure or prosperous. Careless attitudes and rebellious spirits challenge our loyalty to God's will.

If we continue to hold on to the past, if we are unwilling to die out to selfish ideals, we will find ourselves in Israel's position: our hearts will be hardened.

· · · PRAYER · · ·

Father, I want to learn from my circumstances. Help me to always
have the right spirit and attitude toward all things.

· · · TODAY'S THOUGHT · · ·

God grant me the serenity to accept the things I cannot change, the courage to change the things I can, and the wisdom to know the difference .

—Carl Allen

GOD IS ALWAYS FAITHFUL

"And I will pray the Father, and He will give you another Helper, that He may abide with you forever" (John 14:16).

My earliest contact with Christianity came in India when I was 5 years old. I was stricken with symptoms of edema and was unable to walk, eat, or speak. Medical help failed. I grew worse and nearly died. I heard of the missionary Robert F. Cook and requested that he come and pray. Brother Cook anointed me with oil and I was instantly healed. My healing led my parents to Jesus Christ, and they were later baptized in the Holy Spirit.

In December 1934 I accepted Jesus Christ as my Savior. Nevertheless, I continued in sin. Some friends and I attempted to overturn a fully loaded oxcart. One of the iron wheels crushed my foot, smashing it severely. The subsequent pain and worry over this injury helped bring me to the right place and the right frame of mind.

I told God that if He would heal my foot, I would follow Him and obey His commandments. My foot was completely healed and I decided it was time to be baptized in water. Before my baptism, I tarried and sought God for the baptism in His Holy Spirit. On March 16, 1936, I was filled with the Spirit. I worshiped the Lord, spoke in tongues, and continued to sing and pray in tongues for several days.

Many years later I moved to the United States and was living with my two sons when I suffered a severe heart attack. While at the doctor's office I collapsed and was rushed to the emergency room. The doctor told my children to call all the family. It did not seem possible that I could live. The saints prayed. Many of them came to my hospital room. God delivered me and I was able to preach for five more years.

· · · PRAYER · · ·

Lord, we are thankful that You are mindful of us no matter where we live in this world.

· · · TODAY'S THOUGHT · · ·

God is always faithful. His Spirit is our ever-present Comforter and He will not fail.

—A.V. Abraham

ON ALL FLESH

*"'And on My menservants and on My maidservants I will
pour out of My Spirit in those days; and they shall
prophesy'"* (Acts 2:18).

A friend told me about an incident that happened when he was
in college and spent a summer session sharing a house trailer
with a Christian brother. On the kitchen wall a small wooden
plaque of Joel 2:28, from which Peter's recitation of Joel's
prophecy was taken: "And it shall come to pass afterward that I will
pour out My Spirit on all flesh; your sons and your daughters shall
prophesy, your old men shall dream dreams, your young men shall see
visions." When he first read the plaque, it didn't have an impact
because he wasn't baptized in the Spirit and really did not grasp the
importance of the verse.

That little plaque was prophetic! Before my friend graduated from
college, the Holy Spirit taught him the real meaning of those verses
through his baptism in the Holy Spirit. This experience changed his
life. In human terms, he was an unlikely candidate for the baptism of
the Holy Spirit. The church he was raised in did not teach about the
Baptism. He was not attending a Christian college, and he was not taking any Bible or theology courses. Yet the Lord arranged his life so
that he would be drawn to people who had something he didn't have
and who made him come back for more even when his background
said no. When he finally came to himself and submitted to the leading
of the Lord, the Holy Spirit was able to do a transforming work that
changed his focus in life.

· · · PRAYER · · ·

*Father, today we consider the wonder of the gifts that You have
poured out to us through the Spirit, let us never doubt that You are with
us and in us and that you will empower us to speak forth Your Word
and do the things Jesus did. Let us be bold before the throne of grace
to request Your empowerment.*

· · · TODAY'S THOUGHT · · ·

Ministry gifts are available; they are distributed throughout the body
of Christ. We all can walk in and with the Holy Spirit. We don't need
intermediaries or supersaints to make this a reality; all we need is the
Holy Spirit, and He is waiting on us.

—Leonard Albert

April 2 6

THE CHURCH AND THE SPIRIT

For you were bought at a price; therefore glorify God in
your body and in your spirit, which are God's
(1 Corinthians 6:20).

Christ has been my personal Savior for 30 years. For 29 of those years, I have served the Lord in ministry. I have learned that it is impossible to develop and fulfill ministry without the guidance and power of the Holy Spirit. I cannot do ministry in and by myself.

Through the Holy Spirit, I was born again (John 3:5, 6) and adopted into the family of God (Romans 8:15). The Holy Spirit sealed me for the day of redemption (Ephesians 1:13, 14). He lives in me (John 14:17) and gives me true incentive to consecrate myself to Jesus more each day.

He gives me unspeakable joy that does not depend on the circumstances. I have been in the hands of Mexican guerrilla fighters and hostile army troops seven times, in which my life has been in danger. But the Holy Spirit filled my heart and gave me authority to testify of Jesus Christ. The Holy Spirit gives me a love for my adversaries and the ability to forgive them with all my heart.

I love the church, but I get despondent when I see the church depend on plans and methods that are not touched by the power of the Spirit. I fear that the church is guilty of two sins against the Holy Spirit.

First, we grieve the Spirit when we give place to the devil by keeping wrath, resentments, anger, and roots of bitterness. Second, we quench the Spirit when we neglect to do the work of the ministry or when we do not acknowledge, appreciate, and love those who guide us in the Lord.

Let us make plans and methods which God has approved. Then, let us implement these things in the power of the Holy Spirit.

· · · PRAYER · · ·

Prevent us, Lord, from following the same path of failure others have. O God, repeat in us the history of the early church in Acts. As we near the end of the 20th century we pray, Lord, do it again!

· · · TODAY'S THOUGHT · · ·

The Holy Spirit is willing to fill vessels that are clean. Let the church face its sins and put the Word of God into practice. Then, God will give the Holy Spirit to those who obey (Acts 5:32).

—Roberto Aldana Sosa

THE HOLY SPIRIT REVEALED

Now we have received, not the spirit of the world, but the
Spirit who is from God, that we might know the things that
have been freely given to us by God (1 Corinthians 2:12).

 Christian, in the bestowal of His Spirit, God has allowed you to receive something of His own self-consciousness. This gives you the ability to receive His secret wisdom—the things that have been freely given to you by God.

The Spirit who is from God is the Holy Spirit. He proceeds from God and is your personal instructor. As a result, you become the subject of His influence. Since the Holy Spirit knows the deep things of God (vv. 10, 11), He is able to communicate this to you and influence you with divine wisdom.

Part of the divine wisdom is "that we might know the things . . . freely given to us of God." What human reason alone cannot discover, God reveals to those who believe in Christ. Human wisdom leaves us helpless in the face of sin and death, but Christ crucified proves by His redeeming power that He is the wisdom and power of God. This truth is imparted to the believer by the illumination of the Holy Spirit.

As a Christian the light of the Spirit shines in you. Each time you come to the Bible to study or to hear the Word proclaimed, set aside your own wisdom and yield in faith to the wisdom of the divine Teacher, the Holy Spirit. He seeks the sanctification of your life—complete surrender and obedience to Jesus Christ. Acknowledge His dwelling in you; accept His teaching. Reject the vain wisdom of the world and self-confidence. Hear what the Spirit says.

By the revelation of the Spirit your mind can be renewed, enabling you to prove the good, acceptable, and perfect will of God in your own life. The mind renewed by the Holy Spirit wants to know God's will, desires to be taught by the Spirit, and seeks to fulfill God's will. Wait for the wisdom that comes from the Holy Spirit.

· · · PRAYER · · ·

O God, I bless Thee for the wondrous revelation of Thyself in Christ
crucified and for opening my eyes to see by Thy Spirit that He is the
wisdom and power of God for my salvation.

· · · TODAY'S THOUGHT · · ·

An intimate relationship with God by His Spirit always produces a serious desire to purify self and perfect holiness in the fear of God.

—William D. (Bill) Alton

A p r i l   2 8

A PENTECOSTAL TESTIMONY

"These signs will follow those who believe: In My name
they will . . . lay hands on the sick, and they will recover."
(Mark 16:17, 18).

When I was 2 years old I began to suffer from severe bronchitis that almost killed me. With every passing year the bronchitis became more chronic. Every time I had a flu virus or a simple nasal allergy, chronic bronchitis would take over and I would become terribly sick. I developed severe sinusitis and a nasal allergy that was always stimulated when the cycle began. I could not be exposed to extreme cool or hot air, and I reacted to air-conditioning and any kind of fan blowing air in front of me.

Along with all this I developed a continuing dry cough. When I was 32 years of age, a lady from my church, Sister Olga Martinez, prayed specifically for my healing. One night she was praying when she saw me in a vision, and began to rebuke the bronchitis in the name of Jesus. As she kept on praying and rebuking the affliction, something red began to rise up from my stomach and started to travel out through my chest and finally through my mouth. When it left my body, it seemed to fly like a bat and went into Sister Olga's body. She continued to pray and wrestle with it until it left her body just as it had mine, and it disappeared forever.

After that, I started feeling better and began doing things I couldn't do before. For the past eight years I have not experienced a single symptom. The Lord delivered me from it through the prayer of Sister Olga.

When I remember the damage this illness caused me for 30 years, I have no choice but to thank the Lord Jesus Christ, who delivered me by the power of His name and the anointing of the Holy Spirit upon one of His special servants. I thank the Lord for the Pentecostal power available today to deliver and anoint His servants to perform this kind of miraculous works for the glory of the Lord Jesus Christ.

God is still able and willing to heal His children through the power of the Holy Spirit.

· · · PRAYER · · ·

Father, bless us and be with us today. Grant us grace to trust You in all things and to know You are the God who heals.

· · · TODAY'S THOUGHT · · ·

It is a blessed thing to trust in the power of Almighty God for miracles and for daily sustenance.

—Miguel Alvarez

THE MASTER KEY

And such were some of you. But you were washed, but you were sanctified, but you were justified in the name of the Lord Jesus and by the Spirit of our God (1 Corinthians 6:11).

All that God has done for us by His grace in Christ depends on our relationship to the Holy Spirit. From the moment we are saved, the Holy Spirit begins His work in us (Galatians 4:6). He makes our hearts His house. He is our heavenly Guest of Honor.

Yet we may be tempted to treat the Holy Spirit as a visitor and push Him off into a room of our hearts. This reminds me of a friend who was expecting a visitor. She thought there was plenty of time to clean the house and put things in order. But the visitor called and told her there had been a change in his schedule and he would arrive at her home early that morning rather than in the afternoon. She didn't have time to do what needed to be done, so she prepared only one room. When the visitor arrived, she showed him to the room she had cleaned. By doing that, she was saying, "You stay in this room because I don't want you to see this messy house."

At times we treat the Holy Spirit the same way. We try to put Him in one room of our hearts. The Holy Spirit should have the master key and have access to all the rooms of our lives. He can cleanse our hearts and bring order to our hearts. He can remove what should not be there—whether pride, envy, bitterness, wrath, worldly ambitions, lust, or hatred—and impart the wonderful graces of love, joy, faith, hope, and holiness. Mary Margaret Morris' beautiful song expresses it best:

O Holy Spirit, You should have the Master Key,
To every room of my heart, oh, let it be;
Those hidden sins in rooms that others cannot see,
I give to You Holy Spirit; here's the master key.

Beautiful Gospel. Cleveland, TN. Tennessee Music and Printing Co., © 1982. p. 144.

· · · PRAYER · · ·

Father, I know the Holy Spirit is my constant companion. He has taken up residence with me and has made my heart His home. Help me be more sensitive to His presence and more open to His guidance and favor.

· · · TODAY'S THOUGHT · · ·

To abide in the fellowship of the Holy Spirit means to live under the shadow of the Cross.

—French L. Arrington

SUSTAINED BY HIS PRESENCE

He [God] said, "My Presence will go with you, and I will
give you rest" (Exodus 33:14).

In 1933 my wife, Jewell, and I were employed at the Sequoit Cotton Mill in Gadsden, Alabama. Evangelist T.A. Richards came to our neighborhood to conduct cottage prayer meetings and Jewell and I were invited to attend. In a home in Sequoit Mill Village we gave our hearts to Christ and were filled with the Holy Spirit.

While attending the Alabama City Church of God, we experienced our first disappointment as Christians. Our baby boy was born but lived only three hours. Two days later Jewell was still bedridden, so I stood with Donald, my 3-year-old son, beside an open grave, alone. The pastor's wife had forgotten to tell the minister from our new church about the death of our son and the funeral. I prayed a prayer and buried my son without a minister.

The presence of the Holy Spirit consoled me. The Comforter, who is indeed the great Paraclete, stood beside me and my family. Discouragement and disappointment gave way to faith in God as we rejoiced in the hope that we would see Wendel again.

I became Sunday school superintendent at the church. A year later I was licensed as a minister. Seven years from that graveside experience, I took Donald, now 10, to the General Assembly in Chattanooga. During the Assembly I received a call to hurry home for the birth of another child. Don and I left the Assembly, hoping to arrive in Birmingham before Glenda did; but when we arrived at West End Baptist Hospital, she was waiting for us with her mother. Two weeks later I moved my family back to Gadsden, where I had been called to pastor.

The success God gave us in six years of pastoral ministry at the Alabama City church began at a graveside when the comfort of the Holy Spirit took away our discouragement and replaced it with the assurance of His abiding presence. Out of the death of our son Wendel, there came new strength through the Holy Spirit.

· · · PRAYER · · ·

Our Father, keep us near to You. Help us to always be conscious of Your Holy Spirit in times of need. For Jesus' sake.

· · · TODAY'S THOUGHT · · ·

"He is no fool who gives up what he can never keep to gain what he can never lose" (Jim Elliott).

—L.H. Aultman

May 1

WE POSSESS A GIFT OF GOD

*But the manifestation of the Spirit is given to each one for
the profit of all* (1 Corinthians 12:7).

What you possess of the Spirit's manifestation is a gift. If you have much, remember Jesus' words: "For everyone to whom much is given, from him much will be required" (Luke 12:48). Paul emphatically declared that each Christian, not just the "spiritually elite," was given a manifestation of the Spirit—a revelation, an uncovering—to shine forth, like a lantern. Jesus said, "Let your light so shine before men, that they may see your good works and glorify your Father in heaven" (Matthew 5:16). The candle, or lamp, is the manifestation of the Spirit that we possess—we must give light. Pentecostals are called to manifest the Pentecostal light in a world of darkness.

Why are spiritual gifts given to us? "For the profit of all." No spiritual gift is for personal benefit only. True manifestations of the Spirit profit both the individual and the body. Gifts are given "for the equipping of the saints for the work of ministry, for the edifying of the body of Christ" (Ephesians 4:12). The stomach receives food, not just to fill itself, but to feed the entire body. The eye sees, not just to please itself, but to direct the body. All gifts share the same purpose—the good of the congregation.

As a pastor, I long for my congregation to profit from the manifestations of the Spirit. My grandmother scorned the Pentecostal church. But my mother prayed for her, and she received the Baptism. On her deathbed, she said to my mother, "I see a mighty host of angels in the room." And she went to meet the Lord speaking in tongues.

The Holy Spirit gives power to do things you never dreamed of—to smile when your heart is heavy, laugh when you feel like crying, work when you want to rest, and pray when you don't feel like praying. You have the manifestation of the Spirit.

· · · PRAYER · · ·

Father in heaven, when You give us gifts, You give them to us for the blessing of others, for the salvation of sinners, and for the edification of saints.

· · · TODAY'S THOUGHT · · ·

"I need the Lord Jesus Christ for my eternal life, and the Holy Spirit for my internal life."

—Hugh Bair

FAITH—THE VITAL INGREDIENT

To another faith by the same Spirit, to another gifts of heal-
ings by the same Spirit (1 Corinthians 12:9).

Faith is the vital ingredient of spiritual experience. Without faith it is impossible to please God. Faith enables us to enjoy the pleasure of God.

Much talked about but little understood, faith does not work wonders, however. God does. Faith enables us to share a dynamic relationship with the God who performs miracles. The Lord Jesus admonishes us to have faith in God—never to have faith in faith itself.

The writer of Hebrews, in the great treatise on faith, tells us that God "is a rewarder of those who diligently seek Him" (11:6). What is the reward? The answer is perfectly plain: What is the seeker seeking? God! So the reward is obvious; they find what they are seeking—God himself. Faith always has that desire to know Him. Faith brings about a dynamic relationship with God, which the words of Vep Ellis' song aptly describes—"My God can do anything."

Everyone who understands this truth knows there are big moments when you really need God. Paul on the deck of the foundering ship is an example. God graciously endues superabundant faith on believers so that their dynamic relationship with Him can be revealed. The boldness of the apostles caused the Sanhedrin to marvel (Acts 4:13). Apparently this demeanor of the disciples was more impressive than the miracle of a man lame from birth being healed. The gift of faith is a staggering enduement from God that reveals a relationship with the Divine.

Healings naturally follow faith, since faith reveals a relationship with God and the Bible states that God heals. That is what God does. To heal is part of being God. For God not to heal would be for Him to cease being who He is, and that is not possible.

God has placed healings in the church, and the church must thus minister to those in need. That is why we pray, why we anoint with oil, and why we lay hands on the sick. We want God to be revealed as the God who heals His people.

· · · PRAYER · · ·

Thank You, Father, that Your presence brings something wonderful
out of chaos, even the chaos of sickness. Wherever I am, You are there,
faith tells me. How wonderful!

· · · TODAY'S THOUGHT · · ·

Fear knocked on the door; faith opened it; nothing was there.

—Brian Barnett

THE PRIVILEGE TO ASK QUESTIONS

Out of the depths I have cried to You, O Lord; Lord, hear my voice! Let Your ears be attentive to the voice of my supplications (Psalm 130:1, 2).

After I was born again on August 23, 1921, I questioned God, "Lord, You are baptizing others in the Holy Spirit; why don't You baptize me?" I attended church almost every night and had always gone to the altar. I could not understand why others had received the Holy Spirit baptism and I had not.

God spoke to my heart—not with an audible voice but in His own particular way. I readily made my vows to Him and left the altar. I walked about 150 yards to the highway and God inspired me to look up. I said, "Now is the time for me to receive the Holy Ghost." The words *Holy Ghost* was written across the sky, with the first letter beginning where I was and the last one ending in the sky. When I came to myself I was propped on my left elbow speaking in other tongues. My sister, Inez, was standing over me rejoicing and saying, "Glory to God! Buddy has received the Holy Spirit!"

As a child I often thought I would like to be a minister of the gospel. Since I was not a Christian and none of my people were church members, I soon discarded the idea. When I received my baptism in the Holy Spirit, however, I soon realized that one day I would be a preacher. I began to prepare myself for my life's work.

In November 1925, I was ordained a minister by the Pentecostal group which had helped me to find the Lord. I shall always be grateful to them.

Though I had preached whenever opportunity presented itself from the fall of 1921, my real beginning as a preacher was on January 22, 1922, in a home three miles south of Girard, Louisiana. Since then I have considered myself a gospel preacher. Throughout my ministry the picture of the words *Holy Ghost* written across the sky has been fresh in my mind. It was an experience that gave me direction for my life and ministry.

· · · PRAYER · · ·

Lord, thank You for understanding why I sometimes question You. Your answers are always timely and strengthening.

· · · TODAY'S THOUGHT · · ·

Don't be afraid to ask questions. God has answers and He wants us to be fully informed about His will, His ways, and His works .

—A.V. Beaube

THE PRIESTHOOD OF BELIEVERS

*And they were not able to resist the wisdom and the
Spirit by which [Stephen] spoke* (Acts 6:10).

 Jesus was a layman, a member of the synagogue in Nazareth. When He began His ministry He chose fishermen and a tax collector. The church born on the Day of Pentecost was a movement of laypeople.

The church grew in numbers, and administrative problems arose. Grecian Jews complained that their widows were neglected in the daily distribution of bread. Seven deacons were elected to serve tables. This became the ministry function in the early church.

Stephen's life shines like a spiritual diamond in the pages of history of the early church. What kind of man was Stephen? He was sensitive to the call of God. If he had not been willing to wait on tables, God would never have used him to perform miracles and wonders in Jerusalem.

What was Stephen's spiritual secret? He was "full" of God. The Bible repeatedly gives witness that he was "full."

He was *full of the Holy Spirit.* Pentecost means God in us. The third person of the Trinity makes our body His temple. To be possessed by God's Spirit is a sign of greatness in any Christian.

He was *full of power.* The logical result of the infilling of the Spirit is that the Spirit–filled Christian is full of power. His power makes us a hammer to break hearts of stone. He makes us a spade to dig the foundation of a new world.

He was *full of faith*—faith in the Word of God, and faith in the power of God to change things. Those with faith have a titledeed to accomplish things for God.

He was *full of grace and wisdom.* His accusers were not able to resist the wisdom and the Spirit by which he spoke. Wisdom is a right application of knowledge.

· · · PRAYER · · ·

God grant me the serenity to accept the things I cannot change, courage to change the things I can, and the wisdom to know the difference.

· · · TODAY'S THOUGHT · · ·

"You are a chosen generation, a royal priesthood, a holy nation, His own special people, that you may proclaim the praises of Him who called you out of darkness into His marvelous light" (1 Peter 2:9).

—Esdras Betancourt

THE POWER OF FAITHFULNESS

Now may the God of hope fill you with all joy and peace in believing, that you may abound in hope by the power of the Holy Spirit (Romans 15:13).

Sixty–four years ago God called me to Christian ministry. Many of my peers and fellow Christians have already received their eternal welcome, as my wife and I await our invitation. With the call of God resting heavy on my spirit, I followed the advice of my mentor, the Reverend Paul H. Walker, and went to Lemmon, South Dakota, to conduct a revival and start a church. Both of those goals were prayerfully answered and more than 100 came to Christ. Many of them received the baptism in the Holy Spirit.

It was the norm in those days for new converts to be open and ready to receive the precious infilling of the Holy Spirit. It was not a vague wish but a ready response to the commands in the Book of Acts.

Following God was not always without personal fear. Frankly, when I secured the Odd Fellows Hall for our services, I felt like the oddest fellow in town. But God honored my simple messages with His anointing and with signs following. It is so necessary to lean on the Lord and not on just our own understanding in Christian ministry. When our dependence is on Him, the results which follow are God–given and He receives the praise.

· · · PRAYER · · ·

Gracious God, this walk with You is the most precious relationship there is and the most unending. I am grateful for the power of Your Spirit and for the beautiful years You have given me to serve You. I pray today that You will receive praises from my lips and glory from my life and that others may see our good works and glorify You.

· · · TODAY'S THOUGHT · · ·

God places a premium on faithfulness. While He doesn't pay off in full on this earth, there are rewards for the Christian life both now and forevermore.

—David C. Boatwright

THE LAST CALL

And the Lord said, "My Spirit shall not strive with man for-ever, for he is indeed flesh; yet his days shall be one hun-dred and twenty years" (Genesis 6:3).

It seemed to be an ordinary day. I was making hospital visits in Wichita Falls, Texas. As usual I visited patients who expressed no religious preference, along with the members of our congregation. With names and room numbers in hand, I proceeded through the elevator, down the hall, and into the rooms.

I began introducing myself to a man I had never met and realized that he could not respond. Immediately I apologized for the intrusion. Then I said, "I want to pray with you." After prayer I took out my call-ing card, held it before him and told him I was leaving it on the desk so he could call if I could be of further help.

The next morning a nurse called. She said the gentleman was call-ing for me. When I entered his room he said he had suffered a stroke and had been unable to move or speak for seven days. "Yesterday when you prayed, I could hear you. This morning I regained con-sciousness. I want you to tell me about this Church of God."

I asked about his religious background. He said he had not been inside a church in 39 years. I asked if he wanted to pray. He said, "I sure do." I led him in the sinner's prayer, and he accepted the Lord. We had a good visit and expected more, but that afternoon he suffered another stroke that was instant and fatal.

Oh, how merciful God was to give him that last opportunity. I shud-der to think that either of us could have resisted the efforts of the Holy Spirit in His final attempt to save a dying man.

· · · PRAYER · · ·

Heavenly Father, help me to never forget that the call to witness is a life–and–death matter—for me and for the person I am called to wit-ness to.

· · · TODAY'S THOUGHT · · ·

Any call to salvation or service could be the last.

—Wayne Blackshear

THE MINISTRY OF TONGUES

Then they were all amazed and marveled, saying to one
another, "Look, are not all these who speak Galileans? And
how is it that we hear, each in our own language in which
we were born?" (Acts 2:7, 8).

While serving as overseer of New Mexico, my duties included the supervision of Native American churches on the
Navajo Indian Reservation. Jake Ford of Maryville,
Tennessee, missionary to the Navajos, was conducting a
revival at the Church Rock church just outside of Gallup.

One night during an altar call, two ladies went to the altar to be
saved. Everything about our worship and doctrine was strange to
them, and they understood nothing about receiving Christ; so Brother
Ford urged some of the church members to pray with them and explain
how to be saved. No one responded to help pray for the ladies.

When he got no response, he knelt behind the ladies and began to
weep and pray for them, although they understood nothing he was saying. Suddenly, the Holy Spirit came mightily on Brother Ford and he
stepped in front of them. He spoke to them in a spiritual language for
quite some time. Suddenly, they jumped to their feet, weeping and
rejoicing, raising their hands and praising God. They received a wonderful experience of salvation.

After the service, some of the Indian members of the church said to
Brother Ford, "I thought you couldn't speak the Navajo language." He
replied, "You know I can't speak a word of your language." Then they
said, "When you knelt in front of those women, you spoke perfect
Navajo and explained the plan of salvation to them."

Brother Ford never spoke Navajo again, but that night the ministry
of tongues enabled two Navajo women to know Christ as Lord and
Savior.

· · · PRAYER · · ·

Holy Spirit, You are always there when we need You. As promised,
we know You will never leave us nor forsake us. We thank You for this
everlasting promise.

· · · TODAY'S THOUGHT · · ·

The miracle of Pentecost continues today.

—B.G. Hamon

FELLOWSHIP OF THE SPIRIT

Therefore if there is any consolation in Christ, if any com-
fort of love, if any fellowship of the Spirit, if any affection
and mercy, fulfill my joy by being like–minded
(Philippians 2:1, 2).

The idea of communion, or fellowship, with the Holy Spirit began with Jesus. He said, "I will pray the Father, and He will give you another Helper, that He may abide with you for-ever, even the Spirit of truth, whom the world cannot receive, because it neither sees Him nor knows Him; but you know Him, for He dwells with you and will be in you." (John 14:16, 17). Jesus said He was a comfort to them and had fellowship with them, but He was soon to leave. Jesus realized how important it is to have someone to fellow-ship with, so He said, "I will not leave you orphans" (v. 18).

The Holy Spirit is Counselor, Helper, Intercessor, Advocate, and Strengthener.

I am fortunate enough to have friends whom I believe will stand by me in any circumstance. Thank the Lord for friends who will tell you the truth. The Holy Spirit is the Spirit of truth, who also stands by you, as Jesus said in John 14:17. This Comforter and friend will live with you constantly and will be in you.

At times in life we feel sad and alone because friends leave us. But the Holy Spirit will always be there; He will never leave us. Knowing this gives us peace of mind. The Amplified Bible explains John 16:13 like this: "But when He, the Spirit of Truth (the Truth–giving Spirit) comes, He will guide you into all the Truth (the whole, full Truth). For He will not speak His own message [on His own authority]; but He will tell whatever He hears [from the Father; He will give the message that has been given to Him], and He will announce and declare to you the things that are to come [that will happen in the future]."

· · · PRAYER · · ·

Thank You, Father, for this Friend who stands beside us and guides
us into truth. We can know the mind of God concerning our future
because He tells us what He has heard from God. Thank You for this
gift from the Lord Jesus Christ.

· · · TODAY'S THOUGHT · · ·

The human spirit fails unless the Holy Spirit fills.

—Bill Phillips

THE HOLY SPIRIT LEADS

Then the Spirit took me up and brought me in a vision by the Spirit of God into Chaldea, to those in captivity. And the vision that I had seen went up from me (Ezekiel 11:24).

In 1981 I prepared to leave my home near Stuttgart, Germany, to preach in a Pentecostal Fellowship about 40 miles away. My preparations were interrupted by Fritz Pollerman, a German neighbor, who explained:

"Last summer, I attended a tent revival in Heilbronn. I noticed a young American soldier walking by, carrying his boom box. I called for him to come over, and he accepted my invitation to step inside the tent and listen to the evangelist. At the conclusion of the message, this young man prayed to receive Jesus as his Savior. I took his name and address but did not know who to contact. Today, the Lord reminded me of this soldier and that you would know how to contact him."

Fritz handed me a card with the name, rank, and address of the soldier. I explained that I would do my best but perhaps the young man had been rotated back to the United States. After a glance at the card, I stuck it in my pocket and hurried to make the long drive to the service.

The gate guard routinely stopped me and asked to see my pass. I had forgotten it, so the guard assisted in calling someone to come and escort me to the chapel. As he dialed the phone, I noticed his name tag. "Corporal Loudermilk," I asked, "Is your first name Victor, and were you once assigned to C Company, 384th Artillery in Heilbronn?"

"Why, yes," he replied. "How did you know?"

This was the soldier Fritz Pollerman had told me about an hour earlier. After discussing his spiritual encounter of nine months earlier, I prayed with him in the guard shack. Victor confided, "God sent you in answer to my grandma's prayers. She always told me that I could never hide from the Holy Spirit."

· · · PRAYER · · ·

Lord, I am reminded today that Your Holy Spirit can and will lead me in every fruitful path.

· · · TODAY'S THOUGHT · · ·

"Where is the road?" asked a missionary to his guide. The guide replied, "I am the road." And so is the Holy Spirit!

—Robert A. Moore

OBEYING THE SPIRIT

"Remember the words of the Lord Jesus, that He said, 'It is more blessed to give than to receive'" (Acts 20:35).

 Pastoring a congregation in a community with high unemployment and underemployment has often meant dealing with financial stress in our church. But the Holy Spirit is teaching us to experience God's provision. As we have obediently followed the Spirit's leading, God has given us many financial miracles.

Once our church needed nearly $24,000. Members of the church council and I were in prayer about the situation. As I prayed, the Holy Spirit impressed on me a financial strategy for meeting the need—a bold plan calling for considerable financial commitments from church members. Quite honestly, I was reluctant to pursue such a plan in a congregation with so many experiencing financial stress. Later, during a congregation meeting, the Spirit's leadership was confirmed when a council member suggested the same approach for handling the need—with no prior knowledge of how the Spirit had dealt with me. Although economic circumstances did not favor its success, we initiated the plan and God gave the church a financial miracle which met the need.

In another instance, the Spirit directed our church council and me to present a need to the people and to trust God. We did so, sharing with the congregation the amount needed. There was no apparent way for this need to be met. Then, one of our members testified that God had been dealing with him all week to give several thousand dollars to the church. The amount he felt led to give was exactly what the church needed. We obeyed the Spirit, he obeyed the Spirit, and the need was met!

The same Spirit who directed us through pressing church financial crises has led us to minister to those among us with dire financial needs. Sacrificial giving from church members has produced the joy of the Holy Spirit in us and has taught us the importance of trusting God and putting Him first.

· · · PRAYER · · ·

Father, thank You for Your Holy Spirit who teaches us that giving freely and liberally is a way of life.

· · · TODAY'S THOUGHT · · ·

"If you extend your soul to the hungry and satisfy the afflicted soul, then your light shall dawn in the darkness, and your darkness shall be as the noonday" (Isaiah 58:10).

—James P. Bowers

PRAYING IN THE SPIRIT

*Praying always with all prayer and supplication in the
Spirit, being watchful to this end with all perseverance and
supplication for all the saints* (Ephesians 6:18).

The U.S. Air Force Air Demonstration Squadron is called the Thunderbirds. They fly fast, low, and in close formation. I once rode in the backseat of one of the jets and experienced sensations almost beyond words. We flew over 500 miles per hour, barely 100 feet above the ground, within five feet of each other—and upside down! Although I trusted the pilots to keep us safe, I found myself praying with fervency.

The four jets sliced through the sky as one, making loops and turns. Wind gusts and turbulence buffeted our planes, but they held steady. Two elements were crucial to the success of the flight. First, the other three pilots kept their eyes glued to the commander/leader's plane. Second, they all listened and responded to the commands of the leader over the radio. Connected to the leader visually and by radio, they flew beautifully and accomplished their mission successfully.

Paul talked about preparing for spiritual battles. He gave Christians marching orders in Ephesians 6. Be strong (v. 10) and stand firm (v. 14). He pointed to prayer as the source of power to do this (v. 18). Specifically, he said to pray always and pray in the Spirit. Just as Thunderbirds train long and hard, so praying always and being in constant communion with the Lord is training that makes us ready for battle. When contrary winds of opposition buffet us, we can stand our ground in the strength of the Lord.

Praying in the Spirit, being connected to the Source, empowers us to overcome the Enemy. We can pray in the flesh and not touch God, or we can pray confidently in the Spirit and see God win great victories. The Thunderbirds maintained communication visually and by voice. It was not enough for the Thunderbirds to fly near each other, they had to be connected. So we have to be *connected* to the Source!

· · · PRAYER · · ·

Almighty God, more than anything else, I need to be connected to You. Help me to pray always in the Spirit, so that Your power can be released in me to win the victory over the Enemy. Make me Your instrument of power and blessing to those I touch.

· · · TODAY'S THOUGHT · · ·

Prayer in the Spirit enables God to free us.

—Benjamin Perez

THE SPIRIT RESTED ON THEM

But two men had remained in the camp: the name of one
was Eldad, and the name of the other Medad. And the Spirit
rested upon them. Now they were among those listed, but
who had not gone out to the tabernacle; yet they prophesied
in the camp (Numbers 11:26).

Under the old covenant, this was the greatest spiritual experience a man could know—for God's Spirit to rest upon him. From time to time, in order to fulfill the will of God, the Spirit of God would rest on one whom God would choose to perform a special task. Can you imagine how wonderful this must have felt to men like Samson and Gideon, and women like Deborah and Esther? They were anointed for a special task, handpicked by the Spirit and used to accomplish God's will. They were the chosen vessels of God and were almost revered for that reason.

But how about Eldad and Medad! The were contemporaries of Moses and Aaron. Everyone expected God to use Moses and speak through Aaron in a special way, but they were shocked—almost angered—when plain old Eldad and Medad prophesied. Joshua told Moses, "Forbid them!" Moses responded, "Oh, that all the Lord's people were prophets!" (vv. 28, 29). Moses was not jealous or prideful; he knew he didn't have a monopoly on God's Spirit. In fact, the feeling of being touched by the Spirit was so wonderful that Moses wanted everyone to know it.

Now, because of Jesus, everyone can! He told His disciples He would have to go away, but that when He did, He would pray to the Father, who would send One to take His place. Jesus said, "But you know Him, for He dwells with you and shall be in you" (John 14:17). This was fulfilled in Acts 2. Today the Holy Spirit doesn't just come upon us; He also dwells in us. The Spirit resides within the people of God! Moses' desire that all of God's people would know the touch of the Spirit has been fulfilled.

· · · PRAYER · · ·

Heavenly Father, I want to thank You for Your indwelling Spirit.
Help me to understand how marvelous this is, and please help me
never to take Your presence for granted.

· · · TODAY'S THOUGHT · · ·

It doesn't take a great person to do something great; it just takes an ordinary person in whom a great God dwells!

—Ronald D. Brown

VISIONS AND DREAMS

"It shall come to pass in the last days, says God, that I will
pour out of My Spirit on all flesh; your sons and your
daughters shall prophesy, your young men shall see visions,
your old men shall dream dreams'" (Acts 2:17).

Visions, dreams, hope, and change—what a wonderful collection of words! Visions and dreams are a common means of divine revelation to the people of God. There must be hope that things can change.

Sometimes people say, "I can't take it any longer. I can't live like this any more." Those are cries for change. The problem is, they see no possibility of change. They have no hope; thus, their lives are filled with despair. Could this happen in church? In a man's ministry? Recognize that Satan is a thief of visions and dreams. He wants people to be without hope and sink through depression into despair and suicide.

We cannot allow churches and ministries to die. We must see that circumstances can be altered. Revival can come; churches can grow. You will find, however, that human strategies are never adequate for the kind of success necessary for the kingdom of God. Pray for the poured–out Spirit of God. Let's be young men of vision and old men of dreams working the plan of God!

We need an outpouring of God's Spirit. We need a fresh baptism of the Holy Spirit on our lives. We need God to reveal Himself and His plans in dreams and visions. We must be able to see what He wants us to do and how He wants things to change. What we must have is the promise of His Word fulfilled in our lives. His promise is "I will pour out of My spirit upon all flesh."

We are sons and daughters. We are young men and old men. Let's pray for a revival of the prophetic work of God's Spirit. Let's have hope for the church. Let's see change in our lives and ministries so that they may bring glory and honor to the Lord!

· · · PRAYER · · ·

Holy Spirit, baptize us with the freshness of Your inspiring vision,
giving dream–making power.

· · · TODAY'S THOUGHT · · ·

I promise You, Holy Spirit, that I will broaden my horizons so that I can dream dreams and see visions.

—Paul Clawson

FIVE AVENUES OF POWER

"You shall receive power when the Holy Spirit has come upon you; and you shall be witnesses to Me in Jerusalem, and in all Judea and Samaria, and to the end of the earth" (Acts 1:8).

It is the desire, and the command, of God that His people be a people who exert spiritual power. The Holy Spirit is the true source of power. There are at least five avenues by which this power is exerted.

First, we exert spiritual power by what we are. Jesus said, "You are the salt of the earth." As people filled with the Holy Ghost, we give flavor and preservation to our world. Jesus also said, "You are the light of the world." As light, we dispel darkness.

Second, we exert spiritual power by what we say. No matter what our claims may be, our speech will betray us as either people of weakness or people of power. Following the arrest of Jesus, Peter's speech betrayed him when he tried to deny who he was.

Third, we exert spiritual power by what we do. Hebrews 11:7 tells us that Noah's building the ark not only saved his house but also condemned the world. Our godly living will be a rebuke to sin.

Fourth, we exert spiritual power by what we give of our earthly resources. Jesus said we would witness to Him in our tithes and offerings, and in our giving to missions.

Fifth, we exert spiritual power by what we dare proclaim in the name of Jesus. In Acts 3, Peter and John encountered the lame man at the gate called Beautiful. In response to his cry for alms, they proclaimed to him, "In the name of Jesus Christ of Nazareth, rise up and walk" (v.6). As we walk by faith in the promises of God, we give witness to Him by victoriously living above the circumstances, by exploits in prayer, and by walking in righteousness as we follow Jesus.

Let us use every avenue available to exert the power of the Holy Spirit.

· · · PRAYER · · ·

Lord, keep us aware of the power we have through the Holy Spirit. In Jesus' name.

· · · TODAY'S THOUGHT · · ·

"I can do all things through Christ who strengthens me" (Philippians 4:13) remains sure for every believer in any situation.

—H.L. Chesser

GOD'S KINGDOM COMES

"But if I cast out demons by the Spirit of God, surely the kingdom of God has come upon you" (Matthew 12:28).

After He had healed a demon-possessed man who was blind and mute, Jesus was accused of casting out the demons by the power of Beelzebub, the prince of demons. He responded, "If Satan casts out Satan, he is divided against himself. How then will his kingdom stand?" (Matthew 12:26). Jesus reminded us of our authority in Him when He declared, "In my Name they will cast out demons" (Mark 16:17).

The source of power Jesus used in casting out the demons is evident. As the Son of God, He had authority over all circumstances, situations, and evil powers. He said, "'All authority has been given to Me in heaven and on earth" (Matthew 28:18).

Jesus used the same authority, or power, when He met the demon-possessed man in the tombs of Gadara. This man had been a terror to his community; but after meeting Jesus and experiencing deliverance from the demonic powers in his life, he regained his right mind and was seen clothed and sitting at the feet of Jesus.

Many think of the kingdom of God as an earthly kingdom composed of the same structures we see in countries of the world today. The mother of James and John thought Christ's kingdom would be an earthly one and requested that her two sons be given prominent seats next to Jesus himself. Paul stated, "For the kingdom of God is not food and drink, but righteousness and peace and joy in the Holy Spirit" (Romans 14:17). All demonic powers are subject to Jesus Christ and His authority. Satan knows that he was defeated at Calvary and is now a terminal case because his destiny was sealed with his assignment to the bottomless pit.

The followers of Jesus Christ who are filled with the Holy Spirit have the same power and authority over Satan and all his forces. We do not have to be afraid of our Enemy because we have authority over him through Jesus Christ.

· · · PRAYER · · ·

Heavenly Father, may I be daily reminded that Kingdom power and authority belong to us as Your followers to use for the glory of God.

· · · TODAY'S THOUGHT · · ·

"God has not given us a spirit of fear, but of power and of love and of a sound mind" (2 Timothy 1:7).

—Cecil E. Campbell

HOW I RECEIVED THE SPIRIT

*And they were all filled with the Holy Spirit and began to
speak with other tongues, as the Spirit gave them utterance
(Acts 2:4).*

On April 2, 1928, the world was different from today, but the needs of a hungry human heart are always the same. The Lord saved me that night; I was 18 years old. A month later, my mother was killed by a car as she walked home from church on a deserted country road. Her last words to me were, "Son, I want you to go on." My pain was deep.

I withdrew and rarely spoke to anyone. Questions troubled my heart—questions for which I had no answer. Deep in my heart I questioned how God could permit such a thing to happen to a young Christian. *Why, Lord?* was the thought that plagued my every waking moment and haunted my dreams at night.

A year later, when the pain of my heart was little better and the bitterness was more pronounced, I was asked to speak at a small country church in Gotebo, Oklahoma. There were few people present, perhaps 45 or 50 counting the children. I did not speak long, and when I finished, I walked over to the altar and knelt down to pray.

Suddenly, I began to speak in a strange language, in another tongue. This was something very frightening to me. I had never heard of this type thing happening to anyone else; I knew absolutely nothing about the experience we now refer to as the baptism in the Holy Spirit.

What I know now—many years later and after much study of the Word of God—is that God in His mercy took a hurting heart, filled it with His precious Holy Spirit, and has never ceased to be with me ever since.

That was July 14, 1929. God's Spirit has not departed from me, nor I from Him since that day. It has been a wonderful and magnificent journey to this very moment. God has guided me and kept me all the days of my life. To Him be all glory and praise, world without end.

· · · PRAYER · · ·

Lord, let those who read of this marvelous grace in my life be convinced themselves of Your goodness, love, and Spirit. In Jesus' name

· · · TODAY'S THOUGHT · · ·

The Holy Spirit is a present companion in every path of life.

—G.L. Bunch

THE DEEP THINGS OF GOD

These things we also speak, not in words which man's wisdom teaches, but which the Holy Spirit teaches, comparing spiritual things with spiritual (1 Corinthians 2:13).

In order to properly understand this text, read the surrounding verses 9–12 and 14. Observe the phrase "things of God." "But as it is written: 'Eye has not seen, nor ear heard, nor have entered into the heart of man the things which God has prepared for those who love Him.' But God has revealed them to us through His Spirit. For the Spirit searches all things, yes, the deep things of God" (vv. 9, 10).

It is evident in these verses that the "things of God" referred to are not in the realm of man's wisdom, but they are revealed to those who have received the "Spirit who is from God" (v. 12). The "things of God" are spiritual things taught by the Holy Spirit and cannot be understood by the natural man.

Dr. Scofield, in his notes on this scripture, places "man" in three classes: The *Adamic man* is the natural man unrenewed. The *renewed man* is the Spirit–filled man, walking in full communion with God. The *carnal man* walks after the flesh and remains a babe in Christ. The natural man may be learned, gentle, and eloquent, but the spiritual content of Scripture is absolutely hidden from him.

The impact of this forcefully presents the necessity for believers to go beyond being "babes in Christ" and to experience the baptism in the Holy Spirit. The Spirit gives power to witness of Christ (Acts 1:8) and to understand Scripture dictated to men by the Holy Spirit (2 Peter 1:21).

· · · PRAYER · · ·

My loving heavenly Father, thank You for a Pentecostal baptism that opened up Your Word to my understanding. Help me to keep my mind and heart in subjection to Your divine will.

· · · TODAY'S THOUGHT · · ·

We must avoid committing three fatal spiritual errors: ignoring the Holy Spirit, neglecting the Holy Spirit, and substituting for the Holy Spirit.

—W.J. (Bill) Brown

THE HOLY SPIRIT AND WISDOM

*"Therefore, brethren, seek out from among you seven men
of good reputation, full of the Holy Spirit and wisdom,
whom we may appoint over this business"* (Acts 6:3).

Chosen men, full of the Holy Spirit and wisdom, were the solution to a growing pain that could have disrupted the growth, ministry, and fellowship of the early church. Whatever concerns we have today about the growth, ministry, and fellowship of the church, the answer is to have people and leaders who are filled with the Holy Spirit and wisdom.

It avails little for the church if its people and ministers are clever, charitable, kindhearted, and even zealous, but are not filled with the Holy Spirit and wisdom. By all means we must be filled with the Spirit and have the wisdom He imparts.

Some years ago in a growing Church of God, A situation became so difficult that it seemed the church might lose its outstanding pastor. As time went on, the problem was solved and the pastor stayed. When the pastoral preference ballots were received from the congregation, all but four of 500 ballots were in favor of the pastor. He is still the pastor, and the church is one of the largest in the Pentecostal Movement. As state overseer, when I announced the results of the balloting and reappointed the pastor, I suggested that he share with other pastors how a Christian filled with the Holy Spirit and wisdom could differ with others and still remain a shepherd of God's flock.

I was born in 1912, and my parents were filled with the Holy Spirit in the early outpourings of the Holy Spirit in this century. My dad was filled with the Holy Spirit in a revival meeting, and my mother was baptized in a family prayer time at home. Their experiences of being baptized in the Holy Spirit and wisdom has influenced my entire life.

I received the Holy Spirit baptism in 1930, in a Sunday evening service at the East Chattanooga, Tennessee, Church of God. The world around me has changed amazingly since then, but I am thankful that this experience of being filled with the Holy Spirit is still a distinctive of our denomination.

· · · PRAYER · · ·

Father, refill Your people with the Holy Spirit and wisdom.

· · · TODAY'S THOUGHT · · ·

People filled with the Holy Spirit and full of wisdom can disagree and not be disagreeable.

—W.C. Byrd

SPIRIT-DIRECTED DELIVERANCE

*The Spirit of the Lord came upon him [Othniel] and he
judged Israel. He went out to war, and the Lord delivered
Cushan–Rishathaim king of Mesopotamia into his hand*
(Judges 3:10).

The ministry of the Holy Spirit empowers us to fight the forces of darkness. The work of the devil is just the opposite. He continually wars against us to negatively influence our *calling*, our *commitment*, and our *career*. He wants us to live in bondage to a restricted faith and restrained service to God and the church.

Israel had been in bondage to a foreign tyrant, Cushan-Rishathaim, for eight years. The name means "Cushan of Double Wickedness." They were an equipped and trained enemy, and the country was a stronghold of giants. Israel needed a Spirit-directed leader.

In this situation, the Spirit of the Lord came on Othniel and he judged Israel. *Judged* is a military term, meaning to mobilize Israel for God's holy wars. He followed the Lord with all his heart, and the Spirit empowered him to break the yoke of bondage of the enemy.

Othniel's name means "Powerful One." He was powerful because the Holy Spirit took possession of him, clothed him, rushed upon him, and breathed energy into him. This was his source of strength.

God wants us to be powerful Christians and live free from of the bondage that would affect our *faith*, our *family*, or our *future*. Our source of strength is the Holy Spirit.

One of Othniel's relatives was Caleb, the daring man who asked permission to conquer a mountain. Othniel had witnessed the principles of trust and obedience in action and he drew on this experience. Let us draw strength from the example of Spirit-directed leaders around us.

· · · PRAYER · · ·

Father of strength and might, clothe me today with the power of the Holy Spirit. Breathe energy into me so that I can overcome every attempt of the Enemy to defeat me or to detour my spiritual progress. I claim the provisions of Your Spirit to live victoriously.

· · · TODAY'S THOUGHT · · ·

Acts teaches us to focus on the work of the Spirit: Accept His guidance in every aspect of life. Claim His authority over every stronghold. Team with proven Spirit-directed leaders to increase strength. Stand on God's promise of victory for every battle.

—Floyd D. Carey

A GIFT OF POWER

*"You shall receive power when the Holy Spirit has come
upon you; and you shall be witnesses to Me in Jerusalem,
and in all Judea and Samaria, and to the end of the earth"*
(Acts 1:8).

 This promise appears to be Christ's response to a universal
craving for power. Nothing so awakens a person's ambition as
the possibility of personal power. It is sweeter than bread to the
hungry, or a home to the homeless, or a sunrise to the benighted.

Of all the divine attributes, this is the one man most intensely and
incessantly covets. He has a fierce ambition to create but is powerless
to do so. He desperately wishes to control all aspects of his life. He
summons every known element and force in nature to his service and
seeks to compel them to do for him what he cannot do for himself.

From the schoolboy to the statesman, this passion is all–pervading.
Observe the young man with intense features. Watch him closely as he
reads book after book and analyzes author after author. He is in quest
of something you do not see. His whole body, mind, and heart are in a
strain of persistent tension. What is he after? Knowledge? Wealth?
Position? Perhaps! But the end result is that he is after power.

Man, in the final analysis, is a power seeker. But the power man
seeks is not a holy power. Rather, it is a profane power dedicated to
the enhancement and glory of man, not to God and the witness of His
kingdom. The power promised with the baptism in the Holy Spirit is a
holy power which enables us to become the instrument through which
God works and brings glory to Himself.

The high privilege of humans is to receive the best and greatest
power. This is the promise: "You shall receive power." A divine
faucet connects with a pipeline from God and extends to the fainting,
panting heart of the famished. You have only to open a reservoir of
trust in your soul and let the power flow in!

· · · P R A Y E R · · ·

*Father, help me to always remember that it is through the power of
the Holy Spirit that I am enabled to do something worthy of Your holy
name and divine approval.*

· · · T O D A Y ' S   T H O U G H T · · ·

An effective person is powerful. A Christian who surrenders totally
to the sovereign will of God is effective. Commit to do the will of God
and He will fill you with His power.

—R. Leonard Carroll

FROM DEATH TO LIFE

*God has appointed these [gifts of the Holy Spirit] in the
church . . . miracles, then gifts of healings"*
(1 Corinthians 12:28).

Two doctors, a midwife, and the extended family were present. The joyful expectation of the first great-grandchild
turned into a fearful, somber feeling. "The child in the mother's womb is dead, and we must take this woman to the hospital to save her life," the doctors said.

For 10 years Concha Murillo had heard that Church of God people
pray to God and miracles happen, but she had been told that
Pentecostals are evil. Now her granddaughter was suffering excruciat-
ing pain. The child in the mother's womb was dead and the mother
was at the point of death. What should they do? Going to the hospital
was no guarantee the mother would live.

In her confusion and distress, Mrs. Murillo turned to "the Church of
God people." The pastor was awakened, and he called other brothers
and sisters. The group of believers arrived at the Murillo home. Pastor
and people prayed fervently, but nothing happened. The doctors warned
the family and church people that if the mother died, all of them would
be jailed for negligence. "Pray again!" was the reply of Mrs. Murillo.

A second prayer was offered and no answer came. The threat was
made again. "Pray again!" was the order from the lips of the woman
who had been a colonel in the Mexican army. "If nothing happens this
time, take her to the hospital." As the believers prayed the mother gave
birth, but the baby was dead. For some, the miracle was performed.
The mother was saved. There was nothing else to do.

But this was not what Maria Gonzalez was thinking. She had seen
many miracles in answer to prayer and fasting, so she took the baby in
her arms and prayed, "My God, You do not do things halfway. Now,
Lord, do the other half. Give life to this baby as a testimony to these
people that You are a living and merciful God. In Jesus' name. Amen."

As she prayed the child came to life. That child writes this testimony.

· · · PRAYER · · ·

*Thank You, Lord, for the gifts of the Holy Spirit You have placed in
the church so that Your will can be done.*

· · · TODAY'S THOUGHT · · ·

God is the sovereign Creator who, by the Holy Spirit, is able to
accomplish His purposes even if it requires a miracle.

—Cornelio M. Castelo

POWER TO WITNESS

*"You shall receive power when the Holy Spirit has come
upon you; and you shall be witnesses to Me in Jerusalem,
and in all Judea and Samaria, and to the end of the earth"*
(Acts 1:8).

Near the end of combat duty in World War II, I was trans-
ferred to a troop ship to return home. On the ship an
Evangelical and two Pentecostal Christians invited me to a
Bible study. During the 19-day trip, these dedicated young
sailors explained clearly the plan of salvation, which I understood and
accepted for the first time. They outlined the purpose of the baptism in
the Holy Spirit, and I received the experience the night of our arrival
back home. At a Pentecostal mission on Embarcadero Street in San
Francisco I entered my first Pentecostal church.

These Spirit-filled sailors guided me through important scriptures
on this God-given power to witness for Christ. Over the years I have
searched the Word of God and I have discovered that all born-again
believers have the indwelling of the Spirit as a result of the birth (not
the baptism) of the Spirit (John 3:3-5). I learned that the baptism (not
the birth) of the Holy Spirit is power for anointed witnessing and
preaching for Christ (Acts 1:8). It became clear to me that this power
was designed to equip every born-again Christian to carry out the primary mission of Christ (Luke 19:10).

More importantly, I learned that this powerful witnessing gift of the
Holy Spirit was promised to all flesh (Acts 2:17; 10:44-48), to all
future generations (2:39), and to everyone living in the last days
(2:17). These days are much more nearly the "last days" than were
those when the Holy Spirit was first poured out. If the disciples needed Him then, how much more do we need Him now!

· · · PRAYER · · ·

*Lord, continue to strengthen us to boldly witness for You until You
return to gather us to Yourself.*

· · · TODAY'S THOUGHT · · ·

"Moody speaks as if he has a monopoly on the Holy Spirit, " said a
critic of him. "Moody has no monopoly on the Holy Spirit, but the
Holy Spirit has a monopoly on Moody," answered an admirer of
Moody.

—Charles R. Beach

RESISTING THE HOLY SPIRIT

*"You stiffnecked and uncircumcised in heart and ears! You
always resist the Holy Spirit; as your fathers did, so do
you"* (Acts 7:51).

Stephen rebuked the religious community for the sin of resisting the Holy Spirit. What was needed then is needed now: a
circumcision of the heart and ears! As long as a person is
stubborn and rebellious, he or she will continue to struggle
under a heavy yoke.

The message of the Holy Spirit is the message of Jesus: "Come to
Me, all you who labor and are heavy laden, and I will give you rest.
Take My yoke upon you and learn from Me, for I am gentle and lowly
in heart, and you will find rest for your souls. For My yoke is easy and
My burden is light" (Matthew 11:28-30).

A legend says that as a carpenter Jesus made the best yokes in Galilee.
Customers came from all over the country to buy the yokes He made. The
sign above His father's carpenter's shop in Nazareth read: "My yokes fit
well." Whatever Jesus makes or sends fits our needs and abilities.

Before He left this earth, Jesus said, "But the Helper, the Holy Spirit
whom the Father will send in My name, He will teach you all things,
and bring to your remembrance all things" (John 14:26).

The key to a successful spiritual life is accepting the Holy Spirit as
the One standing by to empower us to live as children of God.
Resisting the Holy Spirit leads to spiritual bondage. God's message is
clear: "Do not grieve the Holy Spirit" (Ephesians 4:30). When we
resist the Holy Spirit, we forfeit power, joy, and communion with God.
Like the hearers of Stephen's message, if we willfully resist the Holy
Spirit, we will find ourselves fighting against God.

Are we guilty of the sins of resisting, grieving, and quenching the
Holy Spirit? Let us confess our sins, for the Lord has promised: "If
we confess our sins, He is faithful and just to forgive us our sins and to
cleanse us from all unrighteousness" (1 John 1:9).

· · · PRAYER · · ·

*Heavenly Father, we repent of resisting You and quenching Your
Holy Spirit. Forgive us of the sins of neglect and inaction, as well as
the sins of wrong actions. In Jesus' name.*

· · · TODAY'S THOUGHT · · ·

I am determined to listen for the voice of the Master today.

—O. Wayne Chambers

THE GIFT OF THE HOLY SPIRIT

*Then Peter said to them, "Repent, and let every one of you be
baptized in the name of Jesus Christ for the remission of sins;
and you shall receive the gift of the Holy Spirit* (Acts 2:38).

I remember clearly the day I repented of my sins. Equally
vivid is the day I was baptized in water. Another treasured
memory is when I received the baptism in the Holy Spirit. I
recall the time and place I received this precious gift. No
other gift has impacted my life in the same manner. It is the true treasure of my heart.

The Holy Spirit is more than a mere gift, however. He is a true and
devoted friend.

The Holy Spirit is more than an experience. He is a divine personality who is both with and in true believers. He is a comforter, guide,
teacher, advocate, empowerer, and more.

The Holy Spirit enhances and complements every gift received from
our heavenly Father. An experience with Him is the big, indefinable
satisfaction we have waited for and longed to receive. We do not have
to travel the way of faith without Him.

As with other spectacular gifts, you have to share the news of the
Holy Spirit with others. He is too special to keep to yourself.

Experience Him.

Enjoy Him.

Make sure others know about Him!

· · · PRAYER · · ·

*Father God, thank You for salvation. May the Holy Spirit always
fill our lives. Help us to be instruments through which others may
receive this precious gift.*

· · · TODAY'S THOUGHT · · ·

Some gifts cannot be repaid; they must simply be passed on to others. This describes the gift of the Holy Spirit. Pass the good news on
to others, and be full of the Spirit!

—K. Doyle Allen

A MAN IN WHOM IS THE SPIRIT

*And the Lord said to Moses: "Take Joshua the son of Nun
with you, a man in whom is the Spirit, and lay your hand on
him"* (Numbers 27:18).

Several different pastors had a good influence on my life
while I was growing to adulthood, but the one who first made
a memorable impression on me was W.C. Cudd, pastor of the
Church of God in St. Pauls, North Carolina. I came under the
influence of this good man after my family moved to St. Pauls when I
was 7 years old. This pastor baptized me, received me into the Church
of God, and, when I was 9 years old, officiated at my father's funeral.
Those ministries alone made him an important person in my life, but
there is something else I remember about Pastor Cudd. He had an
uncommon quality about him, a demeanor, a spirit, which demanded
my respect—even my reverence—in his presence.

I knew there was something extraordinary about Pastor Cudd, but as
a child I did not really understand what it was. Later, I would realize
that what I sensed about this man, the thing that made a lasting impression on me was simply this: he was a man in whom dwelt the Spirit.
Now, after many years have passed, I still think of Pastor Cudd as the
ideal of what every minister of the gospel ought to be. He was what
every Christian should want to be—a person in whom is the Spirit.

How can we become one in whom others will recognize the presence of God? People in whom we can sense the presence of the Spirit
do not spend time trying to figure out how they can impress people.
No, people like that spend time with God, cultivating their relationship
with Him, seeking to be filled daily with His Spirit. They are simply
people in whom is the Spirit.

· · · PRAYER · · ·

*Father in heaven, I desire to live in fellowship with You this day.
Fill me with Your Spirit, the Spirit of Christ, the Holy Spirit. Make me
a person in whom others will sense Your holy presence.*

· · · TODAY'S THOUGHT · · ·

It is sometimes said, "Be yourself, but be your best self." There is
something more important than being your best self. Be one in whom
is the Holy Spirit. Be one through whom God comes near to others.

—Daniel L. Black

FULL OF THE SPIRIT

"The Spirit of the Lord is upon Me, because He has anointed Me to preach the gospel to the poor . . . to set at liberty those who are oppressed" (Luke 4:18).

 My father, the Reverend Antonio Collazo, was a spiritual man dedicated to the service of God and the church. He was not a Pentecostal shouting with a loud voice, but he was full of the Holy Spirit. One experience in his ministry I will never forget.

One day while pastoring Santurce, Puerto Rico, he was making pastoral visits and went to see a member with a mentally disturbed son. The boy was so bad that for his and others' safety, he was caged in the backyard. No one, even his mother, dared get near him. His food was slid into the cage with a long pole. My father said he was like an animal with rabies, always screaming and crawling around. His situation caused grief to his family, especially his mother.

After praying for the mother, my father felt compelled by the Holy Spirit to pray for the young man. He asked the mother for the key to the cage. At first she refused because she feared her son would harm him but he insisted, so she gave him the key.

My father went into the yard by himself with the assurance that the Holy Spirit would help him. He opened the cage, went in, and prayed for the young man. He was instantly delivered! My father presented the delivered young man to his mother.

The following Sunday, the young man asked for permission to speak in church. My father was a bit apprehensive; but feeling confident in the Spirit, he gave the young man the opportunity to testify. The youth expressed gratefulness to the Lord for deliverance and began singing a song about the healing. The words of the song mentioned that the young man was living proof of God's saving power. From that day forward, he wrote and sang many songs that the Lord gave him.

· · · PRAYER · · ·

Thank you, Lord, for using my father, who was filled with boldness because of the Holy Spirit.

· · · TODAY'S THOUGHT · · ·

Nothing was too big or scary for my father if the Spirit of the Lord impressed him to do it. The same is true for us if we are full of the Spirit.

—Persida Collazo

THE HOLY SPIRIT WILL CARRY YOU

"And it shall come to pass, as soon as I am gone from you,
that the Spirit of the Lord will carry you to a place I do not
know. . . . But I your servant have feared the Lord from
my youth" (1 Kings 18:12).

My father, the Reverend Ray Collins, accepted a call to full time ministry when he held a responsible position in a Thomasville, North Carolina, furniture factory. Although slated to be the next superintendent of the factory, he resigned his job one day and packed his suitcase. With a Bible in his hand, he stood on U.S. 29 trying to get a ride. He did not know where the Spirit of God would take him.

When Dad saw a car coming down the highway, he stuck out his thumb. Whatever direction a car would be traveling, he would cross the road and stand on that side to try to flag it down. Finally, a car stopped and offered him a ride to Schoolfield, Virginia. In Schoolfield, Dad still didn't know what to expect. He knocked on the Church of God pastor's door and announced in an emphatic voice that God had sent him there for a revival. The pastor told him they had just closed a revival the previous Sunday with no results. Not at all discouraged, Dad asked the pastor if he could just preach on Saturday night. The pastor reluctantly agreed.

After the Saturday night sermon, the alters filled with seekers. The same thing happened on Sunday morning and Sunday night. At the close of the Sunday night service, the pastor told the congregation, "Folks, I don't know who this man is or where he came from; but, church, we are in a revival!"

The pastor was also the state overseer of Virginia. After the revival he asked Dad to stay in Virginia and preach in the other churches. Since that time my dad, now 87 years old, has preached in the largest churches in the Church of God. He has won thousands to the kingdom of God—all because the Spirit of the God carried him where he knew not.

· · · PRAYER · · ·

Dear God, allow us to live our lives expecting the Holy Spirit to guide us into areas of service You have prepared us for. Thank You for your guidance, even when we don't know where You are leading.

· · · TODAY'S THOUGHT · · ·

The Spirit of the Lord will lead me into green pastures of productivity. This removes fear, apprehension, and uneasiness.

—Paul D. Collins

THE SPIRIT WILL COME UPON YOU

And the angel answered and said to her, "The Holy Spirit will come upon you, and the power of the Highest will over-shadow you; therefore, also, that Holy One who is to be born will be called the Son of God" (Luke 1:35).

The role of the Holy Spirit is to empower, energize, and ult-mately bring back to life those who die in Christ.

When Mary received the astonishing word from Gabriel that she was to give birth to a child, she naturally wondered how this could be. By every natural law, it was not possible because she was a virgin. So the modest lady questioned the angel, to which he replied: "The Holy Spirit will come upon you, and the power of the most high will overshadow you."

The Lord does not expect us to always understand His works, only to believe them. I do not know how a weak, vacillating person can suddenly be bold and resolute and confident; but it happens. In the Spirit-filled life it is common. Nor do I know how a shy, timid person can become articulate and communicate the gospel; but it happens all the time. J.R. Moseley, one of the most noted saints of the early days of Pentecost, told this about himself:

"I had no ability to speak, except when I was under the anointing and the control of the Spirit. He can take anyone who will yield and cause to be said things that should be said but cannot be said apart from His anointing."

· · · PRAYER · · ·

Father of life, let Your miracle of living remain forever in us. You who gave us life, now sustain it in us until we shall be called to Thee or Thou shall come to us. Then, holy Father, let us live with Thee for-ever.

· · · TODAY'S THOUGHT · · ·

The Holy Spirit is for sons and daughters, young men and old men—all the servants of the Lord. The Spirit puts life, energy, and ability in us that we would never realize without Him.

—Charles W. Conn

DON'T BLAME IT ON THE SPIRIT

Then they said to him, "Look now, there are fifty strong men with your servants. Please let them go and search for your master, lest perhaps the Spirit of the Lord has taken him up and cast him upon some mountain or into some valley." And he said, "You shall not send anyone" (2 Kings 2:16).

After Elijah's ascension to heaven, Elisha became the prophet's successor. When Elisha returned to Jericho from the place where Elijah had been caught away to heaven, the sons of the prophets at Jericho wanted to send 50 strong men to search for Elijah.

Isn't it amazing to see how professing believers sometimes discount the works of God? Elisha had witnessed the ascension of Elijah, but the sons of the prophets doubted that Elijah had actually been taken up. They speculated that perhaps the Spirit of the Lord had taken him and set him down on some mountain or in some valley.

Elisha strongly objected to the intention of his fellow prophets. "You shall not send anyone," he said. Insisting on searching for the prophet, however, they went and found nothing.

People make statements about God that are as unfair and unfounded as those of the prophets at Jericho. Sometimes when people fail to manage properly and hardship comes, they blame it on God. Through their own carelessness, harm or injury comes and they ask, "Why has God done this?" Saddest of all is when someone does something in total disobedience to God's Word, then attributes his action to God. One man divorced his wife to marry another and said, "I was following the leading of the Lord."

We do not have to fear the leading of the Holy Spirit, and we do not have to fear harm from the Holy Spirit. He will never bring reproach on Christ, act contrary to Scripture, or discredit sincere faith in God.

· · · PRAYER · · ·

Merciful Father, remind us that You are always interested in our good for Your glory and that Your Spirit is our Helper.

· · · TODAY'S THOUGHT · · ·

Trying to discredit the works of God or blaming Him for something He did not do is not an exercise in spirituality.

—James E. Cossey

THE POWER OF SUBMISSION

Then the Spirit came upon Amasai, chief of the captains,
and he said: "We are yours, O David; we are on your side,
O son of Jesse! Peace, peace to you, and peace to your
helpers! For your God helps you." So David received
them, and made them captains of the troop
(1 Chronicles 12:18).

Power for service is a characteristic of the Holy Spirit's anointing. So is submission to God's will. In fact, spiritual power is increased in proportion to one's submission to God's will. Such was the case when the Spirit came upon the powerful warrior-leader, Amasai, as he approached David.

God's anointing on Amasai was clearly evident by his submission to David as king. It was evident by Amasai's alliance with what was right. The divine anointing on Amasai was evident in his prayer for David: "Peace to you and peace to your helpers."

The outcome was that "David received them." By submitting to David, Amasai submitted to God's will for he recognized in David that God was with him. The power of Amasai and his men increased because David "made them captains of the troop."

The Holy Spirit will help us submit to and harmonize with His anointing. The anointing of the Holy Spirit signifies that God has chosen us to be instruments in His work. To have the power of the Spirit, we must learn to submit to the will of the Spirit.

Amasai prepared to help David build the kingdom of Israel because the Spirit prompted him. We, too, are helping to build a kingdom—the kingdom of God and of Christ. We work in response to the Spirit's leading. We need only be submissive to God's purpose by the Spirit.

· · · PRAYER · · ·

Almighty God, I willingly choose to allow You to be Lord of every area of my life. Use me as a Kingdom builder to bring glory to You as I submit to the anointing of Your Spirit.

· · · TODAY'S THOUGHT · · ·

David's men were "mighty" because they were Spirit-anointed and they submitted to David's Spirit-anointed leadership. It is God's will for us to "be submissive to one another" in the Lord (1 Peter 5:5).

—Sam Crisp

THE GLORIOUS GOSPEL

For I am not ashamed of the gospel of Christ, for it is the
power of God to salvation for everyone who believes
(Romans 1:16).

The gospel of God displays the wisdom of God, the power of God, the holiness of God, and the love of God. No wonder the devil has fought the gospel so hard and has tried to stop its spread throughout the world.

To the question "What do you think of the glorious gospel?" John Newton would respond:

Amazing grace! how sweet the sound,

That saved a wretch like me!

I once was lost, but now am found,

Was blind, but now I see.

Ask William Cowper, "What do you think of this glorious Gospel?" His answer:

There is a fountain filled with blood

Drawn from Immanuel's veins;

And sinners, plunged beneath that flood,

Lose all their guilty stains.

I say to Fanny Crosby, "You have been blind all your life. What do you think of the gospel?'" As she speaks the words of her immortal hymn, her face glows with an inward joy. Confidence is expressed in every word she recites:

Blessed assurance, Jesus is mine!

Oh, what a foretaste of glory divine!

Heir of salvation, purchase of God,

Born of His Spirit, washed in his blood.

· · · PRAYER · · ·

We are thankful, Father, for the power of the Holy Spirit to bring the redeeming message of the glorious gospel into our lives.

· · · TODAY'S THOUGHT · · ·

The Holy Spirit gives us the power to glow with the gospel, go with the gospel, and grow with the gospel.

—James A. Cross

THE HOLY SPIRIT CALLED ME

[The] Gospel did not come to you in word only, but also in
power, and in the Holy Spirit and in much assurance
(1 Thessalonians 1:5).

 I went to a cottage prayer meeting conducted by the Toonigh, Georgia, Church of God in September 1912. I was late, but who would notice? Something was urging me on. My sins seemed to overwhelm me, and I felt I would drop into hell.

A beautiful young girl was preaching under the anointing of the Holy Spirit, but I barely saw her. I could see nothing but my lost condition before God. When the invitation was given, I felt I must go to the altar! I had promised God before I got there, "If you will let me get to that prayer meeting, I will give my heart and life to you." And I did. I went back to the altar every time an invitation was given until I received the baptism in the Holy Spirit on February 2, 1913.

In November 1912 I attended the General Assembly. I caught the contagious optimism for the future of the Church of God that pervaded the meeting. Records show that the church had grown to the astonishing number of 3,056 members by this time.

By early spring 1914 I was conducting prayer meetings in locations 15 and 20 miles away. We sometimes continued for 10 days or more in a community, with meetings every night. I would read the Scriptures and talk, and men and women would start crying and kneel or fall. They would pray through to deliverance. Many times people would be sanctified and filled with the Holy Spirit. I did not consider myself a preacher, but in July 1916 I was approved as an evangelist by the officials of the Church of God.

On July 16, 1916, I was married to that beautiful young girl who was preaching the first night I went to the altar to seek God.

· · · PRAYER · · ·

Heavenly Father, I thank You for the reality of the Holy Spirit and for the Pentecostal experience!

· · · TODAY'S THOUGHT · · ·

Trust God's Word. If You are anointed by the Spirit and you deliver the Word, expect God to give results.

—M.P. Cross

THE BAPTISM IS FOR EVERY BELIEVER

*"For the promise is to you and to your children, and to all
who are afar off, as many as the Lord our God will call"*
(Acts 2:39).

As a young person I was told that the baptism in the Holy
Spirit with the evidence of speaking in tongues was not for
my generation. I was told that speaking in tongues was of
Satan.

In 1936 the Reverend C.J. Abbott came to my home town of
Chincoteague, Virginia, with the Pentecostal message. Through the
powerful ministry of this Church of God pioneer, 75 people received
the Holy Spirit baptism in this revival. I, at age 14, was one of them!

Before His ascension, Jesus commanded the disciples to stay at
Jerusalem until they received the Holy Spirit baptism. In obedience to
Jesus, they waited in prayer at Jerusalem until the Spirit came. They
were all filled with the Holy Spirit and began to speak with other
tongues as the Spirit enabled them to speak (Acts 2:4).

The young church, filled with the Holy Spirit, did not remain in the
Upper Room. On the Day of Pentecost 3,000 were added to the church
(Acts 2:41), and the church continued to grow. As the gospel was proclaimed, mighty miracles and healings occurred. In less than 100
years, Christians had evangelized all the Roman Empire and beyond to
the rest of the then-known world.

I have seen in the Church of God the same pattern of the Spirit's
presence and work that we read about in the Book of Acts. Some of
my fondest memories are of times when there were marvelous manifestations of the Holy Spirit. I have seen this in revivals in local churches,
in prayer conferences, in camp meetings, and in General Assemblies.

· · · PRAYER · · ·

*Lord, help us to never forget or forsake our Pentecostal heritage.
Cause the fire of Your Spirit to burn brighter in our lives and in our
churches than ever before.*

· · · TODAY'S THOUGHT · · ·

I am grateful to the Lord first of all—but I am also grateful to the
Church of God and to the Reverend C.J. Abbott—for bringing to me
the Pentecostal message of the baptism in the Holy Spirit.

—Raymond E. Crowley

LOVE NEVER FAILS

Love never fails (1 Corinthians 13:8).

I had been out on an all-night drinking spree with a buddy. Sitting alone in the car, waiting on my friend, I felt a strange wind and heard the Holy Spirit speak: "Frank, today is your last opportunity to be saved. If you harden your heart, you will never have another chance."

I drove through the countryside, weeping. Entering the little community of Granite Falls, North Carolina, I saw a Church of God sign. Turning into the drive, I wept as I walked to the parsonage door. My heart sank when the pastor was not at home. As I was leaving, he drove up. "I have to find God today," I told him. "Can you help me?"

Pastor Moody placed his arm around me, a total stranger, and walked me down the church aisle. Between 4 a.m. and 5 a.m. on Sunday, November 9, 1949, I gave the Lord what was left of a wasted life. He took me as I was and washed every sin away! The load I had carried for nearly 23 years was lifted! The following Sunday in my apartment, I was baptized in the Holy Ghost and called to preach.

Pastor Moody asked me to preach the next Sunday night. All week I prayed and read my Bible, but no message came. Nothing but fear. The time had come. It was Sunday night. I was a two-week old convert with no message. While the choir sang, I retreated to the church basement, where I prayed: "God, I believe You have called me to preach. If You'll give me a message and anoint me tonight, I'll never doubt Your call again."

Powerfully the Holy Spirit spoke to me, "Read 1 Corinthians 13." As I read the Scriptures, inspiration caused the words "Love never fails" to come alive. Unknown to me, those words were the exact words the Lord had given my wife, Kohatha, months earlier as she interceded for me. Divine love never fails—not then, not now, not ever!

· · · PRAYER · · ·

Dear God, forgive my impatience when I don't see my prayers answered immediately. Help me remember that Your love never fails.

· · · TODAY'S THOUGHT · · ·

God's call to serve is not based on education, family background, or financial status. Whom He calls, He equips, qualifies, and anoints for success.

—J. Frank Culpepper

MADE BY THE SPIRIT

*"The Spirit of God has made me, and the breath of the
Almighty gives me life"* (Job 33:4).

The early days of World War II found my fundamentalist
father and mother living near Baywood, Louisiana. During
the day while the men worked, my mother and her cousin
started reading the Bible and attending a ladies prayer meeting. As they read the Scriptures, they developed a desire to pray and
soon experienced the new birth.

One day while they were in prayer, an overwhelming move of the
Spirit filled them so full of joy that they "shouted all over the house."
Continuing to read the Scriptures and pray, these two ladies, who were
ignorant of the Pentecostal experience, read Acts 2:4. They asked, "Do
you suppose this is for us today?" Their conclusion was that they might
be filled, but in any case it wouldn't hurt to pray. So they began praying
for the Holy Spirit to fill them like He filled believers in Acts 2:4.

Their praying so irritated my father that he went off into the woods
until he assumed they were tired of praying. He returned home to find
Mother and her cousin "shouting and speaking in tongues." Soon my
dad found himself in the middle of it all.

For more than 53 years my family has experienced spiritual growth
in the Holy Spirit. For 33 years I have been filled with the Holy Spirit
and have ministered in the Church of God. With the speaker in Job I
can say, "The Spirit of God has made me, and the breath of the
Almighty gives me life."

· · · PRAYER · · ·

*Father in heaven, thank You for the comfort in Your guidance and
teachings. May Your Spirit continue to use us for Your glory and
honor. It is our desire to be sensitive enough to follow You as You lead
us through the paths of life that Your name might be glorified.*

· · · TODAY'S THOUGHT · · ·

The breath of God caused the first man to become a living soul.
Only the breath of God is sufficient to cause dead sinners to become
living spirits.

—Charles Duncan

HAS THE SPIRIT SPOKEN TO YOU?

While Peter thought about the vision, the Spirit said to him,
"Behold, three men are seeking you" (Acts 10:19).

Does the Holy Spirit speak to people today? Are there valid, scripturally based ways in which God communicates to the church today?

To the Bible-believing Christian, the answer to these questions is a resounding "Yes." The Holy Spirit does speak—sometimes through visions, sometimes through dreams, sometimes to our innermost spirit, and, yes, sometimes even audibly.

I have never had a vision such as the apostle had, and I have never heard the voice of God audibly. But I have had the Holy Spirit speak to my spirit so clearly and distinctly that I had no doubt it was the Spirit speaking to me.

Once I was in prayer about a course of action I should take when the Holy Spirit spoke to my inner being and said, "Read Romans 10:20." I had no idea what this scripture was about. I had asked the Lord to speak to me if He wanted me to make myself available for the work at the Home for Children. Church leaders who were in the process of making this appointment did not have me in mind and at that time knew nothing of my burden. When I read Romans 10:20, I knew the Spirit was telling me to make myself and my burden known to the church leaders. This scripture said, "I was found by those who did not seek me; I was made manifest to those who did not ask for Me."

The Holy Spirit had spoken to my spirit through the Word of God. God moved on my behalf, and I was appointed to the Home for Children. Even with so many voices clamoring to be heard, one can know when the voice of the Spirit speaks.

I am convinced that He most often speaks in a still, small voice, and we must be living near to Him to hear His voice.

· · · PRAYER · · ·

Holy Spirit, draw me near that I may hear Your still, small voice.
Grant me the grace and faith to obey You when You speak.

· · · TODAY'S THOUGHT · · ·

The Holy Spirit would speak to us more often if we were more desirous of hearing His voice and would prepare and condition our hearts to hear Him.

—Paul Duncan

June 6

I RECEIVED THE PROMISED BLESSING

*"For the promise is to you and to your children, and to all
who are afar off, as many as the Lord our God will call"*
(Acts 2:39).

Throughout the spring and early summer of 1939, Holy Spirit conviction gripped my life although we were not attending church at the time. I was the 12-year-old son of a farmer. That summer G.N. May conducted a revival at the Hudson Chapel, Mississippi, Church of God. The building had a tin roof and sawdust floors and some simple benches for pews.

When we had laid by the crops, I prevailed on my father to carry me and the family to the revival. For three months I had promised God if He would allow me to get back to church again, I would give my heart to Him. We arrived at the church, and I was thrilled to see a well-attended revival. The service started and Brother May got up to preach. I thought he would never get to the altar service, but he finally did. I almost ran to the altar, kneeling and crying out to God.

The saints came forward to pray for me and the other seekers, and the Holy Spirit fell on me. He lifted me up from a kneeling position to a standing position. I heard someone speaking in other tongues and soon discovered that the person was me. No language on earth can describe the love, joy, and peace that came into my heart that night. My world changed in a moment of time, and I have never been the same since.

· · · PRAYER · · ·

My Father, help me to live the life You wish for me so that I may always be filled by the love, joy, and peace of the Holy Spirit.

· · · TODAY'S THOUGHT · · ·

A person needs only to provide God with a heart made clean by the regenerating power of the Holy Spirit. He will keep it filled with His joy, love, and peace.

—H.L. Evans

174

THE VALUE OF THE HOLY SPIRIT

Do not cast me away from Your presence, and do not take
Your Holy Spirit from me (Psalm 51:11).

 From his youth, David had known and enjoyed the presence of God. That presence guided, protected, and sustained him in the disturbance and delays of life. So intimate was his walk with the Lord that God described David as a man after His own heart (Acts 13:22).

Now David had fallen into sin. There was a cloud upon his soul and a break in his relationship with God. He missed the sweetness of fellowship and unhindered communion with the Lord. He prayed for mercy, cleansing, purging, forgiveness, and change (Psalm 51:1, 2, 7, 9, 10).

In verse 11, however, he prayed a different prayer. Here he considered the dreadful prospect of living outside of God's presence and apart from the Holy Spirit. Perhaps he remembered miserable King Saul, from whom the Spirit of the Lord had departed. Perhaps he was brought face to face with the possibility of life without the Holy Spirit. So he cried out, "Do not cast me away from Your presence, and do not take Your Holy Spirit from me."

At this point David was willing to surrender anything, to pay any price to avoid the loss of the Holy Spirit. This declaration reveals the high esteem he had for the presence of God's Spirit in his life. Everything else was secondary to him.

· · · PRAYER · · ·

Dear God, You are my life; apart from You, I am nothing. I pray for Your presence in my life daily, that I will never grieve You.

· · · TODAY'S THOUGHT · · ·

The Holy Spirit has never failed me. He has been my comfort in sorrow and a friend in loneliness. He is the Helper!

—Donnie L. Fine

THE HOLY SPIRIT

"However, when He, the Spirit of truth, has come, He will guide you into all truth" (John 16:13).

In many years of ministering the gospel, I have had the Holy Spirit to move on me in different ways. Always, He knew what needed to be done and how to do it—if I would yield myself to Him. I was taught this important lesson by a Sunday school teacher when I was a young boy.

As a junior boy in the Eldorado, Illinois, Church of God, I had a teacher named Bertha Summers. She had been teaching boys my age for many years. You knew if God ever let angels live on earth, she was one of them. When she finished praying for our class, she didn't have a discipline problem! We knew someone else was in that room with her as she told us of God and His blessings.

People would call her and she would go and pray for them. She often told how the Holy Spirit would lead her in what to say and how to pray. She never felt she had the gift of healing, but she frequently felt led by the Holy Spirit to minister to the sick. Healing and miracles often resulted from her prayers. This teacher and her life of depending on the Holy Spirit to direct her left an impression on me I will never forget. She became even more precious to me because I married her daughter, Ruth, when I grew up.

Not only did I become a preacher, but many other boys in this church also became ministers. Houston Morehead, Ralph Day, Tommy Day, Estel Moore, and a host of others came from her class over the years. We often got together at the General Assembly and talked about how the Holy Spirit directed our lives into ministry. We all believed that the teaching of Sister Summers and the way the Holy Spirit used her to tell of His goodness got us started on a glorious walk with the Father.

· · · PRAYER · · ·

Thank You, Father, for the presence and power of the Holy Spirit to guide and keep us in the path and ministry You have chosen for us.

· · · TODAY'S THOUGHT · · ·

Each person is a special creation of God that is meant to develop into a unique individual dedicated to the purpose of God. This is accomplished by the Holy Spirit, who continues God's creative work in us.

—T.L. Forester

HE WILL DO IT AGAIN

"Then I will give them one heart, and I will put a new spirit
within them, and take the stony heart out of their flesh, and
give them a heart of flesh" (Ezekiel 11:19).

We cannot touch others for God until we have touched Him for ourselves. We must face the future in the power of the Holy Spirit who enables us to love what is not naturally lovable. In affirming our faith and determination, we believe that He who has delivered us will do it again.

In 1896 the Holy Spirit did not show up accidentally or casually. He came when those who were tired of cold, dead-and-dried services became thirsty. He also came through faith and obedience to God and His Word. Jesus said, "If anyone thirsts, let him come to Me and drink. He who believes in Me, as the Scripture has said, out of his heart will flow rivers of living water" (John 7:37, 38).

According to the Scripture, our outward man is renewed daily, but a new heart will come only to those who are convinced that without it they are helpless. By faith in the Holy Spirit we open the gateway to our heart, from which all the issues of life proceed. We are the temple of the Holy Spirit and the instrument or vehicle through which God shows His mercy and power to this generation.

With little or no religious training in childhood, I was, as Paul, a chief of sinners. My religious contact was a grandfather who was ordained for 80 years in another church. He told me not to have anything to do with the Church of God, which he called "tongue-talkers." However, while in Germany at a servicemen's center, I witnessed a life-changing experience. It was my first real introduction to the power of the Holy Spirit. I wanted the baptism in the Holy Spirit without speaking in tongues; but when I was baptized in the Spirit, He came talking.

· · · PRAYER · · ·

Father, thank You for filling me with the Holy Spirit. Use me to be
Your hands in reaching hurting people.

· · · TODAY'S THOUGHT · · ·

The acceptance I have found within the Church of God family has continually assisted me in overcoming an inbred fear of being a failure and a nobody.

—Tom Frye

SEIZING THE OPPORTUNITY

"And it shall come to pass afterward that I will pour out My
Spirit on all flesh; your sons and your daughters shall
prophesy, your old men shall dream dreams, your young
men shall see visions" (Joel 2:28).

Youth camp had been great that week. Many of the teenagers had experienced an unusual move of the Holy Spirit in their lives. Everyone had gone home except for a small group from the northern part of the state. Finally, their ride came and we watched them depart. Suddenly, the car turned around and came back. Kathy jumped out of the car and ran to us. "I am the only Christian in my school, but it is not going to be that way for long," she declared.

Later, while recording the Christian education reports in the state office, I noticed the reports from the small church where Kathy attended. The September report showed a good increase. The October report indicated a larger increase, and the November report showed the attendance had more than doubled.

I mentioned this to my husband, who was state youth and Christian education director, and we called the pastor to congratulate him on the growth of his church. The pastor asked, "Do you remember Kathy who attended the teen youth camp? When she returned home, she testified of how God had blessed her and poured out His Spirit on her during camp. She didn't stop with her testimony. She witnessed of God's power to her high school friends and brought them to church. Several accepted the Lord as Savior and began to win their families. Each week Kathy would witness and bring others to church. Through the power of the Holy Spirit, Kathy has caught a vision and has been the instrument of bringing revival to our church!"

God is using dedicated youth today to fulfill Joel's prophecy. Through the holy boldness that comes with the baptism in the Holy Spirit, they are catching the vision and seizing the opportunity to witness in the power of the Spirit.

· · · PRAYER · · ·

Dear Father, I pray that You will help our sons and daughters to
seize every opportunity to witness of Your Holy Spirit's power.

· · · TODAY'S THOUGHT · · ·

Power received when a believer is baptized in the Holy Spirit turns the person into an evangelist—be it male or female, young or old, learned or unlearned.

—Barbara Fulbright

A TRUE GUIDE

"He, the Spirit of truth . . . will guide you into all truth"
(John 16:12).

 The Holy Spirit came to me, personally, through the prayers and support of the many good people of my church. I experienced the infilling when I was a teenager. Since then the Holy Spirit has been many things to me.

One thing I learned early, the Spirit works as a guide. One experience that stands out in my memory happened while I was overseas. I was in one city waiting to go to a city of over a million people in another country. I had sent word of my arrival time and assumed that the missionary would meet me at the airport. Believing this, I felt no anxiety and was unaware that the missionary had never received word of my coming.

I was traveling alone. While waiting to leave, I saw a man coming towards me whom I had never seen. Not knowing whether he could speak English or not, I spoke to him in English. He not only knew English but spoke several other languages as well. He was a businessman from Paris and was traveling to the same city I was going to.

On arriving in the destination city, no one was there to meet me. The man whom I had met made provisions for me to get to a hotel. In the evening he came back and said that we would ride through the city and see if we could find the missionary. After traveling around with no success, he stopped in the center of the city, where multitudes of people were milling about. He opened the window and spoke to a group of people in their language. He then turned to me, smiling, and said, "These people are Church of God people. If you go with them, they will take you to the meeting place."

The missionary lived 70 miles away, but there was a meeting in the city, and the missionary's wife "just happened" to be there in the city at this time. Through her help we made connection with the missionary and I had one of the best experiences of my ministry.

· · · PRAYER · · ·

Holy Spirit, You are a true guide, a dependable guide, an eternal guide. Thank You for showing me the way and for preparing people ahead of time to fulfill Your purpose.

· · · TODAY'S THOUGHT · · ·

This experience was not something that happened by coincidence, it is a true example of the Holy Spirit knowing all the schedules.

—Garland M. Griffis

INTIMATE PRAYER

For he who speaks in a tongue does not speak to men but to God, for no one understands him; however, in the spirit he speaks mysteries (1 Corinthians 14:2).

Our regional council met in the council room, and before prayer one member after another related needs from his church. We knelt to pray.

At first the prayers were carefully ordered requests. The phrases were articulated so that an English professor could have been proud of them. Gradually the sounds changed. It was evident that we were sharing one another's burdens at a much more meaningful level.

Soon my own prayer became a flow of unknown syllables, clearly linguistic but unknown to me and to others in the room. The Holy Spirit had so taken over this prayer time, which was intended to last but a few minutes, that we could not get on with the business of our council meeting.

An hour later men began to get up from their places of prayer to move about in the room. We knew that special communion had been shared with God. We had indeed spoken with God. Prayers had been said in a "tongue" that He understood, although we did not.

Much later that day, I was in private conversation with one of the men who was going through a trying time. He shared with me the miracle of the presence of God through prayer in a tongue. The Holy Spirit had ministered to him during that time on a personal, intimate level that is impossible to comprehend.

Speaking to God is as personal and individual as speaking to another person. All relationships have some common qualities. But my relationship with God is special and unique. Praying and speaking to God in a "tongue," expressing feelings so intimate that they are mysterious even to me, makes that relationship real. God alone knows the secrets of my life and the depth of my feelings.

· · · PRAYER · · ·

Lord, lead us into intimate relationship with You.

· · · TODAY'S THOUGHT · · ·

"In other sciences, the instruments you use are things external to yourself (things like microscopes and telescopes); the instrument through which you see God is your whole self" (C.S. Lewis, in *Mere Christianity*).

—Alan O. Hathaway

COMMITTED TO DO HIS BIDDING

"And see, now I go bound in the spirit to Jerusalem, not know-
ing the things that will happen to me there" (Acts 20:22).

I am amazed by the continued prompting of the Spirit which drives an individual to fulfill the Lord's mandate. We are constantly being arrested by the Spirit to fulfill the Great Commission. The constrainment of being bound in the Spirit has been and is the most compelling event that keeps me preaching the gospel.

My parents often remind me about my call to ministry. A 6-year-old growing in the countryside of Jamaica, I would often preach to the animals, goats and dogs, while feeding them. Often, I would lay my hands on them, imitating the clergy I often saw in the local congregation. The sincerity with which I exercised this manifestation of divine intervention soon influenced older young men who frequented a community variety store next to our house.

These young men visited the store on a daily basis, purchasing rum to feed their appetite for alcohol. They sensed my child's passion for spiritual things. They also sensed a spiritual motivation which was "other worldly."

As I grew older and began to choose a vocation in life, I charted a professional course for myself which would not include the Christian ministry. I selected a teaching job instead of ministering the Word. I chose money over mission and profession over commitment. I thought I knew what was best for me, but I was not satisfied.

Then the Spirit bound me. His prompting to fulfill the Great Commission prevailed. The work I do for Christ today is done from a heart committed to Him.

· · · PRAYER · · ·

Father, we desire to be bound in the Spirit so that our lives will be
fully committed to You.

· · · TODAY'S THOUGHT · · ·

True happiness comes to every believer bound in the Spirit. Only then can we fulfill God's will for our lives.

—Joseph E. Jackson

JOYFUL WORSHIP IN THE HOLY SPIRIT

For we are the circumcision, who worship God in the Spirit,
rejoice in Christ Jesus, and have no confidence in the flesh
(Philippians 3:3).

The words *joy* and *rejoice* are mentioned at 14 times in Philippians. The book is often referred to as "the book of joy." Paul wrote this epistle from a Roman prison around A.D. 63-64. The congregations were experiencing trials, persecutions, and hardships because of their faith in Jesus. It is significant that a man in prison, writing to friends going through difficulties, chose joy as his theme. The heart of his message is that Christians can have joy regardless of circumstances. It is often during trying times that true joy is demonstrated in our lives.

While Stephen was being stoned, he saw Jesus standing at the Father's right hand. John was in prison on the Isle of Patmos when he saw Jesus in all His glory. The three Hebrew boys experienced the presence of the Fourth Man while in the fiery furnace. Moses heard the voice of God after 20 years on the back side of a desert.

To worship in fullness of joy, we must be filled with the Holy Spirit. The Spirit comes to live within us after the work of redemption has destroyed our confidence in the flesh. Paul was reminding his Jewish friends that physical cuts or marks are nothing more than mutilation, unless the heart is changed through faith in Christ Jesus. The beginning of true worship is a pure heart, clean hands, and a sanctified spirit.

In Philippians 4:4 the apostle admonished the believers, "Rejoice in the Lord always. Again I will say, rejoice!" When he thought about what was to come to him and what the Christians at Philippi faced, he was saying, "In spite of all these things, I still tell you to rejoice!" Our rejoicing must be independent of earthly circumstances. The source of the disciples' joy must be the continual presence of Christ. Walking with Him, there is eternal peace and joy.

· · · PRAYER · · ·

Dear Lord, continue to fill me with the Holy Spirit and power. May others see the fruit of the Spirit operating in my life. Please allow my cup of joy to always be full and running over.

· · · TODAY'S THOUGHT · · ·

Human happiness is dependent on what happens around us and is often fleeting. The joy of the Lord is constant and steadfast, strengthening every fiber and muscle of the spiritual man.

—Rodney Jeffords

THE SEAL OF THE HOLY SPIRIT

*... who also has sealed us and given us the Spirit in our
hearts as a deposit"* (2 Corinthians 1:22).

We are accustomed to identifications. As a young man I was given a social security number that would always be mine. On entering the military, one was given a serial number. The farmer puts a mark on his livestock. If a cow wanders into another pasture, the mark immediately identifies the owner.

Young people and adults want special labels in their clothing. Peers check labels to see which designer made the garment worn by friends. My wife says that ladies garments made by some designers are readily distinguishable, even from a distance. Men's fashions are also like this. Oxford of Chicago makes what may be the finest suits in the world. They are hand-tailored without synthetic fibers. Even the buttons are made of bone.

God puts His mark on His children. He wants men and women to be identified as His when others see them. He doesn't design synthetic people. His creations are individually tailored by the divine Creator. The world knows we are His disciples because we love one another. The Holy Spirit within us is His seal on us. God's people exhibit His holiness in their hearts, words, and actions. They have a confidence and a peace the world cannot understand. The Holy Spirit is the guarantee of eternal life.

When I was a junior boy, Martha Zimmerman, my Sunday school teacher, had the seal of the Holy Spirit on her life. As a result, she impacted many people. She did not have a college degree and probably could not give a theological definition of the Trinity. But she made biblical truth come alive under the inspiration of the Holy Spirit.

When she was 70 and had taught junior boys for 53 years, I asked her how she had taught for so long without a break. She said, "As a 17-year-old girl, I felt I could do a work for the Lord. I asked the Lord to help me find my place in the Kingdom." She had the seal of the Holy Spirit on her life.

· · · PRAYER · · ·

Father, I thank You for the seal of the Holy Spirit in my life. Help me to represent Your kingdom in this world. Keep my heart right and my experience fresh.

· · · TODAY'S THOUGHT · · ·

Since I have God's mark in me, I resolve to so live that I may impact others.

—James D. Jenkins

GOD AND MAN IN MINISTRY

How will the ministry of the Spirit not be more glorious?
(2 Corinthians 3:8).

In this one short verse the apostle contrasts the old and the new covenants, establishing the superiority of the new. This is the Rosetta stone of a theology of Pentecost. This is man doing his part and God doing His part in ministry.

There is no better illustration of ministry in the Spirit than the Damascus road experience of Saul of Tarsus. His response was, "Lord, what do You want me to do?" (Acts 9:6). Unless we who take the name of Christ respond in kind, our eternal destination will be uncertain. We cannot be like the philosophers of Mars Hill, who waited expectantly for God to reveal some new thing. Instead, we must go on to perfection since we are born again of imperishable seed (1 Peter 1:23). Let us show our confidence in the Word of Truth and earnestly covet the glorious ministry of the Spirit.

The entrance to this ministry may come through "What do You want me to do, Lord?" or "Mold me and make me after Thy will." It must always be accompanied by the biblical commitment to "present your bodies a living sacrifice, holy, acceptable to God, which is your reasonable service" (Romans 12:1). God expects reasonable service of us when He endues with power.

At a conference in February 1995, Dr. Harvey Cox said: "A man with a doctrine is no match for a man who has the indwelling Christ by the power of the Holy Spirit." Draw near to God with fear, meekness, and faith. Give yourself away prayerfully until He comes again.

· · · PRAYER · · ·

Father, grant me the strength and knowledge to fulfill the glorious ministry to which You have called me.

· · · TODAY'S THOUGHT · · ·

No calling is more noble, no ministry more glorious than that of serving Christ and lost humanity in the power of the Holy Spirit.

—Billy Jordan

HE SPEAKS PEACE

I shall not die, but live, and declare the works of the Lord
(Psalm 118:17).

"There isn't anything we can do to help."

"No, there isn't. He's dying, and I can't understand why he's still alive."

I heard these words when I came to after collapsing several hours earlier. A team of doctors stood at my bedside and though I was weak and critically ill, I was alert enough to realize they were talking about me. The doctors spoke openly about the massive brain aneurysm I had suffered, and they agreed there was no way I could survive. They had already given this news to my family.

They said that brain surgery was extremely risky, but to stand by and do nothing would be worse. So after telling these things to Betty, my wife, they scheduled me for brain surgery.

Early on the morning of the scheduled surgery, I was conscious and alert. The devil himself made a hospital visit and began telling me, "Well, this is it. This is how it's going to end. Where is God now? After all these years of preaching, the final chapter of your ministry and life is being written." The devil reminded me of the doctors' conversation about the hopelessness of my illness. He reminded me, too, that the doctors were experts in their fields, specialists who knew what they were talking about.

Before the devil could leave, the Holy Spirit entered. When He did, a calm filled the room. All fear, anxiety, and doubt left with the devil. The Holy Spirit spoke to me and called me by name: "Dave Lanier, I'm here to assure you that when the final chapter of your life is written, it will be by Me, not the devil. Trust in Me; I will see you through this."

And He did! I quickly recovered from the massive aneurysm and major surgery as the Holy Spirit provided the needed calm, comfort, and assurance day by day for me and my family. The Holy Spirit has continued to be our guide. I know that regardless of expert opinion or circumstances, my life is in His hands.

· · · PRAYER · · ·

Holy Spirit, thank You for giving calmness, peace, and assurance during the storms of life. Surely, You are a present help in time of trouble.

· · · TODAY'S THOUGHT · · ·

Through the presence of the Holy Spirit, we can count on peace in every situation.

—David Lanier

MISSION ACCOMPLISHED

So, being sent out by the Holy Spirit, they went down to
Seleucia, and from there they sailed to Cyprus (Acts 13:4).

The early church was praying and fasting when the Holy Spirit spoke to the gathering. The Spirit's message pertained to the mission of the church: God anoints people in order to send them into the world to present Jesus Christ. We note three things about the Holy Spirit through this scriptural account.

The Holy Spirit fills people. When the Holy Spirit spoke, He instructed, "Now separate to Me Barnabas and Saul for the work to which I have called them" (Acts 13:2). Both Barnabas and Saul were filled with the Holy Spirit. The account of Saul's infilling is found in Acts 9:17, 18, and Acts 11:24 says Barnabas was "full of the Holy Spirit."

The Holy Spirit sends people. God uses people by sending them into the world on God's mission. The work of the Spirit is to send, as Acts 13:4 reveals. He directed Saul and Barnabas to go to Seleucia and then to Cyprus.

The Holy Spirit empowers people. The power to accomplish the task is the key to fulfilling God's Great Commission: "Go into all the world and preach the gospel to every creature" (Mark 16:15). Jesus promised to empower the church (Acts 1:8). Supernatural strength is needed to go on God's mission. Because foes will be encountered, an enduement of power is essential.

The god of this world has blinded the minds of unbelievers so that they cannot believe or receive Jesus Christ (2 Corinthians 4:3, 4). The power of the Holy Spirit breaks through this barrier. He enlightens and sparks faith in the unbeliever by applying Holy Scripture. God, in infinite wisdom, gave the Holy Spirit to enable His servants to be more than conquerors in their task (Acts 13:44-49).

· · · PRAYER · · ·

My heavenly Father, in the name of Your Son, I ask You to fill me, to send me, and to empower me.

· · · TODAY'S THOUGHT · · ·

The mission can be accomplished, if we are willing to be part of it at any cost.

—Danny L. May

THE HOLY SPIRIT AND THE GOSPEL

For our gospel did not come to you in word only, but also in power, and in the Holy Spirit and in much assurance, as you know what kind of men we were among you for your sake (1 Thessalonians 1:5).

When the apostle Paul wrote this letter to the Christians at Thessalonica, he commended them for their work of faith, labor of love, and patience of hope. Then he recalled the circumstances in which he had at first proclaimed the gospel in Thessalonica. Despite the presence of religious and political turmoil, many of the Thessalonians believed the gospel. What happened at Thessalonica was like a revival in a riot. Paul recalled these facts to point out that the gospel is effective when it is preached with the power of the Holy Spirit, even in adverse circumstances.

According to Acts 17:1-9, Paul preached in the synagogue at Thessalonica on three consecutive Sabbath days, reasoning from the Scriptures. His message had three main points: (1) the Messiah had to suffer and die, (2) the Messiah was raised from the dead, and (3) Jesus of Nazareth was and is the Messiah. But Paul did more than just simply recite these facts. The truth of his preaching was confirmed by the power of the Holy Spirit, giving such assurance to his hearers that many of them trusted in Jesus as Messiah, Savior, and Lord.

The account in Acts tells that as a result of Paul's preaching at Thessalonica, some of the Jews believed and took a stand with Paul. In addition to these, a large number of God-fearing Gentiles believed, and many of the prominent women of the city were won to the faith.

But while many in Thessalonica embraced the gospel, at the same time a strong resistance to the gospel developed. The Jews who rejected Paul's preaching stirred up opposition to him from the lewd and base people of the city. They set the city in an uproar and created a riot in their attempt to stop Paul's ministry. However, they could not prevail against the mighty move of God's Spirit.

· · · PRAYER · · ·

Lord, give us preachers with the anointing of the Holy Spirit, that many may receive the gospel with joy and come to the full assurance of faith in Jesus Christ.

· · · TODAY'S THOUGHT · · ·

Preaching the gospel by the power of the Holy Spirit can still drive back the forces of evil and liberate people who are bound by sin.

—F.J. May

THE INDWELLING TEACHER

"But the Helper, the Holy Spirit, whom the Father will send in My name, He will teach you all things, and bring to your remembrance all things that I said to you" (John 14: 26).

The infilling of the Holy Spirit gives inspiration to boldly proclaim God's Word. It gives spiritual insight, overcoming power, and inner peace. It gives power to preach the message of salvation, deliverance, future events, and the marvelous works of God.

The Holy Spirit empowers and illumines God's ministers in all circumstances. He gives leadership abilities, provides encouragement, and brings comfort like no other. He is the source of all benefits from the throne of God.

Jesus told the disciples the Holy Spirit would relate to them as Teacher. They were representative of all who would come after them. What He was to them, He is the same to us also.

In the school of the Spirit, we need instruction just as children in school need the personal attention of teachers. Often, we are dull, we lack understanding, and we are slow to learn. But the Holy Spirit is faithful to "teach you all things, and to bring to your remembrance all things" that Christ has said to you.

The Holy Spirit comes to reveal the truth as manifested finally, personally, and objectively in Christ. We have no need for new truth, for in Christ dwells all the fullness of God.

The teaching ministry of the Holy Spirit continues the prophetic office of Christ. Jesus is the great Teacher, and the Holy Spirit is His representative on earth. As the Spirit recalled the message of Christ to the hearts of the disciples, so the Spirit also illumines our minds and brings to our remembrance the truth of Christ. As we ardently long for truth, the Holy Spirit brings the written Word alive in our hearts and minds, giving us guidance in both our physical and spiritual lives.

· · · PRAYER · · ·

Dear Lord, help me keep my heart in harmony with the Holy Spirit's instruction. Thank You, Holy Spirit, for using me.

· · · TODAY'S THOUGHT · · ·

The Holy Spirit is our ever-present Teacher. His instruction is without error. As we pray in the Spirit, He makes intercession for us—groaning for us to God in ways we cannot comprehend.

—Harry M. Miller, Sr.

A SLAVE SET FREE

*For the law of the Spirit of life in Christ Jesus has made me
free from the law of sin and death* (Romans 8:2).

There is no joy like the joy of deliverance. The person who
was a slave and has been emancipated is the person who
should be filled with gratitude and a spirit of celebration.

You may have serious problems—not enough money to pay
the bills, a sickness that is causing you a lot of concern, or a host of
other things. Stop and meditate on God's help to you. You were a
slave, a captive, imprisoned. Romans 7 describes it:

"But I see another law in my members, warring against the law of
my mind, and bringing me into captivity to the law of sin which is in
my members. O wretched man that I am! Who will deliver me from
this body of death?" (Romans 7:23, 24).

These verses sound the depths of human impotence and show the
tragic impossibility of human effort to strip off the poisoned garments
of the fallen nature.

Two tyrants held you captive: sin and death! Sin rules with a
strong hand. It dazzles, dominates, holds its prey captive, and will lead
to death. Knowledge is not enough to liberate; neither is enthusiasm
nor any other outward means sufficient.

Romans 8:2 is a shout of triumph! It is the greatest emancipation of
all times! The slave is set free! It took life to break the fetters of sin's
curse, but not just any life. It took regenerating life, resurrecting life.
Oh, what a day! Out of darkness into light! Out of the power of Satan
unto God!

Celebrate! Give thanks! A slave has been set free, and that slave
was you.

· · · PRAYER · · ·

*Precious Holy Spirit, help me to understand what is really important
in life.*

· · · TODAY'S THOUGHT · · ·

On a street corner a blind man played an accordion. One man in the
crowd heard the music and began crying uncontrollably. When asked
why the music affected him so, he replied, "It is not the music. It is the
man playing the music. You see, I once was blind, but now I can see.
I know the world of darkness that man is living in."

—John D. Nichols

OUR FAITHFUL HELPER

"And I will pray the Father, and He will give you another
Helper, that He may abide with you forever" (John 14:16).

My dad, H.G. Poitier, Sr., a minister of the Church of God for more than 60 years, found this passage of Scripture to be powerful in his life. Jesus gave this promise concerning the Holy Spirit in His last recorded discourse before His crucifixion. Jesus declared that the Spirit of truth is absolutely essential in fulfilling a life of Christian service. How we perceive and welcome the Holy Spirit will determine to what extent He will work through us.

The Christian life is enriched when we realize that dwelling within us is the divine ability to accomplish the tasks committed to our charge. The promised Comforter, or Helper, works inwardly and invisibly, converting and bringing into subjection man's attitude. As the Spirit of truth, the Holy Spirit will be true to you, not leading you astray. He will enlighten your mind with the knowledge of the truth. He will strengthen and confirm your belief of it, and He will increase your love for it.

The Holy Spirit has been sent to help us fulfill the ministry and mission of the church. Being filled with the Spirit is the beginning of a full Christian experience—not the end. As you grow in Him, He searches all things, even the deep things of God (1 Corinthians 2:10). Carnal minds cannot comprehend such heavenly and spiritual wisdom, but believers can know the deep truths through the Holy Spirit.

As our helper, advocate, and revelator, He reveals the deep things in the Word of God that we sometimes find difficult to understand. As glorifier, He exalts Christ and presents a Christ-centered gospel. As our equipper, He prepares us for the work of the ministry.

Let the church claim her heritage and spread the tidings wherever man is found. We are the children of God, and this assures us that we can enjoy all rights and privileges as heirs of God and joint heirs with Jesus Christ.

· · · PRAYER · · ·

O Holy Spirit, You know the hearts of all men. We acknowledge Your divine help that is all sufficient. We ask for Your wisdom and strength today and always.

· · · TODAY'S THOUGHT · · ·

"The Spirit also helps in our weaknesses. For we do not know what we should pray for as we ought, but the Spirit Himself makes intercession for us with groanings which cannot be uttered" (Romans 8:26).

—David L. Poitier

BAPTIZED IN THE HOLY GHOST

"The promise is to you and to your children, and to all who are afar off, as many as the Lord our God will call"
(Acts 2:39).

 On January 12, 1908, I prepared for Sunday school. A man baptized with the Holy Ghost and fire was to speak that day. I wondered how much different he would be from others. The sacredness seemed to increase as the moments galloped past.

On the way to Sunday school, I began to look over the congregation in my mind. Who would be the first to be baptized in the Holy Ghost? I knew it would take the best, most consecrated and spiritual of our sanctified brothers and sisters to receive such an experience. I singled them out one by one. I felt others in the congregation would enter right in and get the experience and be a help to me as pastor later on.

Sunday school was good and well attended. The song service ended, prayers were concluded, and the speaker was introduced. I sat on the platform in a chair. The speaker was going nicely, and I was catching every word. They were sacred to me. The atmosphere was exceedingly sacred.

At about 11:35, a flash struck me. Immediately, I was enshrouded with something I had never experienced. A spirit of weeping took possession of me. The chair disappeared and I was on the floor. I learned afterward that everyone in the house was affected by what was taking place on the platform. The minister closed the discourse and sat down. Other members I had picked out to be baptized in the Holy Ghost before myself were all present, but it was me the Holy Ghost fell on that day.

For three hours I was under the power and operated wholly by Him. From the time I fell to the floor to the time the power subsided and I came to myself, I never moved or said a word except by the power.

· · · PRAYER · · ·

Father, we thank You because the experience of our forefathers is also a contemporary experience today.

· · · TODAY'S THOUGHT · · ·

I appreciate my heritage and resolve to experience and share my faith as never before.

—A.J. Tomlinson

BEGOTTEN BY THE LOVE OF THE SPIRIT

Now I beg you, brethren, through the Lord Jesus Christ, and through the love of the Spirit, that you strive together with me in your prayers to God for me (Romans 15:30).

I had never been in anything like it. I couldn't understand it, but it was absolutely wonderful! For the first time, I had visited a Pentecostal revival meeting. Not quite 12 years old, reared in a traditional family with nominal religious upbringing, I was totally enchanted, enraptured, and enthralled by the special essence of the service.

Then I realized what made this so different: love! These people truly loved each other, and they loved God. It was evident when they greeted each other and when they sang or prayed. Love was present in the tears which overflowed the eyes of the minister speaking of the judgments of God.

When I went to the altar for prayer, I could not pray words born from a knowledge of the theology of salvation. Those terms were unknown to me, but I did know the deep urge and cry of my heart. I simply asked God to help me to love and be loved.

God honored my simple prayer with a marvelously profound experience which has sustained me more than 60 years. The love which flowed into me that night purged me from guilt, fear, and the prison of being alone.

Since then I have experienced many advances in my quest for a deeper life in the Holy Spirit. I have known His baptism and subsequent times of blessed refreshing. I have ministered in many countries of the world. I have written thousands of words that have been printed and distributed worldwide. I have taught in convocations and served as president of a seminary. But I have never been able to improve on the first lesson in Christian theology: Love is the essence of pure religion, for "God is love."

· · · PRAYER · · ·

Father, thank You for the gift of Your Holy Spirit, who fills us with sanctifying love and keeps us in a hostile world. Make Your Spirit flow from us to capture and comfort other lost and lonely people.

· · · TODAY'S THOUGHT · · ·

I resolve to love others as God through the Holy Spirit loves me.

—Lewis J. Willis

THE SPIRIT CAME IN!

*"Nevertheless I tell you the truth. It is to your advantage
that I go away; for if I do not go away, the Helper will not
come to you; but if I depart, I will send Him to you"*
(John 16:7).

In July 1930 my wife and I were living in Morgantown, Mississippi, where I was pastoring two Baptist churches as well as serving in the high school as principal and coach. While in this town, I was privileged to work among members of the Church of God.

In April 1933 the Church of God pastor, Brother W.F. Sharpe, scheduled a revival. On May 11 (with the revival continuing) the pastor asked me to lead a testimony session. I stood by the pulpit, tears running down my cheeks, unable to say anything, but in my heart I was saying, "Lord, what would you have me to do?" I made my way to the altar and prayed earnestly until 2:30 in the morning.

The devil made a pitch the next day that touched all the sensitive areas of my pride. But in my soul I was able to speak back to that evil force: "Go your way; I have found the truth, and I am determined to travel on with God."

When the invitation was given the next night, I made my way to the altar again. With tears, I pleaded earnestly with God. After a while, a peculiar feeling came over me. An overwhelming joy and power took complete charge of my mind, body, and soul. I knew of a certainty that I received the wonderful blessing of sanctification because I experienced joy that tongue cannot express.

I began to pray for the baptism in the Holy Spirit. The mighty power of the Holy Spirit came in and I began to speak in tongues, glorifying and praising Jesus. The Spirit had come in!

· · · PRAYER · · ·

Lord, help me to appreciate and value this wonderful gift of the Holy Spirit, who leads and guides us into all truth.

· · · TODAY'S THOUGHT · · ·

The Holy Spirit will come into our lives when we earnestly seek to be filled.

—R.R. Walker

THE HOLY SPIRIT WITH US

*"And I will pray the Father, and He will give you another
Helper, that He may abide with you forever"* (John 14:16).

 I received the gift of the baptism of the Holy Spirit with the evidence of speaking in other tongues on New Year's Day 1966. The Pentecostal experience made a real impact on my life because the Holy Spirit assured me of His presence as my . . .

- Comforter to console, heal, and restore (John 14:16)
- Advocate to mediate and intercede on my behalf (Romans 8:34)
- Teacher to help me know and understand the Word of truth (John 14:26; 1 Corinthians 2:10-14)
- Guide who leads the way for me (John 16:13)
- Helper in times of need (Romans 8:26)
- Source of power who gives me strength to live a victorious life, with authority to perform the ministry (Acts 1:8; Ephesians 6:12-18).

I depend on the Holy Spirit as my teacher for revelation for what I'm to teach and preach. In my studies and preparation I go to the Word of God while seeking the help of the Holy Spirit for the right message. Thank God for the revelation and inspiration of the Spirit in ministering His Word to meet the real needs of people.

On one occasion, when I was director of a Bible college with 78 students, God took away my appetite for three days. I could not understand why, but I obeyed God. After my three days of fasting and seeking God, a very big and serious disciplinary problem arose among my students. When it happened, I then knew the Holy Spirit had prepared me in advance for handling this delicate situation. God helped me to work it out smoothly.

· · · PRAYER · · ·

*Help us today, dear Lord, to listen to and heed the leading of the
Holy Spirit. We never go wrong when following His guidance.*

· · · TODAY'S THOUGHT · · ·

Many times we face problems that seem impossible to manage—they would be impossible without His aid and intervention—but we can always depend on the Holy Spirit if we will only give to Him a sensitive ear and an obedient heart.

—Marcos M. Ligero

TOUCHED BY HIS SPIRIT

"For the promise is to you and to your children, and to all who are afar off, as many as the Lord our God will call"
(Acts 2:39).

Entertainment in those days around the Boyd house was listening to the radio. Mom enjoyed religious programs, although the family did not attend church. One day in late fall 1949, when the flowers had lost their blooms and the trees were changing colors, she heard a fiery preacher proclaim the gospel. His message included conversion, but he also spoke about more than being saved. He referred to sanctification and being filled with the Holy Spirit. He indicated these experiences were for everyone.

His messages touched Mother, who listened daily. She said, "If that preacher ever comes to this area, I want to go to his services." A few weeks later he came to Greenville, North Carolina, for a tent revival.

Mother went to the altar the first night she attended and was gloriously saved, sanctified, and baptized in the Holy Spirit. Dad also received Christ and was filled with the Spirit. They began attending the Church of God on Broad Street in Greenville.

As the years passed, they led each member of the family to receive Christ and the fullness of His blessings. It was not uncommon for Mom to rejoice and speak in tongues when we offered thanks at the table. Needless to say, we waited reverently for Mom to get through. Sometimes the food was cold, but that didn't seem to matter.

In 1959 Dad answered the call to full-time ministry. Over the past 30 years nine members of my family have been involved in full-time ministry. To God be the glory!

Memories of attending church with my parents recall the happiness and joy they expressed. They made serving God so appealing. Someone asked Mom how she won all of her children to the Lord. She responded, "I just loved them into it."

And she did.

· · · PRAYER · · ·

My loving Lord, fill me with Your presence that I may affect others in a positive way.

· · · TODAY'S THOUGHT · · ·

If I can help somebody as I pass along, then my living will not be in vain.

—Kenneth R. Boyd

WHERE THE SPIRIT OF THE LORD IS

*Now the Lord is the Spirit; and where the Spirit of the Lord
is, there is liberty* (2 Corinthians 3:17).

God has created, by His Spirit, all things seen and unseen. He doesn't dwell in our worship centers or any building made by man. Our daily existence we owe to Him, for every gift great and small. Health, wealth and all other benefits are from and by Him. Our days, hours, and minutes are determined by Him. We cannot add one inch to our height or one minute to our lives.

As heat dispels cold and light dispels darkness, His Spirit dispels all that is not holy—sickness, bondage, habits, chaos, and all sin. I have been a personal witness to these and more. In 1987 I was hospitalized with hemorrhaging and severe pain in my head. The diagnosis was diabetes. After the Mableton Church of God and I fasted and prayed, in a regular church service, no emotional hype, no exciting song service, no dynamic preaching, just "pure God," a brother stood in the back of the church and simply said the word the Lord had already confirmed in my heart and mind: "God has healed you." I knew it to be true. After eight years of testing, I am still healed, because in His presence there is freedom and provision for all our needs.

How do we find that place where He is? We need look no farther than Jesus' own words of instruction. He is found in worship—not a place but an attitude. He is Spirit and seeks worshipers to worship Him in spirit and truth. If He is our Father, then as His child, we will have close fellowship with Him—a daily, abiding, ongoing relationship that is far more important than any other thing on earth.

··· PRAYER ···

Heavenly Father, let our lives glorify You on earth. Help our infirmities that we may magnify Your name to those we meet each day. Anoint us to speak the words that You would be pleased with and to live a life You find no fault in. Enable us through the Holy Spirit to know and to do the perfect will of God.

··· TODAY'S THOUGHT ···

God's love is limitless, His grace is measureless, and His power has no boundaries. Out of His infinite riches He constantly gives to us.

—Henry H. Kinsey, Sr.

CALLED BY THE HOLY SPIRIT

*As they ministered to the Lord and fasted, the Holy Spirit
said, "Now separate to Me Barnabas and Saul for the work
to which I have called them" (Acts 13:2).*

 The Church of God was having a revival in a neighboring village. A close relative urged me to attend. Out of politeness and a certain curiosity, but also with a strong inner opposition, I finally agreed to go.

The singing and the prayers of these people were totally different from what I had known. The gospel made a strong impact on me. Never before had I listened to a sermon as on this evening.

Then something else totally unexpected took place. The evangelist was calling for a decision for Christ. I had taken a seat in the very last row. From that position I was looking directly into the face of the evangelist. His face was shining in a manner I could not explain, and he was looking directly at me. He left the platform, walked through the aisle to the last row, and then stopped directly next to me. He placed his hand on my shoulder and said, "Young man, you are now at a point of decision in your life. Jesus is calling you to leave the street of sin and to come follow him." While he was saying this, a soft yet definitely recognizable stream went through my whole body—from head to foot. Never before had I had such an experience, and I would understand only later about this touch of the Holy Spirit.

I went home that evening with trembling knees. An inner fight started that lasted for months. Finally, unable to shake that touch of conviction, I capitulated and yielded to the King of kings, my Redeemer and my Lord. He accepted me, forgave my sins, and gave me peace, joy, and righteousness in the Holy Spirit.

About a year after my conversion, the Lord baptized me with the Holy Spirit. Within days of my Baptism I felt called to preach the gospel. Brother Herman Lauster visited me and, with hands on my shoulders, confirmed, "The Lord has called you to the preaching ministry."

· · · PRAYER · · ·

*Lord, give us grace to listen to Your Spirit and to obey You in all
that You direct every day of our lives.*

· · · TODAY'S THOUGHT · · ·

When God calls and commissions, there is no other route. But what a glorious privilege to serve the Master.

—Dieter L. Knospe

THE KEY TO PENTECOST

"So God, who knows the heart, acknowledged them, by giving them the Holy Spirit, just as He did to us" (Acts 15:8).

 Peter testified that God is the source of the baptism in the Holy Spirit. The key to Pentecost is God himself—today, on the Day of Pentecost (Acts 2), and when the baptism of the Holy Spirit came to the Gentiles for the first time (Acts 10).

When I received the baptism in the Holy Spirit at age 15, many caring believers stood by me. I grew up in a church in California where love and concern were abundant. In other churches in Hawaii, I saw peace and joy manifested by the believers. I was reared in a godly home with loving parents who nurtured me in security and wisdom.

However, the night I was baptized in the Holy Spirit, as much as my parents cared for me, the peace I felt then was a work of God himself. Though I was aware of others around me, it was the presence of God that overwhelmed me.

As I prayed and expressed my love to Him, suddenly I began speaking in an unknown tongue. God's overflowing Spirit filled me with His love and understanding. Like most youth I had many questions about life; but when God baptized me, He settled my heart.

I had heard my parents testify about "joy unspeakable." Now, I had experienced for myself the power of the Holy Spirit. The key to receiving the power of Pentecost was not in repeating what they had done but in receiving from the Lord himself.

The key to the power of Pentecost is the power giver, God, who is the source and center of Pentecost.

· · · PRAYER · · ·

O Lord, may I receive from You. Thank You for a Spirit-filled spouse, beautiful children, loving parents, and my brothers and sisters who have testified of Your work. My heart is stirred to feel Your very presence about which I have heard them speak. Draw me to Your side, by Your Spirit. Baptize me, know my heart, and bear witness of Your own work in me today.

· · · TODAY'S THOUGHT · · ·

Pentecost is given that the world might know that God is God—the gift giver, not our giftedness; the baptizer, not our baptism; and the fruit producer, not the fruit. He alone is to be praised.

—Oliver McMahan

THE GREATEST EXPERIENCE OF MY LIFE

So, being sent out by the Holy Spirit, they went down to
Seleucia, and from there they sailed to Cyprus (Acts 13:4).

I can never remember a time when I did not know and love God. My father, E.W. Williams, was a pioneer minister of the Church of God, and life was one continuous revival in Florida's swamplands. At 14 years of age, I knew God had called me to preach His Word. My years between 14 and 24 were spent resisting that call. I taught God-centered singing schools throughout Florida's churches and spent three years in biblical studies at Lee College.

In 1937, at the Florida Camp Meeting before 2,000 people, Zeno C. Tharp officiated at my wedding. I looked to the future and found my longing was for more of God and particularly to receive the Holy Spirit. On the fourth Sunday night in January of 1939, I went to the altar. Within 30 minutes, the Holy Spirit came in and changed my life forever.

The joy of that moment cannot be told with mere words. With many rejoicing saints, I went to the telephone to call my parents in North Carolina. My mother and father answered, but I could not speak; the Holy Spirit spoke for me and my parents understood. I had been baptized in the Holy Spirit and completely filled with joy.

When I returned home that night I spoke five words to my wife, "When you're ready, we'll go." She knew exactly what I meant, and within days we left home to tell the world about Jesus.

For 53 years of ministry, the Holy Ghost has continued to lead, guide, strengthen, and comfort me. He walks beside me, speaks through me, and keeps me close to Him each day. I give thanks to God for the infinite richness of His Son and the indwelling glory of the Holy Spirit!

· · · PRAYER · · ·

Thank You, Father, for placing me in Your ministry and for the precious opportunity to witness for You these many years. Please enable me to always be faithful.

· · · TODAY'S THOUGHT · · ·

Beyond eternal salvation, there is no greater gift or higher honor than to be chosen of God to be a worker with Him in His kingdom.

—Ralph E. Williams

REST OF MY SPIRIT

And He called to me, and spoke to me, saying, "See, those
who go toward the north country have given rest to My
Spirit in the north country" (Zechariah 6:8).

The "north country," where God's anger was abiding, was Babylon, the place to which God had banished sinful Israel. His anger was there because of the sins of Israel.

Who were "those" employed in the north country, giving rest to God's Spirit? They were holy angels, spirit creatures who gave strict obedience to God by executing His judgments and thus quieting the anger of His Spirit.

Is not the American nation ripe for divine judgment? Can we doubt that holy angels have been dispatched by God to carry out His judgments against this sinful nation to quiet the anger of His Spirit?

Our nation is plagued with idolatry, selfishness, sinful addictions, promiscuous sex, illegitimate births, crime, abortions, violence, and murder. The holy nature of God demands that He must judge a sinful nation. His Spirit cannot rest content in the face of unbridled sinfulness.

How can God's anger be quieted and His Spirit rested? Is there anything we can do? Yes! We can pray for peace and righteousness to prevail. And in the power of the Holy Spirit, we can wage spiritual warfare to take back what the Enemy has stolen.

We can also ask for wisdom from the Holy Spirit to be able to recognize where Satan has made inroads into our communities and resist Him. Then we can pray that those avenues of evil will be closed as people are convicted of their sins and brought to Christ.

Through prayer, under the anointing of the Holy Spirit, strongholds of evil can be pulled down in your community. You can make a difference!

· · · PRAYER · · ·

Heavenly Father, You have chosen prayer and intercession as means
to bring about Your purposes and execute justice and judgments on
earth. Help me to be among those who give rest to Your Spirit by pre-
vailing prayer and obedience to Your will in warring against evil.

· · · TODAY'S THOUGHT · · ·

It is said that one person's voice represents 100 people. Refuse to keep silent in the face of evil! Stand up for Christ and combat evil in the power of the Holy Spirit.

—Saundra K. Rose

SOVEREIGNLY BAPTIZED

And when they had prayed, the place where they were
assembled together was shaken; and they were all filled
with the Holy Spirit, and they spoke the word of God with
boldness (Acts 4:31).

I came from a hardworking, tenant farmer family in south Georgia, but none of us were Christians. Then, as my little 7-year-old brother lay on his deathbed, he called my father to his bedside and said, "Pa, I want to hear you pray one time before I die."

With tears in his eyes, Pa rose from the bedside and walked out to the porch. Sadly, he didn't know how to pray. A neighbor said to him, "Elisha, I'd go back in there and get on my knees beside that boy and pray if I said nothing but 'Lord, be merciful to me a sinner.'" And that's exactly what Pa did. He was gloriously saved at the bedside of a dying child and later became a Freewill Baptist preacher.

Shortly after Pa's conversion, I went with some friends to a brush arbor meeting. Suddenly, I found myself stretched out on my back in the sawdust shavings, praising God to the top of my voice! At that moment I told God that from that day on I was His and I would preach His gospel.

I began to preach wherever anyone would listen to an excited farm boy. But somehow, I knew there was more; there must be a deeper experience with God. We had never heard of the "Pentecostal experience."

Then S.J. Heath came to south Georgia preaching about this phenomenon. I was anxious to receive whatever was available from God.

I took an unsaved friend to a home prayer meeting, hoping he would be converted. My friend sat in a chair with all of us gathered around him, praying for his salvation. Suddenly, I began speaking in a strange language. I had been sovereignly baptized in the Holy Spirit!

· · · PRAYER · · ·

Lord God, help persons everywhere to know that it is their privilege
to be baptized in the Holy Spirit and to experience His enabling power.

· · · TODAY'S THOUGHT · · ·

Each Christian should prepare himself as well as possible for Christian service but should understand that the ultimate preparation is to be baptized in the Holy Spirit.

—Earl P. Paulk, Sr.

HOLY SPIRIT MINISTRY

And my speech and my preaching were not with persuasive
words of human wisdom, but in demonstration of the Spirit
and of power (1 Corinthians 2:4).

The power of God was falling in the revival services. The hall was packed. The windows were open and filled with people looking in. Many stood in the street—hungry hearts, seeking hearts, angry hearts, and curiosity seekers. I preached on "The Spirit-Filled Life" and many came to the altar. The power of God came down and some were mightily slain before God. Everyone in the mission hall was standing and the aisle was filled.

When I looked toward the door, there stood two cowboys, each holding a manila lariat stretched across the door. A big man stepped under the rope and came down the aisle, shoving people right and left as he forced his way through the crowd toward the front. People turned pale and things looked desperate. The man angrily looked at me, then at the seekers in the altar, and said as he pointed toward the seekers, "Do you call that gospel?" He shouted, "If you or the mayor don't stop this, I will. I am man enough to knock you down and drag you out of here, and I'll prove it to the crowd."

Margaret was sitting at the end of the altar and the power of God came upon her. She jumped to her feet, shouted "Glory to God," and began to spin like a top, whirling around so fast she could hardly be seen. When the man saw this, he turned and left. I thought the battle was over, but soon he returned. This time he meant business. He clinched his fist and took a swing at me to strike me. But in this immediate moment I felt the presence of God like a hedge of fire about me. All fear had disappeared and I felt perfectly secure and cared not what this man could do to me. His fist only came about halfway when God stopped him. He dropped his hand to his side; his eyes filled with fear. His mouth dropped open, and his face turned ashen white as he stared at me. Then he ran out of the building as fast as he could.

The revival continued; miracles were wrought in the name of Jesus. In special prayer meetings many received the Holy Spirit.

· · · PRAYER · · ·

Lord, thank You for the protecting presence of the Holy Spirit.

· · · TODAY'S THOUGHT · · ·

God will always vindicate His message and His messenger.

—Paul H. Walker

MAKING THE RIGHT CHOICES

For if you live according to the flesh you will die; but if by
the Spirit you put to death the deeds of the body, you will
live (Romans 8:13).

 The life of a Dr. Jekyll and Mr. Hyde may make a good story in the world of fiction, but in the real world this dual personality with its dual allegiance is not a desirable lifestyle. This was made clear by Jesus when He said man cannot serve two masters. If we attempt to serve two masters, there will be major conflict.

Many years ago, the apostle Paul wrote to the Christians in Rome and set forth a formula for achieving not only a single-purpose, fulfilling life but also a life which concludes in eternal happiness.

In today's world, even among Christians, there are many who are searching for the good life spoken of by both Christ and Paul. That which they are in search of is readily available through Christ Jesus, who gave Himself so that we might not only live but also live the abundant life. The apostle Paul in his letter to the church at Rome reiterated this concept when he said, "There is . . . no condemnation to those who are in Christ Jesus" (Romans 8:1).

As we survey the future, we need to understand that living according to sinful nature, living without Christ, will lead to an eternity apart from God. We also need to understand that a life dedicated to Christ is filled with love, hope, and assurance and in the end will lead to life with Christ in His heavenly kingdom.

As we make our choice let us hear the glorious words of our Savior: "Let not your heart be troubled; you believe in God, believe also in Me. In My Father's house are many mansions" (John 14:1, 2). He gave us further assurance when He said He was going to his Father and that He will return for all those who through the Spirit have put to death the misdeeds of the body.

· · · PRAYER · · ·

Father, help me to follow the leading of the Holy Spirit so that I may make the right choices in life.

· · · TODAY'S THOUGHT · · ·

We cannot serve two masters. We must choose Christ and allow Him to be the Lord of our life.

—Henry J. Smith

DEVELOPING THROUGH THE SPIRIT

For we through the Spirit eagerly wait for the hope of right-
eousness by faith (Galatians 5:5).

My father passed away when I was 4 years old. After his death, my mother and all her 10 children had to live with our aunts, uncles, and cousins in my grandfather's big house. We, however, were the only Christians. All the extended family members were Muslims.

In 1954 I attended a revival at the Bethel Church of God in Solo, Central Java. The preaching emphasized the fact that God's power had been given to the believer and that God's miracles were still a reality today. I became a regular visitor to the Bethel Church.

My thirst for the Lord's power became bigger. In 1956 I attended 10 days of prayer services. During one of these nightly services, God touched me in a special way. It was as if I were a ship sunk at sea. I was the ship and my praises to Him were the sea. "Sinking" in praises and worship, I began to speak in another language, expressing our Lord's greatness.

As the Spirit continued to work in my life, I realized that there was no other vocation or calling as beautiful as serving in the ministry of our Lord. After graduating from the Bethel School of Evangelism in Jakarta and the Baptist Theological Seminary in Semarang, Central Java, I have been privileged to work in many areas of ministry for the Church of God.

Dr. H.L. Senduk, our esteemed national overseer, was forced to retire because of a serious illness. I never dreamed I would be asked to take his position. I felt there were others who were better qualified, but this seemed to be the will of the church and of God. Therefore, under God and by the guidance and strength of the Holy Spirit, I dedicate myself to the task.

· · · PRAYER · · ·

Father, since You are building Your church and we are Your workers in the building of it, grant grace that we may be always under the direction of the Holy Spirit.

· · · TODAY'S THOUGHT · · ·

A person who is filled with the Spirit must always maintain a balance between the power of the Spirit, the gifts of the Spirit, and the fruit of the Spirit.

—Andres Soerjadi

GOD IS OUR HEALER

*To another faith by the same Spirit, to another gifts of heal-
ings by the same Spirit* (1 Corinthians 12:9).

Shortly after I received the baptism in the Holy Spirit in 1933,
I was in the hospital for several weeks with a heart problem.
One day a lady minister from Arkansas came to pray for me.
The doctors had told my parents that I did not have long to
live. The lady minister came into my room and said, "Brother Charles,
you do not know me. I've heard about you. God spoke to me to come
pray for you. Today is the day you will be healed." She prayed, and I
was healed.

As I testified about my healing, I was able to see many people
healed of many diseases. One of the most outstanding healings took
place during a tent revival that I held at Bastrop, Louisiana. A boy
about 10 years old came to the revival with his parents. He was crippled. His right leg was shorter than the left leg, and he wore a brace
from his waist to his foot. He wore a built-up shoe on his right foot.

The boy and his parents came through the prayer line. I believed
that the boy would walk out from under the tent healed. I asked the
parents if they would agree to remove the shoe and brace. They were
undecided, but their son was so sure he would be able to walk that they
agreed. After prayer the parents started taking the brace off the leg.
They untied the shoe and pulled it off the foot. The instant it was off,
the leg grew out as long as the other. The boy started walking, running, and jumping. He went all around the tent, showing and telling
the people what God did for him. When he went to school, everyone
was amazed to see him walking and playing without the brace. What a
great testimony he had! As far as I know, he never had to put that
brace on again.

· · · PRAYER · · ·

*Lord, Your power works mighty miracles in our lives when we put
our faith in You. Thank You for Your mighty healing power.*

· · · TODAY'S THOUGHT · · ·

What a wonderful God we serve! To Him be the glory and honor!
We can do all things through Jesus Christ our Lord.

—Charles Wesley Kendall

J u l y   8

RECEIVING THE PROMISE

"For the promise is to you and to your children, and to all who are afar off, as many as the Lord our God will call"
(Acts 2:39).

The promises of the Holy Spirit in the Word of God gripped my heart soon after my salvation. My heart began to cry for the anointing of the Holy Spirit. As I fasted and sought His face in prayer, the Lord Jesus Christ graciously baptized me in the Holy Spirit.

I can never forget the day I received the gift of the Holy Spirit with speaking in other tongues. Upon receiving the Spirit, I sensed a new energy to witness for the Lord. One day, while in prayer, a bright light filled my room and I was overwhelmed by the presence of the Holy Spirit. I heard the voice of the Lord saying, "My son, take My yoke upon you and follow Me." That assured me of His call upon my life, and I surrendered myself to the ministry. I can boldly testify to the marvelous workings of the Holy Spirit in my personal life and ministry.

Once I was proceeding to preach in a gospel meeting, but some folks who were against the ministry had set a few men in ambush. I knew nothing about that, but the Spirit of the Lord in me lifted up a standard against the Enemy. God opened my eyes, and I could see the guardian angels on both sides of me. I heard myself speaking in tongues and rebuking the Enemy. Thus, I was saved from those evil men.

There were times when I sensed the prompting of the Holy Spirit to go to a particular church, and upon arrival I would find either the pastor or the believers going through difficult times. If I had not obeyed the prompting of the Holy Spirit, I would have missed being a blessing to that church or that pastor. I am learning more and more to depend upon the guidance of the Holy Spirit. He has never failed me. By the help of the Holy Spirit, I have been able to plant 65 new churches in four years. I praise God for the abiding presence and power of the Holy Spirit.

··· PRAYER ···

Thank You, Father, for the abiding presence of Your Holy Spirit and for the protection You give to Your people.

··· TODAY'S THOUGHT ···

As long as the Holy Spirit directs us, we will always be overcomers.

—P. Wellesly Solomon

THE POURED-OUT SPIRIT

"'And I will not hide My face from them anymore; for I
shall have poured out My Spirit on the house of Israel,' says
the Lord God" (Ezekiel 39:29).

It is an awesome thing to think of a sovereign God turning His face toward mortal man! If this were not mind-boggling enough, add to this the thought of His Spirit being poured out upon mere human flesh. Throughout my life I have been privileged to be present in places where the Spirit of God was being poured out. One of my earliest memories as a child is of my father taking me to a church prayer meeting. I don't remember the particular need or circumstance that brought the church together. Maybe it was simply the desire to seek the face of God. Nevertheless, I remember being ushered into the presence of God through prayer, and I remember the Spirit of God being poured out upon those who came together for prayer.

This experience has been repeated countless times in my life over the past 40 years. I have been an eyewitness to the Spirit of God being poured out in revival services, camp meetings, General Assemblies, youth camps, and in my local church. Our heritage has a close kinship with the pouring out of the Spirit of God. If the Spirit of God was withheld from us, or if God turned His face from us, we would be weaker than Samson when his hair was shorn.

The prayer of the church today must be that God would never turn His face from us—that the Holy Spirit would always be welcome in our services and would lead us into the very presence of God.

The psalmist had an understanding of the need and value of the Lord turning His face toward His people. May the face of God never be turned from us, and may His Spirit continue to be poured out upon us.

· · · PRAYER · · ·

Heavenly Father, we need the Holy Spirit to be poured out upon us today more than ever before. Remove everything in my life that would hinder that flow, and may Your face never be turned from me.

· · · TODAY'S THOUGHT · · ·

It is vital for us to live in the constant flow of the poured-out Spirit of God.

—T. Dwight Spivey

THE DIVINE HELPER

Not by works of righteousness which we have done, but according to His mercy He saved us, through the washing of regeneration and renewing of the Holy Spirit (Titus 3:5).

On April 2, 1941, under the supervision of my state overseer, I stretched a tent in a small southern city in which there was no Pentecostal testimony. The crowds were large and enthusiastic and we were experiencing little or no opposition. However, one day, as I returned home from a funeral, my wife informed me that the police had been there three times and I was to meet the mayor and the chief of police in the mayor's office as soon as I returned, even if it was after office hours.

Realizing it was already after 5 o'clock, I left, praying this simple prayer: "Lord, I can't formulate an answer, for as yet I don't know the questions; but when they ask me the first question, I'm going to say the first thing that comes into my mind, trusting that the Holy Spirit prompted me."

Upon my arrival, the mayor and the chief of police met me with this complaint, "Your services are too long, and the praying is too loud." Then they asked me a direct question, "Is there anything we can do about it?" to which I replied, "I hope you don't think my answer curt or disrespectful, but I don't guess there's a thing you can do about it."

Their response was quick, "We can petition you out of town."

"I don't think so," I said. I named several churches in the city and added, "The same flag that flies over their churches flies over the little tent where I preach."

The mayor said, "Reverend, go back to your tent. Preach as long as you want. Get as many praying as loud as they want. And if anybody bothers you, I'll send every policeman on the force to guard you while you preach."

Today a beautiful church stands in that city as a result of those small beginnings.

· · · PRAYER · · ·

Lord, give us grace to walk always according to Your Word, leaning on the guidance of the Holy Spirit.

· · · TODAY'S THOUGHT · · ·

The same source that was available to me is available to all who trust Him.

—J. Frank Spivey

THE SPIRIT OF JOY AND VICTORY

Then Jesus, being filled with the Holy Spirit, returned from the Jordan and was led by the Spirit into the wilderness (Luke 4:1).

Jesus had just been baptized by John the Baptist. The heavens opened up and the Holy Spirit, in the form of a dove, descended upon Him. It would seem Jesus was now ready for His public ministry to begin. But no, besides the anointing with the Spirit, there must now be temptation by Satan.

Christ's temptation came in three phases. First, there was the temptation to satisfy human hunger. His appetite was innocent; He possessed the ability to gratify it. The sin, however, would lie in using divine power to satisfy His human needs. He overcame the temptation to use His divine power for selfish reasons by the power of the Holy Spirit.

The second temptation was in the realm of earthly ambition. It was a temptation to doubt the power of God, and to be disloyal to Him. Jesus replied to Satan, "You shall worship the Lord your God, and Him only you shall serve." Often we are tempted to compromise with evil to attain our goals. The tempter suggests that the end will justify the means. You can overcome the devil by the indwelling power of the Holy Spirit.

The last temptation was in the realm of intellectual curiosity. It suggested that He experience casting Himself from a great height and then, by the hands of angels, be kept from harm. This is the temptation to place oneself needlessly in a situation of moral peril and then expect to be delivered by God's miraculous power This is not faith, but presumption.

Jesus enjoyed sweet victory and remained full of the Spirit after the battle with Satan. As our perfect example in all things, Jesus would have us to daily live in the power of the fullness of the Holy Spirit and enjoy sweet victory.

· · · PRAYER · · ·

Our Father, fill me with the Spirit, and make me victorious in every trial and temptation so that I may bring glory to Your name.

· · · TODAY'S THOUGHT · · ·

Whenever we face the tempter, we can be assured of victory as we trust in God and live in the power of the fullness of the Holy Spirit.

—Leroy Spivey

VISION AND PROVIDENCE

"I will pour out My Spirit on all flesh; your sons and your daughters shall prophesy, your old men shall dream dreams, your young men shall see visions" (Joel 2: 28).

In the year 1914, when I was just 16 years of age, there was a great outpouring of the Spirit in Sumter County. I attended a tent revival where I received Christ as my personal Savior and had one of the most glorious experiences of my life. The Holy Spirit came upon me, and I began to speak with other tongues as the Spirit gave the utterance, at which time I was slain in the Spirit.

While lying flat on my back on the tent floor, God gave me a vision of a great abyss with smoke and flames coming forth. An awesome burden came upon me to go tell the gospel story. During the vision I was witnessing to hoards of people who were falling into this huge hole or pit. As a result of this great revival, the Church of God was organized in the small town where I lived—Bushnell, Florida. My parents and several of my relatives and even future in-laws were influenced by this great revival and became faithful members of the Church of God until their deaths.

Since God had called me to the ministry, I wanted to avail myself of all the training possible, so in 1921 I attended the Bible Training School in Cleveland, Tennessee. It was just a six-month school, but my wife and I were greatly blessed by what we had learned there.

Upon returning home to Bushnell from Cleveland, Tennessee, our first child, Marion Euverla, was born. As providence would have it, she became the wife of one of our general overseers, Ray H. Hughes. It is marvelous how God directs lives and brings about a chain of events which affect so many people all over the world.

Thank God for the outpouring of the Holy Spirit.

· · · PRAYER · · ·

Thank You, God, that through Your divine power and providence You bring to pass Your holy will for our lives. In Your eternal economy You have created us for Your glory and praise as we serve You and enjoy Your goodness, for which things we give honor to Your precious name.

· · · TODAY'S THOUGHT · · ·

Some things come into our lives that we neither appreciate nor understand. But as people of God who comprehend His providence, we know that in all things He is working for our good. His mercy and goodness follow us throughout our days, ushering us by His Spirit to joys beyond compare.

—U.D. Tidwell

OUR UNSEEN PRAYER PARTNER

*Likewise the Spirit also helps in our weaknesses. For we do
not know what we should pray for as we ought, but the
Spirit Himself makes intercession for us with groanings
which cannot be uttered* (Romans 8: 26).

Often the view of the Holy Spirit by some Pentecostals is narrow and shallow, the sum total of their perspective confined only to what they can see and feel. However, the work of the Holy Spirit in the life of the believer in reality may be more invisible than visible.

Recently, I heard someone tell how they planned to pray about a certain situation. From the start it was obvious that the person's mind was made up, wanting God to answer according to a preconceived notion. However, it was evident to me that this complicated situation needed an answer designed by God's wisdom, not man's.

In many of life's predicaments, the solution may be obvious, not requiring divine mediation. For other problems, however, knowing what approach to take can sometimes be difficult. On those occasions, complex issues must be trusted to the abiding presence of the Holy Spirit, the divine *Parakletos* (the One called alongside us) who actually becomes our divine helper in prayer.

What a marvelous thought! When the right words to God just won't come out and when we don't know the solution to problems, we can give our weakness over to the Holy Spirit who will say the right words and reveal solutions to us. So the uncertainty of times and the difficult circumstances of life should not discourage us.

Our prayer to God is not only a spiritual personality trait but is also an ongoing joy. Nevertheless, in those moments of despair and bewilderment when prayer seems to be so difficult, what a comfort to know that we need not worry. The Holy Spirit stands ready to plead our cause, and God, our heavenly Father, always stands ready to listen and to provide answers in life's most perplexing moments.

· · · PRAYER · · ·

*Father, we know that if we will commit our way to You, You will
surely bring it to pass. Help us to trust You more.*

· · · TODAY'S THOUGHT · · ·

There really is a friend who sticks closer than a brother. Turn your problems over to Him.

—Benjamin B. McGlamery

THE HOLY SPIRIT—A NECESSITY

"When He, the Spirit of truth, has come, He will guide you into all truth; for He will not speak on His own authority, but whatever He hears He will speak; and He will tell you things to come" (John 16:13).

Being raised in a non-Pentecostal home and church, I knew nothing of the baptism in the Holy Spirit. In the summer of 1957, I went to a Church of God revival and was asked if I had received the Holy Spirit. This placed a question in my mind: "Do I have all that God wants me to have, or is there more?"

Under a hickory tree in a cow pasture in Brooks County, Georgia, I told God that if there was more I wanted it. Now, I had heard that the Holy Spirit was a worked-up emotion, or it was illiterate people screaming until they were out of control. I did not want anything to do with that. However, I prayed, "God, if there is anything to this Holy Spirit, I want it. I will ask you for it one time. If I get it, great; if not, I'll forget it."

I went to the revival on Thursday night, saying that I would be the first to the altar. And I was. I simply said, "Lord, here I am." That is all I ever said before the Spirit fell on me, and I have never been the same. That was 38 years ago.

The Holy Spirit has been my Comforter, guide, and companion in my ministry, in the rearing of our children, in my home, and in every walk of my life. I feel the Holy Spirit is a must in everyone's Christian experience.

· · · PRAYER · · ·

Father in heaven, let Your Holy Spirit be with me in all that I do and say today. Guide me into the paths that You would have me go. Cleanse me from every unclean thing that would keep Your presence from me today. Lead me not into temptation, but deliver me by Your precious Holy Spirit.

· · · TODAY'S THOUGHT · · ·

It is urgent that both the clergy and laity tarry until they are filled daily with the Holy Spirit. He, the Holy Spirit, makes the difference!

—James D. Weaver

A WOMAN ANOINTED OF GOD

"The Spirit of the Lord God is upon Me, because the Lord has anointed Me to preach good tidings to the poor; He has sent Me to heal the brokenhearted, to proclaim liberty to the captives, and the opening of the prison to those who are bound" (Isaiah 61:1).

I first received Christ as a 9-year-old boy. However, by the age of 20 the once-fertile ground of my childhood had become hardened and unreceptive to the gospel. While on leave to the States from my overseas duty station, I attended revival services at a Pentecostal church in Pensacola, Florida. A young woman named Gretta Campbell was preaching.

She was a slight woman, rather soft-spoken, not at all what I was accustomed to in a preacher. But her words cut deep. Slowly my every defense was penetrated. By the end of the week, the soil that had only recently been too tightly packed to support life had been broken until it was soft and receptive to the seed of the Word and the life-giving touch of the Spirit.

What is it that sets one preacher above the others in effecting such change? Is it orthodoxy? Eloquence? Love for souls? While each of these is important, none of them is the critical factor in our text. It is the life-giving Spirit alone who enlivens, convicts of sin, and convinces of the power of Christ.

The anointing that brings healing, proclaims liberty, and opens prison doors is first an overflow in the life of the preacher and then an outflow into the lives of others. Gretta Campbell was a woman anointed by God to preach the gospel. As she told and retold the blessed story, the overflow of the Holy Spirit poured from her life into mine, and the consequences were eternal.

· · · PRAYER · · ·

Heavenly Father, let me ever be mindful of my dependence on Your anointing for the effectiveness of my ministry. Anoint me daily to this great task of preaching the gospel.

· · · TODAY'S THOUGHT · · ·

"If I am a man of God, endued with power from on High, souls will break down under my preaching; if I am not, nothing out of the ordinary will take place. Let this be the test for every preacher. By this we stand or fall" (Oswald J. Smith).

—Benny M. Turner

GOING STRAIGHT IN THE SPIRIT

*And each one went straight forward; they went wherever the
spirit wanted to go, and they did not turn when they went*
(Ezekiel 1:12).

Driving across the Mojave Desert, between Blythe and Indio,
California, at not quite 17 years of age, the highway was very
straight, but my life had taken some wrong turns. Brought up
in a Christian home, I was trying to be an atheist. Fatigue and
monotony that hot July night lulled me to sleep, resulting in a crash
with a large truck, a totaled car, and a severed left arm. Bleeding pro-
fusely, with no way to apply a tourniquet, it was a miracle that I
reached Coachella Valley Hospital in Indio alive over an hour later.
Not once did I think of calling upon God for help.

In Ezekiel's day God's people had taken some wrong turns also. In
fact, their sinful, rebellious ways had finally resulted in captivity in
Babylon. But God did not forget or abandon His people. The Lord
gave Ezekiel a vision of four angels who were sent from God's throne
in heavenly chariots to symbolize a message of hope in the midst of
despair. They "went straight forward . . . wherever the spirit wanted to
go, and they did not turn when they went." Heaven came to the rescue
through the Spirit to help God's people walk straight paths, be delivered
from captivity, and be restored to the fullness of the Promised Land

The Lord intervened by His Spirit in my life too. My father, mother,
uncle, and aunt had received the baptism in the Holy Spirit in February
1947 at the East Washington Church of God in Phoenix. As they,
together with Pastor and Sister Hurschel Diffie, were leaving the hospital room the second night, my mother said, "Bill, don't you believe that
God can heal you?" I coldly replied, "No." But through their prayers
afterward at the hotel and the prayers of many back home in Phoenix,
the Spirit broke through that unbelief and rebellion sometime after
midnight. Suddenly a brilliant light filled the room, and I knew when
Jesus touched and healed me. God's Spirit will intervene in your darkest hour and lead you from tortuous paths of sin to life in Christ.

· · · PRAYER · · ·

*Our precious Father, thank You for intervening to bring hope and
deliverance in the time of trouble. Help me to walk straight paths by
the Spirit. Wherever He goes, let me go too.*

· · · TODAY'S THOUGHT · · ·

We need the Spirit to walk straight paths and help others.

—Bill E. Watson

A GIFT OF THE HOLY SPIRIT

Now there are diversities of gifts, but the same Spirit
(1 Corinthians 12:4).

For a hundred years now, the Pentecostal movement has been under way. Manifestations of the Holy Spirit have caused Pentecostals to give much attention to studying what the Scriptures say about the gifts of the Holy Spirit. Most of the attention has been focused on the manifestations of the Spirit commonly referred to as the nine gifts of the Spirit. But how many of us ever think of ourselves as being gifts of the Holy Spirit?

There are many different gifts, but all are of the Holy Spirit. The Bible says that Christ gave to the church "some to be apostles, some prophets, some evangelists, and some pastors and teachers" (Ephesians 4:11). This indicates that those who are called of Christ and gifted by the Spirit to perform certain ministries in the church are, by virtue of their calling, gifts of Christ and of the Holy Spirit to the church.

The servant role we must fill in performing our ministries to the church can sometimes take a toll of our self-esteem. This happens because we see ourselves as less than Christ sees us. With humility and thanksgiving to God, let us remember that we are gifts of the Holy Spirit to the church to do whatever service Christ has called us to do. This is not to be a source of pride, but it should make us aware of what a privilege it is to be a servant of Christ to the church.

Over my lifetime I have received many gifts. I, like most people, value most the gifts given by the people I love the most and who love me the most. In the same way, because we love Christ and He loves us, we should value the fact that we are gifted and given by the Spirit to serve the church.

· · · PRAYER · · ·

Lord Jesus, I praise You for graciously calling me to be a minister of Your gospel. Help me to never take this calling lightly but, realizing my responsibility to Your Spirit and Your people, keep my character above reproach, not for my sake only but also for the sake of the gift I am to the church.

· · · TODAY'S THOUGHT · · ·

Christ is the perfect example of all the gifts of the Spirit. He was the greatest teacher and preacher, and His supreme gift was Himself to serve others.

—Bob Moore

MIRACULOUS PROOFS OF THE SPIRIT

And the multitudes with one accord heeded the things spoken
by Philip, hearing and seeing the miracles which he did
(Acts 8:6).

As long as I can remember I had an intense hunger for God.
As a child I went to the altar to seek the baptism in the Holy
Spirit every time an invitation was given. My father, M.P.
Cross, pastored in Detroit, Michigan, in the 1920s.

One day Sunday school superintendent Houston R. Morehead was
having a special day. My mother, knowing the church would be
crowded and I would go to the altar when an invitation was given, told
me to kneel at a little red chair at the front of the church. The superintendent came by and heard me praying, "God, I'm right here at this little red chair. I'm as close to the altar as my mother will let me get!"

In January 1931, at the age of 9, in a great revival which lasted more
than five months, I received this wonderful experience. My parents
returned from the 1930 General Assembly determined to have revival.
Services began before Thanksgiving with my mother, my father, and
Brother Morehead preaching. After six weeks, a spectacular outpouring
of the Spirit came. Infidels were saved, marvelous healings took place,
and the church experienced phenomenal growth.

Seeing miracles established in me an unshakable belief in
Pentecostal worship. With many others, I heard the organ play beautiful music and no one was at the keyboard. With an entire congregation
I once saw the ceiling of the church engulfed in flames which, like
those at the burning bush, did not consume the building.

One night my father, normally not an emotional preacher, would
speak a sentence and then speak in tongues. This went on throughout
the sermon. After the altar call some visitors asked my father in broken
English where he had learned such beautiful German. When he confessed he did not speak German, they replied, "Oh yes, everything you
said in English you translated into German."

· · · PRAYER · · ·

Father, help us to serve You with fervency and zeal. May the mira-
cle-working power of Pentecost engulf our churches with holy flame
and burn anew in our hearts.

· · · TODAY'S THOUGHT · · ·

I resolve to be completely submissive to the Holy Spirit in my life.

—Louis H. Cross

THE SECRET OF LIFE

"I will put My Spirit in you, and you shall live, and I will place you in your own land. Then you shall know that I, the Lord, have spoken it and performed it" (Ezekiel 37:14).

My son, Jordan, seems to know instinctively that he was made to live. He hates to go to sleep because he doesn't want to miss what's going on around him. In fact, he won't go to sleep unless ordered to do so or until he simply gives in to exhaustion.

The older we become, the more this enthusiasm for life slips away. There are physical causes, of course; we tire more easily the older we get and we are susceptible to energy-sapping maladies.

There is a form of life, however, that need not slip away, which can be ours regardless of age. It is the Spirit of life that transcends physical and emotional infirmities. Paul wrote in Romans, "But if the Spirit of Him who raised Jesus from the dead dwells in you, He who raised Christ from the dead will also give life to your mortal bodies through His Spirit who dwells in you" (8:11).

Oceanographer Jacques Cousteau tells the curious story of a European aquarium that ran short of seawater just before it received a shipment of saltwater invertebrates. Since the formula for saltwater is well known the curators manufactured some. But when the marine creatures were put in it, they soon died. Then, an inspiration! Some real seawater was added and the fragile creatures put in it lived.

This story implies that each of the trillions of drops that comprise the oceans has a life of its own and makes possible the incredible myriads of marine life. And when alive water is added to artifical water, life is restored.

When God's Spirit is put in man, dead in sin, He brings that lifeless man to life. The secret to life, the abundant life, is to be filled with the Spirit!

· · · PRAYER · · ·

Dear God, help me to live the abundant life. When I was dead in trespasses and sin, You brought life to my lifeless soul. I desire to walk with You every day. Fill my new life with Your Spirit.

· · · TODAY'S THOUGHT · · ·

The greatest discovery in life is Jesus Christ. Every day we live in Him, we discover anew the richness of His love for us.

—Gary Lewis

J u l y   2 0

GUIDED BY THE SPIRIT

*And a vision appeared to Paul in the night. A man of
Macedonia stood and pleaded with him, saying, "Come
over to Macedonia and help us"* (Acts 16:9).

Two instances of the Holy Spirit leading me personally stand out in my mind as I think back on the early days my wife, Gladys, and I shared in ministry of the gospel. In 1941 while conducting the business of overseer of Wisconsin, I began to feel an unsettledness within. I had not led one person to the Lord in weeks. Early one morning I said to Gladys, "I feel impressed to board a train and I'm not sure when I will return."

Finding a seat on the next train out, I began to talk with a young serviceman. I asked if he would like to join me for refeshments. The soldier ordered an alcoholic beverage and inquired about doing the same for me. I declined but then added that I knew of Living Water from which one would never thirst again. Right there, this young man came to know Jesus Christ as his Savior. I stepped off the train at the next station and returned home.

In the fall of 1944 Gladys and I attended the General Assembly in Birmingham, Alabama. I was approached by the World Missions Board to go to Jamaica. I gave them a firm answer in the negative. Still, I experienced an uncomfortable feeling.

As the last day of the convention arrived, Gladys prompted me to contact the Missions Board to express appreciation for the confidence they had placed in me by asking me to go to Jamaica. I made the phone call and heard the voice on the other end of the line exclaim, "David, we were just praying for the Lord to send someone who would be willing to go to Jamaica to build a Bible school."

Unknown to these men was a longtime desire of mine to begin schools for the training of Christian workers.   In November 1944, we moved to Kingston and established Bethel Bible College. It continues to fulfill its mission today.

· · · PRAYER · · ·

Great is Your faithfulness, Lord! I release my faith today and ask You to make it fruitful in witnessing and in responding to Your will to teach others.

· · · TODAY'S THOUGHT · · ·

God often places desires in our heart through the work of the Holy Spirit before He arranges the circumstances for their fulfillment.

—David Lemons

THE HOLY SPIRIT—GOD'S SEAL

And do not grieve the Holy Spirit of God, by whom you
were sealed for the day of redemption (Ehpesians 4:30).

 If you were to visit the city of Ephesus today, you would find a completely different geographical scene than when the apostle Paul sojourned there. Now it is completely land-locked and many miles from water; then it was a bustling sea-port.

One of the most important industries was lumbering. Great logs were floated down through the Black Sea and into the port at Ephesus. As logs were brought in, carpenters came to the bay and handpicked the logs they wanted. The next step was to put their mark on the chosen logs, pay a deposit, and then the logs might float in the water for months. It didn't matter how long, because the stamp plainly said, "This log belongs to the owner of this seal."

Just as the mark on the logs signified ownership, a mark has been placed on my life. Paul wrote, ". . . you were sealed for the day of redemption." Sealing refers to a mark of ownership, and I know the Holy Spirit, the third person of the Trinity, has put His seal on me.

With this seal on my life, I daily become more conscious of Paul's admonition to stop grieving the Holy Spirit. The Spirit of God is grieved when we walk carelessly. The Spirit of God is grieved when we do not walk in love. Instead, we are to use the power and authority of the Holy Spirit to put away the negatives in our lives like bitterness, wrath, anger, fanaticism, and ill feelings. Instead, we are to put on the positive. Be kind! Be tenderhearted toward others! Forgive one another as God for Christ's sake has forgiven us!

I am sealed, not with a visible sign, but with the hope that now resides in me. The Holy Spirit's presence in me is a sign that I belong to God. I am no longer my own; I have been bought with a price.

· · · P R A Y E R · · ·

Father, I thank You for the seal of the Holy Spirit. I know it repre-
sents a deposit on my inheritance. It is insurance, a guarantee, to let
me know that He will complete the process that You began in me and
will one day present me blameless before You.

· · · T O D A Y ' S   T H O U G H T · · ·

I am His and He is mine, and I long for the day of total redemption when He redeems our bodies at the resurrection of the church.

—Floyd H. Lawhon

REFLECT THE GLORY OF CHRIST

*But we all, with unveiled face, beholding as in a mirror the
glory of the Lord, are being transformed into the same
image from glory to glory, just as by the Spirit of the Lord*
(2 Corinthians 3:18).

Moses, the leader of Israel, was called of God to climb to the top of Mount Sinai to commune with God. When he came down from the mountain, Moses was so changed by being in God's presence that his face was shining. In fact, his face was shining so brightly that he had to put on a veil so the Israelites could bear to look in his direction. The apostle Paul, in writing to the Corinthians, referred to this incident in the life of Moses.

Paul, calling attention to the amazing transformation of Moses, said that if Moses' reception of the Law at the hands of God could so transform him, we who have received the gospel and the Holy Spirit should so much the more be transformed, so as to be like Christ.

The glory of the covenant God mediated through Moses faded away, but the glory of the new covenant, the covenant of grace by Christ, will never fade away.

Like Moses, we who believe in Christ and have His Holy Spirit dwelling in us are allowed to enter the presence of God. As by faith we behold the glory of God in the face of Jesus Christ, the Holy Spirit works a marvelous transformation in us. He makes us like Christ, so that we reflect the glory of Christ.

Sometimes our faces seem to shine from the glory of Christ's presence, and we rejoice and shout with victory. At other times our way is difficult and tears fall, but still the transformation continues. The Holy Spirit works incessantly to bring us to the full potential of likeness to Christ. Finally, hallelujah, the resurrection awaits us, and we shall see Christ as He is. Then we shall be like Him. But until then, we reflect His glory as we are transformed by the Holy Spirit.

· · · PRAYER · · ·

Lord, we pray that the Holy Spirit will continue to effect a complete metamorphosis in our lives. Change us, Lord, so that we will radiate Your glory and others will be able to see that we have been with You.

· · · TODAY'S THOUGHT · · ·

It is important to grow in our relationship with Christ. By degrees, as our relationship with Christ grows, we are changed more and more by the Holy Spirit into the likeness of Christ.

—Charles Lambert

IN THE SPIRIT

I was in the Spirit on the Lord's Day, and I heard behind me
a loud voice, as of a trumpet (Revelation 1:10).

These words of John constitute a central belief of Pentecostals: that is, that Christians should be "in the Spirit" in their worship and in their living. We sing about it, teach and preach it, and pray for it; but this state of being "in the Spirit" remains a mystery. Although we have the experience, it is difficult to describe or explain.

When John wrote, "I was in the Spirit," he gave expression to the overwhelming richness of his relationship with God. Nothing in the natural world can rival what it means to be in the Spirit.

Even his exile to a lonely windswept island in the Aegean Sea, could not deprive John of the presence of God. In the Spirit, John received visions of glorious and terrible things to come; all to come by the direction of the Sovereign God.

The early Christians knew about life in the Spirit and worship in the Spirit. The forebearers of our own denomination learned about life and worship in the Spirit. The experience set them on a new course. A movement was born—the Pentecostal Movement.

I remember well the testimony times in the church services when I was growing up. The pastor would go around the room giving each member an opportunity to testify. I testified and so did others of being in the Spirit, but I always felt the testimonies somehow fell short of really saying what we wanted to tell.

From a natural standpoint, John could have little hope for the future on that island of Patmos. But in the Spirit, he saw that there was limitless and endless hope for the people of God.

When we look at the world today, we may feel there is not much cause for hope. But in the Spirit, we find our purpose and hope in God.

· · · PRAYER · · ·

Father, help us to wait before You in worship, to experience what it means to be in the Spirit. Reveal to us by Your Spirit that sense of purpose and hope which belongs to all who are in the Spirit.

· · · TODAY'S THOUGHT · · ·

To be prepared for things that shall be hereafter, we need to have the rich experience of being in the Spirit.

—Darrell Smith

GOD LOOKS ON THE HEART

*But he is a Jew who is one inwardly, and circumcision is
that of the heart, in the Spirit, and not in the letter; whose
praise is not from men but from God* (Romans 2:29).

God's plan for salvation and redemption is found in the context of the 16 chapters in the Book of Romans. In Romans 2:29, Paul shows that circumcision was only profitable if the law was kept. If the law was broken, they were as uncircumcised as the Gentiles, for this was the sign of keeping the law of Moses. If Gentiles who were not circumcised in the flesh kept the law by nature, then in reality, they were the circumcised ones, for circumcision was a rite representing something spiritual—the purification of the heart. This is the equivalent of asking, "Of what value is a wedding ring if one is unfaithful to one's marriage partner? Of what value is circumcision? Of what value is church membership? Of what value is outward appearance and forms if the heart and life are not turned to God and walking in His Word and His way?"

Individuals cannot be considered Christians simply because they say they are—because of what they perform externally in the flesh. But a person is a Christian because of what they are inwardly in their relationship to Jesus Christ.

It is through the Holy Spirit in our lives that the Word of God comes alive so that we as Christians can be built up in its most holy faith and be preserved from worldly error. He also makes us progressively more holy in daily life, empowering us to obey God and overcome sin, giving us a pattern of holiness to follow, guiding us in it, and purifying our conscience to bear true witness.

· · · PRAYER · · ·

Our heavenly Father, I pray that You will fill us with Your Holy Spirit, which will empower and enable us to live a life of Christlikeness in heart and practice both in the church and in the world.

· · · TODAY'S THOUGHT · · ·

True Christianity is of the heart, wrought by the Spirit and not in outward performance. The believer's praise comes not from men but from God. Man looks on the outward appearance, but God looks on the heart.

—Donald M. Walker

THE HOLY SPIRIT AS TEACHER

"For the Holy Spirit will teach you in that very hour what you ought to say" (Luke 12:12).

Jesus taught His disciples that unrevealed truth would come to light with the coming of the Holy Spirit. As our teacher, the Holy Spirit will guide us into truth, beginning by drawing us to Christ himself, who is the Truth. The Spirit then empowers us to do the work of God's kingdom. Through the Holy Spirit's teaching, the Scriptures become a lamp to our feet and a light to our path. As the Holy Spirit and the Word are blended in us, the love of God and His truth permeate our lives. We see that the Word without the Spirit is dull and lifeless, dead. We see that the Scriptures come alive as the Spirit breathes on them through a sanctified vessel filled with the Spirit. The truth of Jesus Christ and of the Scriptures become a source of life and hope.

Like a compass that always points to the north, not to itself, the Holy Spirit in the life of the believer points toward Jesus Christ and His teachings, not toward the believer and his or her opinions. In so doing, Christ is glorified. Information imparted by the Holy Spirit is the teacher or the vehicle for communicating the information. Jesus Christ, the person of truth, remains the source of the knowledge and wisdom.

As the Holy Spirit teaches, His gift of comfort comes to us. This comfort is acquainted with the peace, serenity, and security of knowing the revealed Christ, the truth giver. Through the Spirit's teaching, the believer has the courage to speak, based on understanding and truth, not just on opinion. The believer is able to discern lies and false spirits and to respond with boldness and strength even in the most difficult hours. Because the Spirit and the Word have so permeated the believer's life, he or she can wait confidently, knowing that the Holy Spirit will reveal exactly what should be said in the very hour in which it is needed.

· · · PRAYER · · ·

O Holy Spirit, come and dwell with me. Guide me into the truth of Jesus Christ, that I may share Him with the world. Make my spirit teachable and pliable in Your hands, that I may serve the heavenly kingdom on earth today.

· · · TODAY'S THOUGHT · · ·

The Holy Spirit can teach and guide us into all truth so that we as believers are not deceived and can challenge the spirits of this age with Christ's love.

—Cecil B. Knight

GROWING SPIRIT-FILLED CHILDREN

But as for you, continue in the things which you have learned and been assured of, knowing from whom you have learned them, and that from childhood you have known the Holy Scriptures, which are able to make you wise for salvation through faith which is in Christ Jesus (2 Timothy 3:14, 15).

Parents play an important role in the spiritual development of children. Timothy was discipled by his mother Eunice and grandmother Lois (2 Timothy 1:5). The faith of Lois and Eunice had been communicated to Timothy while he was still a small child. Several years later his faith and commitment to Jesus Christ were a reflection of the faith and commitment of both his mother and grandmother. Our children will become thoroughly Pentecostal only if we as parents and church leaders commit ourselves to communicating our Spirit-filled faith and heritage to them.

Discipling children begins with example. Children need God-honoring examples of Spirit-filled living. They need to see their parents worship both corporately and privately. Children need to see Mom and Dad respond to the leading of the Holy Spirit in making daily decisions. They need to see family members demonstrating the fruit of the Spirit in everyday family life. Parents need to demonstrate their belief in spiritual gifts by discovering and deploying their gifts in meaningful ministry in the local church.

Spiritual instruction isn't confined to the Sunday school classroom. Life is filled with teachable moments. Parents must constantly be looking for opportunities to share their faith, whether worshiping, working, or relaxing.

Finally, prayer is essential. God promises a Spirit-filled experience to our children (Acts 2:39). As parents we need to cling to the promise of God. We need to pray daily that our children will give their heart to Jesus and be filled with the Holy Spirit from childhood. Example, instruction, and prayer are imperative to growing Spirit-filled children.

· · · PRAYER · · ·

God, let Your Holy Spirit work in our lives and help us to love, guide, and train our children.

· · · TODAY'S THOUGHT · · ·

As parents we need to be empowered by the Holy Spirit to set a godly example for our children, to instruct them in scriptural truth, and to intercede for their completeness in Christ.

—Chris Goins

THE HOLY SPIRIT, OUR INTERCESSOR

*Likewise the Spirit also helps in our weaknesses. For we do
not know what we should pray for as we ought, but the
Spirit Himself makes intercession for us with groanings
which cannot be uttered. Now He who searches the hearts
knows what the mind of the Spirit is, because He makes
intercession for the saints according to the will of God*
(Romans 8:26, 27).

How marvelous is the thought of the Holy Spirit making intercession for us to the Father. This is a divine plan of God that
cannot be explained with mere words. Those of us who
believe in and have experienced the Holy Spirit working in us
and for us accept this glorious blessing even when we do not understand it.

All of us at some time encounter circumstances in our lives that
seem overwhelming. The pain is so intense, the burden so heavy, and
the despair so deep that we cannot express our prayer with words. All
we can do is cry and groan in sorrow and helplessness. Yet we know
that the Holy Spirit is praying in us for a need that only He fully understands. He receives our burdens and sorrows and presents them as a
prayer before the throne of God. Our prayer is heard, accepted, and
answered in His name because the Spirit prays according to the will of
God.

Our spirit vibrates with His Spirit and we know God has heard us.
A release of peace and unexplained joy fills our hearts, even before the
answer comes. I have cried from the valley of despair that is filled
with dark clouds of depression and pain. I have reached the place
where tears and groans were the only communication I could give. I
have also known when the heaviness lifted as I sensed God receiving
my petitions. Praise enveloped me as I prayed in the Spirit. The
empowering manifestation of God's boundless love replaced the fear
and pain.

· · · PRAYER · · ·

*Search my heart, O God, and keep me in Your abiding presence.
Make me always aware of the gift of the Holy Spirit at work in my life.*

· · · TODAY'S THOUGHT · · ·

The kingdom of God is His Spirit at work in me!

—Pat Bradbury

FIGHTING THE GOOD FIGHT

*"You shall receive power when the Holy Spirit has come
upon you; and you shall be witnesses"* (Acts 1:8).

Daddy was a fighter. He fought in streets and bars. He fought
in the Golden Gloves boxing ring. Anywhere there was a
cause to defend, W. C. Gore was there, with or without his
boxing gloves, listening for the bell, ready to start slugging.

His street fighting and boxing career ended before I was born.
However, I heard him give his testimony many times of the night he
was converted. He went to church to fight the pastor because Mother
had accepted the Lord and become a faithful Christian, in spite of his
resistance. The preacher was his target, but the Holy Spirit interrupted
his plans.

Daddy was saved that night and emerged the victor, with an experience that took him into new arenas. As a soldier of the Cross, he began
fighting for the cause of Christ with a new armor—the Word of God
and a new message, the message of salvation.

The radical change in Daddy's lifestyle was a testimony to people in
Jacksonville, Alabama. His conversion was the talk of the town as he
became a living witness of the truth of Acts 1:8. His turnaround was as
visible and dramatic as that of the apostle Paul. Instead of fighting
against the church, he joined its ranks to "wage the good warfare"
(1 Timothy 1:18).

Daddy was not an educated man but this did not dampen his call.
Limited educational opportunities forced him to become a student of
the Word. With the Bible as his daily companion and the Holy Spirit
his teacher, Daddy embarked on a ministry that lasted years. When
Satan threw his punches, Daddy was ready with an uppercut of faith.

· · · PRAYER · · ·

*Thank You, Father, that through Your power we can fight a tri-
umphant fight.*

· · · TODAY'S THOUGHT · · ·

This truth became a reality in my dad's life: God always equips
those He calls.

—Wanda Griffith

July 29

COOPERATING WITH THE SPIRIT

Who has directed the Spirit of the Lord, or as His counselor has taught Him? (Isaiah 40:13).

The Holy Spirit baptized seekers at Shearer Schoolhouse in 1896, and an embryonic church became thoroughly and decidedly Pentecostal. This small fellowship became the Church of God and has grown into a worldwide Pentecostal denomination, girdling the globe with worship and witness.

This year is the centennial of that North Carolina event. The developments of the past 100 years were not planned or organized by an individual or group of individuals. The Pentecostal/Charismatic revival of the 20th century has occurred "'not by might nor by power, but by My Spirit,' says the Lord of hosts" (Zechariah 4:6). The Church of God was and is a vital part of this last-days move of the Holy Spirit.

The work of the Spirit in this century rivals the Book of Acts. Men and women have ignored persecutions, suffered injustices, and endured hardships to live a life of faith. They've demonstrated the power of God to an unbelieving world.

The Holy Spirit endues men and women with the same power today, but we are better equipped. We have more means and better methods. Communications and technology give us a distinct advantage. As God continues to pour out His Spirit, the church surges forward with new ways to worship, new methods of expansion, and new plans for growth.

The genuine work of God cannot be stopped. Humans cannot dictate the work of the sovereign Holy Spirit. After describing the awesome majesty of God, Isaiah asked rhetorically, "Who directs or gives order to the Holy Spirit? Who presumes to serve as counselor to God, instructing the Holy Spirit?" Israel could not understand the ways of God in the Captivity, and we cannot understand fully what God has done in the 20th-century Holy Spirit revival.

But we don't have to. We only have to believe and receive Him.

· · · PRAYER · · ·

Father, I exalt and hallow Your name by pledging my full cooperation with the Holy Spirit. Teach me to hear the voice of Jesus and obey. Make my life meaningful. In Jesus' name.

· · · TODAY'S THOUGHT · · ·

I resolve to participate fully in what the Holy Spirit is doing today.

—Marcus V. Hand

OVERPOWERED AND EMPOWERED

I say then: Walk in the Spirit, and you shall not fulfill the lust of the flesh (Galatians 5:16).

On Sunday, November 25, 1951, the Holy Spirit arrested me around 5:30 in the afternoon when I saw a friend for the first time in over two years. He had a Bible in his hand and said, "I am a Christian now." His words struck me deeply, and a feeling I had never known before came over me.

That night I followed my friend to church. No one seemed to see me on the back row, but the Holy Spirit saw me and said, "This is your night." The minister preached about the foolish virgins. As he preached, I could see everyone on the inside. The door was shut, and I was the only one outside.

At the altar call, I realized my time had come to get back on the inside. After kneeling for a few seconds, an extraordinary and supernatural presence of the Holy Spirit overwhelmed me. My newfound joy compelled me to write my family members and friends, inviting them to seek this experience.

In May 1952 I joined the Church of God, and five years later the Lord called me to preach. Since that time, I have served my church in every department of the local church. In 1972 I was appointed national overseer of the Bahamas and Turks and Caicos Islands.

Many dramatic experiences have happened during my ministry. Once, during a revival at the church I pastored in Nassau, we had fasted and prayed many weeks for a breakthrough. One night, a young man, under powerful conviction, ran from a bar across the street into the church. He fell at the altar and gave his heart to the Lord. The following night his wife and daughter gave their hearts to the Lord.

The Holy Spirit and His work are just as real today, and He will do the same for us again, if we will pay the price.

· · · PRAYER · · ·

Holy Spirit, You reprove the world of sin, righteousness, and judgment. Touch our hearts today and help us to renew our commitments to You.

· · · TODAY'S THOUGHT · · ·

Like the wind, you cannot see the Holy Spirit, but results boldly declare His presence and power.

—W.M. Johnson

THE HOLY SPIRIT, MY GUIDE

And they were all filled with the Holy Spirit and began to
speak with other tongues, as the Spirit gave them utterance
(Acts 2:4).

I was born into a Pentecostal family near Cluj-Napesa, Romania. My parents were simple people who served the Lord faithfully. At age 19 I made a public witness of faith in Jesus Christ. After being baptized in water, I felt a growing need for the "Promise of the Father." With a group of friends who had the same need, I prayed for the Holy Spirit. On August 21, 1975, we were baptized in the Holy Spirit during prayer.

I will never forget that day. Overwhelmed with a heavenly warmth, my heart filled with divine joy and a great love from God. I began to speak in other tongues. My whole being felt great delight. From that day I was highly motivated to serve the Lord.

I studied in the Polytechnic (school) in my hometown for a year; but in my heart I knew God had something special for me. In March 1976 I dreamed I got off the bus and a policeman in a white uniform stopped me and asked for identification. He marked my card and said, "Very soon you will go to a school for God."

There was no such school in Romania, but only months later the Pentecostal Seminary in Bucharest was approved. God blessed me during four years of study and at graduation I was offered a scholarship to the Church of God School of Theology. The government regime didn't allow studying in the U.S.A. at that time, so I couldn't go. The Holy Spirit helped me keep a pure heart and a good conscience.

From 1980-1989 I taught in the seminary in Bucharest. Simultaneously, I served as pastor of five churches in Cluj County. God gave me health, and I traveled twice a month by train the 500 kilometers between Cluj and Bucharest.

The atheistic regime officially abolished Pentecostal churches in Cluj in 1961. In January 1990 we reregistered more than 170 congregations! After more than five years the Apostolic Church of God in Romania has 440 churches.

· · · PRAYER · · ·

Lord, keep us in Your steadfast love and give us a fresh anointing of the Holy Spirit.

· · · TODAY'S THOUGHT · · ·

The best remembrances are bound up in our victorious suffering!

—Mesares Marinel

THE SAME BLESSING OF PENTECOST

"And as I began to speak, the Holy Spirit fell upon them, as upon us at the beginning" (Acts 11:15).

The Lord baptized me in the Holy Spirit on June 12, 1938. When I think about that unforgettable day, 57 years ago, I believe that I experienced the same blessing as the believers in the Upper Room in Jerusalem on the Day of Pentecost.

On the Day of Pentecost 120 believers were united. Then, when the time was fulfilled, they all were endued with power from heaven, as the Lord Jesus Christ had promised.

At the Isla Maciel Church in Buenos Aires, Argentina, our unity was similar to that of the early church. We were in a revival of teaching, preaching, and seeking the Pentecostal experience. Every day at the end of each church service, the preacher gave a special invitation for those who wanted to pray for the baptism in the Holy Spirit. About 80 to 100 people crowded the altar each service. Many people were receiving the Pentecostal experience, and I became really concerned because I was not one of them.

Then, I remember that day when the Lord was pouring out His blessing, and I was there in the midst of the flowing. I said, "Lord, here I am. I surrender all my life to You. Use me as You will," and the Lord baptized me in the Holy Spirit.

On that day, a complete change happened in my life. I felt as if I were walking on the clouds with a new strength and a strong desire to serve the Lord. Most of all I wanted to do anything to please my Savior, so since that day I have dedicated everything to His glory.

· · · PRAYER · · ·

I thank You, Lord that your truth endures to all generations. The same blessing You poured out on the Day of Pentecost is for all believers today. Thank You for Your power that You still pour out on all flesh around the world.

· · · TODAY'S THOUGHT · · ·

The early constituency of the Isla Maciel Church of God in Buenos Aires, Argentina, was mainly European and predominantly Italian immigrants and their descendants. The church was founded by Marcos Mazzucco, this writer's father. The congregation united with the Church of God in 1940. Much of the work of the Church of God in Argentina today can be traced to the Spirit-empowered ministry of Mazzucco.

—Mario H. Mazzucco

JOY IN AFFLICTIONS

You became followers of us and of the Lord, having received the word in much affliction, with joy of the Holy Spirit (1 Thessalonians 1:6).

We have many blessings of the Holy Spirit, and joy is one of them. Like the Thessalonians, even in times of trouble and suffering we can have "joy of the Holy Spirit."

We cannot afford to allow the troubles of life to keep us from having the joy of the Holy Spirit. Instead of focusing on our troubles, we must focus on the fact that the Comforter, the Holy Spirit, is present with us in our troubles. Jesus promised that He would not leave us comfortless, or as orphans (John 14:18), and He keeps His promises. He sent the Holy Spirit to be our Comforter, our Helper, in times of trouble and suffering.

A woman whose husband had died was left alone with no one to comfort her. She came to the church where I served as pastor, hoping to find some comfort in her grief and loneliness. She was not accustomed to Pentecostal worship, but she kept coming to the services, observing the fact that the members of our congregation had the joy of the Holy Spirit. One Sunday morning while I was preaching, she raised her hands and began praising the Lord. As she was praising the Lord, she was filled with the Holy Spirit and began to speak with other tongues. She found the comfort she had been seeking in the joy of the Holy Spirit.

Though we have received the gift of the Holy Spirit, sometimes the troubles of life can become so intense that they seem to sap our joy. Then, as we seek the Lord in prayer and praise, a spiritual refreshing comes and our joy in the Holy Spirit is renewed.

In times of trouble we must not stop praising the Lord and trusting Him. Never be ashamed to thank and praise the Lord for His goodness. In the midst of affliction the joy of the Holy Spirit comes to those who worship the Lord. When the joy of the Holy Spirit comes, it is as natural for a Christian to praise the Lord as it is for him to breathe.

· · · PRAYER · · ·

God, allow me to have the joy of the Holy Spirit. Make me to appreciate knowing You as my constant companion, Savior, and Lord.

· · · TODAY'S THOUGHT · · ·

The Holy Spirit is always present with us and in us to give us joy in the Lord.

—P. H. McCam

August 3

ARE YOU LISTENING

"He who has an ear, let him hear what the Spirit says to the churches. To him who overcomes I will give to eat from the tree of life, which is in the midst of the Paradise of God"
(Revelation 2:7).

Sometime ago my wife, Marilyn, was concerned about my hearing. She was convinced that something was wrong. It seemed that I was not hearing her as she would attempt to communicate with me unless she spoke louder than she felt was necessary. A physician examined my hearing and said there was nothing wrong. My wife's question was, "Why isn't he hearing me?" The physician's response was, "Perhaps he is preoccupied with other things."

It is possible for Christians to get preoccupied with other matters and fail to hear what the Spirit is saying to us. What the Spirit is saying is important; it is important to us as individuals and as a church collectively. In Matthew, Mark, and Luke, our Lord Jesus said, "He who has ears to hear, let him hear!" The Spirit wants to give guidance for our worship, witness, and work. He desires to give us direction, to guide us in the right paths, and to influence us to make right decisions. We need to hear instructions from Him. In doing so, we will be recipients of many blessings and delivered from pitfalls.

Spiritual battles are won or lost as a result of our listening or our failure to listen to what the Spirit has to say. Renewal and restoration depends on our listening to the Spirit. To be an overcomer and to eat of the Tree of Life is worth everything to us. Those who will listen to the Spirit will have access to the Tree of Life.

· · · PRAYER · · ·

Lord Jesus, I desire to give You my all. Help me always to be attentive to Your voice and hear what You say to me. I promise that I will listen for You to speak to my heart. I want to know Your will for my life.

· · · TODAY'S THOUGHT · · ·

"The Lord came and stood and called as at other times, 'Samuel! Samuel!' And Samuel answered, 'Speak, for Your servant hears'" (1 Samuel 3:10). Let us be sensitive to the voice of God and say with Samuel, "Speak, Lord, I am listening."

—David L. Meadows

August 4

HOLY SPIRIT, TEACH ME WHAT TO SAY

"The Holy Spirit will teach you in that very hour what you ought to say" (Luke 12:12).

In 1982 I was blessed with a 14-day tour. It was exciting to visit Rome, Israel, Egypt, and Africa. The joy I felt was almost uncontrollable.

En route from Cairo, Egypt, to Kenya, I met two Muslims who were returning from Egypt, and I started witnessing to them. Much to my surprise, they challenged me. I wondered what I had gotten myself into. I quoted scriptures. I tried the Evangelism Breakthrough method. I attempted to reason with them. It was to no avail. These issues and others came up: Who was the promised Son? Who really was offered by Abraham on the altar—Ishmael or Isaac? Which religion is right—Christianity or Muslim? Who is our hope—Jesus or Mohammed? Who is God?

Frustrated from listening to these two Muslims attempt to dismantle my faith, I remembered the words of Jesus: "The Holy Spirit will teach you in that very hour what you ought to say" (Luke 12:12). When they said that Allah and his prophet, Muhammad, were "the way" and that Jesus was just a good man and a prophet, I was offended. At that moment the Holy Spirit inspired me.

"Where is Prophet Muhammad? Since he is dead and buried, where is his grave?" They gave me their answer. I felt empowered with a supernatural response: "I've got news for you. If you find the grave of Jesus, you will find it empty. Jesus arose. He did what Prophet Muhammad did not do and cannot do. He conquered death. Jesus is alive. He was seen by many witnesses and He's presently living in my heart and spirit. You have a dead person representing your religion; I have a living Lord representing my faith."

The Muslims were baffled. In fact, when we arrived in Kenya, they invited me to share my faith with their families.

· · · PRAYER · · ·

Father, thank You for the Holy Spirit who inspires us to respond to inquiries about our faith in the Lord Jesus Christ. Enable us to always give an answer for the hope we have in You.

· · · TODAY'S THOUGHT · · ·

In our Christian pilgrimage when we are challenged about our faith, the Holy Spirit will teach us what to say.

—Quan L. Miller

DIRECTED BY THE SPIRIT

Then the Spirit said to Philip, "Go near and overtake this chariot" (Acts 8:29).

My wife and I were in the city of Antofagasta, Chile, establishing a new church, and many people had been saved. While shopping one day, we heard a baby crying in a house. The Holy Spirit impressed us to go to the house. We found a lady in great need and asked her why the baby was crying. She said the child had been sick for days and doctors said her son could not live. She accepted our offer to pray for her baby and accepted Christ as her Savior.

The next day she and her healed son came to our church. For many years now, the Labbe family and their son have been members of the Church of God.

In the city of Necochea, in southern Argentina, Pastor Martin Ponce was reading his Bible. The Holy Spirit told him to get in his car, parked on the street in front of his house. The Spirit then directed him to drive across the city to where the street ended. There the Holy Spirit spoke to him again, telling him to turn left. After driving several blocks, the Holy Spirit told him to stop. He was then directed to go to the door of a house, knock on the door, and say to whoever answered that the Lord had sent him. The person who answered the door was surprised, but informed Pastor Ponce that they had been asking God to send someone to pray for their dying child. When the pastor prayed, the boy was completely healed. The whole family gave their hearts to the Lord.

When we first arrived in Guatemala, we found that most third-generation Pentecostals in the East Territory had not received the baptism in the Holy Spirit. We felt led of the Spirit to strongly emphasize the baptism in the Spirit in all church meetings. After a year we began to see the fruit of this endeavor; sometimes as many as 600 people per month were being baptized in the Holy Spirit.

· · · PRAYER · · ·

Thank You, Father, for the leading of the Holy Spirit. Continue to direct us by Your Spirit into effective ministry for the glory of Jesus Christ.

· · · TODAY'S THOUGHT · · ·

If we have a mind to listen and a heart to do His will, the Holy Spirit will give us direction.

—Jose G. Minay

IN THE FORM OF A DOVE

Jesus, when He had been baptized, came up immediately
from the water; and behold, the heavens were opened to
Him, and He saw the Spirit of God descending like a dove
and alighting upon Him (Matthew 3:16).

All four Gospels describe the descent of the dove during the baptism of Jesus. In the Old Testament the dove is considered ceremonially clean, and its nature and habits reveal this. The dove is selective in its diet, swift in flight, has beautiful feathers, has a sociable way of life, and is monogamous in mating practices. The following characteristics of the dove have special meaning in understanding the ministry of the Holy Spirit: gentleness, tenderness, grace, innocence, mildness, peacefulness, patience, and faithfulness.

The Holy Spirit descended on Christ to empower Him for His extraordinary mission and for His ministry among people. Jesus' ministry is connected to the symbolism of the dove. Jesus, the Son of God, is meek and gentle and brings salvation to those who turn to Him.

The presence of the Holy Spirit in the life of the believer is of great importance. The presence of the Holy Spirit assures us of God's constant care and the fulfillment of His promises. When the Holy Spirit comes, He brings comfort, strength, and peace.

The pressure we live under today is intense. The demands, the pace, the irritations, and the many conflicts of living prove almost too much for us to overcome. Whether it is strength, peace, or comfort we need, the Holy Spirit will come just as we need Him. The Dove does not delay in descending; He comes at the critical point, at the moment of need.

· · · PRAYER · · ·

Heavenly Father, let us be a dwelling place for the heavenly Dove.
Holy Spirit, use Your gentleness, peacefulness, and comfort to assure
us that we belong to God today and forever.

· · · TODAY'S THOUGHT · · ·

The same Spirit that descended on Christ is available for the believer today.

—Carlos S. Moran

August 7

THE SPIRIT OF WISDOM

*That the God of our Lord Jesus Christ, the Father of glory,
may give to you the spirit of wisdom and revelation in the
knowledge of Him* (Ephesians 1:17).

Mother suffered for years with rheumatoid arthritis. On March 19, 1995, this servant of God traded her cross for a crown. But before she became so ill with this terrible affliction, she loved to serve others. She served others with the spirit of wisdom and revelation in the knowledge of God.

As a child I would come into the house from playing outside and find my mother in the back bedroom. The door would be closed, and she would be on her knees in prayer. She was crying out to God for His blessings of the Spirit to flow though her. She wanted to be a servant.

I now understand why I could never fool my mom. There were times I was not totally honest when she asked me about things I was involved in. She was always able to look right into my heart and know that I was not being truthful with her. I know now it was the spirit of wisdom and revelation in the knowledge of Him that gave her this great insight. Ephesians 1:17 should be our prayer.

Paul said in Philippians 3:10, "That I may know Him and the power of His resurrection, and the fellowship of His sufferings." Many want the power of His resurrection but do not want to experience the sufferings. Thank God, it is His suffering that takes us through our time of suffering.

It is obvious that Paul had a genuine love for the saints at Ephesus, he called them "faithful in Christ" in the opening of his letter. And he offered this prayer for them, that God would impart His wisdom and reveal to them His love, so the end result might be that they would know Him better.

· · · PRAYER · · ·

Heavenly Father, give me the spirit of wisdom and revelation so that I may know You better. I pray also that the eyes of my heart may be enlightened so I may know the hope to which He has called me.

· · · TODAY'S THOUGHT · · ·

When we know God better we become servants more pleasing to Him. Remember He promises us that when we draw near to Him, He will draw near to us.

—Darrell Mouser

HELP IN TIMES OF WEAKNESS

*Likewise the Spirit also helps in our weaknesses. For we do
not know what we should pray for as we ought, but the
Spirit Himself makes intercession for us with groanings
which cannot be uttered* (Romans 8:26).

There was a period in our lives when Myrtle, my wife, and I
felt that the Lord just took our hands and led us step-by-step.
Myrtle had had severe back pain for several years. The doctors had told her that some disks and vertebra were dislocated.
The condition was so severe that she was not supposed to walk. It
looked like life in a wheelchair was inevitable. We moved to a new
location for the purpose of erecting a new building. I was faced with
the possibility of my wife being confined to a wheelchair while I
attempted the project alone.

At 2 o'clock one morning, I was sitting on the floor leaning against
the wall in the dining room, praying. The Lord gave me the assurance
that He had healed Myrtle. At the same time she also was praying, but
she was questioning God. The suffering had become so intense that
she could not bear it any longer. Her prayer was "God, if there is a
God, heal me." God's reply was very clear as He spoke to her these
words, "I have already healed you if you will accept it." She
answered, "I accept it."

The pain was gone. The suffering was over. The healing was perfect and complete. She helped raise the walls. She helped nail deck-
ing. She dug ditches and whatever else needed to be done. After more
than 25 years her back is still strong.

God simply took Myrtle and me by the hands and led us through
some hardships and many days of hard work. He also led us to some
glorious heights and wonderful experiences.

· · · PRAYER · · ·

*Accept my thanks, O God, for always being a present help in my
times of need.*

· · · TODAY'S THOUGHT · · ·

God proves His sovereign power by always providing sufficient
grace for all our needs.

—E.L. Murphy

THE SPIRIT PROTECTS

"No weapon formed against you shall prosper, and every tongue which rises against you in judgment You shall condemn" (Isaiah 54:17).

In November 1971 I was in an evangelistic campaign in a northern Guatemala village called El Volcan. The heart of my messages was the salvation of souls, the healing of sick people, and baptism in the Holy Spirit. As I often did, I was sharing the preaching with a fellow evangelist.

This night it was my turn to preach. The service seemed to be a usual one; the atmosphere seemed normal. I looked over the congregation and noticed that there were believers and unbelievers. Many people speculated about the services too.

I began to preach. Suddenly eight men with machetes in their hands came into the meeting place. It was obvious they had evil intentions. When I saw them I was frightened, but I asked God to give me strength. The Holy Spirit filled my heart. I began to speak in tongues, and as the power of the Spirit seized me, I took control of the situation.

They sat down and I began preaching. They were very interested in the message. When the service was over, everybody but those eight men went home.

I testified to the men about Christ, and they began to change. They told me, "We will come to listen to your message every night of this campaign. If anybody tries to bother you, we will protect you!" The pastor later told us that these were wicked men and they had never come to church before. They had intended to destroy the sound equipment and threaten the preachers so they would close the evangelistic meetings.

Who controlled those men? Who changed their minds? Without a doubt, it was the Holy Spirit! The Holy Spirit touched many people, and the little village was shaken by the power of God.

· · · PRAYER · · ·

Eternal Father, anoint us afresh with Your Holy Spirit. Help us to see that no man or power can harm us because of Your care. I thank You for the Holy Spirit.

· · · TODAY'S THOUGHT · · ·

The power of the Holy Spirit is better than personality, enthusiasm, talent, skill, or brilliance.

—David Munguia

ANOINTED WITH A PURPOSE

*"Behold! My servant whom I have chosen, My beloved in
whom My soul is well pleased; I will put My Spirit upon Him,
and He will declare justice to the Gentiles"* (Matthew 12:18).

This is a quotation from Isaiah 42:1, and it is a powerful
scripture. Here the ministry of the Holy Spirit is obvious.
The first thing we can see is how He inspired the prophet to
write precise details about the person, the life, and the ministry of Jesus, the Messiah. Sometimes, reading prophecies leaves the
impression one may be reading a historical narrative, not a prophecy.
This is because the revelation by the Holy Spirit came so clear to the
prophet that a casual reader may forget that he actually wrote it more
than 700 hundred years before the events took place.

We also become aware of the need to be anointed with the Holy
Spirit. The Father, God Almighty, was talking about His Son Jesus, the
only begotten One. The description leaves no room for doubts: "[He
is] My servant . . . chosen . . . beloved in whom My soul is well
pleased."

The eternal relationship between the Father and the Son is a perfect
one. Christ was "obedient to the point of death, even the death of the
cross" (Philippians 2:8). He was a faithful servant. He conducted
Himself in a manner that was always pleasing to His heavenly Father.
He also knew that He had been chosen to drink the cup of death, and
He willingly drank it. Yet in spite of all these virtues in the character
of Christ, and also because of them, the Father said, "I will put My
Spirit upon Him."

· · · PRAYER · · ·

*Father, as we look back to the outpouring of the Holy Spirit that
brought this movement into existence, I pray that You will baptize us
anew. We acknowledge that only when Your Spirit is upon us can we
serve the purpose for which You raised us.*

· · · TODAY'S THOUGHT · · ·

The church is commissioned to continue the ministry of Christ in
preaching, healing, and setting at liberty. Without the Holy Spirit upon
us we would be powerless to accomplish anything.

—Victor M. Pagan

TO THOSE WHO OBEY

"And we are His witnesses to these things, and so also is the Holy Spirit whom God has given to those who obey Him"
(Acts 5:32).

I began preaching in the Church of God in 1960, before I had received the Holy Spirit. When I applied for my first credential, it was denied because I did not have the baptism in the Holy Spirit. I did not want to receive Him the way Pentecostals typically did. I wanted to receive Him in peace and quietness.

I sought for the Baptism at every opportunity. On one occasion someone said, "Brother Palazuelos, you are not going to receive the Holy Spirit until you recognize the supremacy of God, confess your sins, and allow the Holy Spirit to guide you as He pleases." I took the brother's advice, and 10 days later received the Holy Spirit as I had wished to receive Him.

I have learned that God's blessings and guidance come when we deny ourselves and commit to the will of the God. Sometimes His voice seems to say incredible things, but I have always obeyed. He has been faithful to accomplish His word.

The Holy Spirit has guided my ministry for the past 35 years. The experiences I have had have been many: danger of death, sickness and the miraculous healings of my family, ministry in several countries, and administration of church responsibilities. Through all these things, the Holy Spirit has been my Paraclete.

Recently I prayed for 130 ministers in a pastors conference and most of them were slain in the Spirit. The territorial overseer was slain in the Spirit also. This leader told me later that the Lord used this to confirm the reality of the power of God. It pays to be obedient to the Holy Spirit.

· · · PRAYER · · ·

Lord, as we have received Him in obedience, may we continue to follow Him in the same way.

· · · TODAY'S THOUGHT · · ·

The work of the Holy Spirit is sacred, extraordinary, miraculous. In obedience to Him, we serve as vessels through which the world can know hope.

—Regino Palazuelos

BLESSED BEYOND MEASURE

And they were all filled with the Holy Spirit and began to
speak with other tongues, as the Spirit gave them utterance
(Acts 2:4).

 As a minister of the gospel of Jesus Christ, I know the great importance of the anointing of the Holy Spirit in all I do. Many times, I have diligently prepared a sermon that looked great on paper, but it came alive only when the Holy Spirit anointed it.

I was saved January 26, 1946, at Kuhl Avenue Church of God (Orange Avenue Church of God), Orlando, Florida. The Lord called me to preach in January 1948, and I preached my first sermon at Kuhl Avenue in June, 1948. I retired from active ministry in May 1981. However, I still preach, teach, exhort, testify, and minister as the opportunity arises.

On many occasions I have found the Holy Spirit to be my Comforter, even more so since my wife and friend for over 50 years went home to be with the Lord. Truly, He is the great Comforter.

During World War II, I watched mothers, fathers, sisters, and brothers as they received the dreaded telegram, informing them that their loved ones were either dead or missing in action. The grief would have been unbearable had the Holy Spirit not enabled them to pick up the pieces and go on with life.

Over the years I have experienced the work of the Holy Spirit in so many ways. His presence brings joy in time of sorrow, an open door where there is no way out, miracles of healing where death seemed imminent, strength in time of weakness, grace to walk through deep waters, and victory snatched from the jaws of defeat. Time and time again, I have watched the greatest miracle of all as the stony heart of the sinner was melted and transformed into a joyous child of God. My life has been blessed beyond measure!

· · · PRAYER · · ·

In You, blessed Holy Spirit, are joy, peace, and comfort beyond measure. We accept You and all You offer us by Your power and glory.

· · · TODAY'S THOUGHT · · ·

The wonderful experience of the baptism in the Holy Spirit is for believers today. Jesus is alive to give the Holy Spirit to those who believe and receive Him.

—William (Bill) Peeler

August 13

DELIVERANCE IN ALL SITUATIONS

*For I know that this will turn out for my salvation through
your prayer and the supply of the Spirit of Jesus Christ*
(Philippians 1:19).

Anxiety. Worry. Fear. Never before had these emotions hit me with such force as they did when I received that disturbing phone call from my wife. She had taken our oldest—our 4-year-old daughter, Lauren—to the doctor for a routine exam. He discovered something abnormal in her sinuses. His words were few and to the point. "I don't know what it is. I have never seen anything like this. She must see a specialist as soon as possible."

The next day, when the specialist examined Lauren, his words were the same as our doctor's: "I don't know what it is. We must schedule her for a CAT scan this afternoon and surgery tomorrow." Following the second CAT scan the radiologist showed us on the scan that the whole left side of Lauren's maxillary sinus area, the upper region of her nose, and down into her throat was abnormal tissue. He said it could be cancer, and surgery was scheduled for the next day.

There was good news. After the surgery the doctor said the mass was benign. Lauren would be fine!

Through this agonizing trial the apostle Paul's words became real to our family. Our deliverance from those terrible feelings of worry, anxiety, and fear came by means of the prayers of brothers and sisters in Christ on our behalf. In the midst of this trial, the Holy Spirit became for us the Comforter Jesus promised.

How can we be sure of deliverance in any situation? Through the prayers of brothers and sisters in Christ and the continual supply of the Holy Spirit, there is deliverance.

· · · PRAYER · · ·

Father, our God, Your Word says that You know what we need before we ask. Help me by Your Holy Spirit to have deliverance in all situations.

· · · TODAY'S THOUGHT · · ·

"A man's reaction to every situation in time is a witness for or against him in eternity" (William Barclay).

—Derwood L. Perkins

242

WHOM DO THEY SEE WITHIN

*But at last Daniel came before me, (his name is
Belteshazzar, according to the name of my god; in him is
the Spirit of the Holy God), and I told the dream before him
(Daniel 4:8).*

The most important characteristic of a committed believer is
that the Spirit of the Lord lives within. The indwelling of the
Spirit is God's way of manifesting Himself though a person.
When God dwells within, there is a noticeable difference in
character and conduct.

The Spirit of the Lord lived in Daniel. This fact is verified by several manifestations in his personal and public life. It was so discernible
that no method of advertisement was necessary on Daniel's part to
market the special operation of his spiritual gifts. There were no com-
mercials, no neon messages, no marquees, no newsletter with subtle
overtones of self-glorification, and no sly political scheming.

Daniel's method was simple: he maintained a consistent personal
relationship with God, he refused to be intimidated by pressure to
adjust his religion to accommodate the society he lived in, and he was
not inhibited when others noticed and even objected.

Daniel's trademarks should be consistent with those of anyone in
whom dwells the Spirit. They are always selfless. The desire to exhibit
the flesh or to demand personal attention is absent. In fact, all energy
is spent pointing attention to Christ. In the history of Daniel's life, all
of the tremendous spiritual manifestations were observed and recorded
by others. Many biographies reveal the great working of God's Spirit
within individuals, but there are no autobiographies of the same.
Spirit-dwelt individuals consistently exhibit a genuine refusal to accept
attention to themselves. There is a scriptural order of self abandon-
ment in the lives of all who are recognized as dwelling places for the
Spirit.

· · · PRAYER · · ·

*Father, help us to abandon any attempt to rob glory from You. We
pray that we will direct attention to the One who lives inside. By doing
this we will be attributing glory to whom glory is due.*

· · · TODAY'S THOUGHT · · ·

For others to see Christ in us, they must be able to see beyond us.

—Aaron Phillips

August 15

A HYMN OF REAL HOPE

*God was manifested in the flesh, justified in the Spirit, seen
by angels, preached among the Gentiles, believed on in the
world, received up in glory* (1 Timothy 3:16).

I love good music and singing. I grew up in a family of
singers. I can remember Dad and Mom, who pioneered many
churches in the Delmarva-D.C. area, used to sing one of their
favorites, *My God Is Real*. The Holy Spirit would move and
bless many struggling and hurting souls. The message was clear and
without controversy.

Paul affirmed the humanity and divinity of Christ in this text, and
this message is also clear. The heart of the gospel is who Jesus is and
what He can do. Jesus was a man, but He was more than a man. He
was "justified in the Spirit," which speaks of the glorious resurrection
of Christ. Jesus was "seen by angels" (heaven recognizes Him),
"preached among the Gentiles, believed on in the world" (millions
have followed Him), and "received up in glory." He is the divine Son
of God and is in glory now as our intercessor, praying to the Father on
our behalf.

Many struggle to be holy. The how-to of holiness is in Jesus Christ,
"the author and finisher of our faith." We are "confident of this very
thing, that He who has begun a good work in you will complete it until
the day of Jesus Christ" (Philippians 1:6). He loves us where we are,
but He loves us enough not to leave us there.

The Holy Spirit came to convict the world of sin, righteousness, and
judgment. He points out the problem, and the solution is Jesus Christ.

· · · PRAYER · · ·

*Thank You, Holy Spirit, for not only showing me my sin but also
pointing me to the solution. Help me to stop trying to earn my forgiveness and accept Your wonderful grace in Christ Jesus.*

· · · TODAY'S THOUGHT · · ·

Please Jesus! Then you will please the right people and displease
the right people. To be like Jesus is all I ask.

—Jerry A. Price

OVER MY HEAD AND UNDER HIS FEET

"For David himself said by the Holy Spirit: 'The Lord said to my Lord, "Sit at My right hand, till I make Your enemies Your footstool" ' " (Mark 12:36).

Psychotherapy is, literally, the care of the soul and our souls need caring for. David's message through the Holy Spirit is this: Sit at the right hand of the Lord until He gives you the victory over your enemies. This simple formula for victory is often overlooked, but it can give hope to the troubled soul.

In anticipation of gaining the victory over problems or an enemy, the passage in Exodus 23:5 commands that if you should see the donkey of someone who hates you fallen down under its load, do not leave it there, but be sure to help him with it.

Many Bible scholars now admit that there are serious deficiencies in most Christians' understanding of forgiveness. Most tend to embrace what might be called a subjective gospel. This means that whether the message is true does not matter most. Instead, the issue is, What can it do for me? Can it meet my needs? Can it make me feel good? Can it solve my problems? Can it improve my relationships?

Unfortunately, many Christians are not willing to have their situation radically changed by sitting with God in prayer. At least they are not willing to accept the change that sometimes will occur when the Holy Spirit is welcomed without reservation, until an enemy becomes a friend.

Spiritual power flows from God's Spirit to the human spirit, to the mind. With God's enabling of our spirit, our mind, we can have authority in spiritual matters. Our enemies can be made to be at peace with us. Even demons can be vanquished! As we wait at God's right hand, victory will come.

· · · PRAYER · · ·

Heavenly Father, I don't ask You to take away my trials; just for grace to put them under my feet. Pour out your Spirit on me and bring glory to Your name.

· · · TODAY'S THOUGHT · · ·

Faith means not trusting in your own resources but casting yourself wholly, completely, and unreservedly on the goodness and mercy of God through Jesus Christ by the Holy Spirit.

—Tommy Propes

August 17

BUILDING HOUSES AND LOSING HOMES

Now the Spirit expressly says that in latter times some will depart from the faith, giving heed to deceiving spirits and doctrines of demons (1 Timothy 4:1).

Easter Sunday had been great. In four services approximately a thousand people had come to the church to hear the gospel of Jesus Christ. Many had accepted Christ as their Savior. Fifty new families had filled out visitor cards expressing an interest in the church. So why couldn't I get the picture of that one middle-aged, defeated, and embarrassed man out of my mind?

Then I remembered the time I attempted to counsel him and his wife nine years earlier. "Don't let anything interfere with your relationship with God or the church," I pleaded. He had taken on three jobs and was trying to go back to school, and she was working two jobs. Under these circumstances there was little time for God, church, or each other. "Pastor, we want a new house and we believe it is God's will, no matter how many jobs we have to work!" Realizing this seducing spirit was not of God, I replied, "Don't lose your home trying to build a house."

Within a year, the two of them were separated. Divorce soon followed. What had happened? They had accepted one of the "doctrines of demons." The gospel of prosperity had crashed their world in on top of them like a ton of bricks. Enough bricks to build a house, but never enough to build a home.

The good news is that many families are listening to the Spirit, just as the thousand did that Easter Sunday. The Holy Spirit still speaks and guides in these latter times.

Are we willing to listen and follow?

· · · PRAYER · · ·

Father, help us to hear when the Holy Spirit exposes seducing spirits and doctrines of demons. Give us strength and wisdom to follow truth and hold to the faith. In Christ's name, we pray.

· · · TODAY'S THOUGHT · · ·

No Christian is a match against the wiles of Satan without the abiding presence of the Holy Spirit. But "He who is in you is greater than he who is in the world" (1 John 4:4).

—Bruce Rabon

PROTECTED BY THE SPIRIT

Yea, though I walk through the valley of the shadow of death, I will fear no evil; for You are with me; Your rod and Your staff, they comfort me (Psalm 23:4).

I was baptized in the Holy Spirit with the evidence of speaking in tongues in 1956. The Spirit of God has delivered me from death many times. I have been involved in two major automobile accidents, I was in an airplane when it suffered severe damage during a flight, I was in Miami during Hurricane Andrew, and the Lord saved me from a terrible accident.

The Spirit of God also saved me from death when three men broke into my office to rob us. The youth of the Church of God in the United States had just sent me $15,000 to purchase a former synagogue. I was working in the office with another pastor when someone knocked at the door. I opened the door for my secretary and a pastor when three men stepped up, armed with two pistols and a knife.

They ordered everyone to drop to the floor. Then everything began happening fast. I was still standing by my desk, and I heard the voice of the Spirit telling me to be valiant. I picked up something heavy from the desk and threw it to the man who seemed to be the boss. He got very mad and shot me in the chest. When I fell down they thought everything was under control.

Amazingly, I didn't feel any pain so I got up and started fighting with them. They shot me again, in the left arm and in the face. The man with the knife injured my hand. By this time one of them started to run, so the other two followed. A car was waiting at the door for them.

At the hospital I bled a lot, but I was OK. One of the bullets came close to my heart, and the one in the face went just below my brain. The doctor said, "Just a little more and you are dead. Something stopped those bullets. I don't understand it."

The doctor couldn't understand, but I understood perfectly. I was filled with the Holy Spirit, and He protected me from the attack of the Enemy.

· · · PRAYER · · ·

Holy Father, guide my steps and protect me from everything Satan would plan against me.

· · · TODAY'S THOUGHT · · ·

I am filled with the Holy Spirit and armed with the promises of God. I will not be afraid of the Enemy.

—Ricardo Ramirez

LIVING ABOVE STREET LEVEL

For those who live according to the flesh set their minds on the things of the flesh, but those who live according to the Spirit, the things of the Spirit (Romans 8:5).

"The flesh" is man's unregenerate nature, the sinful nature, the seat of sensual appetite and sinful passion. It is identified with the body, for it is through the senses that sinners enjoy sinful pleasures. Therefore, "the things of the flesh" are all the things of this present life that are contrary to God and His will. "All that is in the world" is defined by John as "the lust of the flesh, and the lust of the eyes, and the pride of life" (1 John 2:16).

To set one's mind on the things of the flesh is to set one's affection upon them, to think much about them, and to satisfy oneself with them. Those who "set their minds on the things of the flesh" are interested in sinful pursuits and have little or no regard for God. But those "who live according to the Spirit" are just the opposite of those "who live according to the flesh."

People who live for the things of the Spirit aspire to things excellent and eternal. They seek to please God and live in fellowship with Him. They are spiritually minded, not losing their hold on things eternal while passing through this world. They walk by faith, not by sight, believing the Word of God.

Those who live according to the Spirit live above the common street level of a sinful, worldly existence. Their minds are enlightened by the Holy Spirit to discern spiritual things. They choose good rather than evil. They overcome temptation by the help of the Spirit. They experience daily the work of the Holy Spirit in their walk with Jesus. Their focus is on heaven and heavenly things. Theirs is a way of grace and holiness, life and peace.

The flesh and the Spirit are in conflict with each other (Galatians 5:17). We have a choice: Flesh or Spirit, which will it be? Will we live according to the Spirit, above the street level of the sinful world?

· · · PRAYER · · ·

Lord Jesus, crucify the flesh, my sinful nature, and help me to set my mind on the things of the Spirit. Enable me by Your Holy Spirit to live and serve in the fullness of the Spirit.

· · · TODAY'S THOUGHT · · ·

The Spirit-filled life is lived above the street level of the carnal nature.

—Billy J. Rayburn

THE HOLY SPIRIT

Elect according to the foreknowledge of God the Father, in sanctification of the Spirit, for obedience and sprinkling of the blood of Jesus Christ: Grace to you and peace be multiplied (1 Peter 1:2).

 As a young Christian I somehow thought that praying through to the Holy Spirit was arriving at a terminal position with the Lord. My mom showed me differently; she showed me it was just a beginning.

I had been pastoring for 12 years when I received a call one Sunday morning from Mom. She informed me she was going to be rebaptized in water at the age of 76. I asked her why she was doing this. She said that at an early age she was baptized and she had felt quickened by the Spirit. Now she had a better knowledge of the work of the sanctifying of the Spirit. She wanted a rebaptizing of both the Holy Spirit and in water before she met her Lord.

On Sunday her pastor, with some assistance, put this elderly saint in the baptistery. Later that day, she related to me that as she came up out of the water, the Holy Spirit came on her and in her. She nearly shouted all the water out of the pool. They got her into the dressing room, and then she danced into the sanctuary still speaking in tongues. The whole church received a refilling of the Spirit that day!

To Mom, this was a sanctifying witness of the power of the spirit. For me, it let me know that the Holy Spirit sanctifies and renews on a daily basis. God's grace is multiplied or expanded to us each time the power of the Holy Spirit comes on us.

Mom has gone on to be with the Lord, but the Holy Spirit is still fresh and new to me every day.

· · · PRAYER · · ·

Lord Jesus, let me be even as Mom: never at ease with just a one-time experience of the infilling of the Holy Spirit but with a hunger to be renewed day by day.

· · · TODAY'S THOUGHT · · ·

Redeemed by Christ through grace, I yield to the sanctifying work of the Holy Spirit in my life.

—L.V. Rigney

LED BY THE SPIRIT

*For it seemed good to the Holy Spirit, and to us, to lay upon
you no greater burden than these necessary things*
(Acts 15:28).

In the summer of 1990, I was faced with the possibility of redirecting my ministry. What a challenge it was. Things were going well in the pastorate. The congregation had been gracious to my family and me for six years. I became confused at this crossroads of life, but after spending many hours seeking guidance from the Lord, it seemed good to the Holy Spirit and me to accept another appointment.

As time went on, certain events in life caused me to clearly see that the Spirit had given keen direction for my future. He had ordered my footsteps and brought me to a place where my life was preserved. The Holy Spirit was preparing me for a crisis that would change my life.

Not long after the new appointment, I learned that I had cancer in the left kidney, which ultimately led to radical surgery. Following the surgery, the oncologist recommended nine months of interferon treatments. This medication was very harsh, and there were times I felt I would never be able to endure the side effects. However, during all of this the Holy Spirit was sufficient for every need.

In fact, He had gone before me and had set in motion, years earlier, a turn of events that would prove to be far more than coincidental. While I was visiting in the home of a north Georgia pastor, his wife presented to me my mother's Bible which had been preserved for 14 years. She told me that when she discovered the Bible and observed my mother's name inside, she knew immediately in her spirit that she would one day give it to a member of our family.

This Bible became a powerful force in my recovery. As I perused it, I discovered passages she had marked especially for me. Through the Holy Spirit, His very Word gave me complete assurance that God would sustain me and give me a long, full life (Psalm 91:16).

· · · PRAYER · · ·

Heavenly Father, I feel I have been most blessed. Fill me with Your Spirit so that I too may be a blessing to others.

· · · TODAY'S THOUGHT · · ·

His performance in my past assures me of His ability to handle my future.

—Delbert D. Rose

A NEW DIMENSION OF LIVING

Now hope does not disappoint, because the love of God has
been poured out in our hearts by the Holy Spirit who was
given to us (Romans 5:5).

When we are filled with the Spirit, we are filled with God. Being filled with God means we are filled with love, "for God is love" (1 John 4:8). When God fills our hearts with His love, we feel the warmth of His love radiating from within us, because God has given us the Holy Spirit.

We are admonished by New Testament writers to continue to love, abide in love, dwell in love, be compelled by love, walk in love, put on love, increase and abound in love, and keep ourselves in love.

What an experience to be filled with the fullness of God! When we are equipped by the Spirit, victories become the norm in our everyday experiences. We feel compelled to help another along his way. Love must serve. Love sits by one who weeps, and weeps. Love stands with one misunderstood, and understands. As we lift someone's load this day, our own life will be enriched and blessed beyond measure.

The Holy Spirit lives in me; therefore, God looks out through my eyes. He speaks with my voice. He ministers with my hands. He makes Christ real to us and others. Love makes the difference in our attitudes, actions, and reactions. It is said of Abraham Lincoln that despite the bitterness engendered by the Civil War, he never missed an opportunity to speak kindly of the South. An ardent Union supporter once took him to task for this attitude. "Why try to make friends of your enemies?" the soldier protested. "You should destroy them."

"I am destroying my enemies," gently replied Lincoln, "when I make friends of them." We cannot be truly happy if there is enmity, bitterness, and deep-seated anger in our heart. Love continuing, abiding, compelling, and increasing brings healing, restoration, and joy, for love is of God (1 John 4:7, 8).

· · · PRAYER · · ·

Lord, my soul, mind, and heart are opened to receive the fullness of
Your divine love by the power of the Holy Spirit. Fill me afresh and
anew.

· · · TODAY'S THOUGHT · · ·

The springs of love are in God, not in us. It is absurd to look for the love of God in our hearts naturally.

—Bobby G. Ross

ONE MIGHTIER THAN I

John answered, saying to them all, "I indeed baptize you with water; but One mightier than I is coming, whose sandal strap I am not worthy to loose. He will baptize you with the Holy Spirit and fire" (Luke 3:16).

 When I was about 7 or 8 years old, I heard my mother say, "One mightier than I is coming; He will baptize you with the Holy Ghost and with fire." She was teaching a ladies Bible study, and the other ladies were praising God and shouting.

I wondered who was coming mightier than Mother. She was a great woman of God, and the idea that someone was mightier than my mother was unthinkable. I thought she was talking about herself.

After the meeting I asked "Mom, who is coming mightier than you?"

She replied, "I am not talking about myself but Jesus. John the Baptist preached in the wilderness, 'Repent, for the kingdom of heaven is at hand!'" (Matthew 3:2).

For many days those words rang in my head, "The kingdom of heaven is at hand." I looked for the Kingdom to come at any moment. After all, my mother had said, "Jesus is coming soon; we must be ready." This meant you must be saved and receive the Holy Spirit, as John the Baptist said to the people of his day (Matthew 3:11).

I had a dream about the coming of the Lord. I saw in this dream many people I knew, including my mother, father, and all the ladies of the Willing Worker Band—caught up to meet the Lord in the air. I did not want this to take place without me, so I prayed as a child for the gift of the Holy Ghost with fire. I received Him in my heart.

As a young man I knew that something extraordinary had happened to me that would last a lifetime. I began my journey in the ministry at the age of 17 with the Church of God. The Holy Spirit was burning in my heart, and I had a word from the Lord. I went about everywhere telling anyone I could that Jesus still saves and delivers. After 36 years of ministry in the Church of God, every day with Jesus is sweeter than the day before.

· · · PRAYER · · ·

Dear Father, thank You for the Spirit and for Your great care for Your own.

· · · TODAY'S THOUGHT · · ·

Jesus is the mighty One who has come to us in reality!

—Asbury Sellers

FOREWARNED IS FOREARMED

These are sensual persons, who cause divisions, not having the Spirit (Jude 19).

Nothing is more threatening to the body of Christ than those who cause disunity and division. Indeed, nothing is more sobering than to fall prey to this kind of spiritual apostasy. Jude dealt with a problem facing the family of God. The spirit of apostasy is not the figment of the imagination. To the contrary, it is a real spirit of evil intent, along with unprecedented activity of the vilest nature, that sets itself against the true Spirit of God. Its sole purpose is to destroy the Church of God from within by making a mockery of Christianity in the eyes of the world.

We must possess the Spirit of truth and practice righteous living from day to day. Holy things are being mocked and considered common. Jude gave us an injunction, a word from the Lord as to how we should respond to the terrible apostasy creeping into the body of Christ.

Remember what the apostles told us beforehand, Jude said. They have already warned of those coming in, mocking the true Spirit of God, so do not be surprised. We are not ignorant of the devil's devices!

Jude did not say what the apostates ought to do. What could he say? By definition, the apostate is without the Spirit, and there's nothing more to say to him. The writer to the Hebrews said that it is impossible to renew again to repentance a person who has crucified the Son of God afresh and has put Him to an open shame (6:6). Even John did not recommend we pray for people who get into this particular situation—he called it "sin leading to death" (1 John 5:16).

So Jude said nothing to the apostate. He did say something to the child of God. He was saying, "To be forewarned is to be forearmed." Prepare your defenses with consecrated prayer and be ready for attack. When it comes, don't be surprised, but stand steadfast on the Word of God.

· · · PRAYER · · ·

Dear Jesus, grant that I may be continually filled with Your Spirit and not be deceived by those who make a mockery of your Word through apostasy.

· · · TODAY'S THOUGHT · · ·

I resolve to be faithful to God and His Word!

—James D. Simpson

TO BE CALLED OF GOD

Then the Spirit entered me when He spoke to me, and set me on my feet; and I heard Him who spoke to me (Ezekiel 2:2).

In January 1960 my wife, Rachel, and I moved to South Carolina. Our pastor, W.E. Dowdy, assured us that we would be given a pastoral assignment on the Langley district. As I traveled with my mother-in-law, Louise Corley, who was an evangelist, I had the opportunity to visit many churches on the district.

I went with my mother-in-law to visit the Vaucluse church. As we drove onto the church property, I saw a little brick church that had been built into the side of a very old frame church. The project was unfinished, and the old frame building was in a state of disrepair. There were only 25 to 30 in attendance that morning. I remember thinking as we drove away, "God, please don't send me to pastor this church!"

In August 1960 I was assigned as pastor of the Vaucluse church. For three days I was unable to eat. On the third day, I pleaded with God to lay the burden for the Vaucluse church on my heart or change my assignment. Just as it happened to Ezekiel, the Spirit of the Lord entered me and set me on my feet, and I heard His voice speak to my spirit. The Lord, by the power of the Holy Spirit, turned an assignment into a calling.

On September 4, 1960, I preached my first sermon as the pastor of Vaucluse church. We had 28 in attendance that day. In just a few weeks our attendance rose to 113. During our pastorate in Vaucluse, God gave us 79 conversions, 29 infillings with the Holy Spirit, 15 baptisms in water, 24 added to the church membership, and a new church organized in neighboring Graniteville. This was possible because God placed a calling to the Vaucluse church on my life.

· · · PRAYER · · ·

Lord, help me realize that without the empowerment of the Holy Spirit I am useless; but I am more than qualified when I am called and anointed by the Holy Spirit.

· · · TODAY'S THOUGHT · · ·

"The Spirit of God gave Ezekiel the power to do the job He had given him to do. I believe that when God calls you to do a job, He will give you the power to do that job" (J. Vernon McGee).

—Jesse Wiggins

YOU ARE CALLING ME TO DO WHAT?

So the Spirit lifted me up and took me away, and I went in bitterness, in the heat of my spirit; but the hand of the Lord was strong upon me (Ezekiel 3:14).

In 597 B.C. Nebechadnezzar pillaged the Temple and carried King Jehoiachin to Babylon. Among the captives was Ezekiel, the priest (2 Kings 24:13, 14; Ezekiel 1:3). Away from home, Ezekiel and Judah's leaders were introduced to Babylonian power and influence. Israel's northern kingdom had been destroyed for more than a century, and now the overthrow of Judah was imminent.

Ever feel exiled, abandoned, confined, enslaved, oppressed, or banished? Ever feel like you are being forced to sing the Lord's song in a strange land? Ezekiel did.

In 592 B.C., Ezekiel sat with other captives by the Chebar River. The heavens opened and he saw visions of God. Through a majestic theophany, Ezekiel received his call. The Lord commissioned him to go to Israel, a nation in rebellion against God (2:3). His message was to be filled with lamentations, mourning, and woe (2:10).

The assignment—difficult. The message—judgment. And if that were not enough, God told Ezekiel what the response of the people would be: "The house of Israel will not listen to you, because they will not listen to Me" (3:7).

No wonder Ezekiel felt bitter! When God's servants are disappointed, discouraged, or even bitter, often the hand of the Lord reaches them. It is a hand of encouragement, guidance, and blessing. A hand to uphold. A hand to defend. A hand to direct. A hand to save.

The uplifting power of the Holy Spirit conquers our weaknesses and help our infirmities. He goes alongside—edifying, encouraging, and empowering us. He is the divine enabler, equipping us for Kingdom service. Does your task seem undesirable? Is your commission sometimes painful? You are not alone. Expect His strengthening hand. Get ready for an uplifting by His Spirit.

· · · PRAYER · · ·

Father, I do not always understand Your ways or why You have chosen me for Kingdom service, but I earnestly accept Your call and eagerly welcome the power of the Holy Spirit.

· · · TODAY'S THOUGHT · · ·

Those whom God calls He also equips.

—Mark L. Williams

August 27

THE HOLY SPIRIT AND GIVING

They were all filled with the Holy Spirit, and . . . . neither did anyone say that any of the things he possessed was his own (Acts 4:31, 32).

Alice and E.C. Thomas gave money to buy a needy young woman a coat. Her parents, too poor to pay her way, were encouraged to send their daughter to Lee College by faith, trusting God to supply the need. That was the beginning of a long journey of sharing with Lee students on the part of the Thomases.

Over the years, the Thomases had learned to lean heavily on the leadership of the Holy Spirit. He was miraculously healed of tuberculosis; she was healed as she lay at the point of death. The churches they served grew rapidly, with many manifestations of the Holy Spirit in evidence. In 1970, E. C. Thomas became state overseer of Virginia. The Thomases went to their new appointment with a lot of faith but little in the way of financial resources.

This new challenge was another opportunity to see what God would do through them. Dr. Thomas felt led of the Spirit to make a covenant with God: he would give his salary to God over the next year, and he asked God to baptize 100 people in the Holy Spirit under his personal ministry during the year. The financial commitment was kept and 204 people testified of being baptized in the Holy Spirit that year in the services where E. C. Thomas ministered.

The commitment to give his annual salary to God continued until E. C. Thomas retired as general overseer in 1986. Before his retirement, E. C. and Alice Thomas had reached a major goal of establishing the first $100,000 student endowment fund at Lee College. In recognition of another gift of $35,000, a seminar room in the Vest Building was dedicated to God in Alice's name.

Hundreds of other stories could be told of the Thomas' generosity to ministry needs and individuals. As He did for those early Christians, the Holy Spirit imparted a spirit of giving and sharing to the Thomases.

· · · PRAYER · · ·

Father, all I have comes from Your gracious hand. Thank You for blessing me. I honor You with my finances, my life, and my abilities.

· · · TODAY'S THOUGHT · · ·

Many who never bow before an idol of gold worship at the altar of materialism with its incense of greed.

—Walter P. Atkinson

TRUSTING, NOT TRYING

*"For I will pour water on him who is thirsty, and floods on
the dry ground; I will pour My Spirit on your descendants,
and My blessing on your offspring; they will spring up
among the grass like willows by the watercourses"*
(Isaiah 44:3, 4).

We try harder, but it seems to get harder. We know we should be fruiful, but we find ourselves frustrated. We admit we are trying harder, but we seem to fail more. We are told to be active, be busy, do something—but the harder we try, the less results we see. We know there should be rivers flowing, but we feel the dryness within.

Let's ask ourselves a few questions. We may be trying harder, but are we trusting God? Are we leaning on the flesh, or are we depending on the Spirit? Do we expect might and power to produce, or are we trusting the Holy Spirit? We can get so busy trying that we fail to trust. When that happens, the fulfilled life becomes dry, barren, and empty.

In this verse we see the thirst, the flood, and the fruit. First, there must be a thirst—we must recognize our need. We can no longer excuse or cover up. God said if we thirst, He will fill us. This is our way of preparing the soul for the coming Spirit.

How long has it been since we have broken up the fallow ground within? How long since we have cried out to God to send refreshing, reviving showers of rain from above? We may be looking for a new idea or new program, but we need to look above for the cloud with the water of the Spirit coming to rain on us.

Second, God will pour out a flood on the prepared soul, not a few drops but an abundant shower of blessings, an overflow of His Holy Spirit. He so floods our soul that rivers of living waters flow again. Times of refreshing truly come from the presence of the Holy Spirit.

Finally the fruit springs forth, for the dry desert now is a beautiful garden. It is not something that is manufactured by human effort but produced by the coming of the Holy Spirit.

· · · PRAYER · · ·

Dear God, we are tired of being frustrated and barren; today we trust You for the promised Spirit.

· · · TODAY'S THOUGHT · · ·

God is still looking for better men, not better methods. God wants us to be before we try to do.

—Larry G. Higginbotham

August 29

A SPIRIT-LED REST

As a beast goes down into the valley, and the Spirit of the Lord causes him to rest, so You lead Your people, to make Yourself a glorious name (Isaiah 63:14).

To enjoy the benefits of real rest, there has to be a way to give one's problems or needs to someone else to handle. God has made a way for us to give Him our problems and also to lead us to a place of rest. He does this through the work of the Holy Spirit, but only if we allow Him to work His plan in our lives.

It is evident, as you think of your own life and of the many people you know, that God's people need rest. Most agree on that point; however, many fail to realize that God has provided a rest for them.

Just as God leads the beast down into the valley to rest, He desires to lead His people to a place of rest. Your place of rest will no doubt be different from others' place of rest. When we are ready to yield ourselves to Him and turn our problems and our frustrations over to Him, He is ready to receive them.

Many times during their wilderness wanderings, God provided a place for Israel to rest. However, where and when to rest was always His choice. God knows the best time and place for us to rest.

Two principles of a Spirit-led rest are important for us to remember. First, it is the Holy Spirit who enables us to rest. The leading to that place of rest is a part of His work in our lives. Second, as we receive that rest, it brings honor to God and glorifies His name. God desires for us a proper rest. Only as we yield to the Holy Spirit can we find that place of rest in Him.

· · · PRAYER · · ·

Lord, today I find myself tired and weary and in need of rest. May Your Spirit lead me to that place of safety where I will find rest. And above all else, may Your name receive the honor and glory.

· · · TODAY'S THOUGHT · · ·

The number of hours or days that we rest is not the issue. The real need is for us to be led by the Holy Spirit into that place of rest from which God will be glorified.

—W.F. Waters, Jr.

258

THE SPIRIT OF TRUTH

". . . the Spirit of truth, whom the world cannot receive,
because it neither sees Him nor knows Him; but you know
Him, for He dwells with you and will be in you"
(John 14:17).

The infilling of the Holy Spirit was a most significant event in my life. While I was a Bible college student, I had an unforgettable experience during a campus revival. During an evening service I saw the wind of the Holy Spirit blow across the student body in a wave of glory. That phenomenon awakened my desire to be filled with the Holy Spirit.

The experience of my subsequent infilling made such an impact upon me that it literally changed my life. After ministering my first time in chapel, a number of students remarked, "That cannot be the same Gary Tygart we know." That happening has been a point of reference many times during my life. I've come to find that the Holy Spirit, the Spirit of truth, has given me the confidence that the Lord is directing my life on a daily basis.

God's Word clearly addresses the ills of mankind and reveals the truth by His Spirit. As a young man I experienced through the Word that the Spirit of truth is revealed in me and provides the foundation for my living. When I read the Word of God, it judged me, wounded me, and told me I was a sinner; but I read on further and it acquitted me, healed me, and led me to the Savior. The Word of God, revealed through the Spirit of truth, not only tells me what's wrong but also provides the answers and remedies.

As we know Him better, we learn to trust Him more, thereby strengthening our faith in Him. Our relationships with even our best friends reveal flaws over time; but the longer we know the Lord, the more we realize He has no flaws. Thank God for the Holy Spirit! He brings us into an intimate relationship with our Lord.

· · · PRAYER · · ·

Dear Lord, help me always to do what the Spirit of truth directs me to do. May my life be exemplary of the Spirit-filled life, and may I come to know You better each day.

· · · TODAY'S THOUGHT · · ·

"However, when He, the Spirit of truth, has come, He will guide you into all truth; for He will not speak on His own authority, but whatever He hears He will speak; and He will tell you things to come" (John 16:13).

—Gary D. Tygart

LIVE IN THE SPIRIT

*Are you so foolish? Having begun in the Spirit, are you now
being made perfect by the flesh?* (Galatians 3:3).

In the late 1940s, Dad, the Reverend A.L. Leonhardt, Sr., pastored the Woodfin Church of God in Asheville, North Carolina.
It was state camp meeting time in Charlotte, and Dad had been
promoting and encouraging everyone in the church to go to
camp meeting. One good brother who had never been to camp meeting
wanted to go. He had an old car that he was afraid would not make the
trip. However, he really wanted to go, so—living by faith—he was successful in persuading five other people to go with him.

They started to Charlotte for camp meeting. About 30 miles out of
Asheville, sure enough, the car broke down. It simply would not start
again.

After much trying in their own power, the owner of the car said,
"Wait a minute! I've got some anointing oil in the car. Let's anoint and
pray for this car!"

He got the anointing oil, poured it all over the hood, and then prayed
for God to let the Holy Spirit touch that car, make it crank, and take
them to Charlotte. He then asked God to let the Holy Spirit watch over
the car, transport them around for the week of camp meeting and then
bring them back home!

With faith that God had heard their prayers, the six people got back
in the car. The owner turned the key in the ignition; the car started, and
they drove on to Charlotte!

Throughout the week of camp meeting, the car never failed to start.
When camp meeting was over, they drove back to Asheville. After taking everyone home, the owner drove the car into his driveway, stopped,
and the car would not start again. It finally had to be pulled to a garage
for an overhaul of the motor.

I have wondered what would have happened if he had prayed and
asked God to let the Spirit watch over the car and keep it running for
several years!

· · · PRAYER · · ·

*Lord, give us faith to believe You for the impossible. Help us never
to forget that You can supply all our needs.*

· · · TODAY'S THOUGHT · · ·

God has not promised us more than we need, but He has promised
us all we need.

—Lawrence Leonhardt

WALKING IN THE SPIRIT

*I say then: Walk in the Spirit, and you shall not fulfill the
lust of the flesh (Galatians 5:16).*

Having joined the Church of God as a young boy and witnessing firsthand many significant miracles and healings, I began to equate the work of the Holy Spirit with this area of ministry. Through the years, there has been much preaching on the Holy Spirit and the demonstration of His power but very little instruction on what the work and ministry of the Holy Spirit really is.

I was filled with the Holy Spirit as a young teen but was never quite satisfied with the "power of God" as demonstrated in my lifestyle. For many years I prayed for power to be demonstrated in my life through miracles, healings, and supernatural demonstrations, but I always felt empty, disappointed, and very unspiritual.

One day a miraculous thing happened in my life! In my sincere search for God's power, the Holy Spirit showed me that it takes more of His power to love than it does to pray for the sick or do some other work.

The Holy Spirit wants to reveal Himself to this world through us as we demonstrate the lifestyle and character of God in our daily walk. The Spirit and power of God are demonstrated in and through us in love, joy, and peace. Character is more important than works, and God will reveal Himself through miracles and wonders as—and only as—we live and walk in the Spirit.

· · · PRAYER · · ·

Our Father in heaven, please develop Your character in me, whatever the cost. Holy Spirit, reveal Yourself through me as I walk daily with You. Fill me with the lifestyle and presence of Christ that I will effectively reveal Him to a hurting world.

· · · TODAY'S THOUGHT · · ·

You will be remembered more by your character than by what you do.

—Robert D. (Bob) Pace

LED BY THE SPIRIT

So he came by the Spirit into the temple (Luke 2:27).

Sister Daisy was a hardworking lady in one of our Central American churches. A few months after she became a Christian, she was baptized with the Holy Spirit; a few days later her alcoholic husband left her with their nine small children and one more on the way. Daisy and her family were very poor. They lived in a two-room house, with walls made out of wood, cardboard, and plastic sheets. Daisy prayed and asked the Lord to help her; she could not go out and work because of her big family. The Holy Spirit led her to start a small business at home and God prospered her in a mighty way.

Three years went by and her husband came back. He could not believe all the changes that had taken place where his family used to live. A new house had been built with walls made out of brick and cement; the house had three bedrooms, a living room, a dining room, a nice big kitchen, and a bathroom; and Daisy had a washing machine (very rare among the poor in Latin America).

Daisy told her husband, "When you left me and the children, I made the Lord my friend. I learned to do everything in my life by the leading of the Holy Spirit, and look what He has done for us." A few months later Daisy's husband decided to accept Jesus Christ as his Savior, and he was miraculously delivered from alcohol.

Daisy learned that one of the meanings of being filled with the Holy Spirit is to be led by Him in every single aspect of her life. She has never been disappointed since she came to know the Lord and learned to depend on the guidance of His Holy Spirit.

· · · PRAYER · · ·

Lord, help me to remember at all times that without You, I can do nothing. Help me hear Your voice and allow You to lead me and guide me in every detail of my life. I want to do everything by Your Spirit.

· · · TODAY'S THOUGHT · · ·

I know that victory will be mine, as the Holy Spirit leads me every day of my life.

—Manuel Perez Sanchez

A PROMISE FULFILLED

"Therefore being exalted to the right hand of God, and having received from the Father the promise of the Holy Spirit, He poured out this which you now see and hear" (Acts 2:33).

Oftentimes those seeking a political office will establish their campaign on a platform of promises. It is assumed by the public that once the candidate is elected, the promises made on the campaign trail will be fulfilled. Many times the public is disappointed, for they have been deceived with false promises.

Jesus said, "And I will pray the Father, and He will give you another Helper, that He may abide with you forever" (John 14:16). Peter, in his sermon on the Day of Pentecost, established that the promise of Jesus was fulfilled in the manifestation of the outpouring of the Holy Spirit.

Now that Jesus is exalted at the seat of power and authority, He has received from the Father the promise of the Holy Spirit and has poured it out upon all who thirst. Whereas the Resurrection could only be a matter of testimony by the disciples, acting as witnesses (Acts 2:32), the effects of the pouring out of the Spirit are manifest to all. "For all the promises of God in Him are Yes, and in Him Amen, to the glory of God through us" (2 Corinthians 1:20).

· · · PRAYER · · ·

Thank You, Lord Jesus, that Your promises are true and faithful. Thank You for the fulfillment of the gift of the Holy Spirit that is poured out upon all who will believe and receive. May I ever be faithful to manifest the fruit of the Spirit and to have the gifts of the Spirit operate through me.

· · · TODAY'S THOUGHT · · ·

"Tarry at the promise till God meets you there. He always returns by way of His promises" (The Speaker's Sourcebook).

—Ronald Martin

THE HOLY SPIRIT AND SONSHIP

*And because you are sons, God has sent forth the Spirit of
His Son into your hearts, crying out, "Abba, Father!"*
(Galatians 4:6).

As the firstborn in our household, I was given my father's name
and became Paul, Jr. Yet, throughout my life, Dad rarely called
me by this name but chose for himself a more affectionate term
of "Sonny" or "Son." Later in life he gave me an interlinear
Greek-English New Testament and wrote this inscription in the front:

"It is with pride and pleasure that I give to you this portion of the
Word of God. Your calling is higher than kings and princes of earth. Be
faithful, God pays well. Your Dad, Reverend P.O. Lombard."

The privilege that sonship brings applies both to physical and spiritual birth. Physically, sonship is the result of a paternal and maternal
relationship. Spiritually, the consciousness of sonship is created in each
individual's heart by the Holy Spirit.

God does not use the term son casually or indiscriminately. This status is gained only by His sovereign approval.

It is interesting that Joseph was instructed to call the baby boy Jesus
(Matthew 1). Mary received the same instruction (Luke 1). Everyone
called Him Jesus. But Father God called Him Son.

Stand by the Jordan as He is baptized and listen as God calls Him
"Son." Go to the mountain and listen as Jesus talks with Moses and
Elijah. God breaks into the conversation and calls Him "Son."

The new birth changes our nature, but the Holy Spirit changes our
relationship. We are changed from servants to sons and heirs (Galatians
4:7). We move from servile duty to a position of prestige and authority.
There is no comparison between the portions of a son and a servant.
The son is an heir who inherits the entire estate, while the servant's
portion never increases in value.

Every time Daddy called me, I was reminded of who I was—his
son. When the Holy Spirit speaks to you, remember who you are!

· · · PRAYER · · ·

*Abba, Father, You have bestowed upon the poor blessings and riches
far beyond our ability to acquire. Help me to never forget where I came
from and where I am going.*

· · · TODAY'S THOUGHT · · ·

"A wise son makes a glad father" (Proverbs 10:1).

—Paul O . Lombard, Jr.

NO SECRET TROUBLES YOU

"Belteshazzar, chief of the magicians, because I know that
the Spirit of the Holy God is in you, and no secret troubles
you, explain to me the visions of my dream that I have seen,
and its interpretation" (Daniel 4:9).

Even folk who do not serve God understand that the meaning of life can be found in God. Oftentimes, I have had non-Christians come to me seeking the answer for why certain situations are coming their way. One of the tremendous attributes of the Holy Spirit is that He convicts us of sin and prompts us to do right. He grants us peace in the midst of the adversity. When troublesome times come, His peace passes all understanding.

We may know sometimes what the future appears to hold. But greater knowledge is the realization that the secrets do not have to trouble us, even when revealed by the Spirit. We must remain confident that He who began the work will continue the work until the day of its completion.

There are times that God allows His will to be revealed and the secrets told. There are other times when we have to walk by faith, trusting that He indeed is working all things together for our good.

When my wife and I accepted the call to Iowa-Nebraska as state youth director and pastor of the South Park Church in Council Bluff, Iowa, we did not have all the answers. Certainly, there were times when it appeared that there were more secrets than revelations. However, we learned that guidance and direction granted by the Holy Spirit is the security on which we could depend.

· · · PRAYER · · ·

God, help me to trust You more each day. Allow me to understand that the Holy Spirit will reveal Himself to me daily. And help me to see that His revelation of circumstances and situations should not be cause for alarm. Rather, because of my confidence in Him, I can rest regardless of what is to come. Thank You for calm assurance.

· · · TODAY'S THOUGHT · · ·

Be willing to allow God to do His complete work in you so that even in adversity, when the hard times are revealed, you can remain calm with the assurance that He is in control of your life. Allow His grace to be sufficient so that the revealed secret can do you no harm.

—Tony P. Lane

THE HOLY SPIRIT AND SALVATION

*God also bearing witness both with signs and wonders, with
various miracles, and gifts of the Holy Spirit, according to
His own will* (Hebrews 2:4).

As I read this chapter in Hebrews, the thought came to mind of the time we lived in a church parsonage with a small stream of water located directly behind it. Many times as the girls and I played ball, the ball would end up floating down the stream, carried by the swift current, and I would run quickly to get ahead of the current in order to retrieve the ball. Anxiously, three little girls stood by cheering their daddy on. Many times I rescued the ball, sometimes I didn't.

Early in the chapter, the Hebrews were warned to beware, lest they be carried away from the salvation preached by Christ. One writer says, "Life's ocean is full of currents, any one of which can sweep us past the harbor mouth, even when we seem nearest to it, and carry us far out to sea to be rescued no more."

One of the greatest reasons we drift away from salvation is neglect. In verse 3, the writer asks, "How shall we escape if we neglect so great a salvation?" God's Word is steadfast, and every transgression against God and disobedience to the Word receives a just reward. We cannot afford to neglect our salvation.

How great is this salvation? Its greatness is confirmed by three facts: It was spoken of by the Lord, it was confirmed by the apostles, and it was affirmed by the ministry of the Holy Spirit through miracles and spiritual gifts.

God's affirmation of salvation through the work of the Holy Spirit leads us to believe that the main work of the Holy Spirit is to bring people under the lordship of Jesus Christ. The Holy Spirit is not an impersonal power, and His gifts do not spring from a human source. The Holy Spirit bestows the gifts to whom He wills as the occasion recommends. Each miracle or gift is a manifestation of the Spirit, a visible evidence of His abiding. And each contributes something necessary to the common life and growth of the whole.

· · · PRAYER · · ·

Holy Spirit, work in and through us the miracles and manifestation of Christ. Help us to commune with Him, obey His commands, and receive His promises into our life.

· · · TODAY'S THOUGHT · · ·

The Holy Spirit will keep us from drifting and being carried away.

—Wayne E. Wicker

A HEART TRANSPLANT

*"I will give you a new heart and put a new spirit within
you; I will take the heart of stone out of your flesh and give
you a heart of flesh"* (Ezekiel 36:26).

When trials come, they will make us either bitter or better.
The condition of our heart is not determinded by the person or
peril that strikes out against us but by our decision to either
tackle it personally or let God intervene.

A few years ago, one of the closest friends I had ever known suddenly attacked me for no reason. I had committed endless hours of labor and made numerous sacrifices to show my respect for this friend. Suddenly, I was accused of things that had no semblance of truth. This person has yet to realize the damage that occurred to me and my family. When faced with such a crisis, I had a choice to harden my heart in unforgiveness and bitterness or to forgive and pray for this person. The task of forgiveness was extremely difficult. I could not have accomplished true forgiveness without the help of the Holy Spirit and the comfort of a loving spouse.

The process of a heart becoming hard is not a long process; it can happen in a few days. In a world full of all manner of evil, it is easy to see how an individual could allow his heart to become cold and hard. The promise found in Ezekiel 36:26 is a reassuring word. When the elements of hardship and pain have taken their course; God will restore to us a heart of flesh in place of our heart of stone. God is the specialist in heart transplants.

· · · PRAYER · · ·

Father, search my heart today. Help me keep a clean, healthy heart. If You find in me a heart that has grown cold and hard, transplant a new heart of love and life into me. I desire to have a heart of flesh in me that is made new by the Spirit every day.

· · · TODAY'S THOUGHT · · ·

My mother often said, "When life hands you a lemon, make lemonade." We do not have to understand why we face perilous times. We just have to remember that God wants to use our heart as an instrument of praise. Keep your heart right before God so that heart surgery will not become necessary in your life.

—David C. Blair

WORK OF THE ETERNAL SPIRIT

How much more shall the blood of Christ, who through the
eternal Spirit offered Himself without spot to God, purge
your conscience from dead works to serve the living God?
(Hebrews 9:14).

Many are the times the Spirit has led me back to the altar for a
time of cleansing and refreshing. It is at the altar I am reminded of that first experience I had in coming to God.

From the Word, and by the help of the Spirit, I am told to
repent and do my first works over. One cannot work all day in the field
or shop and stay pressed and clean all day. There comes a time for a
bath and clean clothes. Neither can you walk through this life and live
in the world without needing the help of the eternal Spirit to bring you
back to the altar to once again allow the blood to wash, and the Spirit
to refresh, your soul. The Spirit works continually to bring us before
the Lord without spot or blemish. What you or I cannot do, the Spirit is
willing and able to do.

I know a man who was very discouraged and ready to give up the
ministry. After encouragement to go pray, which he did, this was his
approach to God: "God, You remember what I used to be and all the
things I did in sin." He started to mention many of them, thinking, I'm
sure God will help me again, only to have God stop him and whisper,
"No, I don't remember." God would not remember the sins He had forgiven! The Spirit works for us on an eternal plane with God and with
an eternal relationship.

· · · PRAYER · · ·

Lord, grant that the Spirit may never leave me but continue to draw
me to the foot of the Cross.

· · · TODAY'S THOUGHT · · ·

We can never make it without the Spirit of God. Nothing will wash
away our sins but the blood of Christ. Let us stay at the feet of Jesus,
the best place to be.

—Donald R. Logan

CREATOR AND INDWELLER

*You send forth Your Spirit, they are created; and You renew
the face of the earth* (Psalm 104:30).

The Holy Spirit is divine person. As divine person He creates. He also sustains and directs what He has created.

On the first day the Holy Spirit moved on the face of the waters (Genesis 1:2). It is the breath of God that made man a living being (Genesis 2:7). It was by the Spirit that God garnished the heavens (Job 26:13). Job confessed that his life depended on the presence of the Holy Spirit (Job 27:3). Elihu said that man would return again to the dust if God were to gather His Spirit to Himself (Job 34:14, 15).

In Psalm 104 the worshiper proclaimed that God stretched out the heavens like a curtain (v. 2). He laid the foundations of the earth (v. 5). He set the boundaries of the waters and appointed the seasons (vv. 9, 19, 20).

Our text climaxes these verses and ascribes creation to the Holy Spirit. This demonstrates the personal nature of the Holy Spirit and the unity of the Holy Trinity. The Holy Spirit creates because the Father decrees and the Son mediates the work. The Holy Spirit is the fulfiller of the decree.

Creation and providence place a sacredness on every created thing—but especially on mankind, because God created both man and woman in the divine image. He did this by the Holy Spirit.

Redemption proclaims the sacredness of creation because God in grace restores what man has squandered. The Spirit, through whom God created, is given to redeemed man for indwelling. We had become the temples of evil—the dwelling place of "the spirit who now works in the sons of disobedience" (Ephesians 2:2). Now our bodies have become the temples of the Holy Spirit (2 Corinthians 6:19).

· · · PRAYER · · ·

*Sanctify me, Lord. Prepare me for the descent of the Holy Spirit
upon me to live in me.*

· · · TODAY'S THOUGHT · · ·

We must treat as holy all the things that God calls holy, especially our bodies the dwelling place of the Holy Spirit. We are prepared for his indwelling by the sanctifying work of the blood of Jesus.

—R. Hollis Gause

LIVING TO PLEASE GOD

For the flesh lusts against the Spirit, and the Spirit against the flesh; and these are contrary to one another, so that you do not do the things that you wish (Galatians 5:17).

All who are born-again, Spirit-filled believers have experienced times of personal consecration and sanctification in which we felt that we had finally overcome or had been delivered from a problem area of our lives. We arose from a time of prayer with a sense of peace and joy because of the relief we experienced in our souls. Things actually progressed very well until suddenly the problem we thought had been left at the altar tried to resurface and regain control of our lives.

We are born of the Spirit, but we still have to deal with the flesh. This struggle—sometimes an all-out war—will continue as long as we live in a mortal body. The old corrupt nature must be continually subdued by the power of Christ.

Paul identified some of these sins of the flesh as hatred, anger, envy, strife, idolatry, adultery, and fornication. The nature of these sins is such that they crave to overpower the Spirit of God within us. Paul exhorts us to walk in the Spirit! By walking in the Spirit and by appropriating the power of Christ through the Holy Spirit, we will not only subdue the old sin nature, but we will also experience joy in our daily walk with God.

We must also realize that the antithesis of the work of the flesh is the fruit of the Spirit. The Holy Spirit will produce within us love, joy, peace, long-suffering, gentleness, goodness, faith, meekness, and temperance.

· · · PRAYER · · ·

Heavenly Father, You have declared that I am more than a conqueror through Christ who loves me. You said that if I would receive Christ You would give me power to become a child of God. Help me to daily appropriate Your grace that brings the fruit of the Spirit into my life. My desire is to do the things that will please You.

· · · TODAY'S THOUGHT · · ·

It has been said that grace is God's riches at Christ's expense. Our victory has already been won! Let's walk in the Spirit and bring glory and praise to His name!

— Mitchell Maloney

SPIRITUAL TREASURES TO KEEP

*That good thing which was committed to you, keep by the
Holy Spirit who dwells in us* (2 Timothy 1:14).

Although I didn't realize it at the time, through the Holy Spirit my grandmother taught me basic spiritual truths which I now consider spiritual treasures.

One spiritual treasure she implanted in my heart is that it is not so much how well we pray that matters as what happens when we pray. Nor is it how well we witness or preach but what happens when we witness and preach. It is the anointing of the Holy Spirit within us and upon us that makes miraculous things happen.

A second spiritual treasure she firmly fixed within me is that God's anointing is not an inalienable gift but a conditional gift available to every yielded vessel through the power of the Holy Spirit. It both comes and continues through an intimate spiritual relationship with the Lord.

Grandmother had a time to pray, but she prayed in between times as well. Her prayers were powerful enough to pray heaven down and hell out. Through her I learned the true meaning of the term "prayer warrior."

A third spiritual treasure she imparted to me is that living in the Spirit embodies a supernatural lifestyle day by day, hour by hour, moment by moment. Even as she slept in the next room, I would hear her praying in the Spirit in the night. To her, living in the Spirit was an exciting lifestyle 24 hours a day.

Sometimes I wonder what specific spiritual treasures we are investing in our own families and circle of friends. Are we rearing a whole generation void of many real spiritual treasures to keep in their hearts?

· · · PRAYER · · ·

Father God, we continually realize how much we miss when we fail to commune with You in personal prayer. May we avoid the futility and frustration of prayerlessness, for it results in the weariness of our minds, the exhaustion of our body, and the trial of our faith. Let us experience the constant help of the Holy Spirit in remaking our very lives into lives of constant communion and spiritual intimacy with You through the Spirit.

· · · TODAY'S THOUGHT · · ·

Who we are imparts spiritual treasure more than what we say.

—Carl Richardson

271

THE REALITY CHECK

Then Peter said to her, "How is it that you have agreed together to test the Spirit of the Lord? Look, the feet of those who have buried your husband are at the door, and they will carry you out" (Acts 5:9).

What an awesome message! An instant prophecy of the judgment of God by the Holy Spirit—the ultimate reality check. The offense was lying, but it was also one of not fully considering the obligation for the Christian to be truly fair and real.

Ananias and Sapphira were not absolutely required to sell their possessions. Their selling was a voluntary act, not a compulsory one. It was their right to claim their property or part with it, but their act of deliberately lying to the Holy Spirit by declaring they were bringing the entire proceeds from the sale to the house of God caused them to be immediate recipients of the judgment of God. They were being unreal at a time when they desperately needed total reality.

Ananias and his wife made the fatal mistake of refusing to understand the importance of their action, and they casually lied to the Holy Spirit. They said they had done all they could do. Perhaps, this is one of the greatest problems of today. No one has done all that can be done. We can all do more, sacrifice more, give more, pray more, and live more directly in the light that Christ provides us.

The Holy Spirit empowers us to witness, to serve, and to overcome. He brings help, comfort, and joy. He gives wisdom and knowledge, and it is the Spirit who calls us even closer to God. His gifts enable us to be strong, and the fruit of the Spirit allows us to demonstrate the reality of the overcoming Christian life. However, this same Holy Spirit also examines, reproves, and ultimately judges our behavior. Just as salvation and worship begin in the house of God, so does judgment. Both ends of the continuum are reality, and he who would serve the Lord and be an overcomer would do well to be reminded that the ultimate reality is found in honesty and openness before the Lord.

· · · PRAYER · · ·

Holy Spirit, give me courage to live my life knowing that in all things, circumstances, and times, You require me to be real. Encourage me in right and check me in wrong until that ultimate day.

· · · TODAY'S THOUGHT · · ·

The world needs to see the reality of Christian living in us.

—Delton L. Alford

A DELIGHTFUL SOUL

"Behold! My Servant whom I uphold, My Elect One in whom My soul delights! I have put My Spirit upon Him; He will bring forth justice to the Gentiles" (Isaiah 42:1).

In this scripture God speaks through the prophet Isaiah concerning Christ who was to come to this world, bringing judgment, contrition, confession, conversion, reconciliation, and salvation. Of all that God said about Him in this chapter, there are seven words in verse 1 that should be the heart's desire of every man, woman, boy, and girl as we relate to Him: "My Elect One in whom My soul delights."

As a young boy growing up in the church, I can remember the testimonies of the great Christians as they worshiped the Lord. Time and again they would say as they concluded a fiery praise to the Lord, "Pray for me that I will be pleasing in His sight."

What blesses me as a Christian and student of God's Word is to know that I can be pleasing to the Lord! Everyone can bring pleasure and delight to the Lord!

The basis for this spiritual position is also found in this first verse—again in seven words: "I have put My Spirit upon Him." This wonderful relationship, is a spiritual position which one cannot obtain by election, appointment, or purchase. People who bring joy to the heart of God are they in whom He has put His Spirit!

· · · PRAYER · · ·

O God, I want to please You and serve You fruitfully. I need Your Spirit. Please fill me afresh with Your Holy Spirit!

· · · TODAY'S THOUGHT · · ·

To walk by sight is to discover and experience only those things that can be seen. Walking in the Spirit will take you beyond what you feel or see with the natural senses; it will make of you a servant pleasing to God!

—Jefferson Carl Hart

SOUNDING THE TRUMPET

But the Spirit of the Lord came upon Gideon; then he blew
the trumpet, and the Abiezrites gathered behind him
(Judges 6:34).

Great and gracious things happen when the gospel trumpet is sounded by a Spirit-filled man or woman. When this happens, sinners are called to salvation and the church is called to service. Sinners are convicted, convinced, converted, and the church is challenged to reach and reap the world harvest.

The story of Gideon shows what God's Spirit can do in the life of an ordinary man. He is empowered to do extraordinary exploits for God. This also places him in position to affect the lives of those around him.

Gideon's Spirit-filled message, vibrating from the anointed sounding of his trumpet, caused his people to be gathered behind this mighty man of God! Because he was a yielded vessel, he was clothed with the Holy Spirit and was able to blow the trumpet with a clear, certain, and unmistakable sound.

As Gideon's Spirit-anointed trumpet playing caused the Abiezrites to be gathered to him for a common cause, the sounding of the gospel trumpet will accomplish the same results in our day. Isaiah said, "So it shall be in that day that the great trumpet will be blown; they will come, who are about to perish" (Isaiah 27:13).

"Set the trumpet to your mouth!" (Hosea 8:1). Only the Holy Spirit's anointing can cause us to blow the trumpet with authority.

"Blow the trumpet in Zion, and sound an alarm in My holy mountain! Let all the inhabitants of the land tremble; for the day of the Lord is coming, for it is at hand" (Joel 2:1). "Blow the trumpet in Zion, consecrate a fast, call a sacred assembly; gather the people, sanctify the congregation, assemble the elders, gather the children" (Joel 2:15, 16).

The blowing of the trumpet by Gideon and the gathering of the Abiezrites to his righteous cause speak volumes to the church today.

· · · PRAYER · · ·

Heavenly Father, help us at all times to be under the anointing of the
Holy Spirit when we are called upon to blow the gospel trumpet.

· · · TODAY'S THOUGHT · · ·

It has been said, "God's Spirit will never lead us where His grace cannot keep us." Let us daily live in the Spirit and walk in the Spirit.

—Robert Lee Cary

274

BELIEVE OR NOT

This is He who came by water and blood—Jesus Christ; not only by water, but by water and blood. And it is the Spirit who bears witness, because the Spirit is truth (1 John 5:6).

Skeptics in the time of Christ, along with heretics, wanted to say that the person of Christ had a visitation of God at water baptism which made him God but then that special visitation of God lifted just prior to the cross, making Jesus no longer God. John dealt with this lie head-on. Jesus was proven to be the Son of God "by water" (baptism) and "blood" (crucifixion). He was as much God on the cross dying for your sins and the sins of the world as He was when being baptized and hearing God's approval.

How do we know this? How can we be convinced of the genuineness of Christ? There are three who bear witness of the truth that Christ is God: His baptism, His death on the cross, and the Spirit of truth. Let's look at the witness and testimony of the Holy Spirit. The Spirit cannot lie. He is the ultimate testifier to all truth. The Holy Spirit of God brought validity to the life of Christ by bearing witness to and speaking the truth about Him. The Holy Spirit testifies that we are called to accept Jesus the Son of God for the forgiveness of all our sins.

The office of the Holy Spirit in the world today is to convict men of their sins and to convince them of their need for a Savior. No one can confess Jesus as Lord except by the help of the Holy Spirit. Are you allowing the Holy Spirit to reveal Christ and help you walk in truth?

· · · PRAYER · · ·

Father, allow the Holy Spirit to reveal to me the truth about Your Son.

· · · TODAY'S THOUGHT · · ·

A young man came to church not long ago with no understanding of Christ or his need for salvation. He said, "I didn't know I was a sinner and I needed salvation until I entered a time of worship. Then something made me realize my life was not complete. I found Christ as Lord and Savior." Are you allowing the Holy Spirit to reveal Jesus? Has He spoken to you about your need of salvation? Allow the Holy Spirit to do a special work in your life today!

—Gary Sears

SPIRITUAL INFLUENCE

*And so it was, when they had crossed over, that Elijah said
to Elisha, "Ask! What may I do for you, before I am taken
away from you?" Elisha said, "Please let a double portion
of your spirit be upon me" (2 Kings 2:9).*

My first impression of a life influenced by the Holy Spirit was the night that I gave my life to God. I first attended a Pentecostal church in my homeland, Puerto Rico. It wasn't the preaching or the singing but the presence of the Holy Spirit among those brothers and sisters who worshiped God in spirit and truth that I could not resist. It was that divine influence which led me to the altar and has guided me throughout my Christian life.

Another big influence in my life, similar to that of Elijah and Elisha, was my first pastor, the Reverend Antonio Pauneto. This great spiritual leader impacted my Christian life and influenced me in my personal relationship with the Holy Spirit. In my first days as a Christian, I could see in this man a very special and intimate relationship with God. As Elisha was blessed with a double portion of the Holy Spirit as he followed Elijah, the Lord has blessed my life as I follow the example of Antonio Pauneto.

In the church I pastored for 22 years, before I became overseer of North Central Spanish Church of God, I saw men, women, young people, and children seeking the presence of the Lord as I had never seen in other congregations. In many of our worship services, I saw the Holy Spirit sanctify and baptize many individuals.

· · · PRAYER · · ·

*Our heavenly Father, I pray that I can be an influence on others in
the way my first pastor and the church I pastored were great influences
in my life.*

· · · TODAY'S THOUGHT · · ·

"The key to a victorious leadership today is the influence, not the authority" (Kenneth Blanchard).

—Amado Pantoja, Sr.

THE SOURCE OF POWER

*"You shall receive power when the Holy Spirit has come
upon you; and you shall be witnesses to Me in Jerusalem,
and in all Judea and Samaria, and to the end of the earth"*
(Acts 1:8).

When I was appointed superintendent of the Caribbean, I visited the Dominican Republic. A general service was held at which I ministered. It was held in the central church, with a large crowd in attendance. At the conclusion of the message, speaking through the interpreter, I asked how many of those present had received the Holy Spirit baptism as a personal experience. A very small percentage of the hands were raised. I thought they had misunderstood the question, so I called a senior pastor to come and ask them if they understood. His reply was, "They understood." Yet I insisted that he ask them again. The results were the same.

The work had not been showing much growth, for the people were very resistant to the message. Then and there we purposed that a new direction and a new vision would be stressed. In the altar that night many received the Holy Spirit baptism. A new direction was taken. The emphasis would be the Pentecostal experience first, and then the work would be done through the anointing of the Spirit.

Results were witnessed soon. A dynamic power was realized. Revival and renewal of both emphasis and vision spread throughout the country. The Holy Spirit made the message come alive. He opened hearts to the Word, and literally tens of thousands were saved and thousands were baptized in the Holy Spirit and added to the church. Hundreds of new churches were organized.

It is the anointing that breaks the yoke. It is the anointing that delivers from sin and demon power. The anointing transforms the minister and the ministry. Only in the anointing of the Holy Spirit can the church grow and be effective.

· · · PRAYER · · ·

*Thank You, Father, for the confidence and peace that have come
into my life since I have experienced the power of the Holy Spirit.*

· · · TODAY'S THOUGHT · · ·

There is no greater understanding than to know "if the Spirit of Him who raised Jesus from the dead dwells in you, He who raised Christ from the dead will also give life to your mortal bodies through His Spirit who dwells in you" (Romans 8:11).

—Luke R. Summers

SPIRIT-FILLED LEADERSHIP

And the saying pleased the whole multitude. And they chose Stephen, a man full of faith and the Holy Spirit, and Philip, Prochorus, Nicanor, Timon, Parmenas, and Nicolas, a proselyte from Antioch (Acts 6:5).

In the early church, a serious internal division developed when some Greek-speaking Jewish Christians complained that their widows were not receiving a fair share in the daily food distribution. The whole community of believers were instructed by the apostles to choose seven men known to be full of the Spirit to oversee the ministry.

One of the purposes of the fullness of the Holy Spirit in our lives is to better serve humanity. It is of prime significance that each of the seven leaders were Spirit-filled. Being filled with the Spirit gives one the right perspective—God's glory and not one's own. Therefore, when leaders are empowered by the Holy Spirit, the fulfillment of their responsibilities takes on a new dimension. Spirit-filled leadership is simply living and operating under the complete control of the Holy Spirit. When God wants someone to minister in His church, regardless of the leadership role, He always looks for someone filled with the Spirit. It has been said that the pace of the leader is the pace of the group. The chosen seven were leaders full of the Spirit, and the apostles were looking for men who would focus on the glory of God and not just the divisive problem.

God is looking for Spirit-filled leaders who will exercise their spiritual gifts and know that all service for God is dependent upon the power of the Spirit for its fruitfulness. Although the natural man is limited in his abilities, there is an artesian spring of supernatural enablement for the believer who is filled with the Spirit. Be filled with the Spirit—you are God's chosen leader!

· · · PRAYER · · ·

Dear God, remind us that we belong to You and that all we have and all we are is to be dedicated to Your will. Let us be empowered by the Holy Spirit to fulfill the calling to servant leadership.

· · · TODAY'S THOUGHT · · ·

Being filled with the Spirit calls us as much to character as it does to charismatic activity.

—Mike L. Baker

THE OVERSHADOWING PRESENCE

The earth was without form, and void; and darkness was on the face of the deep. And the Spirit of God was hovering over the face of the waters (Genesis 1:2).

God revealed Himself as He stepped into the pages of time by the moving (hovering) of the unseen presence of the Holy Spirit. He alerted man to His purpose and unlimited power as He sets a chaotic world in order. As God spoke the word, the creative power of the Holy Spirit performed it. As God viewed the developing stages of Creation, He declared that it was good. Humanity—the ultimate creation—made in the image of God, was placed on this earth to live in communion with God and rule over His handiwork.

Our original world has greatly changed. The perfectness of the past was marred by man's sin and disobedience. The resulting fruit has been confused emptiness and an unlighted pathway. But there is hope. The God of the past is still God today. The same Holy Spirit is present in this world. He is still the active agency of Divinity, to bring order and direction to each person who will recognize His presence and respond to His creative abilities.

In Psalm 91 the writer speaks confidently of God's presence. Under the shadow of the Almighty, he found refuge during life's storms. Under the shadow he was fortified against different opposition. There he found deliverance—a covering, a shield against his enemies' fiery darts—and so he journeyed without fear.

The psalmist directs us to the secret of living in the presence of the Holy Spirit and the discovering of God's plan for one's life. With confidence he stated, "You will show me the path of life; in Your presence is fullness of joy; at Your right hand are pleasures forevermore" (Psalm 16:11).

· · · PRAYER · · ·

Lord, may Your abiding presence hover over me and show me the path of life. I desire the fullness of joy that is found in Your presence.

· · · TODAY'S THOUGHT · · ·

Attune your life each day to the person and ministry of the Holy Spirit and His shadow will cover you. His creative presence will make each day's living a treasure-filled journey.

—David A. Barsness

BREATH OF THE HOLY SPIRIT

*And when He had said this, He breathed on them, and said
to them, "Receive the Holy Spirit"* (John 20:22).

A few faithful believers, including Thomas, were gathered in
fear behind closed doors when Jesus appeared before them
suddenly. He spoke words of peace and comfort and then
commanded them, "Receive the Holy Spirit."

In only one other place in Scripture does it speak of God's breathing
on man—in Genesis 2:7. After God had made man from the dust of
the ground, He "breathed into his nostrils the breath of life," and man
became a living soul. The apostle Paul wrote, "'The first man Adam
became a living being.' The last Adam became a life-giving spirit"
(1 Corinthians 15:45).

Thus we can conclude that just as God quickened the lifeless body
of Adam, Jesus—the second Adam—breathed quickening life upon
those believers gathered behind closed doors. The breath of God in
Adam allowed him to bestow life on earth. Likewise, the breath of
Christ on the disciples empowered them to bestow or generate that
same spirit in others.

One writer translated the words of Jesus: "Receive an effusion of
the Spirit." In other words, when Jesus breathed on them and said,
"Receive the Holy Spirit," it was not just a reminder that the Comforter
would come, neither was it the full outpouring that was experienced at
Pentecost, but rather it was a down payment on what was to come once
He had returned to the Father.

Jesus' breathing upon them was an empowerment for ministry that
would carry them forth until He could return to the Father and the Holy
Spirit could come in His fullness and power.

· · · PRAYER · · ·

*Father, I pray that You will breathe a fresh new experience of Your
blessed Holy Spirit into my life today. Fill me afresh with Your Spirit
and empower me to live in fullness and power.*

· · · TODAY'S THOUGHT · · ·

Although the Holy Spirit was given at Pentecost, believers need a
fresh new breath of the Holy Spirit daily.

—David Ray

THE LIFE THAT COUNTS

But the natural man does not receive the things of the Spirit of God, for they are foolishness to him; nor can he know them, because they are spiritually discerned (1 Corinthians 2:14).

There are two kinds of men—the natural man and the spiritual man. The natural man lives under the control of fleshly passions (Galatians 5:19-21). He is the animal man as opposed to the spiritual man. He has no abiding sense of spiritual values nor any relish for them. He counts it the highest wisdom to live for this world and carnal pleasures. Spiritual things are foolishness to him. He cannot see their supreme excellence, due to his animal appetites and being spiritually dead.

The spiritual man lives under the control of the Holy Spirit and minds the things of the Spirit (Galatians 5:16, 22-26). He has the mind of Christ and discerns and esteems spiritual things above all else. He is a new creature, resurrected from death in trespasses and sins.

Twelve blessings provided by the Holy Spirit are freedom from sin, cancellation of the death penalty, fulfillment of righteousness, indwelling of believers, giving of life, quickening the mortal body, mortifying sinful members, leading children of God, adoption into God's family, bearing witness of sonship, helping infirmities, and making intercession for the saints.

We have a choice in life. Though all have sinned and have falle short of the glory of God, it is left up to us to choose the right life and be a spiritual man. Begin today to live in the Spirit.

· · · PRAYER · · ·

Father, thank You for this day You have made. Help me to be a spiritual man so others will see Jesus in me.

· · · TODAY'S THOUGHT · · ·

"Therefore if the Son makes you free, you shall be free indeed" (John 8:36).

—Calvin Anderson

GOD'S SPECIAL ANOINTING

Now when the sons of the prophets who were from Jericho saw him, they said, "The spirit of Elijah rests on Elisha." And they came to meet him, and bowed to the ground before him (2 Kings 2:15).

I was 19 years old when God called me into the ministry. My pastor, L.B. Hammond, gave me much encouragement. He taught me much about God's Word and gave me opportunities to preach.

Pastor Hammond took me under his counsel and love and taught me about the church. He helped me prepare for my first examination for ministerial license. In 1952 I became a licensed minister in the Church of God.

E.L. Simmons, my state overseer, encouraged me to attend Lee College. In the fall of 1953—with little money, no car, and few clothes—I enrolled at Lee College. My faith was strong that God would supply my needs, and He did!

Those who trust in God and lean upon His guidance will not be disappointed. I knew God had called me and was directing my steps. I have found God's grace sufficient through the years. Everyone who trusts Him and obeys His Word will find Him to be the same. When God calls us into His service He equips us with His Spirit.

Elisha never made excuses, nor did he shirk responsibilities. After he was called and anointed, he left the farm and followed the man of God. God used Elisha in a mighty way.

After Peter was filled with the Spirit, he never denied his Lord again. He preached with power, and hundreds came to Christ, for he, like Paul, was "not disobedient to the heavenly vision."

· · · PRAYER · · ·

Thank You, heavenly Father, for the call and the anointing upon my life. Continue to anoint me with Your Spirit and presence so that I may lead others to You.

· · · TODAY'S THOUGHT · · ·

The life I live is not as important as the life I give.

—William P. Colter

September 2 3

COMMUNICATION THROUGH TONGUES

*Now we have received, not the spirit of the world, but the
Spirit who is from God, that we might know the things that
have been freely given to us by God. These things we also
speak, not in words which man's wisdom teaches but which
the Holy Spirit teaches, comparing spiritual things with
spiritual* (1 Corinthians 2:12, 13).

Though our small Church of God congregation was meeting in the half-finished basement of our uncompleted church, the Spirit of God met with us there. While it was more than 40 years ago, I remember well the night the preacher invited us to seek for the baptism of the Holy Spirit with the initial evidence of speaking in tongues as the Spirit gives utterance.

What rejoicing filled the church as I began to speak in a heavenly language. For hours I could not speak English. When I called my parents to tell them about my experience, I was still speaking in tongues. I went to sleep that night praising God and speaking in tongues. I was thrilled with what the Lord had done for me.

A few weeks later, a retired pastor who had been at church when I received the baptism came to me and asked, "Have you spoken in tongues since the night you received the infilling?" I admitted that I had not. "Well," he said, "go back to the altar and tarry until it happens again."

As soon as possible, I took time off from work and went to the camp meeting. I went determined that God was going to refill me—and He did. Since that time the Spirit has used the phenomenon of tongues to teach me many things—foremost among them is this: The Spirit knows my mind and the mind of the Father, and He alone speaks the language of us both.

· · · PRAYER · · ·

Heavenly Father, may I be filled, and filled, and filled again, with Your Spirit. May there never be a time when the Spirit cannot speak to me through clear lines of communication.

· · · TODAY'S THOUGHT · · ·

When we are discouraged and hope is almost gone, the Holy Spirit takes encouraging words of love and divine concern from the mouth of God and whispers them in our ear. When we need help to keep from going under, the Holy Spirit takes the cry of our heart and puts it in the ear of the Father.

—Leroy Kerbo

UNTIL THE SPIRIT IS POURED OUT

*Until the Spirit is poured upon us from on high, and the
wilderness becomes a fruitful field, and the fruitful field is
counted as a forest* (Isaiah 32:15).

When rain has been withheld for a long period of time, the ground becomes dry. But let the rain come—not the torrential downpours but the gentle, consistent rain that brings life with each drop—and soon the dusty barrenness will be a thing of the past. Fruitfulness will become the order of the day as gardens of delight begin to grace the land.

In similar manner, when a church has been void of the Spirit, dryness sets in. The church may still sing, but there will be no joy. The preacher may preach, but there will be no power. Acts of charity may still take place, not with a loving heart but with an attitude of superiority and condescension. Flowing, articulate words may be used to indicate that there is life, but they will be heard as a sounding brass and a tinkling cymbal.

Is there a solution to spiritual dryness and death? The answer is a resounding yes. However, the answer must be divine and not human. When there has been no rain, a farmer can keep on plowing, but he will only stir up the dust. He must have what he cannot produce—rain. Likewise, in a church where there is no life, a new program will only stir up spiritual cobwebs. Any attempt to work up enthusiasm will come across as excessive emotionalism and only magnify the problem. The glorious truth is, however, that we can have what we don't produce.

When the Spirit is poured out on a group of people, dynamic changes take place. The songs have joy, the preaching has power, the giving is generous and cheerful, and the acts of charity are in truth acts of love. Gifted vocabularies are drenched with anointing. In reality, what happens is this: A spiritual wilderness becomes a fruitful field, and a fruitful field becomes a lush forest teeming with life. But it never happens until the Spirit is poured upon us from on high.

· · · PRAYER · · ·

Father, we need what we cannot produce. Please pour Your Spirit upon us again. Please make our wilderness a fruitful field and our fruitful field a lush forest.

· · · TODAY'S THOUGHT · · ·

Never substitute the human for the divine. Only through the Spirit can we have what we cannot produce.

—Howard D. Hancock

BY MY SPIRIT

So he answered and said to me: "This is the word of the Lord to Zerubbabel: 'Not by might nor by power, but by My Spirit,' says the Lord of hosts" (Zechariah 4:6).

People often ask me, "Why, especially now as you are entering retirement age, have you staked everything you own in an old dilapidated building in an inner-city area that is rapidly rising in crime?" God, through dreams and visions, brought us here. The Holy Spirit counsels us and give us encouragement and daily direction. Without the power of the Holy Spirit, we would not be able to withstand the strong spiritual warfare we find ourselves in.

To effectively take back ground Satan has stolen in crime-ridden areas, one must pray in the Spirit, go forth in the Spirit, and claim souls in the Spirit. Having regular fast periods and all-night prayer vigils, knowing we are sealed with the Holy Spirit and that Christ goes before us, we enter the arena God has assigned us.

We are mending cracked walls and broken hearts. Those are the same hearts through which the Holy Spirit desires to do our Father's work. I have been blessed to see the deaf hear, the blind see, and people who had been given a death notice from their doctors rise from their beds healed. In inner-city work, only the power of the Holy Spirit can fill empty hearts hardened by life outside cathedral walls. The Holy Spirit is my assurance. I can do God's bidding only when I allow the Holy Spirit to do His job and when I cooperate with Him.

God has planted me in a harvest field close to the river banks of Chattanooga, but we are not discarded odds and ends nor wreckage washed ashore. Although some of our neighbors find themselves living in what appears to be hopelessness, God's Word tells us differently. We are close to God's heart here. Jesus is here; we yield to Him.

· · · PRAYER · · ·

Creator God, who spoke the universe into existence, whose command breathed life into dust, help us, as those called by Your name, to humble ourselves and pray, seek Your face, and turn from our wicked ways so that You will hear from heaven and forgive our sins and heal our land.

· · · TODAY'S THOUGHT · · ·

"I refuse to accept the idea that man is mere flotsam and jetsam in the river of life which surrounds him" (Martin Luther King).

—C.C. Pratt

September 26

THE SPIRIT OF LOVE

For the law of the Spirit of life in Christ Jesus has made me free from the law of sin and death (Romans 8:2).

The provisions God made under the law were only a school-master to bring us to Christ. All the law and its ordinances were fashioned after man, but Christ is the Son of God, with power to forgive sin and destroy the carnal mind and bring man back into the state of holiness.

Paul said, "For what the law could not do in that it was weak through the flesh, God did by sending His own Son in the likeness of sinful flesh, on account of sin: He condemned sin in the flesh, that the righteous requirement of the law might be fulfilled in us who do not walk according to the flesh but according to the Spirit" (Romans 8:3, 4).

The weakness of the law was that men came often to offer sacrifice to repent and gain favor with God; but Christ, with His power to bless, was offered once for all. And all who come to Him by faith receive pardon that brings them into favor with God so long as they walk in the way He has obtained for them.

It was by the fall of man that the sin of the flesh came, and that same principle is born in every child. But when the righteousness of Christ takes charge, then we can walk in the Spirit and be free from these things that came through the Fall. The perfect work that Jesus came to do, and in His death made possible, may be received by faith. We who receive Him by faith have the evidence by the life we live that we are children of God and made partakers of His holiness. Only those who have been made partakers of His holiness can understand and explain it to others.

Those of us who receive Christ and abide in His love are able to overcome the attacks of the Enemy. As long as we remain in Him, the Enemy cannot pluck us out of His hands. God's blessings and His power are ours by faith.

· · · PRAYER · · ·

Thank You, Father, for the safe walk we have in the Holy Spirit because of the power of the living Christ in our lives.

· · · TODAY'S THOUGHT · · ·

Spiritual union with God is the source of eternal life, which begins at conversion and continues to eternity if one abides in God.

—S.W. Latimer

286

LED BY THE HOLY SPIRIT

Teach me to do Your will, for You are my God; Your Spirit is
good. Lead me in the land of uprightness (Psalm 143:10).

The psalmist prayed for guidance from the Holy Spirit, and so should we. Without divine assistance we can become lost, fall into error, and fail God. With His assistance we will be led to the land of uprightness.

The leadership of the Holy Spirit comes to those who yield themselves to Him. There is a vast difference between companionship and chairmanship. The genuine charismatic experience establishes the Holy Spirit as chairman of our lives. As we surrender self to Christ, the Holy Spirit can be in charge of the direction and decisions of our lives. The nearer we live to God, the more sensitive we become to His presence and the quicker we are to detect the Shepherd's voice and follow Him.

While my wife and I were enjoying a pastorate in San Jose, California, she had an unusually vivid dream, which she related to me the next morning. She dreamed we had just arrived in a strange country, where both black and white Christians greeted us. They had prepared a large banquet for us with lots of food and tropical fruit. The country was verdant with tropical growth. The people asked my wife, "How would you like to be a missionary?" She replied, "If it is like this, I would love it."

Less than two hours later, I received a call from the Church of God superintendent to the West Indies, asking me to consider going to Nassau, Bahamas, to pastor the prestigious Faith Temple Church. I turned him down. I was in San Jose for the long haul. My wife reminded me of her dream. I called the superintendent back and asked him for time to pray about the matter.

We spent four happy, very fruitful years at Faith Temple.

· · · PRAYER · · ·

O Lord, help me to be sensitive to the illuminating, guiding presence
of the Holy Spirit. Enable me to obey His urgings and revelations as
you guide me into all truth.

· · · TODAY'S THOUGHT · · ·

We should remember that God leads us into and through varied experiences. Sometimes it may be to a mountaintop, but then it may be a valley. He led Job through some really dark places, but He faithfully provided sufficient light.

—Robert G. Graham

GUIDANCE FROM ABOVE

*The Spirit lifted me up and brought me into the inner court;
and behold, the glory of the Lord filled the temple
(Ezekiel 43:5).*

Within the heart of every man exists the need for divine direction. Every day we make decisions that affect our well-being as well as that of others. The world needs God's guidance that comes through His manifest presence. In this text, three observations concerning the Spirit in Ezekiel's life apply to us.

First, the Holy Spirit will lead and guide your steps. In John 16:13, Jesus promised, "The Spirit of truth . . . will guide you into all truth." We seek guidance from many good professional sources when necessary. However, man also needs the guidance that only God can give. He is the only source for direction into "all truth." Nothing—past, present, or future—is ever hidden from God. Through the Holy Spirit, He appropriately leads us into the full provision He has waiting for us, just as He had waiting for Ezekiel.

The Spirit brought Ezekiel to the place where he could receive from God. We also must get near the source just as Ezekiel was drawn to God's presence in the Temple. Sometimes it takes the unusual or the extraordinary to lead us to the place of revelation. Upon arriving, we must be willing to hear His voice.

Suddenly, God's plans and will are revealed to us. Acts 7:55 illustrates this. Stephen, a man full of faith and the Holy Spirit, had just preached God's will and direction to a rebellious people. Upon hearing the message of Stephen, the rebellious group went into a rage. The Bible says, "But he, being full of the Holy Spirit, gazed into heaven and saw the glory of God, and Jesus standing at the right hand of God." The glory of God is made manifest when one is led by the Spirit to the place of anointing.

· · · PRAYER · · ·

Heavenly Father, may I be led by You today. Give guidance unto my feet and light unto my path. Guide me toward righteousness and truth. May the words of my mouth and the meditations of my heart be acceptable in Your sight.

· · · TODAY'S THOUGHT · · ·

If we accept God's leading, we will be enriched by His manifest presence and the satisfaction that comes from being in His perfect will.

—Stephen P. Darnell

UNDERSTANDING GOD'S WORD

Teach me, O Lord, the way of Your statutes, and I shall
keep it to the end. Give me understanding, and I shall keep
Your law; indeed, I shall observe it with my whole heart
(Psalm 119:33, 34).

The psalmist who wrote these verses realized there were conditions he must meet and do, since his well–being depended on his personal responsibility to the Word of God. He was aware there were commands from God he must learn. But he also knew he could not teach himself. God, through the Holy Spirit and the written Word, must teach him.

The knowledge he had motivated him to move in the direction of God, but soon he became ready to slow down or stop altogether his pursuit of understanding. God must help if he was to continue on. But with confidence that God would help, he determined to get away from any halfhearted effort in his relationship with God. Rather, his prayer to God was that he would observe the law with his whole heart.

· · · PRAYER · · ·

Lord, teach me Your Word through the Holy Spirit's guidance. Give
me determination to pursue with my whole heart a close, growing rela-
tionship with You.

· · · TODAY'S THOUGHT · · ·

A church in London, England, regularly distributed Bibles to the poor of the city. A lady whose possessions had been destroyed in a fire received one of the distributed Bibles. She sent a note to the church saying, "Thank you, and thank God, I now have a Bible. With the help of the Holy Spirit, it was the guide of my youth, and it is the staff of my age. It wounded me and healed me. It showed me I was a sinner, and it led me to the Savior. It has given me comfort and understanding in life, and I know it will give me hope in death."

—James E. Humbertson

S e p t e m b e r   3 0

THE ANOINTING MADE THE DIFFERENCE

"The Spirit of the Lord spoke by me, and His word was on my tongue" (2 Samuel 23:2).

One Sunday in 1970 I stood in the pulpit of our church as Sunday school superintendent to encourage the people to improve their attendance. That morning something at once wonderful and frightening happened. A bold power came over me, and I began to preach with anointing! It was such a fluid, subtle transition that it happened before I recognized it. In that exhilarating moment I was soaring! It was a miracle! It was the Spirit!

When I realized what I was doing, I was stunned. I stopped in mid–sentence and sat down quickly, without explanation. The pastor looked at me with a puzzled expression, then he stood and continued the service.

In the days that followed, I mulled over that moment many times. I began to understand what should have been obvious to me the whole time. Preaching that matters is not by might nor by power but by His Spirit! It's a timeless truth: the anointing makes the difference!

Now twice every Sunday, and many other times each week, I become a miracle. I do regularly what I know I cannot do—I preach! How? By His Spirit and with His word! Everything I need—the word to speak and the power to speak it—is mine from God.

· · · PRAYER · · ·

Heavenly Father, help me always to remember that I cannot do any ministry without Your Spirit and Your Word. Help me to remember that what I began to do in the power of the Spirit, I cannot continue to do in my own strength.

· · · TODAY'S THOUGHT · · ·

I will never forget that I am an earthly vessel, fashioned by God's caring hand, and that His is the kingdom and the power and the glory forever!

—F. John Colbaugh

290

A MINISTER OF JESUS CHRIST

That I might be a minister of Jesus Christ to the Gentiles,
ministering the gospel of God, that the offering of the
Gentiles might be acceptable, sanctified by the Holy Spirit
(Romans 15:16).

There was never a question in Paul's mind about his being a vessel chosen to bear the name of Christ. I look back to a time when I had to settle this question for myself, once and for all. I had spoken on a few occasions but I was confronted with doubt. I became willing to return to the places I had preached and acknowledge to the people that I had missed the will of God and was not chosen to be a minister. In tears I asked for special grace and was directed to Ezekiel 33:7-9. When chosen a watchman, failure to warn results in condemnation upon the minister—obedience brings deliverance to the soul of the minister. Through this scripture God gave me grace and assurance that I was chosen and called.

Before King Agrippa, Paul recounted his encounter with Christ and declared, "I was not disobedient to the heavenly vision" (Acts 26:19). Paul's ministry was apostolic and specific. "I am an apostle to the Gentiles, I magnify my ministry" (Romans 11:13). From among the prophets and teachers in the Antioch church, Paul and Barnabas were called and sent forth by the Holy Spirit to witness and minister throughout the Roman Empire. When warned of bondage, persecution, and affliction, he said: "None of these things move [or deter] me . . . that I may finish . . . the ministry which I received from the Lord Jesus, to testify to the gospel of the grace of God" (Acts 20:24).

· · · PRAYER · · ·

Father, grant us a fresh anointing and a refilling of the Holy Spirit, who sanctifies our labor and makes it acceptable in Your sight.

· · · TODAY'S THOUGHT · · ·

Leaving a moving service where a great minister spoke, a visitor said, "What a preacher!" Leaving a great worship service, the same visitor said, "What a Savior!"

—Bobby A. Brown

October 2

THE SPIRIT'S TIMELESS REVELATIONS

*To them it was revealed that, not to themselves, but to us
they were ministering the things which now have been
reported to you through those who have preached the gospel
to you by the Holy Spirit sent from heaven—things which
angels desire to look into* (1 Peter 1:12).

The gospel of Jesus Christ comes to us by the Holy Spirit. If the body of Christ is successful in evangelizing the world, it will only be done only through the Holy Spirit's empowerment. This is the principal work of the Spirit. The Holy Spirit speaks through us to those with whom we come in contact where we live, work, and play when we are sensitive and yielded to Him. He brings to our remembrance the things that have transformed our lives through the inspiration of the Word of God. He gives us a word of knowledge, wisdom, or discernment beyond our own ability.

This empowerment enables us to articulate the answers to the longings of unbelievers for peace, contentment, and fulfillment in life. Interestingly, our ability to be effective witnesses and ministers of eternal, life-giving truth is directly proportionate to our personal relationship with the Holy Spirit. Is it any wonder the apostle Paul determined within his own life to be renewed in Him daily?

The Holy Spirit's purpose has never been changed. The manifestations of God's Spirit are designed to glorify and exalt Christ.

· · · PRAYER · · ·

My Lord and my God, breathe on me and refresh me by Your Spirit. I acknowledge again my need for the leading, guidance, and direction that is available only through Him. Cause me to be more sensitive than ever before. I need You, Holy Spirit!

· · · TODAY'S THOUGHT · · ·

Talent, abilities, and education are important and necessary gifts and tools to assist one in communicating the gospel. Let us never forget, however, that it is "'not by might nor by power, but by My Spirit,' says the Lord of hosts" (Zechariah 4:6).

—Forrest Bass

October 3

GOD'S PLAN FOR YOUR LIFE

"He will also be filled with the Holy Spirit, even from his mother's womb" (Luke 1:15).

John the Baptist was a special person. He was the answer to the prayers of his elderly parents, Zacharias and Elizabeth. He had the distinction of being filled with the Spirit from his mother's womb, and he was the divinely designed forerunner of the Messiah.

God had a plan for our lives long before we were saved. The psalmist declared, "The steps of a good man are ordered by the Lord" (Psalm 37:23). Our task may not be as momentous as that of John, but it is important in the overall scheme. Each part in the body of Christ is important to the functioning of the whole (1 Corinthians 12:12-27).

To follow God's plan is to enjoy God's best. He has established an inseparable connection between our obedience to Him and our enjoyment of His richest blessings. We are always losers when we sin; we are always winners when we obey God's will. As we diligently follow His plan, He empowers us through His Spirit to accomplish His purpose.

As John the Baptist was given the Holy Spirit to enable him to fulfill his task, so we need the anointing and baptism in the Spirit to accomplish the work given to us. John's work was to turn the nation back to God, reconcile families, preach and teach in the power of the Spirit, and prepare the people for the coming of Christ (Luke 1:15-17). This is also our work!

Many become burned-out because they attempt to do the work of God in their own strength. As John ministered in the Spirit, we must seek daily the Spirit's anointing and guidance for the tasks He has ordained for us.

· · · PRAYER · · ·

Father, help me to follow Your plan for my life and recognize that I can fulfill it only through the power and anointing of the Holy Spirit.

· · · TODAY'S THOUGHT · · ·

The Holy Spirit can take our talents, regardless of how small, and accomplish His highest purposes.

—Kenneth R. Bell

MORE ABLE MINISTRY

For none of us lives to himself, and no one dies to himself
(Romans 14:7).

One may be an orator and speak as fluently as a nightingale can sing; but without the Spirit of God, he will have a form of religion without power or fruit. On the other hand, one may stammer in broken English and be as ignorant as Peter and John; yet filled with the Holy Spirit and zeal for God, that person can preach the gospel with power and bring men and women into the kingdom of God.

Jesus said, "The Spirit of the Lord is upon Me, because He has anointed Me to preach the gospel" (Luke 4:18). As He preached under the Spirit's anointing, people marveled at the gracious words that proceeded out of His mouth. Paul said, "My speech and my preaching were not with persuasive words of human wisdom, but in demonstration of the Spirit and of power, that your faith should not be in the wisdom of men but in the power of God" (1 Corinthians 2:4, 5). What one does for God without the Holy Spirit can be done better after being baptized in Him.

When one receives the Spirit, he renders better service to God and has the assurance that the anointing dwells in him. John wrote, "But you have an anointing from the Holy One, and you know all things. . . . But the anointing which you have received from Him abides in you, and you do not need that anyone teach you" (1 John 2:20, 27). "By this we know that He abides in us, by the Spirit whom He has given us" (3:24). "By this we know that we abide in Him, and He in us, because He has given us of His Spirit" (4:13).

Whatever we say or do, we need the baptism in the Holy Spirit, for not only does he have the answer, but He also is the answer.

· · · PRAYER · · ·

Father, keep us filled with Thy Holy Spirit every day of our lives. In Jesus' name.

· · · TODAY'S THOUGHT · · ·

Just as I cannot do service for God without the Holy Spirit, so I cannot live without Him.

—Albert Batts

THE SPIRIT—ANOTHER HELPER

*"I will pray the Father, and He will give you another
Helper, that He may abide with you forever"* (John 14:16).

At 16, I went to a Pentecostal revival in Oklahoma City. I felt convicted and vowed to go back. The next night I got on a streetcar and prayed for Jesus to lead me back to the church. I didn't know where to get off, but as the streetcar approached 32nd Street, a voice said, "Get off here and go left." I soon found myself at the brush arbor revival. I was saved and sanctified that night. Years later I was baptized in the Holy Spirit.

In 1932 we moved to Selman City, Texas, where I joined the Church of God. Through the years I had felt I was called to preach the gospel, but I was shy and timid. When I received the Holy Spirit, however, God took the fear away.

Left to raise three girls alone, I started a home laundry because I wanted to stay home with them. We always knelt down and prayed before they left for school each morning on the school bus that stopped in front of our house. One morning in March we were running late, but I said, "Come on, girls. Let's pray." I felt uneasy that day, and I will never forget my prayer: "Dear God, I'm not putting my children in the hands of the bus driver or the teachers but in Your hands. Please protect them and bring them home safely."

Ten minutes before the last bell that day, a gas leak caused an explosion, and the school blew up. Although 307 children and adults were killed in the terrible disaster, God spared my girls—Inez, 13; Louise, 12; and Lottie, 10. Inez crawled through the rubble, past the injured, mutilated, and dead to find her younger sisters. When I got to the school, they were waiting for me by the school bus.

· · · PRAYER · · ·

*Thank You, Father, for Your protection. Your Holy Spirit abides
with us always!*

· · · TODAY'S THOUGHT · · ·

Nothing is too small or too large for Jesus to do. We only have to pray and have faith in Him.

—Zoe Brown

TO BE SPIRIT-FILLED IS GOD'S WILL

"Oh, that all the Lord's people were prophets and that the Lord would put His Spirit upon them!" (Numbers 11:29).

During the 1960s I became aware of the Charismatic Movement. Names like "Jesus Movement," "Full Gospel Business Men's Fellowship," and others became prominent in church circles. In the midst of it all, we heard that Baptists, Methodists, Presbyterians, Episcopalians, and even Catholics were receiving the Holy Spirit baptism and were speaking with other tongues as the Spirit gave utterance. Then we heard of healings and deliverances from tormenting depressions and oppressions among these groups.

It seemed strange that these things could happen outside the Pentecostal framework. Many of us were so taken aback that we may have missed, for a time, the things that God wanted to do in and through us.

A fellow worker in New Jersey once asked me, "What if all churches begin to preach and experience the baptism in the Holy Spirit with the evidence of speaking in tongues as the Spirit gives utterance?" My immediate response was, "There would be no change in our message; we would be joy-filled that God's purpose was coming to pass."

The message on the Day of Pentecost was Acts 2:17, 18.

There is a certainty in the Word of God that all of God's people should be Spirit-filled. As we count down to the 21st century, let there be no jealousy in anyone about the Holy Spirit filling all!

· · · PRAYER · · ·

Father, may we be filled with the Holy Spirit and bring to fulfillment Christ's words: "Your kingdom come. Your will be done on earth as it is in heaven" (Matthew 6:10).

· · · TODAY'S THOUGHT · · ·

Jesus said, "I will build My church" (Matthew 16:18). I want to be a part of what Christ is building.

—C. Irvin Burris

MINISTRY OF THE HOLY SPIRIT

*"But when the Helper comes, whom I shall send to you
from the Father, the Spirit of truth who proceeds from the
Father, He will testify of Me"* (John 15:26).

What is the work of the Holy Spirit in the world? More importantly, what is the work of the Holy Spirit in your life? What does He do for you?

Recently, I began to think about the Upper Room of the New Testament. God spoke to my heart and assured me that the Holy Spirit is not focused on a place but in a direction. We are currently seeing the greatest ministry of the Holy Spirit that history has ever known. God is renewing hearts, minds, and experiences. He is bringing vitality, hope, love, power, and joy into the lives of millions of people. I pray that God will help us learn to live in anticipation of what He might do next.

A boy was fishing one day when a passerby ask him how many fish he had caught. He responded, "When I catch the one that's nibbling my hook and one more, I'll have two." Anticipation! Living in anticipation of what the Holy Spirit can do is demonstrated by the pastor who prayed, "God, do something for us today that is not in the bulletin."

What is the ministry of the Holy Spirit in the contemporary church? The Holy Spirit bears witness of Christ. The purpose of Pentecost was not to highlight the Holy Spirit but to empower the church to bear witness of Jesus. This is evidenced by the first Pentecostal sermon in Acts 2. After explaining the phenomenon of Pentecost, Peter quickly changed the subject and preached Christ to the multitude. Our primary message is the crucified, resurrected Christ.

· · · PRAYER · · ·

Lord, help us to keep Christ central in our message as we are anointed by the Spirit.

· · · TODAY'S THOUGHT · · ·

God gives His peace to those who follow His will and keep Jesus in clear focus as the reason for living and ministering.

—Dan R. Callahan

297

THE SHAPING OF A SPIRITUAL LEADER

And the Lord said to Moses: "Take Joshua the son of Nun with you, a man in whom is the Spirit, and lay your hand on him" (Numbers 27:18).

Moses had come to the final days of his ministry. The crossing of the Red Sea, the manna from heaven, the Ten Commandments, the water from the rock, and the building of the Tabernacle were past. The conquest of the Promised Land lay ahead.

Moses was not permitted to enter Canaan. Joshua, a younger man, gifted with boldness and possessing strong qualities, would take his place. The deciding factor had been "a man in whom [was] the Spirit." This is the secret of godly leadership. Spiritual matters demand Spirit-filled individuals.

God instructed Moses to lay his hand on his successor. Mentoring is often an ingredient of successful leadership. Laying on hands spoke of the continuity of God's redemptive plan. Joshua was not on a solo flight or a Lone Ranger adventure.

Joshua was presented publicly to the congregation. The church is a community of faith. Whatever we do for God as individuals must be done within the corporate body of Christ. God told Moses to transfer his authority to his successor. That was not an easy task. He had talked face-to-face with God; yet he prayed, "Lord, send them a true shepherd."

When Moses died the Lord spoke to Joshua: "Arise, go over this Jordan, you and all the people, to the land which I am giving to them" (Joshua 1:2). Joshua called the people to a renewed covenant with God, crossed the Jordan, took Jericho—and in 10 years had conquered all the Land of Promise.

· · · PRAYER · · ·

Lord, give me strength to overcome obstacles, humility in my accomplishments, and the wisdom to give You glory in all things.

· · · TODAY'S THOUGHT · · ·

I affirm that God is good. It is only through the anointing of His Holy Spirit that we can succeed in any ministry for Him.

—Loida Camacho

THE SPIRIT CAME

*"The Helper, the Holy Spirit, whom the Father will send in
My name, He will teach you all things, and bring to your
remembrance all things that I said to you"* (John 14:26).

 The Holy Spirit came as Christ promised. Jesus' followers
had doubts and questions after His resurrection and the
announcement that He was going back to the Father. Those
things changed when the Spirit came.

The Spirit came to bring to their remembrance what Jesus said.
There was much for them to remember, much that would bring comfort
and hope. He knew they would need to be reminded of His promises,
provisions, and admonitions.

The Spirit came to comfort. He fulfilled Christ's promise to send a
Comforter (Helper) after He departed. So the Spirit comes to us today
to bring comfort and to abide with us. He brings peace and joy no
matter what may be our circumstance.

The Spirit came to guide His children. The Holy Spirit guides those
who are filled with Him.

The Spirit came to give power for Christian service. Effectiveness
and joy in Christian service is made powerful when the Spirit operates
in the life of the believer.

The Spirit came to convict of sin and judgment to come. The Holy
Spirit works through conviction to reach the unbeliever. This work of
the Spirit has not changed since Jesus walked among men; He still
comes to touch us all.

· · · PRAYER · · ·

*Heavenly Father, thank You for bringing to my life Your Holy Spirit.
Teach me, guide me, and reveal to my heart Your truth and Your will.*

· · · TODAY'S THOUGHT · · ·

What a blessing to have His Spirit in our hearts and lives to bring us
strength and empower us for ministry to others.

—Dee Cason

THE HOLY SPIRIT AND PRAYER

*We do not know what we should pray for as we ought, but
the Spirit Himself makes intercession for us with groanings
which cannot be uttered* (Romans 8:26).

Henry Nouwen writes, "Prayer is not what is done by us but
rather what is done by the Holy Spirit in us." This is the purpose and intent of prayer. Many seem anxious about their
prayer life and carry around guilt because of the small amount
of time they dedicate to prayer. Guilt is a tool used by others to motivate us to pray more. Scripture makes clear that prayer is to relieve
anxiety, not create it. God's peace is the result of prayer, not the
removal of it.

When we view prayer as the work of the Holy Spirit in us, not as
something done by us, we are freed from anxiety and standards of performance that others may place on us. Even our own agendas are laid
aside as we stand in God's presence with open hearts, honest and vulnerable, proclaiming to ourselves and others that without God we can
do nothing. Prayer is supremely the work of the Holy Spirit in us.

How this truth should encourage us! We are not groping in the dark.
The divine voice issues out of the depths of our soul more profoundly
than anything our weak humanity can ever speak. I am inarticulate; He
is articulate. My aspirations and desires are immature; His petitions
are with perfect knowledge. He transcends the restricted sphere of self
and personal interest.

Be open to what the Spirit says in prayer. Discern the presence of
God's life-giving Spirit in the midst of your hectic life. Let the Spirit
constantly transform you.

· · · PRAYER · · ·

*Holy Spirit, speak to me and through me. Take control of my prayer
life and do Your will and work in me. Teach me to listen to what You
are speaking to my heart today.*

· · · TODAY'S THOUGHT · · ·

I resolve to set aside time every day to be alone with God and listen
to His Spirit.

—Ron Cason

THE SPIRIT WANTS YOU

The Spirit who dwells in us yearns jealously (James 4:5).

 My 12-year-old son, Jeremy, lost an expensive electronic game. He wanted to replace it, and I told him he would have to save his money and repurchase it on his own. He managed to save $127 over several months to buy the game he wanted.

One Sunday morning at church the pastor was sharing his vision of the new building program the church was entering. The pastor spoke of the need for total commitment and sacrifice. A few weeks later Jeremy began talking about the church and the building program. He asked his mother if it would take a lot of money.

"Yes, it will," she replied.

After pausing a few moments Jeremy said, "I have the money I've saved. Perhaps Pastor needs it to help build the church."

"Are you sure that's what you want to do?" she asked, knowing how long he had saved to buy the electronic game.

"Yes, Pastor needs it for the new church."

I was touched to realize that he was willing to give all he had.

Different things test the willingness of different persons because circumstances and dispositions are different. The design of the gospel is not to set us free to do as we please. It is to place us in our true position as children of God, to turn the heart wholly to Him so that His law is written by His Holy Spirit in the fleshly tables of our hearts.

· · · PRAYER · · ·

Holy Spirit, who dwells in us, touch our lives daily so that we yearn eagerly after You. Our prayer is that we will willingly give You all our possessions, affections, and desires exclusively!

· · · TODAY'S THOUGHT · · ·

You give willingly when you give knowing full well that you will not receive anything in return.

—John D. Childers

THE SPIRIT IN UNUSUAL PLACES

*When they came up out of the water, the Spirit of the Lord
caught Philip away, so that the eunuch saw him no more;
and he went on his way rejoicing* (Acts 8:39).

My unit was getting ready for a series of battles in the area of
Dak To, in the Vietnamese highlands. Thirty-seven new converts had expressed a desire to be baptized in water prior to
this operation. In my heart, I knew it was absolutely necessary. In fact, several of those baptized on that sunny, humid afternoon
were killed in battle within the next few days.

Against the clamor of those who were worried about security, we
took 37 new converts to a nearby river for baptism. This was no easy
task. We had to secure the area—set up a perimeter of guard posts to
protect us from snipers and other enemy intrusion.

As those young converts made their way into the river for baptism,
the sergeant and this chaplain were so caught up in the Spirit that it is
easy for me to understand what the Scripture meant when it said,
"When they came up out of the water, the Spirit of the Lord caught
Philip away." We were oblivious to the dangers we were facing. We
were so focused we could almost feel the covering of the Lord, as if the
whole valley was surrounded by an army of angels.

As we baptized these young men, the Spirit of God fell in a marvelous way. Several began speaking in a heavenly language that
echoed through that Vietnamese valley. When I feel stale in my spiritual life, God recalls for me afresh when truly He did meet with me and
my flock and carried us away in His Spirit.

· · · PRAYER · · ·

*O God, in the deserts of our lives meet with us for a new baptism in
Your Spirit, so that we can witness to the stranger.*

· · · TODAY'S THOUGHT · · ·

We cannot live all our lives in this carried–away state, but we must
have it occasionally as a resource, like Philip, to preach the gospel in
all the towns.

—Robert D. Crick

SPIRIT BAPTISM: A CRISIS EXPERIENCE

He said to them, "Did you receive the Holy Spirit when you believed?" And they said to him, "We have not so much as heard whether there is a Holy Spirit" (Acts 19:2).

 I take no issue with my Christian brethren who do not have the same understanding of the person and work of the Holy Spirit as I and other Pentecostals do. However, I'll never forget my experience of receiving the Baptism.

I was around 14 years old when my dear old grandmother, Agnes Crouch, in her long black dress with white starched cuffs and gleaming blue eyes, literally made me get on my knees to seek the Baptism. She said, "Son, you've just got to receive the baptism in the Holy Spirit with the evidence of speaking in tongues."

Just a young boy, I wasn't nearly as excited about receiving the baptism in the Holy Spirit as she was about my receiving it. But that precious saint of God prayed for me until she prayed the "glory" down. I'll never forget as long as I live that night when I received the enduement of power from on high.

I call it a crisis experience, because it is a crisis of the will. One must yield oneself completely. It is also a crisis of faith. One receives the baptism in the Holy Spirit by faith, not by intellectual reasoning.

Finally, it is a crisis of commitment. One is endued with power for service in the kingdom of God.

The pertinent question to ask yourself today is, "Have I received the Holy Spirit since I believed?"

· · · PRAYER · · ·

Heavenly Father, help me today to submit my will completely to Your will and by faith claim the promises of Your Word.

· · · TODAY'S THOUGHT · · ·

The first step in knowing God's will is being willing to accept it, whatever it might be.

—Paul Crouch

DEVELOPING SPIRITUAL LEADERSHIP

*They rebelled against His Spirit, so that he spoke rashly
with his lips* (Psalm 106:33).

I spent my childhood years in the Church of God on the Island of Jamaica under the leadership of the Reverend C.A. Morris. He dedicated me as an infant. When I was 8 years old, on a Sunday morning in Sunday school, the Holy Spirit spoke these words to the pastor: "This little boy will some day be a minister of the Church of God." As I grew up, his life and ministry impacted mine so much that I accepted the Lord Jesus as my personal Savior at age 16.

In 1955 I became a minister of the Church of God. How wonderful it has been to yield to the will of God as the Holy Spirit has empowered me these 40 years to preach God's word.

The need for dedicated, Spirit-filled leaders is urgent because humanity is constantly rebelling. It will take committed leaders to carry the torch forward, blazing for God so that others may follow. Leaders are called of God to become great warriors for the Lord. The best example to follow is that of an anointed servant of God who submits his will to the lordship of the Holy Spirit.

A leader must be aware of the consequences of his or her actions when the Holy Spirit is not in control. An awesome responsibility rests on those the Holy Spirit empowers to carry this great gospel to dying souls.

The Spirit makes the difference as we follow from victory to victory. Reliance on the Holy Spirit is not just for a special time or for one project only. We must seek to be led of Him every step we take.

· · · PRAYER · · ·

Heavenly Father, I pray You will fill me with Your Holy Spirit so that I will have communion and fellowship with You. Let the light of Christ shine in me until others may see and glorify You.

· · · TODAY'S THOUGHT · · ·

An axiom is that leaders are developed by other competent leaders. Spiritual leaders can only be developed as they are nurtured by the Holy Spirit.

—Peter Gayle

THE LEADERSHIP OF THE HOLY SPIRIT

After they had come to Mysia, they tried to go into Bithynia,
but the Spirit did not permit them (Acts 16:7).

Many choices, decisions and opportunities come our way. Giving our lives in God's service in the right place at the right time is so important. Paul came to realize that he could not evangelize Europe and Asia Minor at the same time. But he was sensitive to the Holy Spirit, knowing that God would direct him to the places of greatest fruitfulness and benefit.

Timing is important in the work of God! There are times of planting, times of waiting, and times of reaping the harvest. There are times when people are open to God and times when they have hardened their hearts. God wants us to be in the place where we can freely follow His leading and devote our energies to His will.

Most of us at some point in our lives have wanted to go to a certain place but it didn't work out. The door seemed to be blocked. When this happens, it is easy to get discouraged and feel upset with people who seem to stand in our way. In reality, God may have intervened in our lives as He did in Paul's. God closed one door but opened a greater one!

A key to success in life and ministry is to be sensitive and obedient to the leadership of the Holy Spirit. We must earnestly seek to do His will, not ours; and to go where He leads, not where we want to be. God leads and guides us when we obey. Then we can make an eternal difference in people's lives.

· · · PRAYER · · ·

Father, help me to always be sensitive to the leadership of the Holy Spirit. I want to be tender and open to the Spirit.

· · · TODAY'S THOUGHT · · ·

Seeking God's will involves a conscious surrender to God and a commitment to follow the Word.

—Larry G. Hess

THE SPIRIT STILL SPEAKS

*So when they did not agree among themselves, they depart-
ed after Paul had said one word: "The Holy Spirit spoke
rightly" (Acts 28:25).*

Fear gripped Mary Land's heart as she saw alcoholics, prostitutes, addicts, homosexuals, and criminals around her. The
sign outside the Atlanta urban ministry said "Mission
Possible." Most members of the small staff were bivocation-
al; and when they weren't at work, they were on the streets witnessing.
In those early days Mother would be alone with the needy in the 27-
room run-down building. She helped repair the building and feed 20-
30 people a day, but now she was afraid.

Mother grew up hard—abused, fighting, struggling, often hungry.
But her mother, a charter member of the Church of God in Jasper,
Alabama, had loved her and taught her to pray. As she prayed this
day, the Holy Spirit reminded her that He had called our family into
urban mission work. Suddenly, the Holy Spirit came on her. Feeling
as though she were 20 feet tall, she marched through each room of the
mission, praising God and rebuking the devil. The Holy Spirit said, "I
have sent my holy angels to stand guard around this place, and they
stand with their swords drawn." Freedom and courage replaced
bondage and fear.

A few years later, the Reverend J.F. Rowlands, Church of God apostle to the Indians of South Africa, visited the mission for the first time.
Before introductions were completed, he silenced the conversation
with a finger to his lips and began walking through the house. He said
to Mother, "Sister, you have great need of patience!"

"Yes, I do," she answered through knowing tears of long-suffering.

Then Pastor Rowlands exclaimed, "God says to tell you that His
angels are still around this place with their swords drawn!"

· · · PRAYER · · ·

*Spirit of the living God, I pray that You would cleanse my heart and
hands by the blood of Jesus, that I may be a clear channel through
whom You can speak in words and deeds.*

· · · TODAY'S THOUGHT · · ·

What the Holy Spirit speaks to us and through us is always biblical.

—Steven J. Land

THE SPIRIT-FILLED LIFE

And do not be drunk with wine, in which is dissipation; but
be filled with the Spirit (Ephesians 5:18).

Only a Spirit-filled church can affect a wine-filled world. Changes so desperately needed in our world will not come from a more efficient government or by a more efficient social system. If it comes, it will be through the church's being filled with the Spirit.

To be filled with the Spirit means to be under the control of the Spirit—to live one's life in accordance with the dictates and desires of the Spirit. As a sailing ship is carried along by the wind filling its sail, so the Holy Spirit fills or controls believers who submit to Him.

Paul said to be filled with the Spirit. This filling is not optional. Nor is it a once-for-all past experience we look back at with complacent satisfaction. It should be a daily, continuous experience.

When the Holy Spirit controls our lives, He not only makes us more like Jesus, but He also puts a song in our hearts and praise on our lips. One inescapable mark of the Spirit-filled Christian is joy that wells forth in songs of praise to God.

Four things result from a Spirit-filled life: *Fellowship* is implied in "psalms and hymns and spiritual songs" sung in the congregation (v. 19). *Worship*, or "making melody," includes vocal and instrumental music (v. 19). *Gratitude* is "giving thanks" (v. 20). Finally, there is *mutual submission* (v. 21). The absence of these characteristics in a congregation indicates the church is not Spirit-filled.

Paul alluded to the need for dependence on the Holy Spirit when he wrote to the Ephesians, "Finally, my brethren, be strong in the Lord and in the power of His might" (6:10).

· · · PRAYER · · ·

Lord, help me to live a Spirit-filled life that will be a witness to my neighbors and point them to Jesus.

· · · TODAY'S THOUGHT · · ·

The sooner we learn the importance of the power of the Spirit, the sooner we will endeavor to live a Spirit-filled life through which God can flow.

—George Peart

THE SPIRIT CONNECTION

"They tried to go into Bithynia, but the Spirit did not permit them" (Acts 16:7).

The elderly lady testified: "I'm glad I'm saved!" Then she danced in the Spirit. She continued, "I'm glad I'm sanctified!" and she danced again. She finished her testimony with, "I'm glad I have the Holy Spirit with the fire of Pentecost burning in my soul!"

This was my first experience with the "Spirit Connection," and my life has never been the same. More than 50 years have passed and I am still studying and experiencing that spiritual connection that occurs when you "do not walk according to the flesh, but according to the Spirit" (Romans 8:1).

The law of gravity keeps our feet solidly on the ground, but the Holy Spirit gives us the power that takes us directly into the presence of Jehovah God. If our minds are carnal and we walk according to the flesh, then we become totally grounded (see Romans 8:5-7). But if we have the mind of Christ (Philippians 2:5) and are "led by the Spirit" (Romans 8:14), then He is in full control and we find ourselves following the perfect will of God.

It can happen in a worship service when the Spirit simply moves us to dance under the anointing. Or it can happen when the Spirit directs us. The bottom line is if we are truly connected to Him, wherever the Spirit wants us to go, we will go.

· · · PRAYER · · ·

Father, search me, try me, and know me. Remove anything that hinders the Spirit from taking full control of my life. I give You permission to do what You have to do—break, mold, renew. I want the Spirit connection. I want to go wherever the Spirit goes.

· · · TODAY'S THOUGHT · · ·

The secret of the victorious life is balance; the secret of balance is the Spirit connection.

—C. Annette Watson

A SURE GUIDE

"When He, the Spirit of truth, has come, He will guide you into all truth; for He will not speak on His own authority, but whatever He hears He will speak; and He will tell you things to come" (John 16:13).

Life is similar, in some ways, to climbing a mountain. You never really know what you are facing next. The possibility of danger can never be dismissed. Each day is a new challenge. You have never been this way before, so decisions are often based solely on your own limited experience. You must live with the consequences of your decisions. Circumstances, like the weather, are constantly changing and we have little control over them.

Sometimes we think it would be helpful if we could preview our lives and be alerted to prepare for some of the difficulties ahead. Unfortunately, we lack this ability. Wouldn't it be great to have a guide who has this capacity? The future would lose some of its fear, and we would be much more secure in facing tomorrow.

Jesus had this need in mind when He said to the disciples, "I will not leave you orphans" (John 14:18). He had seen the effect His absence had on the disciples. They were at a loss; they had lost their sense of direction. How easy it is to get lost without a guide.

Jesus said of the Holy Spirit, "He will guide you" (John 16:13). Consider this guide sent from the Father if you need knowledge or lack power (Micah 3:8).

· · · PRAYER · · ·

Heavenly Father, I pray that each of us will receive in faith this heavenly Guide to be with us and in us.

· · · TODAY'S THOUGHT · · ·

I am never alone; my friend, the Holy Spirit, is always with me.

—Richard L. Tyler, Jr.

A MAN OF FAITH

"These signs will follow those who believe" (Mark 16:17).

The origin of E.O. Kerce's faith can be traced to his family's spiritual beginnings. In the sparsely settled woods of north Florida, this family was ready for the refreshing winds of revival that swept through the area in the early part of the century.

Church of God pioneer, R.P. Johnson, was mightily used of the Holy Spirit to fan the flames of revival throughout this area. During one of these revival services, S.W. Kerce took his family to the meeting. The crude altar in that building marked the birthplace of the spiritual heritage of the Kerce family in the Church of God. S.W. Kerce was called into the ministry and was followed by three sons. Five generations of this family have found ministry in the church.

In that meeting in 1909, E.O. Kerce was saved. A few years later, after his call to preach, he made a trip from Florida to visit relatives in Tennessee. He carried with him the simple faith and fervent spirit of those early days of the church. He also carried the zeal to witness and preach.

Due to the lack of church buildings, prayer meetings were held in homes. While preaching during one of these services, the anointing of the Spirit weighed heavily on God's servant. Spontaneously, he reached out and grasped a red-hot stovepipe. Such acts of faith in the early church were never programmed or planned. They were, rather, simple acts of faith, unencumbered by logic or unbelief.

The outgrowth of that experience was an irresistible outpouring of revival fervor. People were saved, healed, and filled with the Holy Spirit. News spread rapidly through the community and revival fires were ignited.

· · · PRAYER · · ·

God, help me to have faith in You, and let my life be a testimony of my faith.

· · · TODAY'S THOUGHT · · ·

True believers never follow signs, but signs do follow true believers.

—Betty Roberts

THE PRINCIPLE OF THE ZERO FACTOR

*I waited patiently for the Lord; and He inclined to me,
and heard my cry. He also brought me up out of a horrible
pit, out of the miry clay, and set my feet upon a rock, and
established my steps* (Psalm 40:1, 2).

 Many face times of bitter hopelessness in their lives: a child
is stricken with an incurable disease; a job is lost at a time
when the household faces a mountain of debt; a son is hooked
on cocaine;, a divorce is pending in the judicial system.

In the Bible many turned to God when all hope was gone—when all
their physical resources had been exhausted. In fact, when no banker,
lawyer, or doctor can help, that's an excellent time to trust God!

Remember the woman with the issue of blood? For 12 long years
she sought the help of doctors. She had spent her life's savings trying
to get well. All hope was gone—until she çaught sight of Jesus.

Something within her began to stir when she remembered that she
had heard about the miracle worker. As she reached out in faith, grasping the hem of His garment, she was instantly made whole.

Are you at the point of hopelessness now? Get a glimpse of Jesus.
He is still performing miracles.

Reach out and touch Him in faith.

Your miracle is on the way!

· · · PRAYER · · ·

*Thank You, Father, for the miracles You give us every day! Help us
to always live worthy of Your love and grace.*

· · · TODAY'S THOUGHTS · · ·

I am a miracle. I experience miracles daily. I will share God's miracles with others through the Holy Spirit.

—R.W. Schambach

CONTROLLED BY THE SPIRIT

The fruit of the Spirit is love, joy, peace, longsuffering,
kindness, goodness, faithfulness, gentleness, self–control.
If we live in the Spirit, let us also walk in the Spirit
(Galatians 5:22, 23, 25).

Those who live in the Spirit, Paul says, walk in the Spirit. They who walk in the Spirit bear the fruit of the Holy Spirit. Examine this fruit:

1. *Love* is the ability to see beyond yourself and care for others.

2. *Joy* is the ability to take the unexpected difficulties of life in confidence, knowing that God will see your through it all.

3. *Peace* comes from living in harmony with God and knowing you are led by the Spirit.

4. *Patience* helps you withstand adverse circumstances until God's work is completed.

5. *Kindness* is the oil of a civilized society. This grace should be evident in Christians, of all people.

6. *Goodness* manifests itself in generous, upright living. Goodness is an honorable quality.

7. *Faithfulness* means dependability. A Spirit-led Christian is reliable and loyal.

8. *Gentleness* adds strength to kindness and goodness. It is velvet but it is firm.

9. *Self-control* is the governor on the appetites of the flesh and spirit. It keeps us from being slaves to our own desires and to evil lusts.

Fruit grows naturally when the tree is properly tended and gets the proper nourishment. The Holy Spirit carefully tends and guards those who follow His leading. Life in the Spirit is sometimes demanding and difficult. Yet, only the Spirit-filled life will yield the fruit of the Spirit.

· · · PRAYER · · ·

Our Father, we ask You to lead us faithfully as we follow You faithfully. May the fruit of the Holy Spirit be evident in my life every day, in every way!

· · · TODAY'S THOUGHT · · ·

I am born of the Spirit and baptized in the Holy Spirit. Therefore, I will walk in the Spirit and bear His fruit in my live.

—Dave B. Lorency

SPIRITUAL UNITY

Endeavoring to keep the unity of the Spirit in the bond of peace (Ephesians 4:3).

 "That was fun!" sighed John in exhausted pleasure as he sat down in his easy chair, knowing the whole family had worked together on Mr. Alexander's wheelchair ramp. This was the first time in four years the whole family had been together. John enjoyed seeing his children and grandchildren working together on a worthy cause for a neighbor.

Jesus, through the Holy Spirit, teaches us to pray, "Our Father in heaven." He is leading us to acknowledge our family relationship and to understand our uniqueness in His family. Paul encourages us to go beyond what is expected, and do more to keep unity and peace in the family. The key to family strength is unity. The cause of family weakness is division and fragmentation. In the previous verse, Paul says we bring about unity "with all lowliness and gentleness, with longsuffering, bearing with one another in love." And this is how we, "walk worthy of the calling with which we are called."

As Christians we are part of our natural family and a part of God's family. The family of God is derived from the fatherhood and love of God. God our Father, loves all His children. We are loved because He is love. Since He is spirit, His family is spiritual. This is why Paul tells us to "endeavor to keep the unity of the Spirit," because spiritually we are all equals in His family.

We have peace in our natural family when we work together in harmony. We enjoy the bond of peace in the family of God when we dedicate to doing of the will of our Father in heaven. In this way we experience a unity in purpose and understanding, with peace in our daily lives.

· · · PRAYER · · ·

Our Father in heaven, let Your will be done through me today, for Your glory, through the power of the Holy Spirit.

· · · TODAY'S THOUGHT · · ·

"My peace I give to you. Let not your heart be troubled, neither let it be afraid (John 14:27).

—Robert D. "Bob" McCall

STRENGTHENED BY GOD'S SPIRIT

... that He would grant you, according to the riches of His
glory, to be strengthened with might through His Spirit in
the inner man (Ephesians 3:16).

No matter how confident we are, we are not strong enough to conquer temptation, sin, grief, and death. If we allow the Spirit to strengthen us, however, we shall be more than conquerors. When we allow Him to strengthen us, we will be strong in the deepest part of our being—in our spirits that God has renewed.

The man who has had the greatest impact on me is my father, the Reverend Orphilus Noel. In his years of pastoring in the southern part of Haiti, the way he allowed the Holy Spirit to strengthen him was always a mystery to me. He never failed to let me know that the Holy Spirit was the One doing the great works through him. That was the constant testimony that led me to Christ.

I have learned to allow the Spirit of God to strengthen me. He never fails to exhibit His power through great works. The secret is in letting go of self and allowing the Spirit of God to strengthen you.

· · · PRAYER · · ·

Heavenly Father, help me to be strengthened with might by Your
Spirit in the inner man.

· · · TODAY'S THOUGHT · · ·

I will let the Holy Spirit comfort me, thus assuring that I will be victorious.

—O. Othon Noel

POWER FOR LIVING

"But you shall receive power when the Holy Spirit has come upon you; and you shall be witnesses to Me in Jerusalem, and in all Judea and Samaria, and to the end of the earth" (Acts 1:8).

If our needs met and we are to address the needs of others, we must have power. Power for living is available through a personal relationship with the Creator. As His Word declares, "Power belongs to God" (Psalm 62:11). Power for living, therefore, is God's power shared with man. This is an awesome thought but it is a Biblical reality. Jesus promised His followers "you shall receive power."

My older son was in his early teens when I was serving as State Youth and Christian Education Director in Florida. As I traveled trying to help other young people, it was impressed on me that my sons were not baptized in the Holy Spirit and, therefore, did not have the essential power needed for living.

In a convention in the northern end of the state, I watched young people fill the altar and pray, but my thoughts were back home where my sons were. Returning home, I learned that my wife had the same impression I had. Together, we decided to go back to the pastorate where our sons could have a regular church to attend.

Several months later, we found ourselves in a pastorate and not long after that—on a balmy summer evening—the Lord graciously baptized our older son in the Holy Spirit. What a wonderful experience for our family! Later, our younger son was baptized in the Spirit. We had been taught all of our lives that one could not live a powerful, victorious life without the baptism in the Holy Spirit and clearly God has made that power available to His people.

· · · PRAYER · · ·

Father, fill us with your Spirit according to Your promises. May that Spirit flow through us in the power that you have so designed.

· · · TODAY'S THOUGHT · · ·

By faith, we appropriate God's power for living so that we do not exist in confusion, weakness, or weariness.

—Donald T. Pemberton

LOVE IN THE SPIRIT

. . . who also declared to us your love in the Spirit
(Colossians 1:8).

God is love (1 John 4:8) and love is the essential nature of God. The fruit of the Spirit—love, joy, peace, long-suffering, kindness, goodness, faithfulness, gentleness, and self-control—is God's nature being produced in our lives. God's nature of love is manifested through us as we do for others when they cannot do for us. God's manifested love goes the extra mile in service with joy.

Love is primary in Christian character and conduct. God, by the Holy Spirit, drew us to salvation with love. This love affects our intellect, our will, our emotions, and our being. God is so good to communicate this divine attribute to us. Love begins and continues in God, but He lets us share this love in the Spirit.

When we are privileged to have love in the Spirit, it results in our being like Jesus. This love is not self-promotion, self-effort, or self-improvement. Love in the Spirit is God's nature flowing through us. It is being like Jesus.

Love is God's way of reaching others through us (Matthew 5:43-46). Love in the Spirit will cause us to love even our enemies, will cause us to bless those who curse us, will help us meet hate with goodness and persecution with prayer.

Love in the Spirit is the fruit from which the other virtues flow.

· · · PRAYER · · ·

Lord, help me to demonstrate love in the Spirit so that all I say, do, or think will be motivated by You.

· · · TODAY'S THOUGHT · · ·

I resolve to show love in the Spirit in all my words, actions, motives, and attitudes . . . with all my being.

—Travis Porter

ASSURANCE IN THE RESURRECTION

He who raised Christ from the dead will also give life to
your mortal bodies through His Spirit who dwells in you
(Romans 8:11).

The indwelling of the Holy Spirit is the common mark of all believers. It is the Shepherd's mark of the flock, distinguishing them from the rest of the world. It is the goldsmith's stamp on the genuine sons of God, separating them from the dross of false professors of the faith. It is the King's own seal on those who are His peculiar people, proving them to be His own property. The indwelling Spirit of God brings life and peace which enables the believer to walk in newness of life.

The Holy Spirit has many titles in Scripture, but none is more exciting than "the Spirit of Life." He originates in the Father, the Author and Sustainer of life, and takes up His abode in the lives of believers. He will give life to our dead bodies.

Our bodies, indeed, are not exempt from the death brought by sin; but our spirits have in them an undying life—life in the Son. If the Spirit who raised Jesus from the dead dwells in us, our bodies will experience the same resurrection.

The life within is a gift from God. Further, the indwelling of the Holy Spirit is the "Spirit of Him who raised Jesus from the dead." Resurrection comes "through His Spirit who dwells in you."

· · · PRAYER · · ·

Father, help us to live a life of obedience to Your divine will and experience the resurrection to eternal life.

· · · TODAY'S THOUGHT · · ·

What joy it brings the believer to know that dwelling in Him is the Spirit of God who raised Jesus from the dead.

—Julian B. Robinson

THE HOLY SPIRIT'S ASSURANCE

By this we know that He abides in us, by the Spirit whom
He has given us (1 John 3:24).

Paul's definition of assurance is described in Romans 8:15-16. When a believer cries "Abba! Father!" it is the Holy Spirit Himself bearing witness with our spirit that we are children of God. There come to us an inner sense of a new relationship with God. Thus, we are made aware of the eternal realm, and we clearly perceive our status as justified children of God at peace with our Father.

Because of the indwelling of the Holy Spirit, we are able to calmly appropriate God's promises. Assurance is an indispensable and welcoming ministry of the Holy Spirit.

We have the Holy Spirit's assurance Christ lives in us. It is the office of the Holy Spirit to reproduce in our lives the graces and qualities that reside in their fullness in Christ. When we hunger for love, patience, purity, power, or courage, we may draw from the One who lives in us. Our lives are enriched and empowered by the presence of Christ. Christ dwells in the heart of the believer who is obedient to His commandments. He makes our hearts His abode and the Holy Spirit makes His presence real.

Christ overcomes for us and His overflow becomes the outliving of His inliving.

· · · PRAYER · · ·

Heavenly Father, thank you for giving us the Holy Spirit to assure us of the fact that we are your children and that Christ abides in us.

· · · TODAY'S THOUGHT · · ·

I commit my life to Christ and to His Holy Spirit. I want my actions and my words to overflow from a Spirit-filled heart and bless others.

—Lazaro Santana

I WAS IN THE SPIRIT

Immediately I was in the Spirit; and behold, a throne set in heaven, and One sat on the throne (Revelation 4:2).

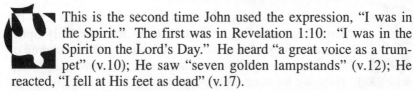 This is the second time John used the expression, "I was in the Spirit." The first was in Revelation 1:10: "I was in the Spirit on the Lord's Day." He heard "a great voice as a trumpet" (v.10); He saw "seven golden lampstands" (v.12); He reacted, "I fell at His feet as dead" (v.17).

When one is in the Spirit, something wonderful happens. John was so awed with the sight of Jesus, whom he knew so well on earth, now resplendent in the symbols of divinity, that he said, "And when I saw Him, I fell at His feet as dead." Oh that we too might be so awed by the presence of the Son of God in our midst.

At age 8 I felt the call of God on my life to preach the Gospel. I was attending a church that did not believe in the baptism in the Holy Spirit with the initial evidence of speaking in tongues as the Spirit gives utterance. By the time I was a teenager, I had heard all negative teaching concerning the Pentecostal experience. One night a friend took me to a Church of God in Atlanta, Georgia. Though I had all the answers as to why these people were wrong about the infilling of the Holy Spirit, a hunger for this experience began to rise in me.

On Thursday before Easter Sunday in 1978, I attended a revival at the Riverside Church of God in Atlanta. When the altar call was given, I went forward. Those praying in the altar had their hands on me, and immediately I was in the Spirit. I became intoxicated and captivated by the Holy Spirit. My life was invaded with a wonderful joy from heaven that I had never known.

· · · PRAYER · · ·

Lord, it is my desire to be always filled with your Holy Spirit.

· · · TODAY'S THOUGHT · · ·

The power and the glory of the church is the fire of Pentecost.

—George Stephens

IT'S OUR CHOICE

They made their hearts like flint, refusing to hear the law
and the words which the Lord of hosts had sent by His Spirit
(Zechariah 7:12).

Pharaoh had many opportunities to make a noble and right choice concerning the Israelites. But he turned his heart "like flint" from God, and the Lord hardened his heart.

In my own moments of stubbornness and self-reliance, I find my problems getting bigger and more complex. Only when I turn toward God and allow Him to touch my heart do I begin to see positive results. Only then does my heart become soft and pliable and useable.

Years ago we pastored in Florida, and that particular church needed a leader for young adults. This was something I had not done before, had no desire to do, and did not feel capable of doing. I felt I was in no way responsible for filling this need. One Sunday as we stood in prayer the Holy Spirit impressed me with these words: "That's your Sunday school class." My answer was quick and emphatic: "Not mine! I can't do that and I won't volunteer for something I'm not able to do."

Wouldn't you think that would have settled the issue? Not so! Once again I sensed the Spirit telling me, "That's your Sunday school Class!" No one was more surprised than I was when I heard myself offer to take the class and try to make it grow. Now as I look at pictures of "my" class of 25-30 young adults meeting at the parsonage and walking from Sunday school with me, their teacher. I am grateful I made the right choice.

· · · PRAYER · · ·

Lord, my desire is that my heart be firm enough to ward off the Enemy yet, soft with compassion for hurting people and alert to Your voice.

· · · TODAY'S THOUGHT · · ·

Choose this day whom you will serve.

—Betty Lanier

HOLY SPIRIT'S GUIDANCE

Let them do good, that they be rich in good works, ready to give, willing to share, storing up for themselves a good foundation for the time to come, that they may lay hold on eternal life (1Timothy 6:18, 19).

My grandfather A.H. Argue was in his 20s when he moved from the Red River Valley of North Dakota to Winnipeg, Canada. He was a committed Christian and involved in the Holiness Movement. Just before the turn of the century, he invested in real estate and almost overnight became very wealthy. One of his grandsons has estimated his holdings in 1996 dollars, and they amount to several million dollars.

In 1906, A.H. Argue heard of the great revival at Azusa Street in Los Angeles. As a man of means, he was able to travel to Los Angeles and be part of the revival. His life was dramatically changed when he felt the call of God to leave his business and enter full-time ministry.

Most Pentecostal churches in those days were small and struggling, and many cities did not have a Pentecostal witness. With the wealth that God had provided, my grandfather and members of his family were able to conduct revivals in established churches and in communities and cities that had never had a Pentecostal meeting. He was able to support himself and his family through the funds received from the sale of his business.

There are cities and churches all over the United States and Canada that were profoundly impacted by the ministry of A.H. Argue and his family. He was one of the true pioneers of the Pentecostal revival.

When A.H. Argue passed away at 91 years of age, his estate was valued at $1,600. In his will he directed that those funds be equally distributed among three of his grandsons who were enrolled in college and preparing for the ministry. I was one of those grandsons.

· · · PRAYER · · ·

Thank You, Lord, for the leadership of Your Holy Spirit, and for a grandfather who was willing to be led.

· · · TODAY'S THOUGHT · · ·

The late J. Paul Getty, one of the world's richest men, wrote in his memoirs, *As I See It*, that he had tried to live by his father's credo: "It's not how much money a man has, it's what he does with it that counts."

—Don Argue

THE SPIRIT DIRECTS

*Paul was constrained by the Spirit, and testified . . . that
Jesus is the Christ (Acts 18:5).*

My husband, Randall, accepted our first pastorate in Fortuna,
California. Our first child had died and we were expecting
our second. I was experiencing a lot of stress. A special lady,
Margaret Bolt, ministered to us during this time with extraordinary grace and spirit.

Now, 17 years later, we are pastoring a thriving church in Vacaville,
California. We have seen a great revival among the youth.
Subcultures of all kinds, including Satanists, have been born again. I
accompany our youth group to the streets to witness to troubled kids
every Friday night.

One night, three years ago, the Holy Spirit prompted me to ask a
young man whom I'd never seen, what his name was. Reluctantly, he
said, "David Bolt."

Under the unction of the Holy Spirit I blurted out, "David, I know
your grandma, and she is at home right now on her knees praying for
you."

His eyes grew as big as saucers. Then I thought in my mind, Sister
Bolt might not even be alive. I hadn't heard from her or seen her in
years. Besides, this boy might be from a different Bolt family.

Suddenly I laid my hand on his blond head and began to pray. He
threw his cigarette away and began to pray. Later I discovered that she
was praying for him that very night. The next Sunday morning David,
along with his mom and dad, was in Sunday school and church.

If we allow the Holy Spirit to guide us, lives can be changed. The
Bolts are now faithful members and a great blessing to our church.

· · · PRAYER · · ·

*Heavenly Father, I thank You for Your Holy Spirit who not only
gives us boldness to witness of Christ, but who impresses us and leads
us in our endeavors.*

· · · TODAY'S THOUGHT · · ·

Keep praying for your children and grandchildren. God listens.
And He directs.

—Cheryl Ann Bailey

THE SPIRIT ALSO WITNESSES TO US

The Holy Spirit also witnesses to us . . . "This is the
covenant that I will make with them after those days, says
the Lord: I will put My laws into their hearts, and in their
minds I will write them" (Hebrews 10:15, 16).

 His name was George; he was well into his 80s. A big barrel-chested veteran of World War I, he made it clear he was not interested in church. Everyone in the neighborhood knew George, but no one seemed to be able to become close to him.

One early spring, George's wife suffered a stroke and was placed in a nursing home. My wife and I visited her and eventually led her to the Lord. She prayed with us and accepted Christ, but George remained adamant. Suffering from diabetes, George eventually had to have his right foot amputated. We visited regularly and helped him with his mail and personal affairs. Still he resisted our efforts to lead him to the Lord.

It was Saturday and I was busily preparing for Sunday, and quite frankly I had forgotten about George for the moment. Driving down North Avenue, I felt the Holy Spirit whisper to my heart, "You need to visit George today." As I drove on, the Holy Spirit continued to press—"Visit George!" I drove to Veterans Hospital, and when I entered his room George was weeping. He spoke through tears and said, "I've been waiting for you to come. I want to make things right with the Lord." We wept and prayed together. The angels rejoiced in heaven as George's name was written down!

I excitedly returned to the hospital the next day to see how George was doing, but a message was waiting at the front desk. George had passed away during the night. He had gone home. Clearly the Holy Spirit had spoken the day before, and through sensitivity to Him another precious soul had made it safely home.

· · · PRAYER · · ·

Father, help us to keep our hearts always sensitive to the leading of
Your Holy Spirit so that He might make us effective soulwinners.

· · · TODAY'S THOUGHT · · ·

So often we relegate the working of the gifts of the Spirit to the sanctuary and large meetings. However, we must be mindful always that the Spirit works in the hustle and bustle of everyday life. Let us listen!

—Gale A. Barnett

THE SPIRIT FLOWS

Do not quench the Spirit (1 Thessalonians 5:19).

The Christian life is really very simple. Often, we try to make the Christian life complicated. If we cannot understand a teacher or his teachings, we label them "profound." But the Spirit walk is so simple, many don't believe it. We think we must produce something or accomplish something to walk in the Spirit. But, no—the price has already been paid. Although that seems too simple, we finally accept it. At that very moment the Holy Spirit moves into our house to live.

When He comes in, several things begin to happen. First, He comes in to lead us according to the Bible. He leads us by His book because, after all, He wrote it. That's why I don't understand why some people are always looking for men to lead them. Of course, God does use people, but why take second-best. The Holy Spirit-inspired Bible provides all the guidance we will ever need. But that's not all. The Holy Spirit comes to teach us. This wonderful Holy Spirit comes in to comfort, to strengthen, to fill, and to cleanse.

No one has to tell a river to flow. If no one blocks it, it will flow automatically. No one has to tell the Holy Spirit to do His work. If we quit bothering and blocking Him, He will do His work. It's the natural thing, just as it is natural for birds to fly and fish to swim and the sun to shine and the river to flow. No one needs to encourage Him; we just must not discourage Him.

It is the natural thing for the new nature that comes in with the Holy Spirit to receive the work of the Holy Spirit, so let Him who is now within you do what He will.

· · · PRAYER · · ·

Holy Spirit, I yield myself to You and I pray that You will allow my path to cross the paths of those whom Jesus would help if He walked in the shoes I walk in today.

· · · TODAY'S THOUGHT · · ·

I have found that all God wants is for us to yield ourselves. He will do the work if we just get out of the way and let Him.

—Tommy Barnett

HANDLING CRITICISM SPIRITUALLY

Then Peter, filled with the Holy Spirit, said to them, "Rulers of the people and elders of Israel . . . (Acts 4:8).

In the beginning of my Christian experience, I often made mountains of molehills. I sometimes felt that every time I did something for God my brothers in the Lord would criticize me for it, and I allowed the criticism to hinder my service for the Lord.

One day someone phoned and called me everything but a brother. He criticized me for neglecting to give proper counseling to his family. I was not to call on his family ever again. Did I ever want to give him a piece of my mind! But while he was shouting on the phone, I felt the Holy Spirit come over me and anoint me to listen to him and respond in love. I did, but I wondered what good God would get from this. A month later he called me and said, "I'm sorry." He went on to say that his daughter had been in a severe automobile accident and was in a coma. When she awoke, she said she didn't want to talk to anyone but the pastor, and that was why he was calling.

I thank God for the anointing of the Holy Spirit. I could have responded in the flesh, but thank God for His Holy Spirit. He will take every situation and cause it to bring glory, honor, and praise to Him.

· · · PRAYER · · ·

Heavenly Father, thank You for wanting to bring out the best in me. I want to be led by the Holy Spirit. I know You care for me and will not allow me to encounter anything that will destroy me. May Your will be done in my life.

· · · TODAY'S THOUGHT · · ·

My beloved brethren, let every man be swift to hear, slow to speak, slow to wrath (James 1:19).

—Timothy James Bass

HELP ME FIND A JOB

"When He, the Spirit of truth, has come, He will guide you"
(John 16:13).

Our finances were so low that I was going to have to return to work. How I dreaded all that was involved in the process of filling out applications and knocking on business doors to find a suitable job. "Lord," I prayed, "help me find a job soon."

Since I had worked at a credit bureau in another town and enjoyed my job, I decided to call the local credit bureau to see if there were any openings. I knew I should make contacts in person rather than call, but the urge was so strong that I called. The man in charge said the office was only a two-person operation. He suggested a similar business where I might inquire. This was Friday afternoon. I knew that on Monday I would have to start making contacts.

Saturday came, and my telephone rang. "Are you the lady who called yesterday looking for a job with the credit bureau?" the man asked.

"Yes," I replied.

"Well, the girl who works here came in Friday afternoon, turned in her keys, and left. I would like for you to come down and apply."

I started to work on Tuesday and was eventually offered full management of the bureau.

So many times we try to solve all of our problems, while Christ stands ready to help if we ask. We are instructed in 1 Peter 5:7 to cast all our cares upon Him because He cares for us.

· · · PRAYER · · ·

Thank You, Father, for the guiding hand of Your Holy Spirit. May we always be sensitive to Your leadership and listen for the compelling inner voice of the Spirit.

· · · TODAY'S THOUGHT · · ·

God's Word reminds us that He knows our needs before we ask. Yet, He still wants us to ask so we may receive and our joy may be full.

—Edith Bean

GOD'S POWER IS NOT FOR SALE

Now when Simon saw that through the laying on of the apostles' hands the Holy Spirit was given, he offered them money, saying, "Give me this power also" (Acts 8:18, 19).

Simon Magus was a powerful man, a sorcerer. When Philip came to town preaching Christ, his ministry was accompanied by signs and miracles. Many of Simon's followers were converted and began to follow Christ. Simon also believed and was baptized. He had quickly recognized that Philip had access to a source of power greater than his own.

When news of the revival reached Jerusalem, the apostles sent Peter and John to inspect the work. When they arrived, Peter and John prayed for the converts, laying their hands on them, and they received the gift of the Holy Spirit.

Simon desired to also possess power to lay hands on others and have them receive this spiritual gift. Coming from his background in sorcery, perhaps he felt he was getting close to the heart of these mysteries. So intense was his desire that he offered Peter and John money for a share in their secret power. It is this act that has given the term *simony* to our ecclesiastical vocabulary.

Simon was quite unprepared for the stern words his carnal request elicited from Peter. "Your money perish with you," was the denunciation, "because you thought that the gift of God could be purchased with money!" (v. 20).

God's gifts and power are free. They are bestowals of His grace. They cannot be merited or purchased but are available to "whosoever will." It is just as wrong today for someone to feel that God's power is somehow deserved as it was in that day for Simon to try to buy it. Yet it is available to all who believe!

· · · PRAYER · · ·

Father, thank You for the free gift of Your Holy Spirit. I surrender my will and open my heart to You. I am available for whatever You want to do. Work Your will in me so that Your Spirit may flow through me to bless others and bring You praise.

· · · TODAY'S THOUGHT · · ·

"If the gift of God could be purchased with money, it would not be a gift!" (H.A. Ironside).

—David S. Bishop

CHRIST THE BAPTIZER

"And as I began to speak, the Holy Spirit fell upon them, as upon us at the beginning." (Acts 11:15-17).

Peter confirmed that Cornelius, a Gentile and an earnest seeker, had been baptized in the Holy Spirit. Peter was quick to point out that this was the same experience he and the other Jewish disciples had received in the Upper Room at Jerusalem. When Peter saw the Holy Spirit poured out upon this man and his household, he concluded that he had no power to withstand God in His choice to sovereignly extend His grace to a hungry, seeking soul, even if that person happened to be a Gentile.

We must remember that God knows no limitations. There are times when God is ready to do something, but because of our religious orientation or dogmatic mind-set we find ourselves standing in God's way. Peter felt "Who am I that I should be able to thwart God's plans?" God can and will manifest Himself to anyone who will truly seek after Him wholeheartedly.

Cornelius was a devoted, poised, dutiful man, who feared God. He gave much alms and prayed often. He was a just man in the eyes of other men, and he had a good reputation. Yet, it was only when he became truly hungry for the knowledge of God that deliverance and power came to his life. We see the seeker sending for help (Acts 10:7, 8). This was an exercise of great faith, and the result was amazing. It helped Peter to learn a wonderful truth which changed his attitude and his ministry. Peter's testimony sounded like this: "God led and I followed; He taught me and I believed." And God sealed Peter's work with the witness of the Holy Spirit by baptizing Cornelius and his household.

· · · PRAYER · · ·

Lord, send us a fresh outpouring of Your Holy Spirit, empowering us to go forth into the harvest field and reap the last-days harvest.

· · · TODAY'S THOUGHT · · ·

It is comforting to know that God still opens His truths to individuals today. If we seek for a fresh outpouring of His Spirit, He will grant our desire.

—Canute Blake

THE COMFORT OF THE SPIRIT

*I will pray the Father, and He will give you another Helper,
that He may abide with you forever, even the Spirit of truth,
whom the world cannot receive, because it neither sees Him
nor knows Him; but you know Him, for He dwells with you
and will be in you* (John 14:16, 17).

In my darkest hour I came to know the reality of the Holy Spirit's abiding presence as Comforter and friend.

After a dynamic service in Georgia, I joined the pastor at the parsonage for a time of warm, pleasant fellowship. The telephone rang and after a brief conversation, the pastor walked straight to me. Kneeling before my chair, he looked me straight in the eyes and with trembling voice spoke words that would change my life forever: "Steve . . . there's been an accident. David's dead!"

It felt as though my heart had been ripped from my chest. "Oh, God, not my boy, David," I cried, over and over. Despair and agony filled the next long, lonely hours, and the darkness of the night seemed to hold me captive for an eternity.

Darkness gave way to dawn the next day and I realized that this terrible nightmare was real. Returning home to Ohio that morning, I did not go alone, however. The Holy Spirit was with me, comforting me, helping me through the pain and grief.

The Holy Spirit is aware of our pain in times of need. He is our Paraclete, "one called alongside to help." When we are grieving or overwhelmed with the trials of life, He is our Helper, our buckler, our shield. He is the One who goes before us to overcome whatever would try to steal our peace and joy.

· · · PRAYER · · ·

Precious Holy Spirit, I thank You in Jesus Christ for being there every time I have needed You. Help me to be a comfort to others, as You are to me.

· · · TODAY'S THOUGHT · · ·

God's Word promises the Comforter will abide forever. No matter what you're facing, remember that you are not alone!

—Steve Brock

WHO'S YOUR FATHER?

For as many as are led by the Spirit of God, these are sons of God (Romans 8:14).

We cannot evolve into sonship. It is God's plan to lead us by His Holy Spirit into a relationship in which the Holy Spirit will confirm that we are the children of God (v. 16).

God taught man about His leadership by degrees. During Israel's wilderness wanderings, the Lord directed that a small ark be built. This ark contained sacred relics and was carried wherever the people went. It was the centerpiece of God's leadership of Israel. He told His people that He would dwell above the mercy seat and between the cherubim and that He would lead them from there.

The ark led the way across the flooded Jordan River and past the fallen walls of Jericho to ultimate possession of the Land of Promise. The ark symbolizes God's leadership of His children—He leads them; He does not drive them. He leads us today in several ways:

First, God leads through His Word. The more we read, memorize, and meditate upon it, the more sensitive we are to His leadership.

Then God leads through His church. Just as the family teaches the child to walk, talk, play, and eat, the church family teaches its children to seek the leadership of the Holy Spirit and the guidance of God in all things.

God also leads through the personal working of the Holy Spirit within us (John 14:17). "The Holy Spirit Himself bears witness with our spirit that we are children of God" (Romans 8:16). The Holy Spirit guides us when we don't know what decision to make. God's Word says, "Your ears shall hear a word behind you, saying, 'This is the way, walk in it'" (Isaiah 30:21).

· · · PRAYER · · ·

Thank You Father for the privileges of sonship. Enable me, this day and always, to remain sensitive to the tender leadings of Your Holy Spirit.

· · · TODAY'S THOUGHT · · ·

Who do *you* obey? "Who's your Father?"

—Robert E. Daughtery

TONGUES ARE REAL

I thank my God I speak with tongues more than you all
(1 Corinthians 14:18).

My wife, Hazel, and I moved to Arizona in 1936. We attended the Bisbee Church of God because we liked the singing and because they showed a love we had never experienced in church. We did not believe their doctrine, especially the Pentecostal emphasis on the gift of the Spirit and speaking in tongues.

I bought a good reference Bible to prove to them that their doctrine was wrong. The more I studied to prove them wrong, the more I realized by my own intensive study that they were right.

I began seeking the baptism in the Holy Spirit without telling my wife. One night as we had our devotional prayer, we continued to pray. When we went to bed, our prayers continued. Suddenly, I found my speech was not in English; it sounded more like an Oriental language. This went on for some time.

I knew the Bible said, "If a son asks for bread from any father among you, will he give him a stone? Or if he asks for a fish, will he give him a serpent instead of a fish? Or if he asks for an egg, will he offer him a scorpion? If you then, being evil, know how to give good gifts to your children, how much more will your heavenly Father give the Holy Spirit to those who ask Him!" (Luke 11:11-13).

I had been told that speaking in tongues was of the devil or, at best, gibberish. I did not want something which was not from God or which was not real. As I continued to speak in tongues, I asked the Lord to show me that this experience was real, that it was from Him. In an instant, my speech pattern was changed completely. Both Hazel and I knew immediately that this was my confirmation from the Lord. Honest seekers need not worry about questioning God. He can and will prove Himself to those who are sincere.

· · · PRAYER · · ·

Lord, thank You for sending the Holy Spirit to be our Comforter. Help us to always live in such a way that others will know that our experience is real.

· · · TODAY'S THOUGHT · · ·

I have never been afraid to stand for our Pentecostal heritage. God has always proven Himself to me during my 55 years of ministry.

—Hurschel L. Diffie

YOU SHALL RECEIVE POWER

*"But you shall receive power when the Holy Spirit has come
upon you; and you shall be witnesses to Me in Jerusalem,
and in all Judea and Samaria, and to the end of the earth"*
(Acts 1:8).

When the departing Savior said "You shall receive power," He was not merely trying to soften the shock of His departure. It was not an idle promise, it was an inspired announcement. Jesus was preparing the disciples for the power that was about to be provided them in the person of the Holy Spirit.

Power implies to have resources, to possess capability, to be able to do, to be strong enough for the task at hand. The early church had supernatural resources through the Holy Spirit. They possessed powerful capabilities. They were able to do mighty deeds for God. Through the Spirit they were more than a match for the task at hand!

The church went forth—witnessing from house to house, town to town, country to country—in the power of the Spirit, lifting up the Lord Jesus Christ and filling the earth with the gospel message. When extreme persecution drove them from Jerusalem, they didn't run and hide; instead they carried the gospel to new towns and new people.

The power of the Holy Spirit gave people the resources to witness boldly and win thousands of people to Christ, so that "the Lord added to the church daily those who were being saved" (Acts 2:47).

They had power because they had the Spirit's presence. Jesus said, "He dwells with you and will be in you" (John 14:17). Later He promised, "I will send Him to you" (John 16:7).

God said, "My Presence will go with you" (Exodus 33:14). The psalmist exclaimed, "In Your presence is fullness of joy" (Psalm 16:11).

The Holy Spirit is Divinity come to man. If He is working through us, we do not have Him so much as He has us. We are His! We go in power, yielding ourselves for Him to work through us to accomplish His will.

· · · PRAYER · · ·

*Father, I praise You for the power You have provided Your church.
Help us to go forth in the harvest in the power of the Holy Spirit.*

· · · TODAY'S THOUGHT · · ·

The power that has been given to the church will always exalt Jesus Christ, the Savior of the world.

—Tom George

FULL OF THE HOLY SPIRIT

*And it happened, when Elizabeth heard the greeting of
Mary, that the babe leaped in her womb; and Elizabeth was
filled with the Holy Spirit* (Luke 1:41).

A person once asked an evangelist, "Do I have to have the Holy Spirit to go to heaven?" The preacher replied, "I'm not sure I understand that question; I wouldn't want to go from here to the next room without the Holy Spirit!" In the passage we are given for today's devotion, we learn, first, that belief is blessed. Zacharias was stricken with the inability to speak due to his unbelief of Gabriel's announcement concerning Elizabeth and the child she would soon deliver.

Jesus said, "Have faith in God" (Mark 11:22). He also said, "According to your faith let it be to you" (Matthew 9:29). C.H. Dodd wrote that "faith is an act which is the negation of all activity, a moment of passivity out of which the strength for action comes, because in it God acts." Faith is the quiet surrender of the self to the Spirit of God within, which then takes hold and brings to fulfillment in us the faith that is His gift. The Scripture does not show that Elizabeth needed a sign; she accepted the annunciation by faith, as did her cousin, Mary.

Second, we learn that the Holy Spirit is a gift for all believers. Acts 2:38 states, "Then Peter said to them, 'Repent, and let every one of you be baptized in the name of Jesus Christ for the remission of sins; and you shall receive the gift of the Holy Spirit.'"

Paul issued an injunction to the church at Ephesus: "And do not be drunk with wine, in which is dissipation; but be filled with the Spirit" (Ephesians 5:18).

· · · PRAYER · · ·

Father, forgive us for our unbelief; forgive us when we ask for signs, indicating disbelief. Overshadow us, as You did Mary, and fill us, as You did Elizabeth, with Your Holy Spirit!

· · · TODAY'S THOUGHT · · ·

The salutation uttered by Elizabeth is certain to have been inspired of the Holy Spirit. No intimation had been made to her of Mary's pregnancy. The leap in the womb of Elizabeth was a spiritual leap of joy (v. 44).

—B. Gary Harris

DEFINING THE CHURCH'S ROLE

"I [Jesus] also say to you that . . . on this rock I will build My church, and the gates of Hades shall not prevail against it" (Matthew 16:18).

 What should the church be doing in these last days before the return of Christ? What is the role of church administrators? Pastors? The laity? It is vital that we understand what the Bible says in regard to the mission of the church.

The best example of the true church is found in the Book of Acts. The early church adhered to the confession of truth. They practiced the fellowship of public family worship. They demonstrated their faith through works of self-denying love. In Acts the church is pictured as the family of God. It is always centered on Christ and empowered by the Holy Spirit.

God expects no less of the body of Christ today. Remember that the church is people, not architecture. We as the people of God are called to be salt, light, and leaven in our world.

The church is guilty at times of overemphasizing one aspect of its mission to the exclusion of the others. At times we seek to win the sinner with little regard for his physical and social needs. We want to expand the Kingdom yet ignore societal injustices where the Kingdom should be most influential. At other times we focus on social issues and overlook spiritual needs.

The truth is that the role of the church is to do both evangelism and social ministry.

· · · PRAYER · · ·

Lord, help me to be salt, light, and leaven to my neighbor. Help me to show forth Your love to my brothers and sisters in Christ as a testimony to them and the world that You died for us, rose from the dead, and are living with us.

· · · TODAY'S THOUGHT · · ·

Since the church is people, not buildings or programs, I am part of the church. I resolve to make the church Spirit-filled by seeking continually to be filled with the Spirit myself.

—Robert P. Herrin

A SPIRITUAL HERITAGE

When the enemy comes in like a flood, the Spirit of the
Lord will lift up a standard against him (Isaiah 59:19).

When I was a young Christian military man, a superior once asked me, "Roy, I notice you are different. What do you believe?" I began to tell him about the things I did not believe in doing. "Roy," he said, "I am not interested in what you don't believe. I want to know what you do believe."

I walked away sad. I had let him down, and I had let the Lord down—for I did not know what I believed. I promised the Lord that day that I would never again present a "negative gospel."

As I look back to that sad encounter, I realize that I began then to look for a human but also Christlike man of God after whom to pattern my life. Townsend Garland was that man.

We were a very poor family. My mother and father were Christians who made their children live right but did not teach them how to live a Christian life. Providing that example was left to Townsend Garland.

Often, this Spirit-filled preacher would stop by our hose on his way home from the grocery store, see that our cupboard was bare, bring all his family's food in, and say, "Here, God has provided." Instead of wondering where his own groceries were coming from, he would shout and speak in tongues all the way to his car—happy that he had been able to share with someone less fortunate.

Sometimes he held revivals in an old tent. I listened to him preach and watched him pray for the sick. Sinners were saved; the sick were healed. When the power of God came upon this man, things happened!

Even now, when I get sick or despondent, I think, *If Townsend Garland were here, I would be all right.* His life in the Spirit was his heritage to me. To be like Townsend Garland is, for me, like saying, "Oh, to be like Jesus!"

· · · PRAYER · · ·

Lord, let the young men and women to whom I minister be so blessed that they will remember me as I remember Townsend Garland.

· · · TODAY'S THOUGHT · · ·

I know in whom I have believed, and I know that no matter what circumstances I find myself in, the Lord has lifted up a standard against Satan, and I am on the winning team.

—Roy L. Humphrey

EDIFYING THE CHURCH

I will pray with the Spirit, and I will also pray with the understanding (1 Corinthians 14:15).

 Tongues are the spiritual gift bestowed by the indwelling Holy Spirit and are beyond the natural powers. They edify the speaker himself, who speaks not to men but to God. No man understands him, for in the Spirit, he speaks mysteries.

In pouring the gifts on His church, God gives their purpose. They are given to equip the saints for the work of the ministry and for the edifying of the body of Christ (Ephesians 4:12). When one blesses with the spirit, his spirit is directly influenced by the Holy Spirit; his speaking is an activity of his spirit but not of his understanding.

The guidance is this: "Therefore let him that speaks in a tongue pray that he may interpret" (v. 13). For the sake of edifying others, it is good to speak with understanding.

In the church, said Paul, "I would rather speak five words with my understanding, that I may teach others also, than ten thousand words in a tongue" (v. 19).

On the Day of Pentecost, at the first outpouring of the Holy Spirit, the disciples spoke in other tongues as the Spirit gave them utterance: "When this sound occurred, the multitude came together, and were confused, because everyone heard them speak in his own language. Then they were all amazed and marveled, saying to one another, "Look, are not all these who speak Galileans? And how is it that we hear, each in our own language in which we were born?" . . . So they were all amazed and perplexed, saying to one another, 'Whatever could this mean?'" (Acts 2:6-8, 12).

Speaking in other tongues brings amazement to some and confusion to others. It must be accompanied by interpretation in order to lead to perfect edification.

· · · PRAYER · · ·

Father, allow Your Spirit to flow through us that others may be blessed. May we be used by the Spirit for the edification of Your church.

· · · TODAY'S THOUGHT · · ·

Let all things be done decently and in order. God is not the author of confusion but of peace.

—Honore Jacques

THE HOLY SPIRIT SENDS

So, being sent out by the Holy Spirit, they went down . . .
from there (Acts 13:4).

Of the prophets and teachers in the church at Antioch, four are mentioned: Barnabas, Simeon, Lucius, and Manaen. These men ministered to the Lord; they also fasted and prayed. They were wholly consecrated to God and the Holy Spirit spoke to them, declaring the calling of Paul and Barnabas to a certain work.

For years, both of these men had preached the gospel, and this is definite proof that they were called of God. Here is also evidence that the Holy Spirit speaks to good men about the callings of others. Paul and Barnabas, dedicated ministers of the gospel, were subject to their brothers in the church.

The brethren laid hands on Paul and Barnabas, praying for them and blessing them. They prayed for the two ministers to be successful in the work that God had called them to do. The Holy Spirit made known their calling to the church leaders. Then the two men submitted themselves to the church and were sent forth by those in authority to carry out the work they had been divinely called to do.

Years later Paul recognized the authority of the church, and the importance of being sent to preach the gospel, in the words of his letter to the Romans: "And how shall they preach unless they are sent?" (10:15).

In our consecration to God and in the dedication of our service to become laborers in His vineyard, we must recognize the authority of the Holy Spirit in the church. We must come to realize that no man has full jurisdiction of himself. It is God's plan for men to direct each other, submitting themselves to each other, under the guidance of the Holy Spirit.

· · · PRAYER · · ·

Heavenly Father, I thank You for the work of the Holy Spirit in the church. May we always be submissive to Your promptings, especially when they come from others.

· · · TODAY'S THOUGHT · · ·

The Holy Spirit speaks to anointed men and women about the callings and gifts of others.

—John C. Jernigan

LIFE AND GODLINESS

*. . . as His divine power has given to us all things that per-
tain to life and godliness, through the knowledge of Him
who called us by glory and virtue* (2 Peter 1:3).

My parents raised a family of 14 children on a farm near Campaign, a small rural community in middle Tennessee. They were among the first in this area to receive the Holy Spirit. I was 5 years old when they joined the Church of God in 1914. Although I grew up in the church, I was not saved until August 8, 1928, at the age of 19.

As a young boy, I dreamed I was preaching to a multitude of people with black faces. This caused me to be reluctant to accept the Lord for fear that I would have to become a missionary. This dream was fulfilled years later in my association with the Missions Department. Two nights after I was saved, I was baptized in the Holy Spirit. Less than two weeks later, I was baptized in water, joined the church, and immediately started preaching.

After being filled with the Holy Spirit, I developed a love for evangelism and foreign missions. In the middle 1930s, as a young pastor, I attended the Tennessee State Convention where I was so touched by the appeal of a missionary that I pledged a full month's salary. The pledge was almost due, and I did not have the money. Through a miraculous incident, I was able to sell a car for the exact amount I needed. God had provided.

From the time I was filled with the Holy Spirit, I found 2 Peter 1:3 to be true, "as His divine power has given to us all things that pertain to life and godliness."

· · · PRAYER · · ·

Lord, through Your enabling Spirit I have served You faithfully for 74 years. Thank You for the fullness of the Spirit.

· · · TODAY'S THOUGHT · · ·

A life in the Spirit assures us of God's presence and provision.

—W.E. Johnson

THE CHRISTIAN'S GUARANTEE

In Him you also trusted, after you heard the word of truth,
the gospel of your salvation; in whom also, having believed,
you were sealed with the Holy Spirit of promise, who is the
guarantee of our inheritance until the redemption of the
purchased possession, to the praise of His glory
(Ephesians 1:13, 14).

By our measuring line—the prophecies of Scripture—we know that troubles will soon be over for the Christian. We have determined that we are now in shallow water, and day by day we are drawing nearer to the shore of complete deliverance. The Jews have been given their homeland; now they are there. There was a time when we knew nothing of the fire of atomic energy or the pillar of smoke from the blast; but now it has become a common occurrence. There were days when false christs were never heard of; now you constantly hear of someone's calling himself such.

"We also have the prophetic word made more sure, which you do well to heed as a light that shines in a dark place, until the day dawns and the morning star rises in your hearts" (2 Peter 1:19). Events in the Scripture point out the set schedule and timing of the ages. It is by these prophecies that those who are interested in keeping time with the ages can determine our position in God's arranged schedule. It is only by the Scripture that such knowledge can be gained.

Jesus gave two promises before He went away. First He said, "And I will pray the Father, and He will give you another Helper, that He may abide with you forever" (John 14:16). Second, "And if I go and prepare a place for you, I will come again and receive you to Myself; that where I am, there you may be also" (John 14:3). The Holy Spirit has come, and lives are being blessed. Jesus is soon to return, and the church will realize a glorious landing away from the storms of life.

· · · PRAYER · · ·

Thank You, Lord, for the assurance You give us of our redemption
and entrance into the glories of the Lord.

· · · TODAY'S THOUGHT · · ·

The trials of this life are only temporary; our redemption is eternal.

—G.W. Lane

I HAVE HEARD OF YOU

"I have heard of you, that the Spirit of God is in you, and that light and understanding and excellent wisdom are found in you" (Daniel 5:14).

Daniel was God's witness in the palace of the Babylonian empire that ruled the world during the period of 606 to 534 BC. He had been captured by Nebuchadnezzar, in the first year of his reign as king, and brought to Babylon from Jerusalem. Daniel was not as prominent in Belshazzar's kingdom as he had been in earlier years during Nebuchadnezzar's time; but his integrity and his faith in God had not changed.

Daniel's leadership and influence in the kingdom at Babylon was the result of his being full of the Spirit of God. It is this power source alone that can produce light, understanding, and the wisdom needed for the hour.

The same rebellion and resistance exhibited in the life of Belshazzar is ever present in this generation. Our only answer to this troubled and turbulent world is for men and women to be filled with the Spirit. It is our only power source.

Daniel had the opportunity to make known by divine revelation God's power in his life, not only for the king but for all those he was associated with. How important it is for each of us who are involved in the latter-day harvest to be able to demonstrate the power of God in our lives. It is the only true power source. Being filled with the Spirit is such a contrast to the definition of power today. It will motivate such remarks as "I have heard of you."

· · · PRAYER · · ·

Eternal Father, may we who have been given the enabling power of God be diligent in Your vineyard and be sensitive to the moving of Your Spirit as we reap Your harvest in anticipation of Your soon return.

· · · TODAY'S THOUGHT · · ·

It is not important what we say about ourselves concerning our relationship with God but, rather, what those we serve recognize to be in us. It is important that they see the Spirit of God in us. Reaping the spiritual harvest requires our dependence upon a power greater than that of the world.

—Franklin D. Meadows

A SPIRITUALLY CONTROLLED LIFE

Walk in the Spirit, and you shall not fulfill the lust of the flesh (Galatians 5:16).

 Early in life I was forced to choose between advancing my business career and following God's lead. Business lost.

I worked for a large grocery chain. I was offered a store manager's slot, even though I was a few weeks shy of my 21st birthday. And that was the catch. Company policy insisted that all store managers be at least 21 years old—no exception.

I moved my birthday up enough to qualify me for the job. But the lie soon became a major burden when I met Christ at the altar of a small Detroit church.

So on a snowy Michigan morning, I took a streetcar to my company's regional headquarters downtown. I walked up to the manager's office and told him I was Christian now and God had convicted me about lying.

He was not impressed.

"What if we put you in a store," he asked, "and one of the departments wasn't making the profit it should? Say the meat market was in trouble. Would you be willing to adjust the scales a little if you had to?"

"No sir, I couldn't do that."

"Then you'd better forget the chain store business."

That ended my career as a merchant, but within a year I entered the ministry.

· · · PRAYER · · ·

Thank You, Father, that we can be assured that if our lives are under the control of the Holy Spirit, our lives will bear the fruit of a Christian.

· · · TODAY'S THOUGHT · · ·

Success is never to be measured by the accumulation of earthly wealth but by treasures in heaven.

—Houston R. Morehead

341

A MIRACLE FOR TARA

. . . to another faith by the same Spirit, to another gifts of
healings by the same Spirit (1 Corinthians 12:9).

 On April 19, 1979, God gave us a beautiful baby girl, Tara. At 3 months, Tara became seriously ill. For the next 15 months she lived on antibiotics. Tara had pneumonia five times by the time she was 15 months old.

Her doctor advised us to move from the Mississippi Delta country. We moved to Philadelphia, Mississippi, hoping Tara's health would improve. Surely divine direction and care dictated the move. Tara collapsed and was admitted to the hospital with a temperature of nearly 105 degrees.

On Wednesday afternoon Dr. Ross Smith diagnosed Tara with severe urinary tract infection and said it would take a miracle for her to survive. She would have permanent kidney damage and would always have to take medication, if she survived.

By Friday, she had not responded to medication. I had gone to the parsonage for a short reprieve when I received a call from my wife. Dr. Smith had just reported that the situation for Tara looked bleak.

Suddenly, the months of carrying this load overwhelmed me. I called State Overseer W.P. Atkinson who prayed with me on the telephone and directed me to read Psalm 27 and place my daughter in God's hands. While on my knees by Tara's bedside, weeping uncontrollably, the Spirit spoke: "Get up, the work is done." Within 30 minutes Tara began to respond. By Sunday she was normal.

Tara then had eyesight problems and was prescribed very strong glasses, which she wore for several years. In 1984 the Reverend Paul Henson prayed with her and the Holy Spirit performed another miracle; Tara's eyes are healed, and she now has 20/20 vision.

· · · PRAYER · · ·

Father, I praise You for the miracles You give to Your people. Thank You for Your healing touch.

· · · TODAY'S THOUGHT · · ·

The blessed Holy Spirit is God, the third person of the Godhead—coequal, coeternal, consubstantial with the Father and Son—and He is relevant in our lives, performing the mighty works of God.

—Bobby Myers

DO NOT QUENCH THE SPIRIT

Do not quench the Spirit (1 Thessalonians 5:19).

 "Do not quench the Spirit" is one of those short exhortations in 1 Thessalonians that are easy to remember and extremely helpful in the conduct of our Christian lives. Others are "rejoice always, pray without ceasing, in everything give thanks" (5:16-18).

John the Baptist said of Jesus, "He will baptize you with the Holy Spirit and with fire" (Luke 3:16). To quench denotes "to put out completely, or to extinguish." Instead of extinguishing the blaze of the Spirit, we should be feeding the flames. There are several ways the Spirit may be quenched.

First, *the cares of this life* can cause us to quench the Spirit (Matthew 13:22). In this age of stress and anxiety, even Spirit-filled believers can be overcome if the fire inside is allowed to burn low.

Second, we can quench the Spirit through the *lust of the flesh*. Peter tells us to "abstain from fleshly lusts which war against the soul" (1 Peter 2:11). Nothing turns away the Spirit of God like an unclean temple. We must recognize sin and abstain from the very appearance of it.

Third, we can quench the Spirit through *neglect*. Paul advised Timothy, "Do not neglect the gift that is in you" (1 Timothy 4:14). It is not necessary to blaspheme (Matthew 12:31) against the Holy Spirit to expel Him from our lives. If we neglect Him long enough, He will leave on His own. When we fail to use the spiritual gifts and display the fruit of the Spirit in our lives, we run the risk of quenching the Spirit and putting out the fire.

There are ways also to fan the fire, to keep the Spirit burning bright in our lives. The fuel of the Word of God, fanned by the oxygen of prayer, works wonders towards maintaining the Spirit-filled life.

· · · PRAYER · · ·

Father, please allow the Spirit to use us in any way He desires. Help us to empty ourselves and let Him fill us with His love. Let nothing draw my attention away from staying in the center of Your will.

· · · TODAY'S THOUGHT · · ·

Peter said, "For these are not drunk, as you suppose" (Acts 2:15). He did not say they were not intoxicated, only that they were not drunk on wine. They, like us, were intoxicated on the Spirit!

—Richard E. Porterfield

THE HOLY SPIRIT— OUR HELPER

"But the Helper, the Holy Spirit, whom the Father will send in My name, He will teach you all things, and bring to your remembrance all things that I said to you" (John 14:26).

On March 15, 1991, I crossed the Angolan/Namibian border with the Reverend Gabriel Josef. I was determined to get the Full Gospel Church of God registered with the government. Eventually after many trials, including traveling over roads on which it took eight hours to travel 75 miles, we arrived in Luanda, the capital of Angola.

By this time I was feeling tired from our trip; and while having an informal session with our pastors, I suddenly fell asleep where I was sitting. No one was alarmed because they all thought I was just tired. Over the next few days, matters got worse. I was finding it difficult to get up from a sitting or lying-down position. Eventually I collapsed and went into a coma. The brethren wanted to take me to the hospital, but I refused because I had not finished registering the church.

The brethren had to carry me in a semiconscious state to the taxi and up the three flights of stairs at the government office. The elevators were not working because battles on the outskirts of Luanda had affected electricity and water supplies. The brethren there testified later that when they got to the doors of the various government departments, I suddenly regained consciousness, stood firmly on my feet, entered the offices with them, and discussed our registration application lucidly with the authorities. Once out of the relevant offices, however, I again collapsed and became semiconscious. Once again the Holy Spirit's timing was impeccable, and He gave me all the answers for those who had always been opposed to Pentecostalism. A year later our church's registration was officially announced in the Angolan government gazette.

On reaching the mission compound, I slipped into a deep coma and the brethren decided to take me to the hospital. I ended up in the hands of a doctor who happened to be a member of our Luanda congregation.

· · · PRAYER · · ·

Father, I praise You for the miraculous guidance of Your Holy Spirit.

· · · TODAY'S THOUGHT · · ·

If we put our trust in God, He will prepare the way for us.

—R.H. Roberts

PENTECOSTAL POWER

For this reason the gospel was preached also to those who are dead, that they might be judged according to men in the flesh, but live according to God in the spirit (1 Peter 4:6).

The old evangelist was well past retirement age. I was a 21-year-old evangelist, conducting a revival at the church he attended. One night he said, "I want to tell you a story."

His story began when he was a young preacher. He was preaching in a small country church to just a few people. The door opened and a man came in. The man was tall, slender, handsome, youthful, and dressed impeccably. His suit, shirt, tie, and shoes were all white. There was not a wrinkle or a stain anywhere. He seemed to glow. He had a pleasant expression. His eyes were fixed on the young preacher as he moved up the aisle.

He stepped directly in front of the preacher and said, "Do not stop preaching. You can see me but the other people cannot. I am the Holy Spirit. I have come to help you. From this time forward I will be with you, and I will bless your ministry and use you." With those words, He stepped onto the platform and stood beside the minister. "This is how I will be with you and within you." And He stepped into the preacher and disappeared. In a moment He stepped out on the other side. "You will not see me again, but you will know I am with you." Then He stepped back into the evangelist.

The young preacher's words began to flow in an unusual way. There was a power present that had not been there before. People were wonderfully saved and healed by the power of God. In a few nights, the little building would not hold the people who came. The services lasted for several weeks. Multitudes were blessed of God.

"That," said the old soldier of the Cross, "was the beginning of a signs-and-wonders ministry which the Holy Spirit gave to me."

I felt the Spirit. Chills went up my spine. Tears filled my eyes. Silently, I prayed, "Holy Spirit, step inside me."

· · · PRAYER · · ·

Lord, come into my life in all Your fullness. I yield myself now to be used in Your kingdom work.

· · · TODAY'S THOUGHT · · ·

Will you invite Him in and ask Him to take complete control.

—Bobby Rose

WHERE THE SPIRIT FLOWS

*"But you shall receive power when the Holy Spirit has come
upon you; and you shall be witnesses to Me in Jerusalem,
and in all Judea and Samaria, and to the end of the earth"*
(Acts 1:8).

Desperately backslidden and suicidally depressed, I knew no
place to turn. By Thanksgiving Day 1975, I was a hopeless
shell of a man. The bitter drought in my own soul was produc-
ing its totally predictable fruit in what I brazenly dared to call
my ministry. My preaching was of no effect. My prayers were hollow
and futile. My marriage was poisoned with rancor. Despair, not thanksgiving, filled my heart that day.

An earlier attempted suicide was followed by a second. I knew that
eventually I would succeed. I was afraid of myself and angry at my
religion. I believed in Christianity, but it would not work for me.

Then on December 5, 1975, I learned about the Holy Spirit. At 4
p.m. that frosty December afternoon, I fell before God and asked for
the full blessing of Pentecost. An explosion! An eruption! A tidal
wave! I know that different people receive His Spirit in different ways,
but He always comes with power!

Power for preaching was suddenly *real* to me. Power to live, to
relate, to love, and to give filled our marriage. The power of His presence is a glorious promise. Without the Holy Spirit I am bankrupt and
dangerous to myself and others. But where the Spirit flows there is
power!

· · · PRAYER · · ·

*Father, thank You for the blessing of Pentecost and for the power
You give me to live victoriously.*

· · · TODAY'S THOUGHT · · ·

For ministry and for life, the promise of power is precious indeed. In
a world of striving, laboring self-worshipers, the rested child of God
moving in the power of the Spirit is an awesome sight. Ask and you
shall receive power.

—Mark Rutland

THE LIGHT OF THE LORD

For you were once darkness, but now you are light in the
Lord. Walk as children of light (for the fruit of the Spirit is
in all goodness, righteousness, and truth)
(Ephesians 5:8, 9).

 After Robin came home from school that Thursday, Wanda and I were able to enjoy one of those increasingly rare trips to the mall with our daughter accompanying us. While Robin and Wanda looked for clothing from store to store, I walked the mall.

I spotted the young man who had preached in our most recent youth rally. I stopped to have a chat with him, but the chat developed into a deeper Christian sharing. While we were talking, the place where we were standing suddenly became daylight bright. I immediately looked up to see what had happened. I discovered myself looking straight at the sun through the skylight. Bright sunshine! What a rare sight over Lynchburg skies during that past week! The young brother said, "I thought someone had turned a spotlight on us."

I began thinking afterward that God frequently uses light in His dealings with man. To make the earth habitable for man, God said, "'Let there be light'; and there was light" (Genesis 1:3). Psalm 119:105 says, "Your word is a lamp to my feet and a light to my path." And we think of judgment in terms of the white light of God's judgment. Thank God, our conversation was holy. That bright sunbeam was a quick reminder that God is up there!

· · · PRAYER · · ·

Father, I praise You for the marvelous light of Your love that shines upon us daily!

· · · TODAY'S THOUGHT · · ·

"Let your light so shine before men, that they may see your good works and glorify your Father in heaven" (Matthew 5:16).

—Mack A. Shires

LED BY THE HOLY SPIRIT

*For as many as are led by the Spirit of God, these are sons
of God* (Romans 8:14).

In my early years I lived on a farm near Paris, Texas. I fell in love with and married a Church of God lady, Alma McCain. I did not know much about Pentecost, and I received a lot of persecution from friends and neighbors who tried to persuade me against the Holy Spirit baptism.

After moving to Electric, I'd take my wife to church and stay outside in the car. Since there was no air conditioning then, the windows were wide open. The singing and preaching came out loud and clear. I would put my fingers in my ears to keep from hearing the message.

Sometimes on Sunday we had the pastor come with us for dinner. My object in this was to argue the Scriptures, for I still was not convinced about the Holy Spirit. One Sunday in a discussion about the Holy Spirit, my wife joined the conversation. In a few minutes, the pastor's young daughter came to me and said, "She is right."

I finally decided the Holy Spirit was for me. After many times of seeking the Lord, the Spirit fell. I heard someone speaking in a language I did not understand, then realized it was coming from me.

I was farming and had to gather grain when it was ready. My neighbors would use the combine on Sunday to miss the rain. I would not gather my grain on Sunday, and the Lord always protected my crops. This made an impression on my neighbors.

The Spirit began dealing with me about preaching. I did not want to preach. I feared I might have to go to a foreign country as a missionary. I worried over this until I had a dream one night that I was preaching to a crowd out in the open by the courthouse. I was standing on the back of a truck. This was my witness that I should preach the gospel of Jesus Christ in my area.

· · · PRAYER · · ·

Thank You, Lord, for the gift of the Holy Spirit and for His empowering presence throughout my many years of ministry.

· · · TODAY'S THOUGHT · · ·

My advice to everyone is to seek Him, for the power of Pentecost is real.

—W.L. Shires

THE HOLY SPIRIT'S YEARNING

*Or do you think that the Scripture says in vain, "The Spirit
who dwells in us yearns jealously"?* (James 4:5).

 God showed us His desire to have a relationship with His creation when He came down in the evening to walk and talk with
Adam and Eve (Genesis 3:8). Even after the Fall, God continued to show His love by reaching out to fallen humankind.

God showed us His greatest love when He gave His only begotten
Son, Jesus Christ, to bring us back into the proper relationship. No one
can come into relationship with Him without being purified and made
righteous by the cleansing blood of Jesus. God created humankind
holy, pure, and righteous. Therefore, in the beginning we had an ongoing relationship with God.

God again is saying to all humankind, "You are important and I
want a relationship with you." Once you have given your life to Him
and have been filled with the Spirit, He yearns jealously for an ongoing relationship with you.

When Satan and temptations come our way, there is no room for
worldly ways. "Do you not know that friendship with the world is
enmity with God?" (James 4:4).

God wants to have a relationship with you that includes your affections. His feeling at the withdrawal of these affections to any degree is
spoken of as "jealousy." Therefore, this verse means that the Spirit of
God dwelling in you demands the absolute rule in your heart and longs
for you with something akin to envy of any other influence that would
gain the mastery over your heart. God has never left his created
humankind. Humankind has left Him. The Holy Spirit's dwelling in us
is one of the ways He desires to relate to us today. The Spirit yearns tenderly over us for relationship with Him.

· · · PRAYER · · ·

*Father, help me accept today that I am loved by You and that You
long to influence my every thought. O Lord, I love Your desire to love
me and have a living relationship with me.*

· · · TODAY'S THOUGHT · · ·

God has chosen to share Himself with us through the Holy Spirit's
leading us in understanding His Word. The Holy Spirit is both teacher
and minister to assist me in knowing His loving care for me.

—Douglas W. Slocumb

LED BY THE SPIRIT OF GOD

For as many as are led by the Spirit of God, these are sons of God (Romans 8:14).

In 1932, when I was 3 years old, the Holy Spirit descended on several members of my family gathered for the evening family worship. One of my uncles, Pierre Nicolle, a French Baptist minister who had been filled with the Holy Spirit a few months before, spoke on the Holy Spirit. During the prayer which followed, six people among those present started to praise God and to speak in tongues. Although I was very young, this meeting impressed me so much that I cannot forget it. It is from this humble kitchen that the Lord showed me His greatness, and the joy of those who are filled with the Holy Spirit.

In 1959 I was a minister in a Pentecostal church in Charleroi, Belgium. My wife and I had been praying for God's will concerning our desire to leave that church. A minister from the Full Gospel Church of God of South Africa, J.H. Saayman, was traveling through Europe with his wife. I had met him a few weeks before in Brussels.

The Lord spoke clearly to him telling him to come to get me and take me to Germany to see Walter Lauster. The Lord had something for me there. Since we had been praying for a change in the ministry, we felt that it was God's leading, so I went with Brother Saayman. When we arrived at Lauster's home, Saayman asked him immediately if he needed a Frenchman. Lauster said, "Yes, but how did you know?"

Saayman said, "The Lord told me, and here is your Frenchman." The Church of God in Germany had started a new church in Colmar, France; but due to the Alsatian laws, that church would have to close if it was not officially recognized elsewhere inside France. For this they needed a Frenchman to start a new church and have it registered officially to save the church in Colmar. This we did. The Lord led us to go to Troyes, and we started a new Church of God there.

· · · PRAYER · · ·

Father, I am thankful that You know us and that You know how to lead us to the place of service You have chosen for us.

· · · TODAY'S THOUGHT · · ·

I marvel at the power of the Holy Spirit, at the way He inspires me each time I speak for the Lord.

—Andre Weber

THE WORK OF THE HOLY SPIRIT

*"Nevertheless I tell you the truth. It is to your advantage
that I go away; for if I do not go away, the Helper will not
come to you; but if I depart, I will send Him to you"*
(John 16:7).

Our heavenly Father made no mistakes in His divine plan of
sending the Holy Spirit to us upon Jesus' return to heaven. I
was surprised recently at the ease with which my two small
daughters have grasped a clear understanding of why Jesus is
where He is—in heaven.

The works of the Holy Spirit on earth are numerous. In fact, the
longer I serve the Lord, the more beneficent acts I discover on the part
of the Holy Spirit.

The word translated "Helper" in this verse (*Parakletos*) means "one
who stands alongside another." This word has received considerable
treatment by Bible scholars.

In ancient secular Greek writings, however, this term often was used
to describe a helper or one who stood alongside another in a courtroom
setting. Thus, the Holy Spirit might be understood as an advocate on
our behalf.

With Christ as our advocate in heaven (1 John 2:1) and the Holy
Spirit as our advocate on earth, how can we lose?

I once was reminded of this in a courtroom situation. As a young
lawyer, I entered a court hearing, thinking to myself that I didn't have
much chance of winning. I did win the case, however; and walking
out of the courthouse, I felt as if the Holy Spirit was saying, "How
could you lose? I was right beside you in that room!"

From that point on, I have always tried to remember that in a courtroom or any other place, the Holy Spirit is right beside me, ready and
willing to help.

· · · PRAYER · · ·

*Father, thank You that Jesus Christ is our advocate in heaven, while
the Holy Spirit is our helper on earth.*

· · · TODAY'S THOUGHT · · ·

In whatever setting I find myself today—whether the workroom,
classroom, courtroom, or hospital room—may I always recall that the
Holy Spirit is in me and right beside me, offering His divine assistance.

—Dennis W. Watkins

INTO HIS MARVELOUS LIGHT

*There is therefore now no condemnation to those who are in
Christ Jesus, who do not walk according to the flesh, but
according to the Spirit* (Romans 8:1).

I was born in China and raised in a completely atheistic environment both at home and in school. I was indoctrinated early in life that there is no God. I joined the Red Guards of Mao and the Communist Youth League and was promoted to be a party secretary of the Communist Youth.

In 1983, when I was studying English and American literature at a university, I encountered many references and allusions to a book called the Bible, which I had never seen. Despite tremendous difficulties, I obtained authorization to receive the Bible. I found it in the library, classified as Western pornographic literature which could pollute and poison the people.

As I studied the Bible, I felt great joy and peace I had never known before. I learned that I was God's creation—created to love, worship, and serve Him. The Holy Spirit convicted me and I confessed my sins and received Christ into my heart as my Savior. Praise the holy and precious name of Jesus, who saved me, sanctified me, and, before I knew much about Pentecostal theology, wonderfully baptized me in the Holy Spirit. I spoke in tongues as the Holy Spirit gave me the utterance. Jesus Christ also called me to be a minister of the gospel.

Since December 1983, when God saved me, I have been serving Him heart and soul. My experience with the Lord is a dynamic, daily, and personal love relationship between my Lord and me, enabled and empowered by the sweet Holy Spirit. I thank God daily for the privilege of serving Him. I proclaim with authority and anointing wherever I go that Jesus is the Christ. I am not ashamed of the gospel of my Lord Jesus Christ, for indeed I know experientially that it is the power of God for salvation for all who will believe.

· · · PRAYER · · ·

*Thank You, Father, for the light of Your love that shone into the heart
of a communist youth and made me a new creature in Christ Jesus.*

· · · TODAY'S THOUGHT · · ·

The same light that shone into my life can reach into the life of anyone, anywhere. Open your heart to Him and let the light shine in!

—Hong Y. Yang

352

THE MANY GIFTS OF THE HOLY SPIRIT

There are diversities of gifts, but the same Spirit
(1 Corinthians 12:4).

While on the earth, Christ was able to meet the needs of mankind. The Lord knew the time would come, however, when He would go to His Father and the ministry of the church would be placed in the hands of His disciples. Jesus also knew the disciples could not perform ministry in their own power and strength.

Thus, Jesus promised that when He went away He would ask the Father to send them the Holy Spirit. The purpose was to give them power to do the works of God. Through the Holy Spirit, God would provide and distribute specific gifts to the church: the word of wisdom, the word of knowledge, faith, gifts of healing, the working of miracles, prophecy, discerning of spirits, various kinds of tongues, and the interpretation of tongues (1 Corinthians 12:8-11). These gifts would equip believers for service to God.

All the varieties of gifts proceed from the Holy Spirit. God is the author of the gifts, not man. The Holy Spirit administers the gifts to meet the needs of the church. All the gifts are manifested through individuals in the body of Christ by the Holy Spirit. They are not given to glorify any individual but to meet the needs of the local church. Therefore, the ability to exercise any and all of these gifts does not reside with man but with God.

This was God's method for the early church, and it is still God's method today. He still manifests the gifts of the Spirit through dedicated men and women. The early church went forth in the "power of the Spirit," and the church of this day cannot go forward in the strength of men or in the wisdom of men. Every need can still be met if men and women will depend on the Holy Spirit and be open and receptive to the operation of His gifts.

· · · PRAYER · · ·

Dear God, help me to rely on the gifts of the Holy Spirit and be a yielded vessel, used to the praise and glory of God.

· · · TODAY'S THOUGHT · · ·

I will not attempt to do the work of God in my own strength and knowledge.

—Troy A. Baggett

GRACE AND SUPPLICATION

"I will pour on the house of David and on the inhabitants of
Jerusalem the Spirit of grace and supplication"
(Zechariah 12: 10).

It seems that the spirit of supplication comes before the spirit
of grace, yet grace is present all the time, making supplication
for wounded spirits. Both words come from the same Hebrew
root, *chanan*. Grace bends or stoops in kindness to an inferi-
or—this is what God does; *supplication* is what I do.

Once, my dreams had toppled. Hope was gone. Darkness had
invaded my spirit. As I lay on my face before the Lord, He said,
"Sandy, you're My child." Though circumstances did not change, I
did. Then hope invaded my spirit. I received unspeakable joy and the
peace that passes understanding. He gave me His amazing grace.

Sufficient for every need. Jesus says, "My grace is sufficient for you,
for My strength is made perfect in weakness" (2 Corinthians 12:9). I
become strong in the Lord and in the power of His might (Ephesians 6:10)
as I learn that I am more than a conqueror through Jesus (Romans 8:37).

Accessible in the time of need. Hebrews 4:15, 16 says that Jesus
was tested the same way I am. He feels my pain. I can now boldly
enter the throne room of grace to obtain mercy—not what I deserve. I
find grace—what I don't deserve—in the time of need. G. Campbell
Morgan says this phrase actually means "in the nick of time"—just
when we need it.

Available in time of need. Hebrews 12:15 says to look diligently
(take the oversight) lest we fail the grace of God and become bitter
(Greek: *pikria*, poisoned). We must receive His sufficient and accessible grace, not allowing bitterness to spring up and defile us.

The spirit of grace and supplication has been poured out! Praise the
Lord, we are the recipients!

· · · PRAYER · · ·

Father, thank You for the sufficiency of Your grace. Thank You for
making it available to Your people today.

· · · TODAY'S THOUGHT · · ·

Grace is the desire and ability to do God's will. Perhaps you have
the ability today but do not want to do God's will. Or perhaps you
have the desire but lack the ability. Either way, ask Him for His grace,
that you may be willing and able to do what His Word commands.

—Sandy Bishop

COPING POWER FOR LIFE

*Then the churches throughout all Judea, Galilee, and
Samaria had peace and were edified. And walking in the
fear of the Lord and in the comfort of the Holy Spirit, they
were multiplied* (Acts 9:31).

Before the time of peace, growth, and comfort mentioned in
Acts 9:31, the church had experienced an intense period of
persecution. Chief among the persecutors was a young Jew
named Saul. After his conversion (9:6), Holy Spirit infilling
(v. 17), and subsequent acceptance by the brotherhood (vv. 26-30), the
church entered into a new time of peace and blessing. At first glance,
this welcome change looks like happenstance. Closer examination
reveals a process plan orchestrated by the Holy Spirit. He indeed pre-
sides over the process of our lives.

It was the Holy Spirit who precipitated life's process for Jesus: His
birth (Luke 1:35); temptation (Luke 4:1); ministry (Luke 4:14; Acts
10:38); death (Hebrews 9:14); and resurrection (1 Peter 3:18).

How should a Spirit-filled believer respond to the process?

Remember. Nothing in life takes the Holy Spirit by surprise. He
sees the blessings or bruisings long before they arrive . . . and He is
praying for you—now!

Rest. He who has begun a good work in you will see it through to
completion (Philippians 1:6). He will, not you.

Realize. You can be successful, but not always. You can be faithful
every time.

Rely. Our greatest ally in times of success or stress is the Holy Spirit.

Resist. The temptation to cave in will be great in times of stress.
Likewise, the tendency to puff up will be increased in times of success.

Rejoice. The process will be complete one day. "To him who overcomes I will grant to sit with Me on My throne, as I also overcame and
sat down with My Father on His throne" (Revelation 3:21).

· · · PRAYER · · ·

*Dear God, teach me to appropriate the comforting presence of the
Holy Spirit through life's process. Help me to remember that the Holy
Spirit is praying for me in and through each period of my life.*

· · · TODAY'S THOUGHT · · ·

The Holy Spirit is always there to help me avoid taking life too seriously in times of perplexity.

—Raymond F. Culpepper

WE ARE WITNESSES

*"We are His witnesses to these things, and so also is the
Holy Spirit whom God has given to those who obey Him"*
(Acts 5:32).

A third-generation Pentecostal preacher, I have observed
Spirit-filled individuals all my life. My childhood memories
include going to church and seeing a move of God's Spirit on
people. As a boy, I sat in awe and watched the saints rejoice.
Today, I am still amazed to see the Holy Spirit move on people and
drive them into the world to witness for Jesus Christ.

As a lad, I wondered about this motivating power that I had not yet
experienced nor fully understood. In my dad's congregation everyone
was a bearer and sharer of the good news. They all acted like preachers, testifying at every opportunity and witnessing in every open door.
They couldn't keep from sharing the good news.

They witnessed of the resurrected Lord. They had not seen the
empty tomb nor heard the angel's announcement, but the Holy Spirit
constantly confirmed that the Lord was alive in their hearts. This truth
enabled early church pioneers to endure persecution and survive. Their
focus and level of operation were in the realm of the Spirit; their main
objective was to obey the commands of Jesus. They marched to a different drumbeat. Though the world tried to silence them, they could
not help but teach and preach the things they had seen and heard!

My grandfather told me stories of the early days of his ministry.
Despite threats on his life and persecution, he preached about
Pentecost. At times, he did not know where the next meal was coming
from. I still remember the glint in his eye and the smile on his face as
he shared those things. How could he smile while talking about hard
times? Because he was a witness to these things through the Holy
Spirit who dwelt in him.

· · · PRAYER · · ·

*Dear Jesus, help us to be so full of Your Holy Spirit that we never
fail to share the good news with those we meet each day. May we
never let the world and its threats silence our Pentecostal witness.*

· · · TODAY'S THOUGHT · · ·

A witness is motivated by what he has seen and experienced. Truth
propels one across the hurdles of adversity and persecution. The Word
of God we share is the truth that sets men free!

—Terance R. Hart

THE PROMISE OF PENTECOST

*"It shall come to pass afterward that I will pour out My
Spirit on all flesh; your sons and your daughters shall
prophesy, your old men shall dream dreams, your young
men shall see visions; and also on My menservants and on
My maidservants I will pour out My Spirit in those days"*
(Joel 2:28, 29).

 The outpouring of the Holy Spirit originated in the heart of
God and was gloriously fulfilled in the New Testament. Joel
prophesied the Spirit would be poured on "all flesh." John
said Christ would baptize believers with the Holy Spirit
(Matthew 3:11).

On the Day of Pentecost, "suddenly there came a sound from heaven, as of a rushing mighty wind, and it filled the whole house where
they were sitting. Then there appeared to them divided tongues, as of
fire, and one sat upon each of them. And they were all filled with the
Holy Spirit and began to speak with other tongues, as the Spirit gave
them utterance" (Acts 2:2-4).

He came to fill up and fire up the church for the task ahead. He
filled it with spiritual power to withstand evil forces. He filled it with
holy zeal and warmth, and set 120 on a mission to take salvation to the
whole world. Their actions provoked stern rebuke and mockery from
the staid religionists of the day. Many take the same position today.
Some say it's emotional excitement, neurotic disturbance, or plain religious fanaticism. Luke states that it came from heaven.

Joel and Peter made it clear the Holy Spirit baptism is for every
believer. *First*, the Spirit was to be poured out on "all flesh" (Joel
2:28). *Second,* it would happen "in the last days" (Acts 2:17). Third,
Peter's words are unmistakably clear that Christians at Pentecost and
beyond are included in the promise (Acts 2:39).

Have you received the Holy Spirit, the promise of the Father, since
you believed? Have you been endued with power from on high? The
Spirit is available to asking, believing, obedient believers.

· · · PRAYER · · ·

*Heavenly Father, thank You for the gift of the blessed Holy Spirit.
He fills believers with His love, His gifts, and His power to witness.*

· · · TODAY'S THOUGHT · · ·

I affirm my belief in the Holy Spirit!

—Wade H. Horton

THE HOLY SPIRIT FELL ON US

While Peter was still speaking these words, the Holy Spirit fell upon all those who heard the word (Acts 10:44).

As a third-generation Church of God member, all my life I heard preaching and teaching about the baptism in the Holy Spirit. But it was not until my 18th year that I experienced the baptism in the Spirit.

The year was 1959; the place was the Isle Maciel Church of God in Buenos Aires, Argentina. As a member of the church youth group, I received good biblical teaching about the need to be filled with the Holy Spirit. We would often pray together and for one another to receive the Pentecostal experience.

One day I was among a large group of people who came forward to the altar to pray at the invitation of World Missions director Vessie D. Hargrave. Suddenly, as we began to pray, the Holy Spirit fell on us. I, along with many others, was filled with the Spirit and began to speak with other tongues. This manifestation and spiritual ecstasy went on for more than an hour. When finally the leaders of the church came to speak to me, I couldn't say anything to them in my own language. I could only smile and continue speaking in the language I did not know.

That experience marked the beginning of a more in-depth life with the Lord. After receiving the Pentecostal experience, I was more able to receive additional spiritual strength from the Lord, and I gave more attention to building my relationship with God and better relationships with my family, fellow Christians, and people in general.

The gift of the Holy Spirit caused me to have a new vision for and interest in the things of God and service in His kingdom. I was highly motivated to grow in Christ and to prepare for ministry.

The day the Holy Spirit fell on me was a milestone in my spiritual journey in Christ that I can never forget.

· · · PRAYER · · ·

Thank You, Father in heaven, for pouring out the Holy Spirit on me. Thank You for calling and equipping me by Your Spirit to be of service in Your church.

· · · TODAY'S THOUGHT · · ·

When the Holy Spirit falls on a person and the individual is baptized in the Spirit, the purpose is to make him or her more useful in the kingdom of God.

—Osvaldo Pupillo

DON'T INSULT THE SPIRIT OF GRACE

Of how much worse punishment, do you suppose, will he be thought worthy who has trampled the Son of God underfoot, counted the blood of the covenant by which he was sanctified a common thing, and insulted the Spirit of grace?
(Hebrews 10:29).

In the words of the old hymn of the church: "What can wash away my sin? Nothing but the blood of Jesus; What can make me whole again? Nothing but the blood of Jesus. Oh! precious is the flow, that makes me white as snow; no other fount I know, Nothing but the blood of Jesus." There is no remission of sin without the shedding of blood.

Anything we try in an attempt to work out our own salvation, the writer of Hebrews says, is an insult to the Spirit of grace. Jesus Christ is the Lamb of God, slain from the foundation of the world. When one rejects Jesus Christ as personal Savior, he or she rejects God's plan of salvation. There is no other remedy for sin.

To trample the Son of God underfoot is to reject the only provision God has provided for sinners to be reconciled to God. Jesus said, "I am the way, the truth, and the life. No one comes to the Father except through Me" (John 14:6). As the Holy Spirit speaks to our spirit, we must respond to enjoy the blessings of God. A rejection, or trampling of His blood, will cause one to be lost eternally. Through the shed blood of Jesus Christ we can have life and have it more abundantly!

· · · PRAYER · · ·

Father God, I thank You for Your Son, Jesus Christ. Thank You for Your Spirit, who leads me to Your Son. I sincerely recommit myself to You. May Your Spirit lead and guide me as I follow Jesus.

· · · TODAY'S THOUGHT · · ·

A granddaughter of Aaron Burr gave her heart to Christ in an evangelistic meeting. That evening she said to her grandfather, "I wish you were a Christian, too." He replied, "When I was a young man, I went to an evangelistic meeting. I felt my need of God's mercy and forgiveness and knew that I should give my heart to Christ, but I walked out without doing it. I stood under the stars and looked up toward heaven and said, 'God, if You don't bother me anymore, I'll never bother You.'

"Honey, God has kept that bargain. He has never bothered me; now it's too late for me to bother Him."

—Bill Reid

HAVE YOU RECEIVED THE SPIRIT?

[Paul] said to them, "Did you receive the Holy Spirit when
you believed?" And they said to him, "We have not so
much as heard whether there is a Holy Spirit" (Acts 19:2).

Paul's primary purpose for asking these followers if they had received the Holy Spirit was to see if they had received power. It was not to see if they might be speaking in tongues, though he thought that was important. He wanted them to receive power for personal edification, power to die to the flesh in everyday living, power for boldness in their witness.

Paul knew the mission set before the early church was to evangelize the world through a Christlike lifestyle and a witness to the death and resurrection of Jesus. Of all people, he knew the perils, the temptations, the ridicule and persecutions these people faced if they acknowledged they were believers in Christ. Yet it would take more than just believing; it would take the undergirding and indwelling of the supernatural Spirit to make them victorious.

Paul wanted them to witness in the unction, anointing, and power of the Holy Spirit. They needed power to live, serve, worship, teach, and witness of what they had seen, heard, and received. But how could they receive the experience of power if they were not aware that it existed?

It is evident by this scripture that they did not receive this power at the time of their conversion. Rather, it was separate from conversion and was evidenced by speaking in tongues. This was the power that enabled ordinary people to turn the world upside down.

The baptism in the Holy Spirit is an experience vitally relevant to our time. The world is examining the Pentecostal experience with sincere interest. The test must be "Do we have the power since we believed?" The ecstasy of speaking in tongues is not the ultimate goal. The goal is living in supernatural power which causes the world to take notice of the holy life of a believer.

· · · PRAYER · · ·

Lord, help me manifest the attributes of a dedicated believer through
the strength and power of the Holy Spirit.

· · · TODAY'S THOUGHT · · ·

Those who fail to live in the power of the Holy Spirit are like the man who bought a new power saw yet insisted on cutting wood by hand!

—Ray H. Sanders

BY THIS WE KNOW

By this we know that we abide in Him, and He in us,
because He has given us of His Spirit (1 John 4:13).

We need to know many things. When we are hungry, we need to know where to find food for the body. When we lack understanding, we need to know where knowledge and enlightenment can be found. In time of peril, we need to know where to find protection. When sickness comes, we need to know a good physician. To avoid loneliness, we need to know a friend with whom we can find fellowship and companionship.

The privilege of knowing God and being known by Him involves a personal walk with God. Trust is the basis of this relationship. The wonderful news that makes this kind of trust possible is that God is not a dictator bent on punishing us. Nor is He a tyrant waiting to pounce on us. God is good and He loves us.

Of all the things we need to know, the most important is to know that we abide in God and He in us. The Bible says, "The Spirit Himself bears witness with our spirit that we are children of God" (Romans 8:16). If God is living in us, His Spirit will make us aware of His presence.

"He has given us of His Spirit." By the Holy Spirit in us we not only come to understand where we stand with God, we also know three very important facts about God:

We know that God is love. He sent His Son to be the Savior of the world. By this we know the love of God for us.

As believers in Christ we also must love others. If we do not love, we do not know God, for God is love. As Christians we live in His love.

Loving one another tells us that we abide in Him and He abides in us. This is evidence that we are saved from sin and that we have the nature of God in us.

· · · PRAYER · · ·

Heavenly Father, help me to know by Your indwelling Spirit that You abide in me and I abide in You. Thank You for the Holy Spirit who gives this assurance to Your people.

· · · TODAY'S THOUGHT · · ·

Godly love for others is not something we make happen. Only by the Holy Spirit dwelling in us can this kind of love take place.

—Bobby G. Scott

SPIRIT CONSCIOUSNESS

*By this you know the Spirit of God: Every spirit that con-
fesses that Jesus Christ has come in the flesh is of God*
(1 John 4:2).

I visited my 85-year-old mother. For more than 45 years she trusted God for her health, never even taking an aspirin. At an early age God revealed Himself to her as the healer of her body. Her favorite verse was Isaiah 26:3: "You will keep him in perfect peace, whose mind is stayed on You."

Until three years ago Mother was active—cutting her grass, planting her garden, cleaning her house. She had 43 years of perfect Sunday school attendance. Gradually, it became evident her memory was beginning to fade. At first, we thought it was her age; and then came the stunning, heartbreaking report that Mother has Alzheimer's disease.

We sat on Mother's enclosed porch in the old swing. She doesn't remember my name, just that I'm the "young'n who lives way up yonder in Toledo." As we sat there, I asked her about Jesus. Immediately she told me how good the Lord had been to her and how she had served Him all her life. Then we sang "Amazing Grace" and "O Happy Day." Incredibly, she remembers the words and the tunes. With a smile on her face and hands clapping, you would never know she has Alzheimer's.

The aging process and disease take their toll on the body. Slowly but surely, the body begins to decline in strength and agility. The mind may lose its ability to recall even the most familiar things. But spirit consciousness is totally different. As the mind and body decline, the human spirit has the amazing ability to grow stronger through the Holy Spirit. "Our outward man is perishing, yet the inward man is being renewed day by day" (2 Corinthians 4:16).

Mother doesn't remember most names, but she acknowledges Jesus as Lord, Savior, and Healer. Knowledge deteriorates, the body loses strength, but Christ in our spirit becomes stronger. Spirit consciousness cannot be defeated by aging, dementia, or even Alzheimer's.

· · · PRAYER · · ·

God, let Your Holy Spirit flood my spirit when my body is ravaged by pain or slowed by age. When my soul loses its mental edge, let my spirit soar with renewed knowledge and power.

· · · TODAY'S THOUGHT · · ·

It is not our bodies but our spirits, in the power of the Holy Spirit, that keeps us going.

—Tony Scott

LOOK WHAT GOD HAS DONE

But as many as received Him, to them He gave the right to become children of God, even to those who believe in His name (John 1:12).

April 19, 1939, is the date of my conversion. I was born again and became a child of God. This wonderful experience had led me in the new life until this very day. As the first disciples were called by Christ to become fishers of men, so am I (Matthew 4:19). Seven days after my water baptism, I received the baptism in the Holy Spirit. What a wonderful experience!

The radical change in my life made the world seem as nothing and meaningless to me. The Holy Spirit opened my eyes to see the glory of His kingdom to be established on earth. I must fight to establish His kingdom. Since then I have one desire and one objective in my life: to serve Him with dedication according to His holy will. The Bible is a living, powerful book to me.

In 1939 the Lord used me to open my first congregation in Bandaneira, Moluccas, in East Indonesia. During this time of ministry I became stronger in faith, and in 1952 the Lord used me to establish the Bethel Church. In 1967 this church amalgamated with the Church of God in Cleveland, Tennessee, U.S.A. For further growth the Lord used me to establish a more dynamic church, the Gereja Bethel Indonesia Church of God in Sukabumi, West Java, in 1970. I served as national overseer and leader until 1994.

In 1970 the Lord used me to erect and establish the Bethel Seminary in Jakarta. Then followed 10 Bible schools in the different regions for multiplying workers in Indonesia. By God's grace the ministry has grown to 3,330 churches. One can never tell what the Holy Spirit can do until full trust is placed in Him. I pray and believe that He will "turn Indonesia upside down" and draw the masses to our Lord Jesus Christ.

· · · PRAYER · · ·

Lord, thank You for Your work in Indonesia and for using me to reach people and plant new churches. You commanded us to go into all the world; may we always obey You.

· · · TODAY'S THOUGHT · · ·

Little is much when God is in it. When we give ourselves to God, He turns the impossible into the possible.

—H. L. Senduk

FULL OF THE HOLY SPIRIT

He was a good man, full of the Holy Spirit and of faith
(Acts 11:24).

Barnabas was a man full of the Holy Spirit. It is one thing to respond to the Spirit's call and be saved. It is quite another to be full of the Spirit. Being full of the Spirit suggests being overcome by, submerged in, and controlled by God's Holy Spirit. Barnabas had reached that spiritual place. God needs men and women today who are not only touched by, or even occasionally helped by, the Holy Spirit but who are also dominated and directed by Him.

I've known people who I believe were totally committed to the control of the Spirit.

I once saw a church member in Chicago who cranked up an old school bus on Sunday morning in zero-degree weather and joyfully rounded up ghetto children to attend church. Before he returned these children home, they were fed a hot meal, taught the Word of God, and given a small gift.

I know someone with a Ph.D. who could be making a six-digit annual salary but is working instead among the drug addicts and prostitutes in New York City . . . and making a difference.

I am closely acquainted with a 70-year-old college professor who speaks four languages and has a doctoral degree. This man visits hospitals and nursing homes daily to bring sunshine to those who are physically and mentally sick.

Another person I know prays two hours a day for his local church, his denomination, and for other needs as they are presented to him.

These people are full of the Holy Spirit. Receiving the gift of the baptism in the Spirit with the evidence of speaking in other tongues is a marvelous, joyful, and very real experience. Our relationship with the Spirit does not stop there, however. This is only a beginning.

God is calling us to be full of the Holy Spirit.

· · · PRAYER · · ·

Father, fill us with the Holy Spirit. May Your Spirit so overshadow us that we are always effective in doing God's work on earth. I want to live with the fullness of Your Spirit expressed through me daily.

· · · TODAY'S THOUGHT · · ·

Pray until you have the Holy Spirit, then pray until the Holy Spirit has you.

—Bill F. Sheeks

THE SPIRIT OF TRUTH

"However, when He, the Spirit of truth, has come, He will guide you into all truth; for He will not speak on His own authority, but whatever He hears He will speak; and He will tell you things to come" (John 16:13).

Before Jesus went away, He told His disciples He was not going to leave them alone. He said He would send another Comforter, the Spirit of truth. Christians today need the Spirit of truth to guide them. The Holy Spirit guides believers in three distinct ways:

1. *He guides by speaking the truth.* Jesus tells the Spirit what to say and how to guide believers. Christ knows the infirmities and needs of men. He is appointed by God to instruct the Spirit in His guiding ministry. This should cause our hearts to leap with great joy and confidence, for the Lord knows exactly what we face. He knows through personal experience (Hebrews 4:15, 16)!

"For as many as are led by the Spirit of God, these are sons of God" (Romans 8:14). "You will guide me with Your counsel, and afterward receive me to glory" (Psalm 73:24).

2. *The Holy Spirit guides by leading into all the truth.* He is called the Spirit of truth. He speaks only truth and guides into "all truth." The Truth, of course, is Jesus Christ himself. The Spirit leads the believer to Christ, the Truth, and teaches him *all* the truth.

"When the Helper comes," Jesus said, "whom I shall send to you from the Father, the Spirit of truth who proceeds from the Father, He will testify of Me" (John 15:26).

3. *The Holy Spirit guides by showing us things to come.* He led the apostles to write the New Testament and foresee the things revealed in its pages. Today, the Holy Spirit takes things revealed in the Word and shows them to believers. "Eye has not seen, nor ear heard, nor have entered into the heart of man the things which God has prepared for those who love Him. But God has revealed them to us through His Spirit" (1 Corinthians 2:9, 10).

· · · PRAYER · · ·

Father, in the decisions I must make today, help me to lean heavily on Your Spirit of truth. Make me one with You that I may be led into all truth. I place my footsteps in Your hands.

· · · TODAY'S THOUGHT · · ·

True freedom is yielding to God's way, not choosing our way!

—Tony M. Weaver

THE HOLY SPIRIT BUILDS THE CHURCH

They continued steadfastly in the apostles' doctrine and fellowship, in the breaking of bread, and in prayers. . . . And the Lord added to the church daily those who were being saved (Acts 2:42, 47).

One Sunday night in 1936 I walked past the North Chattanooga Church of God and heard singing inside. The music was so good I felt in my heart they had something real and knew what they were singing about. Suddenly I knew I was a sinner and my life was a mess.

Pastor Jeff Wilson preached and the Holy Spirit convicted me. I went to the altar feeling ruined, lost, dirty. Everything bad you can think about the sin-life, I felt that night. I knew if I did not get right with God, I was going to hell.

After I knew I was saved, I still could not quit praying. The Reverend C.B. Godsey came over to anoint me and prayed for God to sanctify me and fill me with the Holy Spirit. I thought, *I wish he would go pray for somebody else and not muss up my hair.* He left, but I felt cold and empty. I couldn't get anywhere after he left, so I prayed, "God, send C.B. back over to pray for me, and I don't care if he does muss my hair up!"

Before long, C.B. came back and started praying for God to fill me. I felt I would die if I did not have the Baptism. When I came to myself later, I was lying on my back talking in tongues. C.B. Godsey was standing over me shouting and praising God.

Throughout my life the Holy Spirit has helped me. I have pastored small churches, and I have pastored the largest church in the Church of God. In every work I ever did for the Lord, the Spirit gave me the direction I needed and the answer to difficult situations. Whether serving as a pastor or a state overseer, helping people or preaching, it was the Holy Spirit who always gave the victory.

· · · PRAYER · · ·

Heavenly Father, help us to be as faithful to our calling and our mission as were our Pentecostal forefathers. In Jesus' holy name.

· · · TODAY'S THOUGHT · · ·

I will affirm the power of the Holy Spirit to change lives and make a difference in the world today.

—John D. Smith

AN EAR TO HEAR

"He who has an ear, let him hear what the Spirit says to the churches. He who overcomes shall not be hurt by the second death" (Revelation 2:11).

God created us with five senses: sight, hearing, smell, taste, and touch. Hearing is the only one that remains active up to the moment of death. In a comatose state a person is still capable of physically hearing all that is spoken. Yet, hearing sounds is not enough; one must be able to know, understand, discern, and perceive what is being spoken.

Hearing is an intellectual and a spiritual process. Hearing the Word of God increases our faith (Romans 10:17). It is vital for us to give attention to what the Spirit of God is speaking, and thereby overcome the spirit of the age.

Throughout the earthly ministry of Jesus, the disciples demonstrated by their words that they didn't understand the truth just revealed to them. Jesus rebuked them: "Do you not yet perceive nor understand? Is your heart still hardened? Having eyes, do you not see? And having ears, do you not hear?" (Mark 8:17, 18). How often do we find ourselves in the same position—having heard what the Spirit was saying yet not perceiving the truth. Do we interpret the Word by our situation or experience instead of by the Word of God itself?

Today, we must be alert and attentive to what the Spirit of God is saying to the church. There are many voices trying to speak to us—people, our feelings, cares of this world, and angels of darkness disguised as angels of light. We cannot listen to every voice we hear, to every spirit that speaks; but we must test the spirits by the Word of God. With a sensitive ear that hears what the Spirit of God is saying to the church, we will overcome!

· · · PRAYER · · ·

Lord, I desire to hear what You are saying. Help me to listen to only Your voice and follow only Your Word. I ask for Your Spirit of discernment to teach me truth from error and show me light from darkness.

· · · TODAY'S THOUGHT · · ·

Listening is hearing with intention. Let us listen to what the Spirit is saying, with the intention of willingly and obediently following His instructions.

—Marion M. Spellman

THE NEEDED INGREDIENT

"You shall receive power when the Holy Spirit has come upon you; and you shall be witnesses to Me in Jerusalem, and in all Judea and Samaria, and to the end of the earth" (Acts 1:8).

I was saved at the age of 5, and I was 15 when I received the baptism in the Holy Spirit with the initial evidence of speaking in tongues. The wind of the Spirit blows where He wills it to blow. We hear the sound and see the evidence, but we don't know exactly how the mysterious breath of God touches human hearts. Upon receiving the Baptism I had great joy and a sense of fellowship with God.

The Spirit gave me a boldness I had never experienced before. It was the same kind of boldness the early church received. In the Book of Acts believers assembled in the Upper Room in obedience to the Lord's command. They waited there in continuous prayer and were of one mind. Then the Spirit came and gave life to the church. The church, in turn, transformed the world.

The longer I live, the more important the work of the Holy Spirit is to my life and work. When people are saved, it is the power of the Holy Spirit that convicts sinners. When sick people are healed, the Holy Spirit does the work. When opposition confronts and frustrates, the Holy Spirit gives calm assurances. He who is in me is greater than whoever or whatever comes against me (1 John 4:4).

I am convinced that a Christian cannot overcome the world in his or her personal life without the baptism in the Holy Spirit. The needed ingredient in our lives is the power and boldness that believers had in the early church. "The promise is to you and to your children, and to all who are afar off, as many as the Lord our God will call" (Acts 2:39).

· · · PRAYER · · ·

O God, fill us today with Your Holy Spirit and power. Make us realize that we cannot do the work You have for us to do without the Spirit. Fill all of us! In Jesus' name.

· · · TODAY'S THOUGHT · · ·

I resolve to proclaim the gospel every day through the power and anointing of the Holy Spirit.

—A.M. Stephens, Jr.

PENTECOSTAL AFTERGLOW

{Peter and John], when they had come down, prayed for
them that they might receive the Holy Spirit. For as yet He
had fallen upon none of them. They had only been baptized
in the name of the Lord Jesus. Then they laid hands on
them, and they received the Holy Spirit (Acts 8:15-17).

When the day is long and hot and you are tired, isn't it nice to sit and relax in the afterglow of sunset, listening to the sounds of evening . . . waiting for the moon and letting the backed-up weariness drain away? Pentecost carries its own unique afterglow. So satisfying and exhilarating is the afterglow of receiving the Holy Spirit that one is never content to be without His influence and inspiration.

We who are filled with the Spirit should always pray for others to receive this wonderful experience. We should be burdened for our own families who have not been filled with the Holy Spirit. Why do we need this experience? Because real Pentecost brings humility, unselfishness, reliable guidance, faithfulness, solidarity, and sincerity. The Spirit also gives power to live victoriously, to pray effectively, and to witness courageously.

Thank God for a Spirit-based heritage! My father and mother had the Holy Spirit before I was born. Many people have made a great impact upon my life, but none like my parents. As a boy, I heard my mother and father speak in tongues and glorify the Lord. My mother died at the age of 39, speaking in tongues.

In 1937, at age 17, I attended a watch night service at the Osborne Avenue Church in Anderson, South Carolina. John Childers was pastor; A.V. Beaube, state overseer, was the guest speaker. He gave the invitation for those who wanted to receive the Holy Spirit at 11:30 p.m. At 2 a.m. the Spirit fell and I began to speak in tongues. Joy filled my soul. After 58 years, I am still rejoicing in the Holy Spirit.

· · · PRAYER · · ·

Our Father, keep us so filled with Your Spirit that we may influence
others to accept Christ and to be filled with the Holy Spirit.

· · · TODAY'S THOUGHT · · ·

The Spirit-filled life brings joy, integrity, and credibility. Live a good life; then when you are older and look back, you'll get to enjoy it a second time.

—Floyd J. Timmerman

December 19

LIFTED BY THE SPIRIT

He stretched out the form of a hand, and took me by a lock
of my hair; and the Spirit lifted me up (Ezekiel 8:3).

There are times when we come face-to-face with the painful reality that God's children are not exempt from life's process of pain and sorrow. So often we find ourselves standing in the path of such a dreaded circumstance. Struggling against the raging current of life's steady problems, we exhaust our strength and eventually realize that the rain falls on both the just and the unjust.

In 1985, standing in a lonely hospital corridor, my wife, Becky, and I heard the dreaded news that our son had an incurable disease of the spinal cord. Dismayed and confused, we struggled against a constant current of blame and doubt. Painful imaginations crept into our thoughts and minds with each medical announcement that our son would succumb to death or paralysis. Watching him suffer through seemingly endless treatments and painful surgeries, we continually grasped for the hope of his healing.

We rode the emotional roller coaster of ups and downs for nine years, searching for a glimmer of hope and watching his body become deformed and twisted. We too asked the questions "Where is God? Why did this happen?" We found the answer in the revealing presence of God's Spirit: "He stretched out the form of a hand, and took me . . . and the Spirit lifted me up."

In our darkest moments God chose to demonstrate again His omnipotent power to bring hope where despair ruled. Through the presence of His Spirit, darkness dissipated and the light of His marvelous love, care, and compassion came shining through. When earth's problems hold us down, God will surely lift us up.

· · · PRAYER · · ·

Holy Spirit of strength and everlasting deliverance, grant to all who
are in despair the uplifting power of Your loving grasp.

· · · TODAY'S THOUGHT · · ·

We watched God perform miracle after miracle for our son's healing. He no longer sits on the sidelines, unable to participate, burdened with pelvic and back braces; he now stands tall in body and spirit as a testimony to God's uplifting Spirit.

—T. Ron Wood

WHEN GOD BECOMES YOUR ENEMY

But they rebelled and grieved His Holy Spirit; so He turned Himself against them as an enemy, and He fought against them (Isaiah 63:10).

The prophet described the abundant mercies and blessings of God that had been extended to Israel. God's compassion toward Israel was evident; for when they suffered under some distress or hardship, He felt their pain and sent His messengers to deliver them. He was personally and intimately involved in their lives.

But Isaiah also told of God's reaction to Israel when they deliberately rebelled against His commandments and would not change. They grieved His Holy Spirit. Then God, who had been their Savior, "turned Himself against them" and became their enemy. He allowed His displeasure with their rebellion to be seen and felt by them.

God's purpose in turning Himself against rebellious Israel was not destructive, however, but remedial. He assumed the role of their enemy in hopes that this would bring them to repentance. His Holy Spirit was grieved by their attitudes and conduct, so He devoured their pride with humiliation and took away their idols by depriving them of their freedom.

As Christians in whom the Holy Spirit dwells, we are able to sense God's attitude toward us. We know that God is love, and more than anything He wants to give us peace and joy and blessing. But if we willfully disobey Him, the Holy Spirit of God is grieved.

God will not stand by impassively while we deliberately transgress or try to bypass His commandments. He is personally and intimately involved in our lives. To change us, to turn us around, to bring us to repentance, He will set Himself against us and become like an enemy if He has to. But He does this to halt our rebellion and save us, not to destroy us.

· · · PRAYER · · ·

Dear God, I want to live in obedience to Your will, so that You will continue to be for me the Captain of my salvation. Help me to be submissive to Your authority, that I may not grieve Your Holy Spirit by attitudes, words, or deeds.

· · · TODAY'S THOUGHT · · ·

On God's side I can fight the good fight of faith and win. But when I am not on His side, there is no possibility for victory.

—Robert M. Varner

PENTECOST AND MISSIONS

*In mighty signs and wonders, by the power of the Spirit of
God, so that from Jerusalem and round about to Illyricum I
have fully preached the gospel of Christ* (Romans 15:19).

Over 27 years of missionary ministry, I have witnessed the
fact that God's method of world evangelism has not changed.
Around the world, wherever church growth is taking place, it
is being done as described in the Book of Acts and by the
apostle Paul in his letter to the Romans.

The church was born in the fire of the Holy Spirit. Signs, wonders,
and miracles occurred as the apostles preached the gospel of Christ in the
power of the Holy Spirit. God confirmed the truthfulness of their preaching by manifestations of His mighty power. The result was the steady
growth of the church as sinners were saved and added to the church daily.

On the Day of Pentecost, when the Holy Spirit was first poured out on
the church, three activities of the Spirit were prominent:

1. The 120 believers were filled with the Holy Spirit and enabled by
the Spirit to speak in languages they had not learned.

2. With the anointing of the Holy Spirit, the gospel of Christ was
preached to the assembled multitude.

3. Three thousand souls were added to the church that day.

These three phenomena of the Holy Spirit cannot be separated from
ministry in the life of the church. Where the Holy Spirit is active,
whether in the life of an individual or in the church, the Word will be
proclaimed and confirmed by supernatural manifestations of the Holy
Spirit. Souls will be saved.

The manifestations of the Holy Spirit still go hand in hand with
soulwinning.

· · · PRAYER · · ·

*Christ, our Lord, we acknowledge with grateful hearts the gift of the
Holy Spirit. We are thankful that the age of miracles has not passed,
and You are still working by the power of Your Spirit to save people
and add them to Your church.*

· · · TODAY'S THOUGHT · · ·

For souls to be saved by the preaching of the gospel, the message
must be accompanied with and confirmed by mighty, convincing evi-
dences of the Holy Spirit's presence.

—Roland Vaughan

HE KNOWS WHAT'S BEST

*"Nevertheless I tell you the truth. It is to your advantage
that I go away; for if I do not go away, the Helper will not
come to you; but if I depart, I will send Him to you"*
(John 16:7).

 How can something so bad turn out to be good? No doubt the
disciples were filled with dismay at the thought of Jesus'
announcement that He would be leaving them. But He said
this was in their best interest. How could it be? His leaving
was the worst thing they could imagine happening to them.

A sailor shipwrecked on a South Seas island managed to salvage a
few things from the wreck. He built a small shelter to live in and to
house his meager possessions. One day he was on another part of the
island when his shelter caught fire. He returned in time to see the last
of everything he had go up in smoke. He was devastated. When he
awoke the next morning, he saw a ship approaching the island. When
the rescuers arrived, they said they had come in response to his smoke
signal! What had seemed at first a disaster had turned out to be in the
best interest of the stranded sailor.

The disciples knew they could trust Jesus' words, but at the moment
they could not see how His departure would be to their advantage. But
He assured them that everything was moving according to plan; and in
the end, they would realize that His going was for their benefit.

Jesus knew the loss of His physical presence would be more than
compensated for by the coming of the Holy Spirit. But there was a
condition for the fulfillment of this promise. The Holy Spirit could not
come until He departed. The disciples would have to let go of Jesus
and trust that He knew best.

· · · PRAYER · · ·

*Lord Jesus, help me remember that Your plans for me are best. I
want to walk with You daily in complete submission to Your will, so the
Helper, the Holy Spirit, can do in me and through me all You intend
Him to do.*

· · · TODAY'S THOUGHT · · ·

We can live by our own rationalizations and perceptions, or we can
believe the promises of the Savior. He has promised the Helper to all
who will submit to His will.

—Raymond Wall

HOPE DOES NOT DISAPPOINT

*Now hope does not disappoint, because the love of God has
been poured out in our hearts by the Holy Spirit who was
given to us* (Romans 5:5).

Children are born with two fears: the fear of falling and the fear of loud noises. They learn other fears from painful experiences. Three-year-old Chase is different. Toss him, lift him by one leg, hold him by his ankles upside down and pretend to drop him—he won't cry, scream, or show fear. He only laughs and asks for more. He is totally secure because he is totally loved. His parents, Todd and Danielle Hibbard, have cushioned his world with their love. Chase knows he is safe and his needs will be met. He knows the absolute security of perfect love (1 John 4:18).

Paul speaks of three great virtues: *faith, hope,* and *love.* Love is the motivation, hope is the objective, and faith is the means of attainment. These criteria for true spirituality are the focus of Romans 5:1-5.

Faith brings peace with God and access into His grace (vv. 1, 2). Hope overcomes severe testing (vv. 3, 4). Faith and hope enjoy total victory because of love (v. 5). Love produces a faith that cannot fail and a hope that never disappoints. Love equips faith and hope for ultimate victory. The Holy Spirit brings that love and pours it into our hearts like a flood.

What kind of love produces such powerful faith and hope? A love *for* God, causing us to seek passionately after Him, comes later. A love *from* God, causing us to seek passionately the good of others, comes still later. We grow in love for God and for others only when we discover how much He loves us (John 13:34; 15:12).

The starting point for triumphant faith, hope, and love is His love. From the Holy Spirit we learn what it is like to be truly loved. We believe, hope, and love in proportion to our knowledge of His love for us!

· · · PRAYER · · ·

Father, let Your Holy Spirit reveal more fully Your love for me, so that faith, hope, and love may grow in me.

· · · TODAY'S THOUGHT · · ·

The God of love my Shepherd is,
And He that doth me feed,
While He is mine, and I am His,
What can I want or need? (George Herbert)

—Horace Ward

THE HOLY SPIRIT AS GUIDE

"However, when He, the Spirit of truth, has come, He will guide you into all truth; for He will not speak on His own authority, but whatever He hears He will speak; and He will tell you things to come" (John 16:13).

The leadership of the Holy Spirit should be significant in the life of every Spirit-filled believer. For the minister of God, it is absolutely essential that the Holy Spirit be one's guide. In every decision, question, response, task, work, and in every other area of our lives, we must allow Him to fulfill His office of guide. Without His supernatural leadership, we stand in danger of becoming powerless and without purpose.

Since the beginning of my ministry in 1952, I have been acutely aware of the essential benevolence He provides. For me, dependence on His guidance is total and has become a way of life. It is paramount in my sermon preparation, decision making, and appointment acceptance. The last word must come from Him. He is my counselor, my friend, and my companion. I am as aware of His presence in my life as I am of the purpose that I fulfill.

As a result of this fellowship, every task of ministry takes on a higher meaning. Every problem becomes solvable. Every adverse situation becomes a shared burden. Every appointment becomes a joyous task. All this because He is my guide! I would never make a move in my ministry without first consulting Him. In giving Him this latitude, He is involved with the entirety of my ministry.

In a recent building program at Middletown, Ohio, we determined to submit all plans and decisions to His scrutiny before proceeding. Every obstacle was overcome, and a three-phase building program that was supposed to last six to eight years was completed in just three years! A loan was secured as a result of His arrangements, and the work of the congregation is progressing as a result of His guidance.

· · · PRAYER · · ·

Thank You, God, for the baptism in the Holy Spirit! By His revelation we can know God's perfect will, and by His guidance we can avoid costly and damaging errors.

· · · TODAY'S THOUGHT · · ·

One of our greatest promises from God is that in all our ways, if we look to Him, He will direct us.

—Walter D. Watkins

A SONG IN MY DARKEST NIGHT

I call to remembrance my song in the night (Psalm 77:6).

I met Jesus at an altar in Memphis when I was 19 years old. I accepted the call to preach and attended Central Bible Institute in Springfield, Missouri, for a year. I began to evangelize, and for six months I devoted my life to fasting, praying, and preaching. But success eluded me. I seemed to preach too long or not long enough.

Going home for Christmas was a great relief. All the family was home. Everybody was happy. But in the midst of this happy family group, I was lonely, discouraged, and depressed. In my mind I decided to abandon preaching and pursue a secular profession. After Christmas dinner I went to the bedroom to take a nap. Feeling too unworthy to even lie on the bed, I fell to my knees—a miserable, wretched soul—and cried out to God. Job 35:10 kept ringing in my ears and pounding in my heart: "Where is God my Maker, who gives songs in the night?"

In a state of exhaustion and desperation I fell asleep. I don't remember how long I lay there, but suddenly I was awakened. Half-asleep and half-awake, I was aware of brilliant white lights flooding the entire room. Far away I could hear a choir singing. The sopranos, altos, tenors, and basses were blending into one intense stream of harmony; but I didn't recognize the song. As I lay there, awed by this great happening, I was afraid to move.

In a moment the room reverberated with the sound of music. I could understand the words the heavenly choir was singing: "God is still on the throne, and He never forsaketh His own; When troubles oppress us and burdens distress us, He never will leave us alone."

God gave me a song in the midst of my darkest night! That song refreshed my spirit, renewed my strength, and reminded me that my calling from God had never left me.

· · · PRAYER · · ·

Thank You, Father, for lifting my spirit with the presence of Your Spirit through dreams, songs, and spiritual insights.

· · · TODAY'S THOUGHT · · ·

In our darkest and most trying circumstances, the Holy Spirit will give us a song of encouragement in the night.

—James L. Slay

THE SPIRIT SET ME ON MY FEET

*Then the Spirit entered me and set me on my feet, and spoke
with me and said to me: "Go shut yourself inside your
house"* (Ezekiel 3:24).

Ten years ago, the passing of my mother caught me in a vulnerable state, unprepared for the pain that followed. It knocked me down emotionally and spiritually. I have had numerous battles in my life before and some since, but none can compare with the pain I endured as a result of my mother's death.

It was as though faith was but a mere shadow. All I had preached was nothing more than empty rhetoric. All the words that I had encouraged others with were sounds of brass and tinkling cymbals. My faith and confidence were on trial.

The adversary buffeted, urging me to forsake my ministry and my godly covenant. He tempted me to bid farewell to a belief in the omnipotent power of God. He was not going to settle for a hung jury. "Then the Spirit entered me and set me on my feet."

Boxers are sometimes knocked down during the early rounds of a match yet come back to win the bout. A sports team will trail throughout a game, only to be victorious in the final minutes or seconds. What drives those with great odds against them to persevere? It is an energy that says to be knocked down does not mean to be knocked out. If that is the attitude of those who do not embrace the Spirit of God, how much more so should those of us in the kingdom of God know that we can do all things through Christ who strengthens us?

This is the awesomeness of the Spirit of God: He excels even in times of our failures; He is encouraging even in our times of despair; His strength is made perfect in our weakness. The Spirit of the Lord will minister to us and cause us to receive strength to endure the battle and the humility to relish the victory.

· · · PRAYER · · ·

Spirit of God, in the midst of my greatest battle, my most grueling struggle, may You be so near that Your Spirit would lift me to a place higher and stronger than I.

· · · TODAY'S THOUGHT · · ·

The Spirit gives the ability to rise from every hurt and disappointment and face every challenge. "For a righteous man may fall seven times and rise up again" (Proverbs 24:16).

—Dannie Williams

THE FIRE OF THE HOLY SPIRIT

The Spirit Himself bears witness with our spirit that we are children of God (Romans 8:16).

I had heard about the Holy Spirit as a child, but no one told me about being baptized in the Spirit until I was an adult. At conversion, I was released from the power and dominion of sin. When I received the Holy Spirit, power rushed into my life and gave me victory over the works of spiritual darkness.

When the Holy Spirit baptism took place, I learned that His power was all-subduing, all-encompassing, and all-important. The burning bush typifies my soul set on fire with holy zeal and fervor. The experience of the baptism was that wonderful promise of the Father in which speaking with tongues as the Spirit gives the utterance is the initial evidence. There is no place in the Bible where the promise has been canceled. I can testify that this experience is real.

He comforts me. The Holy Spirit not only gives comfort, He is the Comforter. The very fact of His presence in my heart gives me assurance of peace and joy.

He teaches me. This great Teacher who comes from God does not speak of Himself but of Him who sent Him. A carnal mind cannot understand the language of the Spirit.

He gives me power in prayer. The Holy Spirit comes to my aid and bears me up in times of weakness. "The Spirit Himself makes intercession for [me] with groanings which cannot be uttered" (Romans 8:26).

He gives me power to witness. I received power to witness for the Lord after the Holy Spirit came on me. The figure of fire expresses more fully the intensity and power of my experience. Fire is the most forceful and suggestive of natural elements and is used to symbolize the Holy Spirit. Fire is a penetrating element. It goes to the very fiber of my soul and is internal in its action.

· · · PRAYER · · ·

Father, let the Holy Spirit quicken my mind so that I can grasp spiritual truths and reflect a holy boldness in all my actions and activities.

· · · TODAY'S THOUGHT · · ·

Through faith in His Word I have received the Holy Spirit. He makes me glow with His presence; He makes me go with His message; He makes me grow in favor with God.

—H.D. Williams

WHEN THE SPIRIT COMES

But this He spoke concerning the Spirit, whom those believing in Him would receive; for the Holy Spirit was not yet given, because Jesus was not yet glorified (John 7:39).

The words the Lord spoke in verses 37 and 38 told of living water and the outpouring of the Spirit at Pentecost—a future and then-unrealized condition. Untold multitudes had been inwardly cleansed by the Spirit and had come to know they were sons and daughters of God. Eternal life is a present gift to the thirsty soul and an immediate bestowal of Christ to those who believe. And the work and person of the Holy Spirit throughout the Old Testament sanctified and equipped individuals, increasing the kingdom of God.

John says here, however, that "the Holy Spirit was not yet given." This reference looked forward to a new and nobler flowing of the Spirit to those who believed in Christ. The blessing would be conditioned by what was yet to happen. Christ was to be glorified, and those who believed would receive their overflowing baptism of the Spirit at Pentecost.

Jesus promised the Paraclete in John 16:13, 14: "He will not speak on His own authority. . . . He will take of what is Mine and declare it to you." He also said, "It is to your advantage that I go away; for if I do not go away, the Helper [Comforter] will not come to you" (v. 7). The Holy Spirit was not yet given because Christ was not yet glorified. Jesus had to return to the Father. He reassumed His antenatal glory and carried our nature, dishonored by man but now clothed with an infinite majesty, to the throne of God as the condition of the gift of the Holy Spirit.

When divine atonement was made and God glorified His Son, the facts were ready and the truth was revealed for the salvation of men. Then the streams of living water, the Holy Spirit baptism, was ready to flow from heart to heart.

I am glad that Christ died, rose again, ascended to the Father, and has sent back the Paraclete. We are blessed!

· · · PRAYER · · ·

Father, thank You for Your Son and for the gift of the Holy Spirit. Help us to glorify You and lift up Your Son through the power of the Holy Spirit in our thoughts, words, lives, and service.

· · · TODAY'S THOUGHT · · ·

The Holy Spirit enables us to do a great work for God and His Kingdom.

—Harvey Turner

THE SPIRIT LIFTED ME

*Then the Spirit lifted me up and brought me to the east gate
of the Lord's house, which faces eastward* (Ezekiel 11:1).

My parents, J.R. and Bessie Woodard, were saved and Spirit-filled in the revival in which the Church of God in Talladega, Alabama, was born. They introduced me to the reality of the Holy Spirit. I learned more by observing the Spirit's work in them than by their words.

During a Nebraska blizzard, our family had no food, heat, or money. We had no means of obtaining any, but a miraculous provision came just in time. The Spirit lifted us and every need was met!

One night while preaching, Dad took coals from a red-hot potbellied stove. He walked and preached with the coals in his hand, yet suffered no burns, blisters, or harm. The Spirit lifted him up!

Of all the experiences I have had in life, however, nothing prepared me for the crushing blow of my father's death. Dad and I were more than father and son—we were buddies, colleagues, confidants. I received hope, joy, and strength from him—and now he was gone! What of the Spirit's lifting now? "The Spirit lifted me," Ezekiel testified, "and brought me to . . . the Lord's house." When Dad died, I discovered this is the victory in all of life's devastations! The Spirit lifted and comforted me. I received strength in God's house.

Jesus promised "another Comforter" would come and abide with us forever. David called Him "the One who lifts up my head" (Psalm 3:3).

There is no substitute for the lifting, comforting presence of the Spirit in all circumstances.

• • • PRAYER • • •

Jesus, thank You for the lifting of the Spirit! You transform my feelings from the despair of merely surviving to joy and triumph. May I ever avail myself of the lifting that occurs in Your house and in the presence of the Holy Spirit!

• • • TODAY'S THOUGHT • • •

No immunity from the pain of life's transitions exists, but the Holy Spirit is available to lift the human spirit!

—Roger R. Woodard

FILLED WITH THE HOLY SPIRIT

And they were all filled with the Holy Spirit and began to speak with other tongues, as the Spirit gave them utterance (Acts 2:4).

On the Day of Pentecost the disciples were all filled with the Holy Spirit. Every area of their being became possessed by Him as they yielded themselves. There was no portion of their lives not submitted to His lordship. It was imperative that they be endued with power from on high, since the Great Commission (Matthew 28:19, 20) could not be effectively fulfilled through human abilities alone. He endowed them with supernatural enablement.

The filling of believers with the Holy Spirit in this manner signified Christ had indeed ascended to heaven and thus it was time for them to begin the work of witnessing—the work for which they had been selected and commissioned. Now they were equipped for service. The Spirit-filled life is not merely a once-in-a-lifetime experience; it is a powerful ongoing actuality for every believer.

The Holy Spirit came upon their entire beings, and the overflowing manifested itself with speaking in other tongues. They all began to speak with tongues as the Holy Spirit gave them utterance, giving them a supernatural endowment of power for service. Speaking in tongues became the vehicle through which they expressed praise and worship without preplanned thinking and articulation of known words.

The Holy Spirit, speaking through them in tongues, offered praise, worship, thanksgiving, and adoration to God. This sign arrested the attention of the multitude and at the same time served as God's divine stamp of approval upon the lives and ministry of those who were experiencing the phenomenon. The people who heard them speaking in their own language were anxiously desirous to know what it all meant. So when Peter stood to proclaim the gospel, there was a ready audience!

· · · PRAYER · · ·

Father, may all believers be filled with the Holy Spirit today, just as the believers were on the Day of Pentecost. May we speak in other tongues as the Holy Spirit gives the utterance so that all humanity may be convinced of the gospel message and be saved.

· · · TODAY'S THOUGHT · · ·

The Holy Spirit flowing in and through us gives life to our witness and work.

—L. Martin Wright

HEARING THE HOLY SPIRIT

"Thus says God: 'Why do you transgress the command-
ments of the Lord, so that you cannot prosper? Because you
have forsaken the Lord, He also has forsaken you'"
(2 Chronicles 24:20).

Joash, king of Judah, lived a remarkable life. When his grandmother Athaliah conspired to murder all the heirs to the throne of Judah, he alone was rescued by his aunt. Under the godly influence of Jehoiada, the high priest of Israel, Joash did right. However, it seems Joash never developed a personal relationship with God so that he could hear and understand the Spirit of God. After Jehoiada died, Joash came under the influence of the enemies of God.

After the princes of Judah had led Joash and the nation away from God, the Holy Spirit spoke to Joash through Zechariah, the son of Jehoiada. But Joash rejected the message from God and had the messenger put to death.

Whose voice has your attention? What counsel directs your life? A thousand voices want your attention—on television and radio, where you work, on the street, in your home, and in the church. Amid and above all these voices, are you able to hear the voice of God's Spirit?

Do you hear a word from the Lord? Are you listening to the right voices? How can you know? Be filled with the Holy Spirit. Know Him personally so you will be able to recognize His voice.

With the massive amount of information and knowledge and communication available today, it is imperative that we be able to hear the Holy Spirit, whether His message comes to us in thundering tones or in a still, small voice.

Who is speaking to your heart? Who is God using today to get His message through to you? Listen.

· · · PRAYER · · ·

Father, help us through Your Word and Holy Spirit. Let us never be
led away from You by strange voices and evil influences.

· · · TODAY'S THOUGHT · · ·

There are many sources of information and direction in life, but there is no one who can lead us in the paths of righteousness except the Holy Spirit, who has been sent to guide us "into all truth" (John 16:13).

—R. Edward Davenport